Ludwig Büchner, Peter Eckler

Man in the Past, Present, and Future

A popular account of the results of recent scientific research regarding the origin,

position and prospects of mankind

Ludwig Büchner, Peter Eckler

Man in the Past, Present, and Future
A popular account of the results of recent scientific research regarding the origin, position and prospects of mankind

ISBN/EAN: 9783337427825

Printed in Europe, USA, Canada, Australia, Japan

Cover: Foto ©ninafisch / pixelio.de

More available books at **www.hansebooks.com**

MAN

IN THE

PAST, PRESENT, AND FUTURE:

A POPULAR ACCOUNT OF THE

RESULTS OF RECENT SCIENTIFIC RESEARCH

REGARDING THE

ORIGIN, POSITION AND PROSPECTS OF MANKIND.

FROM THE GERMAN OF

DR. LUDWIG BÜCHNER,

AUTHOR OF "FORCE AND MATTER," "ESSAYS ON NATURE AND SCIENCE,"
"PHYSIOLOGICAL PICTURES," "SIX LECTURES ON DARWIN," ETC.

———

In the past, man appeared to be a creature foreign to the earth, and placed upon it as a transitory inhabitant by some incomprehensible power. The more perfect insight of the present day sees man as a being whose development has taken place in accordance with the same laws that have governed the development of the earth and its entire organization — a being not put upon the earth accidentally by an arbitrary act, but produced in harmony with the earth's nature, and belonging to it as do the flowers and fruits to the tree which bears them.—PROF. PERTY.

———

NEW YORK:

PETER ECKLER, PUBLISHER,

35 FULTON STREET.

PUBLISHER'S PREFACE.

———

AMONG the popular scientific writers of the present day in Germany, Dr. Büchner stands pre-eminently in the foremost rank, and the publisher of the present translation of his able work, which defines *the Position of Man in Nature*, takes great pleasure in placing it before the American public, at a price so reasonable that it brings it within the reach of all classes.

A number of engravings, which have not appeared in former editions of this work, have now been added, to assist in illustrating the text.

Theologians, and naturalists whose scientific views are in accord with the so-called sacred revelations, have long contended for the specific unity of the human race,—a race destined, as they believe, to an eternal existence after this life,—whilst all other sentient beings are doomed by them to annihilation and oblivion. But Dr. Büchner teaches us a more equitable and righteous doctrine. He grandly broadens and enlarges this unjust and restricted view, and ably contends, not only for the unity of the human race, but also for the unity of all races that exist,—indeed, we may say, for the unity of the universe. He sees that man has risen from the lowest position to his present exalted state, by the slow and gradual process of evolution—that "in the animal as in man, the eye serves for vision, the ear for hearing, the tongue for tasting, the stomach for digestion, and the liver for the secretion of bile ; the feet serve for locomotion, the lungs for breathing, the kidneys for the separation of water, etc. By means of chloroform the animal is stupefied just like the man — they live, sicken and die by the same processes and causes."

The same thought "concerning the estate of the sons of men" is even more tersely expressed by the author of *Ecclesiastes ; or, the Preacher*, chap. iii, verses 19 and 20 :

"For that which befalleth the sons of men befalleth beasts ; even one thing befalleth them : as the one dieth, so dieth the the other ; yea, they have all one breath ; so that a man hath no pre-eminence above a beast : for all *is* vanity.

"All go unto one place ; all are of the dust, and all turn to dust again."

Whilst many animals excel man in strength, courage, swiftness and endurance, he has nevertheless attained an ascendency over them by his superior reasoning powers, which result from the exercise of his larger and more perfectly developed brain. But even if he possesses the power to govern, it gives him no right to abuse that power. Justice and mercy should prompt him to act as the friend, not the persecutor of the inferior races. And above all, he should cease to ruthlessly destroy, for so-called sport and pastime, the lives of innocent animals — lives which are their only possession — and which it is impossible for him to again restore.

We are told in Clarke's *Travels*, vol. IV., page 544, that a traveller, alighting from his horse, killed a serpent which was crossing the way. Carrying it to the ambassador, who was seated in his Arabah, he received a mild but pointed reproof against the wantonness of depriving an animal unnecessarily of life. "Bey Zedeh," said he, "had that poor serpent done any thing to injure you? Are you the happier because you have deprived it of life? Do not carry with you a proof of your cruelty ; it may be unlucky : the same Power who made you created also the serpent ; and surely there was room enough in this wilderness for both of you."

PETER ECKLER.

PREFACE.

THE following book has resulted from a series of public discourses by the author upon the great scientific discoveries of recent times with regard to the *Antiquity* and *Origin of the Human race*, and the *Position of Man in Nature*.

The great and almost unexampled interest in the subject, and its importance in the development and further evolution of our general conception of the Universe and of life, from the point of view of philosophical realism, (an importance which is still far from being sufficiently acknowledged), will justify the author in abstaining from any prefatory explanation of his motives in deciding to communicate in the present compilation, the essential parts of these discourses to a more distant or larger public, in a form suited for general comprehension.

In order to avoid confusion by the particularly copious abundance of materials at hand, the author has arranged the actual, or more exact proof of what is given in the Text, (consisting of quotations, scientific details, and further particulars or remarks,) in a separate *Appendix*, brought into connection with the Text by continuous numbers, and also in a series of foot notes. He hopes that this method will augment the scientific value of the book without injuring its usefulness with the general public, to whose wants he has paid particular attention in the text itself.

The extraordinary favor which the public has hitherto man- .
ifested towards all the literary productions of the author without exception, and which has been his principal incitement to
proceed in the same course will, he hopes, not be wanting to
this new book, the principal tendency of which is towards
culture and intellectual progress.   The author believes that he
is the more justified in this expectation, since the book contains in its second section a popular exposition of one of the
most prominent questions of the day—a question which, in
the last few years, has excited the minds of men in a most
remarkable manner.   This question, which has been so often
misunderstood, and answered in the most varied forms,
relates to the *Ape-genealogy of man* as it has been called.
If the author should succeed by means of credible and scientific evidence in diffusing correct views, free from prejudice
and ignorance, and resting upon the truths of nature in
regard to this new doctrine which has called forth so much
opposition, this result alone will appear to him of sufficient
importance to compensate for the trouble which he has bestowed upon the subject.

No doubt in this, as in former cases, there will be no lack
of those opponents and calumniators who seek to displace
light by darkness, truth by falsehood, and facts by phrases.
The author, who has neither time, leisure nor inclination for
futile polemics, thinks that he cannot meet such opponents
better than by closing his preface with the following passages
from an English writer, who has so brilliantly and resolutely
defended the author's standpoint against his own assailants
and censurers, that it is unnecessary to add a single word to
what he has said.

" There is nothing more frequent," says David Page, (*Man*,
&c., Edingburgh, 1867), " than denunciations from the pulpit
and platform against the tendencies of modern science, by
men who are not only ignorant of the rudiments of science,

but who have bound themselves by creeds and formulas before their minds were matured enough or their knowledge sufficient to discriminate between the essentials and non-essentials of these restrictions. And here it may be remarked, once for all, that no man who has subscribed to creeds and formulas, either in theology or philosophy, can be an unbiased investigator of the truth, or an unprejudiced judge of the opinions of others. His sworn preconceptions warp his discernment, and adherence to his sect or party engenders intolerance to the honest convictions of other enquirers.

" Beliefs we may and must have, but a belief to be changed with new and advancing knowledge impedes no progress, while a creed subscribed to as ultimate truth and sworn to be defended, not only puts a bar to further research, but as a consequence, throws the odium of distrust on all that may seem to oppose it. Even when such odium cannot deter, it annoys and irritates ; hence the frequent unwillingness of men of science to come prominently forward with the avowal of their beliefs.

" It is time this delicacy were thrown aside, and such theologians plainly told that the skepticism and infidelity — if skepticism and infidelity there be — lies all on their own side. There is no skepticism so offensive as that which doubts the facts of honest and careful observation,—no infidelity so gross as that which disbelieves the deductions of competent and unbiased judgments."

These golden words deserve to be engraved on metal and displayed in all Churches, Lecture-halls and Editorial rooms.

POSTSCRIPT TO THE ENGLISH EDITION.

ON the appearance of this English edition of his book on
the *Position of Man in Nature*, the author thinks it
necessary to express to the English Public his regret, that he
was unable, in the preparation of its second section, to make
use of the admirable arguments upon this subject, which have
recently been published in England by the distinguished naturalist Darwin, in his book upon the *Descent of Man*. This
was impossible, as the printing of the greater part of the
translation was already completed when the work just mentioned made its appearance. The author's regret at this circumstance was however abundantly compensated by the satisfaction which he could not but feel when, on reading Darwin's
work, he remarked the great and remarkable agreement
between his views and those of the celebrated English
naturalist, although he had been unable to arrive at any
definite opinion upon the subject in question from Darwin's
previous writings. Quite independently of any personal feeling, this circumstance may serve as a proof how completely a
correct interpretation of facts, and consistent and unprejudiced
thought in scientific matters, but especially in Natural History,
must lead to the same clear and simple results, no matter in
what brain the necessary process of thought is carried on, or
whether it is in England or in Germany, or in any other part
of the civilized world.

Dr. L. Büchner.

Darmstadt, February, 1872.

CONTENTS.

WHAT ARE WE?

WHERE ARE WE GOING?

INTRODUCTION.

"The great business of life—even that which lies most immediately before us—will be more fully understood and more rationally performed, the better man knows the place he holds and the relations he bears to the plan of Creation."—D. PAGE.

"When we glance over the results of modern research, now flowing in from all sides, and consider them in their significance for the knowledge of man, it can no longer be a matter of doubt that we have come to the end of established notions, and that we are approaching a different conception of nature."—SCHAAFFHAUSEN.

"Natural history in the present day gives us a higher conception of the Universe than that entertained by the ancients; it no longer regards the material world as the plaything of mere caprice, or history as an unequal contest between God and Man; it embraces the past, the present and the future as a magnificent unity, outside of which nothing can exist."—A. LAUGEL.

IN his admirable *Essay on Man's Place in Nature*, the celebrated anatomist and philosopher, Professor Huxley, compares the process of development by which the human intellect is constantly advancing towards truth, with the periodical moultings of a *feeding and growing grub*. "From time to time," he says, "the old integument becomes too straitened for the growing animal, it is therefore burst asunder and replaced by a new and larger growth. Precisely the same thing occurs in the history of the intellectual development of man. The human mind, fed by constant accessions of knowledge, grows too large for its theoretical coverings, and periodically bursts them asunder, to appear in new habiliments."

Since the revival of learning in the fifteenth century, there has been an abundance of strong food for the human intellect, the education of which was indeed commenced by the Greek philosophers, but then suffered the interruption of a long intellectual stagnation or sleep of fourteen centuries. I will not stop to enquire, by what influence this stagnation was brought about, although this is clear enough to the eyes of those who are acquainted with *true* history, and not merely with that substitute for it which has been concocted by theologians and philosophers for their own purposes.

But this revival of science being once set on foot, it was inevitable that a more frequent bursting of the old integuments would take place, and this process of intellectual moulting must be frequently repeated. And so it was in the sixteenth century, by the overthrow of the old astronomical system and the influence of the Reformation! and at the end of the eighteenth century, by the period of intellectual enlightenment and the influence of the great French Revolution!

And now once more the human intellect has received such a quantity of strong and stimulating nourishment by the extraordinary progress of the natural sciences during the last fifty years, that a new and great change and a repeated bursting of the old integuments appears to be inevitable.

Nevertheless, as Huxley remarks in carrying still further his admirable simile, just as these periodical moultings are not effected without superinducing various diseased conditions, disturbances, and general debility in the animal undergoing change,—so also in the intellectual world these metamorphoses are likewise attended with perils and discomforts of all kinds. Therefore, it is the duty of every good citizen and patriot to aid with all the strength and means at his command, (however small they may be), towards the speedy and satisfactory completion of this process or necessary crisis, or at any rate to do what he can to assist in bursting and stripping off the old integuments, and thus give room and liberty to the growing body.

This masterly comparison, by which at the outset of his Essay, Professor Huxley seeks to show, that it was his *right*, or better still his *duty* to take part in the public discussion of the greatest scientific question of his age, may also serve to excuse or justify the author of the present book for having undertaken to treat in a familiar style a question so important and difficult as the position of man in nature, and to present to the general public an exposition of the results attained by modern science for its elucidation, and for the refutation of old-world errors and prejudices.

Professor Huxley is undoubtedly in the right in describing this question of Man's place in nature and his relations to the universe, as *the question of questions* for mankind,—as a problem which lies at the root of all others and interests us more profoundly than any other.

"Whence our race has come;" he says, "what are the limits of our power over nature and of nature's power over us; to what goal are we tending; are the problems which present themselves anew and with undiminished interest to every man born into the world." More simply expressed, these are the old questions which have in all times occupied the human mind, and which run as follows:

Whence do we come? What are we? and whither are we going?—Problems which formerly seemed to be veiled in the deepest obscurity of impenetrable secrecy, and which first received some elucidation or illumination from the science of our own day.

In former times, the answer to such questions as these could, of course, but accommodate itself to the general philosophical and theological ideas of the age, and that mystery especially with which we are now chiefly occupied, lay until quite recently buried under such a load of ignorance and prejudice that, from a scientific standpoint, it could only be regarded as insoluble and incapable of any scientific treatment. Hence it came about, that the fundamental problem of all, namely, that of the origin and production or genealogy of the human race, was almost unanimously declared, not merely by the philosophers of former days, but also in unison with them by general opinion to be *transcendental*, that is to say, beyond the reach of human powers of conception and comprehension, (at all events, so far as these rested upon observation and experience.)

Who could have suspected, even a few years ago, that within so short a period the progress of knowledge and of scientific induction would throw a light so clear and certain upon this mystery of mysteries—upon the earliest past history and the first commencement of our race upon the earth?

We may say without exaggeration, that *this* step stands in the first line of all the advances made by the human mind ; that the discovery of the *natural* origin of man, and the demonstration of his *true* position in the universe, deserves to be ranged side by side with the greatest scientific discoveries of all times, if indeed it should not be raised above them.

Those men of science of our day who have applied their minds most thoroughly to this subject, have found themselves constrained to express themselves in the same or a similar manner.   Thus Professor Schaaffhausen says : "To have ascertained the real origin of man is a discovery so fertile in its consequences for all human conceptions, that futurity will perhaps regard this result of investigation as the greatest of which the attainment was allotted to the human mind."   And from the opinion expressed by Professor Ernest Haeckel in his *Natürliche Schöpfungsgeschichte*, (Berlin, 1860, p. 487), the recognition of the natural (and especially the animal) origin of man must sooner or later bring about a complete revolution in our entire conception of the relations of mankind and the world.

There is perhaps only a single scientific discovery, which in point of importance and far-reaching consequences is to be placed on the same level with this, and that is the discovery that the earth moves and that the sun is stationary, or the establishment of the so-called Copernican system of the universe.* Of all those "burstings forth" or "moultings" of the human mind, already spoken of, and which we may count so many of greater or less importance in the history of the development of human civilization, this great astronomical discovery is undoubtedly one of the most important and conspicuous. Nowadays we can hardly form a notion of the immense influence which the great discovery of Nicholas Copernicus, about the middle of the sixteenth century, after the long intellectual lethargy of the middle ages, exerted upon the men of that and the following century; in this respect, and as enlarging the intellectual horizon of the men of that time, there is nothing to compare with it except perhaps the discovery of America.

Starting from this idea, Professor Haeckel, in an admirable lecture on the origin and genealogy of the human race, (Berlin, 1868,) indicates *two* errors as the greatest and most serious in their consequences, which still, as formerly, stand in opposition to the development of the human intellect.

These he very appropriately calls the *geocentric* and the *anthropocentric* errors. The *geocentric* error consisted in regarding the earth as the central point and chief object in the whole universe, the other parts of which were considered only to

---

* In the year 1543, Nicholas Copernicus published his celebrated book on the *Paths of the Heavenly Bodies*, which effected a complete revolution not only in astronomy, but also in the whole conception of the Universe of that day. In gratitude for this he was regarded as a fool by his contemporaries! Even the great reformer Dr. Martin Luther, who, however, like his opponents, was a theologian, was so unable to comprehend the new discovery that he came forward as a bitter opponent of Copernicus, and expresses himself with regard to him as follows in his *Table-Talk :* " The fool wishes to upset the whole art of Astronomy. But as Holy Scripture shows, Joshua commanded the sun and not the earth to stand still." Might not our zealots against modern science take an example from this?

serve the purposes of this central point and its inhabitants; the *anthropocentric* error, which even still governs the great majority of mankind, regards man as the centre and sole object of the whole organic creation—as the image of God, or the ruler and centre of the terrestrial world—the whole mechanism of which has been organized and exists solely for his use and with reference to his special needs.

The former of these errors, as is well known, was overturned and swept away by Copernicus, Kepler, Galileo and Newton; the second by Lamarck, Goethe, Lyell, Darwin and their adherents and followers.

It is of this second error and its removal, or rather of what is to be put in its place, that the present book will particularly treat. But before entering into details upon the subject, the author will venture to refer to a phenomenon which, as history teaches us, has always repeated itself with every new and great discovery, and of course is not wanting in the present case. This is the entirely unbounded fear which takes possession of the minds of men with regard to the supposed terrible consequences of such discoveries—or of the promulgation of a new scientific or philosophical conception of the universe. When the Copernican system began to prevail, not only religion but the whole moral order of the world was supposed to be fearfully shaken and imperiled, and people thought that, with the change in opinion as to the relative positions of the heavenly bodies, faith and civilization, religion and morality, government and society must at once go to the wall, or at least undergo the most serious injuries. In reality, however, as is well known, not one of all these dreaded consequences and terrible prophecies was realized, but on the contrary mankind has since progressed in the most remarkable manner, not merely intellectually, but also in morality and civilization, and actually by the aid and in fact by the influence of this very enlargement of knowledge.

As it was then, so it will be now. All the innumerable declamations and tirades of the votaries of darkness and victims of fear, in opposition to the recent step in advance, will not only have no effect against the truth, but the apprehensions raised by them will in no way be fulfilled. In the eyes of the writer and probably of every thinking man, every intellectual advance of mankind, every great approximation to the truth, is at the same time an advance both materially and morally!

With regard to the so-called *anthropocentric* error, against which the recent discovery of the true position of man in nature must be regarded as especially directed, it is in itself, equally intelligible and excusable. For without the knowledge of the numerous facts which the indefatigable spirit of research has now placed at our command, man appears, at the first superficial glance, to be so thoroughly and fundamentally different from surrounding nature, that we can scarcely blame our ancestors for not having known or even suspected the intimate and insoluble connection that exists between all the phenomena of nature and life, not excepting those presented by man himself.

"In the past," as Prof. Perty says in his *Anthropologische Vorträge*, (Leipzig, 1863,) "man appeared to be a creature foreign to the earth and placed upon it as a transitory inhabitant by some incomprehensible power. The more perfect insight of the present day sees man as a being whose development has taken place in accordance with the same laws that have governed the development of the earth and its entire organization,—a being not put upon the earth accidentally by an arbitrary act, but produced in harmony with the earth's nature, and belonging to it as do the flowers and the fruits to the tree which bears them."

These ideas are also clearly and tersely expressed by an English writer, as follows : "In the opinions of former philosophers, man was an exceptional instance in the grand scheme of creation ; he formed an isolated phenomenon in the great plan of nature, to make free with whom, after the ordinary fashion of inductive inquiry, was little other than an act of open and scandalous impiety." (*Anthropol. Review*, 1865, No. 9.)

The state of things here pictured has now indeed been radically changed : for as soon as we investigate the position of man from the standpoint of modern science and the great discoveries of recent days, setting aside all old prejudices, we come at once to results which are completely opposed to former views. We find, that man is most intimately connected with surrounding nature, not only in his *bodily* but also in his *intellectual* qualities, and that his elevated position is due only to the higher and more varied development of his powers and faculties.

Formerly, with a strange and wilful blindness, Nature, from whose bosom man has sprung, was regarded, not as his friend and relative, but on the contrary as the greatest obstacle in his course of life, and especially in the way to the evolution of his highest intellectual powers. I could cite innumerable passages from our most celebrated philosophers, in which these notions are expressed in the clearest manner. Nay, they sometimes even went so far as to declare positively, that nature was merely a revolt of the mind against itself, and therefore they loaded *matter*, which forms the foundation of all nature, with the coarsest invectives. Truly such conduct as this was as irrational as that of a child who raises its hand against its parents.

We know only too well how far this contempt for nature in contradistinction to the world of the spirit, was carried by those whose conceptions of the universe were drawn from religious and especially from Christian sources. This senseless fanaticism of rage against our own flesh must soon come to an end in the presence of the great discoveries now under discussion. For what we have now especially to seek in the interests of the individual man and of the human race, is not a contempt and rejection of nature, but the most intimate acquaintance with it, in order that by this knowledge we may understand it, honor it, and conquer it.

To the gradual diffusion of this knowledge are due the great influence and authority which the natural sciences have acquired in the last fifty years, and this will become more and more striking as time goes on.

It is true indeed, (and in the interests of historical accuracy this must not be forgotten), the real position of man in nature was partially understood or recognized by a few remarkable thinkers at a very early period, long before the promulgation of the observations which we have now at our command. But theirs were isolated guesses, resting upon an intellectual intuition destitute of the necessary basis of empirical proof, and therefore could never arrive at general acceptance. The science of our time could alone furnish them with the necessary foundation.

As regards this science itself, we must place in the first rank the recent and interesting investigation into *the antiquity of the human race upon the earth ;*—an antiquity which seems to us primeval and leaves far behind it all historical tradition. Of this so-called *prehistoric* existence of man, no one formerly had the least knowledge or suspicion, and this circumstance alone must have almost completely barred the way to a right recognition of the position of man in Nature.

For if we imagine man, in accordance with the universally prevailing opinion of former times, created and placed upon the earth by an Almighty sovereign or creative power about five thousand or six thousand years ago,—if we suppose that he was then in all essential points the same thing or creature that we now behold him, or even perhaps still more perfect,— as a matter of course every thread which could bind him in accordance with regular laws with the rest of the universe, is entirely wanting, and there is no room for any other opinion than the old one which we have here indicated. But the late discoveries and investigations as to the primeval existence of man upon the earth have proved that man, although the highest and perhaps the youngest member of the organic creation has already lived upon the earth during a period in comparison with which the few thousands of years covered by human history and tradition shrink almost to a single moment.

The facts proving this assertion will form the subject of the following section, the first of the three great divisions of our book.

OUR ORIGIN.

THE ANTIQUITY AND ORIGINAL STATE OF THE HUMAN RACE,
AND ITS DEVELOPMENT FROM A BARBAROUS BEGINNING.

" Natural history has traced back the history of Man to a period which lies far beyond all historical tradition. It has put back the antiquity of our race into that far past time when the European man fought with the cave animals of the diluvium, and not only ate the flesh of the Mammoth and Rhinoceros and the marrow of their bones, but even laid cannibal hands on the flesh of his own kind, —into a time when in our regions man fed his herds of Reindeer amongst the glaciers, or lived in the pile-dwellings of our lakes, or heaped up on the northern coasts great mounds of shells, the relics of his meals."—PROF. SCHAAFFHAUSEN.
(*Vortrag über die anthropologischen Fragen der Gegenwart.*)

" Modern science is not contented with breaking down the foundations of classical chronologies, which indeed were already in a very dilapidated state, and throwing back the origin of man to a period so distant, that in comparison with it, our written history appears like a passing moment in a series of centuries which the mind is unable to grasp. It goes still further," etc.—A. LAUGEL.

IN the year 1852, or some forty years ago, an ancient cavern was accidentally discovered in France, on the southern slope of the Pyrenees, and close to the little town of Aurignac, in the department of the Haute Garonne. This has since become celebrated under the name of the " Cavern of Aurignac." It was closed by a heavy slab of sandstone, and in it were found the skeletons or bones of at least seventeen human beings, men, women and children, which had been deposited there. At first, unfortunately, a very imperfect examination of the cave was made, and the bones were again deposited in some other place.

It was only after an interval of eight years (or in the year 1860), that a careful and scientific examination and description of the place was made by the famous French palaeontologist, M. E. Lartet, who had long been familiarly acquainted with the numerous bone caves of the south of France and with their contents.

By this examination it was established beyond the reach of doubt, that the cave of Aurignac was a primeval sepulchre of the stone age,—of a period when a great number of what are commonly called *antediluvian* animals, of species long since extinct, were still living in our part of the world.

When the rubbish which covered the slope was cleared away, it appeared that the floor of the cave had in former times been continued forward, so as to form a spacious open place or terrace in front of it. This terrace had evidently served the important purpose of furnishing the scene of the funeral ceremonies. Upon it a layer of ashes and fragments of wood charcoal, six inches thick, was found, and beneath this a sort of rough hearth, composed of several flat pieces of sandstone reddened by the action of fire and resting immediately upon the underlying limestone. But the most remarkable thing was, that among the ashes and in the soil which covered them, a great quantity of the bones of animals and many articles of human handiwork were found. Of the latter at least a hundred were discovered. They were all made of stone and chiefly of flint. Among them were knives, arrowheads, slingstones, flint-flakes and other objects, besides one of those flint nodules, which occur so abundantly in the chalk hills of France, and from which the flint implements were manufactured; this also had its surfaces chipped. With these was found a sort of hammer, consisting of a rounded stone with a hollow place on each side; this was made of a kind of rock not found in the district. It was probably held by placing the thumb and forefinger in the two opposite cavities and may have been employed in the manufacture of the flint implements. Besides these stone implements, others were found, made from the bones and horns of the Roe and Reindeer, such as needles, arrow-heads, awls, scraping knives, etc., and also the canine tooth of a young Cave Bear, bored lengthwise and worked in a peculiar manner, apparently to represent the head of a bird. This probably was suspended from the neck as an amulet or ornament.

The bones of animals were very numerous, and for the most part belonged to species which lived in that Quarternary or Diluvial period of geological history which immediately preceded our own epoch. No fewer than nineteen species were counted, and among these were the very animals which are most characteristic of the Diluvial period, such as the Cave Bear, the Cave Hyena, the Mammoth or primeval Elephant, the Wooly Rhinoceros, the Gigantic Irish Deer, Horse, Reindeer and Aurochs. Bones of herbivorous animals were by far the most numerous ; those of the Carnivora and also those of the Mammoth and Rhinoceros occurred but rarely. Hence we may conclude, that the last named animals were too formidable or too powerful to be hunted and killed by these early men. All the marrow-bones, without exception, were broken and split up to enable these primitive people to get at the marrow, which was one of their great dainties. Most of the bones were also scratched or furrowed lengthwise, as if they had been scraped with some rough instrument, such as a flint knife, to detach the last morsels of flesh adhering to them. Many of the bones also showed marks of the teeth of predaceous animals, and the spongy portions of them were gnawed off. This must have been done by the Hyenas, of which the petrified fæces (coprolites) were found lying about in abundance. Many bones showed evident traces of the action of fire, and these were of such a kind as to prove that the bones were in a fresh state when exposed to it.

Of human bones not one was found outside the cave.— Within it, however, many were found, chiefly those of the hands and feet, which had been left behind in the first clearing out. Their general condition was precisely the same as that of the bones of the extinct animals, the Cave Bear, Mammoth, etc., and their chemical examination showed them to contain exactly the same quantity of organic matter. All the bones whether of men or animals presented the signs of high antiquity ; they were friable and porous, and adhered to the tongue.

Besides the human bones the interior of the cave contained a number of bones belonging to the same species of animals that were found outside it, but these presented one very remarkable difference,— no traces of any violence, of gnawing, breaking, or the action of fire, could be detected upon them. Amongst others, all the bones of the leg of a Cave Bear were found lying together in their natural position, from which we may justly conclude, that this limb was put into the cave in an uninjured state and whilst still covered with flesh. There were also eighteen small, flat plates of a pearly substance, evidently derived from a cockle-shell (*Cardium*). These were all perforated in the middle and were probably strung upon a cord for the purpose of being used as a necklace. Lastly, the cave contained a great number of well preserved flint-knives, which apparently had never been used, a few instruments made of horn, and other objects of the same kind. There were however in the interior of the cave no traces of the charcoal and ashes which were so plentiful on the outside of it.

On his third visit to the cave M. Lartet examined the rubbish, which had been heaped up near it when it was first cleared out. In this he found many specimens of worked flint-stones and teeth of men and animals, together with a great number of fragments, pottery roughly made by hand and dried in the sun or half burnt, and various ornaments made of hard bone. There is little difficulty in seeing what is the significance of this remarkable discovery. The cave of Aurignac was evidently a primeval sepulchre of the so-called Stone-age, in which the remains of seventeen human beings had been successively deposited. These people were of small stature. More than this, unfortunately, we cannot say, as the skeletons could not be found in the place of their second interment. The objects found in the interior of the grotto seem to indicate that, in accordance with the custom still prevailing among barbarous people, food, implements, weapons and even ornaments, were placed in the grave with the dead. The heavy sandstone slab before the entrance to the cave evidently served to close it temporarily and to protect it from the visits of wild animals.

The flat place or terrace in front of the cave is even more interesting than the cave itself. Upon this, evidently, the relations and other mourners of the deceased held the funeral feasts. This is clearly proved by the hearth, the fragments of charcoal, the bones, with traces of the action of fire and of violence upon them, and the instruments with which the flesh was cut and scraped from the bones. After each interment, when the place was left by its human visitors and the cave itself was closed with the sandstone slab, the Hyenas came at night to regale upon the relics of the feast, as is proved by the marks of gnawing upon the bones and the coprolites scattered about.

Thus this discovery gives us a pretty distinct picture of the life and doings of the primitive European man at a period when history did not exist, and when Europe was still inhabited by those large and powerful quadrupeds which have hitherto been regarded as characteristic of a geological period antecedent to our own, and which have since given place to a very different set of animal inhabitants. The antique picture thus unrolled before us, agrees in its details most remarkably with that which we obtain from the accounts of travellers of the customs of savage nations in distant parts of the earth. Thus, amongst others, we have the journal of an English traveller, John Carver, who journeyed through North America in the years 1766–68 and witnessed the funeral ceremonies of an Indian tribe in what is now the state of Iowa, at the junction of the Mississippi with St. Peter's River. He describes these ceremonies perfectly in accordance with the data furnished by the discovery at Aurignac, and, as Sir Charles Lyell states, (*Antiquity of Man*), his account served our great poet Schiller as the model of his well-known *Nadowessische Todtenklage*, in which the rites observed at the funeral of an Indian chief are described in precisely the same manner.

The actual antiquity of the cave of Aurignac has been estimated at 50 — 10,000 years. Whether or not this estimate is correct, this remarkable discovery certainly justifies us in coming to the following conclusions :

1. That long before the existence of any history, or even of any tradition, a savage tribe of men must have lived in Europe in a barbarous condition, or displaying such rudiments of civilization as we now find among existing savages ;

2. That this tribe of men must have lived *contemporaneously* with the Mammoth, the extinct Rhinoceros, the Cave Bear, etc., that is to say, with animals which have long since become extinct and which, as has already been stated, are generally regarded as characteristic of a prehuman geological period.*

These conclusions, which carry back the presence of man upon the earth to an unsuspected distance in the past, would be perfectly justified, even if we had no other evidence to stand upon than that furnished by the cave of Aurignac. But the fact of the very ancient existence of man, of his contemporaneity with certain extinct animals, (a proposition long disputed with the greatest violence, but now perfectly demonstrated), does not rest only on the discovery at Aurignac, which is cited here merely as a simple example ; but similar

* See Appendix No. 1.

discoveries in proof of it have been made in nearly every part of the world — in England, France, Italy, Spain, Germany and Belgium, nay even in America, Asia, Australia, etc. Everywhere the same or very similar conditions have been found to prevail,— everywhere caverns have occurred, in which remains of Man or indubitable evidences of human handiwork are found associated with the remains of supposed prehuman animals, and in many instances under circumstances which, when carefully examined, leave no doubt that the men and animals must have been contemporaries. From a comparatively early date the discoveries of Schmerling and Spring in the numerous Belgian caves have been particularly celebrated; as early as 1833–34, Schmerling, with perfect justice, deduced from them the contemporaneity of man with the animals of the Diluvial period.* But in opposition to the general prejudices, his testimony was wasted like that of one preaching in the desert. The same fate had previously befallen the French naturalists Journal and Christol, who, as early as 1828-29, had made similar discoveries, and drawn similar conclusions from them, in the equally numerous caves of the South of France, (such as Bize near Narbonne, Gondres near Nîmes, etc.); and the assertions of the English Geologist Buckland, in his *Reliquiæ Diluvianæ*, (1822), and of the German palæontologist Baron von Schlotheim, had met with no better reception. The last named naturalist had made some discoveries in the years 1820–1824 in the gypsum quarries near Gera in Thuringia, which led him also to infer the contemporaneity of man with the Diluvial animals. The Danish naturalist Lund was so much under the

---

* The book in which Schmerling gave his important observations to the world is entitled: *Recherches sur les ossements fossiles découverts dans les cavernes de la province de Liége (1833).*

"It is impossible," says Professor Fuhlrott, "to read his report without sympathy; we feel with him the difficulty of the task of establishing an opinion which offends against the firmly rooted prejudices of the day. And in fact neither by the solidity of his arguments, nor by the warmth of conviction, with which he supports them, could he at that time gain any adherents to his opinions."

influence of this prejudice, that not even his interesting discoveries in the numerous bone-caves of Brazil, could thoroughly
convince him of its falsehood.   But since this period numerous
and careful investigations of other bone-caves have been made,
especially in England, France and Belgium, (partly at the
expense of the respective governments of these countries,) and
all have led to the same results.   Among the Belgian caves
the so-called *Trou de Frontal*, situated in the valley of the
Lesse, is particularly worthy of mention, because, when it was
discovered, it presented so precisely the same character as the
the cave of Aurignac that the two caverns might almost be
described in the same words.   Here again the mouth of the
cave was closed by a slab of sandstone ; within it the remains
of fourteen human beings of small stature were deposited ;
whilst in front of it there was an esplanade for the funeral
feasts, with its hearth and traces of fire and with many flint-
knives, bones of animals, shells, etc.

But all these early discoveries were incapable of overthrow-
ing a scientific prejudice which had for so long a period enjoyed
an unrestricted dominion over the learned world, and indeed, in
spite of all evidence to the contrary, still maintains itself in great
force in some scientific and in very many non-scientific circles.

This prejudice consists in the assumption, that man cannot
have had a more ancient existence upon the earth than the
latest of known geological periods, namely that of the so-called
Alluvium, which is a deposit produced by the action of our
existing rivers upon their banks and at their mouths.

The formation of this deposit necessarily presupposes that,
when it took place, the surface of the earth was of the same
form as at the present day ; the equilibrium between land and
water must likewise have been the same, and the same fauna
and flora must have been in existence as at present.

The existence of man upon the earth was therefore believed

not to date more than a few thousand years before the Christian
era. This prejudice, sanctified by age and, as it was supposed,
supported by great scientific authority, had indeed been nourished and strengthened by many circumstances, among which
a principal part must be ascribed to the numerous disappointments, which had been experienced with regard to discoveries
of supposed fossil human bones, which afterwards turned out to
be those of animals* and to the asserted opposition of the great
anatomist and naturalist Cuvier.† But another circumstance
may have contributed even more than these to the misapprehension of the truth, and this was that the prejudice in question
agreed remarkably with a widely diffused philosophical opinion,
which had by degrees become the darling of the general public.
According to this opinion, man, as the final flower or crown of
creation, its corner-stone as it were, could not have appeared

* See Appendix No. 2.

† Cuvier, who, by his celebrated work, the *Recherches sur les ossements
fossiles*, (1812), was the first to introduce system and order into the previously
very imperfect knowledge of the remains of a former world, and whose immense
knowledge certainly quite justified his undisputed claim to the leadership in this
field, has generally been supposed to have declared the existence of fossil or antediluvian man to be an impossibility. But in reality his authority has been and
still is cited quite erroneously on this point. For, far from expressing himself
in any such terms, Cuvier only says *that no fossil or petrified men or apes have
yet been found*. Most certainly if Cuvier were living at present he would have
taken his stand with his weighty authority on the side opposed to his opinion of
that time.

The affair is, however, so important that I cannot abstain from giving here
Cuvier's own words. In his great work *Sur les Revolutions du Globe*, (1825),
he says expressly: "But I will not conclude from this (*i. e.*, from the fact that
as yet no remains of man or apes had been found), that man did not exist at all
before this epoch. He might inhabit some countries of small extent, from
whence he re-peopled the earth after these terrible occurrences; perhaps also the
places where he dwelt have been entirely submerged and his bones *buried* at the
bottom of the present seas, with the exception of a small number of individuals
who have continued the species."

It may serve for the explanation of this quotation to state that Cuvier in the
spirit of his time still believed in isolated, great and universal revolutions of the
globe, which, however, in reality have not taken place. It will be seen, however, from the quotation, that Cuvier's followers and disciples were more ortho-
dox or more limited in their views than the master himself, a case which indeed
is by no means unfrequent.

upon this theatre of his being until the last and most recent geological period, (the Alluvium), and thus he forms not only the highest fulfillment, but also the final conclusion of all organic creative activity.   Of course this comfortable opinion was in danger of being greatly diminished in value, or perhaps even altogether upset by the investigations to which we have referred, and as the majority of men, in their fondness for intellectual repose and comfort, dread nothing more than the shaking of old established articles of faith, they prepared to fight against the new ideas to the very last drop of their blood.   It must be confessed, that there was *one* circumstance much in favor of the opponents of the new doctrine in their struggle against the fossil man* and the evidence derived from the cave-discoveries. So long as we had only these cave-discoveries to appeal to, it was said: Granting the truth of all these discoveries and their results, how is it, that we find no human remains and no traces of human action in the regular strata of the period before the alluvium, in deposits open to the light of day? Why do we always meet with them only in these dark caves and grottos, where there is always a possibility that the remains of man and animals may have been swept together by great floods of water, and where at any rate the peculiarity of the conditions, under which these remains are discovered, leaves so much enveloped in obscurity and mystery?

But even to these grave questions the indefatigable spirit of

* In using the expression " fossil" we must take care to avoid the frequent misconception that the idea of " petrifaction " is necessarily connected with it. For although undoubtedly many fossil objects are found in a petrified state, this condition is by no means always their essential characteristic. Even in our times organic bodies are petrified under favorable circumstances, whilst others which have lain much longer in the earth do not become petrified. Moreover the word " fossil" itself (derived from the Latin "*fossilis*") by no means signifies a petrified object, but only something *that is dug out of the depths of the earth.* According to Professor Pictet of Geneva, the word is applicable to all organic remains which lie buried in those strata of the earth which have been formed under certain conditions *different from those of the present day.* Therefore in order that organic remains should be recognized as fossil, they must belong to a period which preceded the present state of things on the surface of the earth.

investigation has found an answer. And here we might narrate the touching history of a man who, for twenty long years, in spite of misapprehension and scorn, contended in vain against the great prejudice in favor of the late appearance of the human race upon the earth, until finally he was rewarded by victory and general appreciation. We refer to the celebrated French antiquary and discoverer of antediluvian flint axes, Boucher de Perthes, of Abbeville on the Somme.

The Somme, as is well known, is a river of the North of France, (in Picardy), and falls into the English Channel. In the greater part of its course it runs through a district of white chalk, partly covered with Tertiary deposits. Above these Tertiary strata there are great beds of rolled pebbles, sand, gravel and loam, belonging to the Diluvial period which we have already so frequently mentioned. In the vicinity of the towns of Amiens and Abbeville these beds were laid bare to a considerable extent, partly by the formation of great gravel pits and fortifications, and partly, in more recent times, (1830 to 1840), by the construction of a canal and railway. Years ago the bones of diluvial and extinct animals, (such as Elephants, Rhinoceroses, Bears, Hyenas, Deer, etc.), had been found in these diluvial deposits at a depth of 20 to 30 feet and close to the underlying chalk; these were sent to Cuvier in Paris, who determined and described them. And it was here and in precisely the same places that Boucher de Perthes found those famous flint axes of the rudest form, which have given a totally different aspect to the whole question of the antiquity of the human race upon the earth. Boucher de Perthes had seen, (probably in 1805 and 1810), certain worked flints in Italian caves and was led to ascribe to them a high antiquity on account of their peculiar coloration. His archæological knowledge enabled him to distinguish these flint axes from the so-called *celts*—the polished stone weapons of a much latter date—which have been found in a great many places and may be seen in abundance in every collection of antiquities. In the year 1838, Boucher de Perthes first exhibited the flint axes found by him to the scientific Society of Amiens, but without any result. With equal want of success he took them to Paris in 1839. In 1841 he began to form his collection, which has since become so celebrated. In 1847 he published his *Antiquités antédiluviennes*, but even this work attracted no attention, until, in 1854, a French *savant* named Rigollot, who had long been a determined opponent of Boucher de Perthes' views, became convinced of the correctness of his statements by personal examination, and then made a successful search for these flint implements in the neighborhood of Amiens. He was soon followed by others, especially Englishmen, among whom were the celebrated geologist, Sir Charles Lyell, (in whose presence during two visits to the locality no fewer than seventy flint hatchets were turned out), Mr. Prestwich, M. A. Gaudry and others.

Scientific men soon assembled in the valley of the Somme from all quarters, and all those who came and examined for themselves went away converted to the new opinions. Of course, as might be expected, objections of all kinds were raised. Some declared, that the hatchets had been thrown out of a volcano; others that they were natural products of the action of water or frost. Others again, without venturing to deny their artificial origin, maintained that they had reached the depth, at which they lay, either by a gradual sinking caused by their own weight or by falling into fissures of the soil. However, all these objections were soon shown to be untenable. Commissions of scientific men, including the most celebrated names of England and France among their members, assembled repeatedly to investigate the matter, and the general result of their examinations was expressed in the following important statements:

1. The flint hatchets are undoubtedly the work of human hands;

2. They lie in virgin or undisturbed deposits of the Diluvial age, which have not undergone any alteration or reconstruction by natural phenomena since their original deposition, and therefore in deposits the formation of which presupposes a structure of the surface of the earth essentially different from that which now exists;

3. They occur associated with remains of fossil animals now entirely extinct; and they *prove that the antiquity of man upon the earth reaches far beyond all historic times and indeed far beyond all tradition.**

These flint axes have been found in such abundance in the Valley of the Somme, that their number, several years ago, must have been some thousands, not to mention the innumerable chips, flakes and imperfect specimens that have been met with.

Manufactured from the flint-nodules so abundant in the white chalk of France, these implements represent the first and lowest stage of human industry. They were produced merely by knocking together the flint-nodules, which, when thus treated, split up with a sharp, conchoidal, (or shell-like), fracture. Flint, hard as it is, is in fact very easy to split, especially when it is operated on in a fresh state with its pit-moisture still in it, or when it has been soaked for a good while in water. When the nodules had been split up roughly, the fragments were worked at with little taps until they attained a useful form, and then the instrument was complete. That this was the process really adopted, and that it effects the desired purpose, has been proved by experiment.

* Carl Vogt expresses himself in the same way in his *Vorlesungen über den Menschen*.— At p. 52 of his first volume he says: "It is now incontestably proved, that these flint weapons could only have been fabricated by man, that they owe their existence to no other natural cause, that they lie in great quantities in beds which have never been disturbed or moved since their first deposition, and that they undoubtedly belong to the same period as all the extinct animals that I have already mentioned."— And A. Laugel in his *L'homme antédiluvien* says: "The greatest skeptics now admit, that the stones found in such considerable numbers by Boucher de Perthes are indebted to the hand of man for their peculiar form and their sharp edges."

In these rudest forms of flint implements we find no trace of any finishing process; they are neither polished, ground, nor ornamented in the same manner usual with stone weapons of a latter date.*   Nor do we find in them a hole for the handle or an external excavation or contracted part for reception in a haft embracing the stone on the outside.   These flint axes were either held in the hand itself or merely stuck into a piece of wood, as is done to the present day by many savage people,

* In prehistoric times flint was the most sought for and indeed almost the only material that was worked in Europe, and it has exerted a much more powerful influence upon the course of civilization than is commonly supposed, as for a long time the articles manufactured from it were the only implements that man could produce.   Even now, savage tribes are anxious to obtain it, partly on account of its hardness, partly on account of its mode of fracture and the readiness with which it is worked in consequence.— If one strikes strongly with a round hammer upon the smooth surface of a flint-nodule, a *conical* fracture spreading through the whole mass of the nodule is produced ; whilst, if one strikes upon a projecting angle of the nodule, fragments split off which have rather a half-conical, flat and knife like form.   When the four projecting angles of an angular flint-nodule have been cut off in this manner, the same process can be repeated with the eight angles then formed, and so on, until at last an axe-like nucleus is left.   Of course a certain amount of practice and dexterity is required for this purpose, as also care in the selection of the pieces for working.—A flint-fragment worked in this manner is, according to Sir John Lubbock, as sure a proof to the Archaeologist of the presence of man, as the traces of human footsteps in the sand were for Robinson Crusoe.

The flints served sometimes as *weapons*, sometimes as *implements*.   The former purpose was fulfilled especially by the larger fragments or true axes; whilst the smaller fragments and chips were employed as knives, saws, awls, arrowheads and lance-heads, etc.   Even to the present day by means of the same or similar stone-implements assisted by fire, our existing savages fell trees and hollow them into boats, and also fight with each other.   In the year 1809 an old stone-grave, ascribed by tradition to King Aldus McGaldus, was opened in Scotland.   There was found in it the very brittle skeleton of a man of very large stature, one arm of which was nearly separated from the trunk by a blow with a stone axe.   A fragment of the axe was broken off and remained wedged into the bone.

The stone itself was *diorite*,— a rock which does not occur in Scotland. Other stone-implements, some of them polished, were also found in the grave, but no trace of metal.

In latter times the working of flint advanced, and we find all kinds of axes, knives, arrow, and lance-heads, daggers, saws, etc., of this and similar materials. (From an Essay by Sir John Lubbock in the *Revue Littéraire*, 1865-66, No. 1.)

who usually wedge their stone weapons into the cleft branches of trees and endeavor to fix them firmly by tight binding above and below the stone.

At the places where these flint axes were found in the Valley of the Somme, no other traces of human handiwork were met with, not one of those articles made of horn, bone, shell, etc., which have been so frequently found in deposits of later date, and in the numerous ossiferous caves especially have scarcely ever been missed. From this we may conclude that the objects found in the Valley of the Somme are certainly more ancient than the cave of Aurignac, which has already been described, and in which there was a great collection of articles made of bone and horn, together with flint knives, which also indicate a later stage of civilization.

We may therefore regard the flint axes of the Valley of the Somme, commonly known to archæologists from the special localities where they are found, as stone implements of the *Amiens*, or of the *Abbeville-type*, as the earliest known trace of human industry, or as indicating the first and rudest beginning of the arts of civilization. As representing such a commencement as this, these objects, notwithstanding their simplicity and roughness, possess the highest significance, and must excite our deepest interest. For they show us with what rude and primitive steps man must have commenced his long and weary march towards civilization, and how poor and insignificant were the first beginnings of a culture which has since yielded such grand and noble results. They furnish us with the best guide to the recognition of the great fundamental law of nature and of man, according to which every thing great and admirable that man or the universe can yield or possess, is not a gratuitous gift from above, but only attained by slow and laborious development from simple and rude beginnings, by gradual evolution of the powers and faculties slumbering in nature and in man.

"*Evolution* is henceforward the spell by means of which we may solve all the mysteries surrounding us, or at least put ourselves in the way of solving them." (*Haeckel, Natürliche Schöpfungsgeschichte*, Berlin, 1868.)

To use the words of the celebrated discoverer of the flint axes, Boucher de Perthes, in his well known memoir, *De l'Homme antediluvien*, (Paris, 1860): "Let us not then disdain these first essays of our forefathers; if they had not made them, if they had not persevered in their efforts, we should have neither our towns nor palaces, nor any of those masterpieces which we admire in them. The first man who struck one pebble against another to give it a more regular form, gave the first blow of the chisel which produced the Minerva and all the marbles of the Parthenon."

We must not, however, omit remarking, that the Valley of the Somme is no longer the only place where rude flint implements of the character just described have been found. Since these axes and their appearance have become so well known, and general attention has been called to them, they have been found in many other parts of France, and especially in the Valley of the Seine, where their occurrence in the lowest Diluvial deposits, associated with the bones of Diluvial animals, was very accurately ascertained by Gosse. And they have been discovered not only in France, but in many other parts of Europe, Asia, America, etc., and in all cases in the same Quaternary or Diluvial deposits, in company with bones of the same extinct animals to which reference has already so frequently been made, and, singularly enough, with the same absence of all products of a more advanced state of civilization. It must not be supposed, however, that we merely find single bones of the animals mixed with the products of human industry, but sometimes the bones of entire limbs or other parts of the body are met with in their normal position in the gravel-beds which contain the axes, (Baillon), so that the idea of subsequent intermixture or sweeping together by water is at once excluded. A very convincing discovery of this kind was made on the banks of the Manzanares, near Madrid, by Casiano de Prado. In 1845 to 1850, a large portion of the skeleton of a Rhinoceros was found in the diluvial sand occurring there, and soon afterwards a nearly perfect skeleton of an Elephant. In a bed of rolled pebbles lying *beneath* this ossiferous Diluvial sand several flint axes of human workmanship were discovered. According to Carl Vogt, (*Archiv für Anthropologie*, 1866, Part I.), this discovery removes all doubt.

The flint axes have hitherto been found most abundantly in old river-valleys in England and France, and in England also, on some parts of the coast. Their number, which was at first small, has gradually become so considerable, that Sir John Lubbock estimates at more than three thousand the flint implements of the earliest stone-age or the *palaeolithic* period, as he calls it, which have been exhumed in the north of France and the south of England alone. None of these utensils are ground or polished, and they are nowhere associated with worked metals or pottery, or with objects made of bone, horn, etc. From an historical point of view it is certainly worthy of notice, that, as soon as the discoveries in the Valley of the Somme were made known, people remembered that in England, as long ago as the year 1797, these same flint axes had been dug out in great numbers from a brickfield near Hoxne, in the county of Suffolk, where they occurred at a depth of twelve feet in company with the bones of extinct animals. As no one knew what to make of them they were thrown by baskets-full upon the neighboring road. The English Antiquary, John Frere, had noticed them, however, and in the year 1801 he read a paper upon them at a Meeting of the Society of the Antiquaries, but the matter was not regarded as of any importance. Nevertheless Frere even then remarked quite justly, that the discovery pointed to a very remote and indeed to an antediluvian period.   Short as his communication is, it contains the essence of all subsequent discoveries and speculations as to the antiquity of the human race.

Even before this time, in the year 1715, one of these flint instruments of the most ancient kind had been exhumed, in company with Elephants' bones, from the gravel of London; but people were then in a less favorable position than at the later period to draw definite conclusions from this circumstance.*

The great resemblance that prevails throughout all these axes found in England and France is very remarkable, and is so great that the workmen in the gravel-pits where they occur have given them the general name of "*cat's tongues*."   This circumstance may be partly explained, if we consider that at the time of the deposition of the diluvium, England and France were not yet separated by the Channel; they were then directly united by land, so that reciprocal communication between the inhabitants of the two countries was very easy.

Lastly, in connection with this, it must be borne in mind, that the cave-discoveries have also furnished an abundant supply of rude stone-implements, although these are in part of a different character and generally belong to a rather later date.

So much for the flint axes of the Diluvial period, of which such numerous and remarkable specimens are now to be seen in the Museums of London, Paris and elsewhere.   An attempt

* At a still earlier period people had so little notion of the nature and significance of the stone axes and weapons of earlier and later times that they were regarded with superstitious fear and hope and as productions of lightning or thunder.   Hence for a long time they were called thunderbolts (ceramia) even by the learned, and popularly, in common with some fossil remains of animals, they still bear this name.   "Albinus (in his *Meissener Land- und Berg-Chronik*) says, that the thunder throws down these stones, and Happelius *Kleine Weltbeschreibung* describes their production from the vapors in the atmosphere as pleasantly as if he had himself been a witness of it.   As late as the beginning of the last century (1734) when Mahndel explained in the Academy of Paris that these stones were human implements, he was laughed at, because he had not proved that they could not have been formed in the clouds.   Even at the present day they are reverenced and carried about by the common people as talismans, love-charms, etc."— (Schleiden.)

has been made to weaken the force of their evidence as to the high antiquity of the human race by raising the following question : Why do we not find associated with these axes other human remains, especially human bones, seeing that plenty of bones of animals are to be found with them? This point was seized upon with avidity by the numerous opponents of the new doctrine and has, in fact, given rise to much doubt. The explanation of this obscure matter given by Lyell, in his work upon the *Antiquity of Man*, is exceedingly ingenious and, as it appears to us, perfectly satisfactory. But this explanation has become unnecessary since Boucher de Perthes, the original discoverer of the flint axes, succeeded in satisfying even this requirement. On March 28, 1813, Boucher de Perthes took with his own hands from a gravel pit at Abbeville, in which the axes had been found, and from a great depth in it, and close to the subjacent chalk, a human lower jaw, the same which has since become so celebrated as the jaw of Moulin Quignon.

This is now in the Anthropological Museum at Paris. It is of a very dark, blue-black color, and in its conformation shows some tendency towards an animal character. Some objections to the genuineness of the jaw were made, especially by the English *savants*, who were perhaps a little jealous of the French discoveries, and these led to long discussions in the scientific world. But on May 13, 1863, an international scientific commission decided that the jaw was genuine, that it had not only lain where it was discovered, but that it was actually contemporaneous with the diluvial flint axes.*

* The details of this discussion will be found in the *Procès-Verbaux des Séances du Congrès réuni à Paris et à Abbeville sous la présidence de M. le Professeur Milne-Edwards, etc.*, printed in Paris. The French savants Quatrefages and Broca, also express themselves in the same way. In his report on the labors of the Anthropological Society of Paris for the year 1863, the latter says :—" All this has convinced you of the authenticity of this fossil jaw of Moulin-Quignon,"—and Quatrefages says, in his Anthropological Lectures for the year 1865 :—"The question of the authenticity of the discovery at Moulin-Quignon is fully solved. No one any longer doubts this authenticity, unless it be in England."

Until July 16, 1869, this interesting discovery remained an isolated fact. But on that day Boucher de Perthes found a number of human bones presenting the same character as the jaw, and amongst these was a skull of a very low type. These were found not far from the locality of the first discovery, under the same circumstances, and at a depth in the ground of three metres (about ten feet).

These, however, are not the only fossil human bones which have been found out of caves. In his celebrated book on the *Antiquity of Man*, Sir Charles Lyell enumerates several cases, some of them of comparatively early date, such as the *fossil Man of Denise*, discovered by Dr. Aymard in 1844, whose remains were found enclosed in the old volcanic tuff of a long extinct volcano of Central France, (Auvergne). The man to whom these remains belonged must have lived when the volcanoes were still in activity ; and that this activity pertains to a long-past geological period, is proved by the circumstance that the remains of the Cave Hyena and Hippopotamus have been met with in similar blocks of tuff in the same region. Sir Charles also notices the human fossil of Natchez on the Mississippi, which was found in the so-called Mammoth fissure, associated with bones of *Mastodon* and *Megalonyx*, (animals long since extinct and belonging to a past geological period). Further, a human skeleton found in 1823, by Ami Boué,* near Lahr in Baden, (opposite Strasbourg), in the so-called *Loess* of the Rhine valley, (a product of the glacial period), and the human jaw from the *Loess* near Mæstricht, (in Hollerd), which was found during the construction of a canal, (1815 to 1823), together with the bones of extinct animals, and is now preserved in the Museum at Leyden. All these bones were discovered under such circumstances and in such a condition that, if they had only been the bones of animals, no one would have thought of doubting their being fossils. But as they were human bones,

* See Appendix No. 3.

doubt seemed to be perfectly legitimate so long as the old general prejudice still existed. Now, however, Sir Charles Lyell, who has seen and examined them all, declares them to be decidedly fossils, that is to say, belonging to a different geological period from that in which we live. Sir Charles comes to the same conclusion with regard to the skeleton of the celebrated Neanderthal man,* found in 1856, in a limestone

* The details of this remarkable discovery, which attracted so much attention, may be found in Professor Schaaffhausen's memoir, *Zur Kenntniss der ältesten Rassenschädel*, as also in an essay by Professor C. Fuhlrott, entitled: *The fossil man from the Neanderthal and his relations to the antiquity of the Human Race*, (Duisburg, 1865.) The last mentioned author, who was also the first investigator and describer of these remarkable bones, says: "The position and general arrangement of the locality in which they were found, of which I published a description at the time, place it in my judgment beyond doubt, that the bones belong to the Diluvium and therefore to primitive times, *i. e.*, they come down to us from a period of the past when our native country was still inhabited by various kinds of animals, especially Mammoths and Cave-bears, which have long since disappeared out of the series of living creatures." The human bones discovered agree in all essential respects with the fossil remains of antediluvian animals which were brought to light under perfectly analogous circumstances from other caverns and fissures of the same limestone range and in the immediate vicinity, and they possess properties which plead in favor of a high antiquity for them. The whole of the bones, but especially the cranium, are characterized by their uncommon thickness and by the very strong development of all tubercles, crests and ridges which serve for the attachment of muscles, a peculiarity such as is usually observed in the bones of savage and very muscular men (and animals.) We shall refer hereafter to the very peculiarly formed skull of the Neanderthal man.

The fossil state of the Neanderthal skeleton is still further strongly confirmed by the discovery in the summer of 1865 of numerous fossil bones and teeth of animals (Rhinoceros, Cave-Bear, Cave-Hyena, etc.,) in the loam-deposit of the so-called Teufelskammer, a cavern situated only 130 paces distant from the Feldhofner Cave (in which the Neanderthal man was found) and on the same side of the Neanderthal. According to the report upon this discovery given by Professor Schaaffhausen to the Natural History Society of the Lower Rhine and published in the *Kölnische Zeitung*, of April 1, 1866, a great part of these bones, especially those of the Cave-Bears, agree in color, weight, density and the preservation of their microscopic structure with the human bones found in the Feldhofner Cave, and both are covered with the same *dendrites* or tree-like markings.

Finally it is to be remarked that the loam-deposit which partly fills the caves of the Neanderthal and the clefts and fissures of its limestone mountains, and in which both the Neanderthal bones and the fossil bones and teeth of animals were imbedded, is exactly the same that, in the caverns of the Neanderthal, covers the whole limestone mountain with a deposit from 10 to 12 feet in thickness, and the diluvial origin of which is unmistakable. (See, for details, the essay of Fuhlrott already cited.)

cavern in the valley of the Neander, near Düsseldorf. To this we shall have to refer in more detail hereafter, on account of the peculiar interest which it possesses in connection with the primitive history of man. Since Sir Charles wrote, a whole series of discoveries of human bones, in caves and elsewhere, have been made. In their texture and mode of deposition all these remains possess more or less of the same significance as those already referred to, and have a similar claim to be regarded as fossil, but their enumeration here would detain us too long.* Many of them, however, will be mentioned more particularly in connection with other matters.

* I refer here to the discoveries (not mentioned by Lyell) of human bones in the caves of L'hombrive and L'herm, which are described more particularly by Carl Vogt in his *Lectures on Man*, (Giessen, 1863,) and which justify the conclusion, *that man must have lived contemporaneously with the extinct cave-animals;* to the human bones discovered by Lartet and Christy in the cave of Les Eyzies, (Perigord), probably belonging to the period of the Mammoth; to the human lower jaw found by the Marquis de Vibraye in the grotto of Arcy in Burgundy; to the extremely animal human jaw of the Mammoth period found in the cave of La Naulette in Belgium, and to the flint axes of the diluvium, as well as to numerous analogous discoveries made in many bone-caves in France, Belgium, England, Germany and other places. Everywhere human remains or productions were found together with the bones of primeval, extinct or displaced animals under conditions which exclude the idea of subsequent fortuitous admixture. Among the discoveries of human bones *outside the caverns* we may also cite: The teeth described by Jaeger and Quenstedt from the *Bohnerz* of Würtenberg,— the human teeth found in an ancient travertine near Rome upon which Ponzi has reported,— the human skull in the Natural History Museum at Stuttgart, which was dug out in 1700 from the calcareous tuff of Canstatt in company with bones of the Mammoth, and which resembles the Neanderthal skull in its low, narrow forehead and strong superciliary arches; the fossil human jaw from the gravel-pits of Ipswich in Suffolk, which was exhibited to the Ethnological Society of London in April, 1865, and which, besides its very low structure and the great amount of iron contained in it, exhibited all the characters of very high antiquity; the remains of a human skull found quite recently by Professor Cocchi in the valley of the Arno near Florence in diluvial clay, together with various bones of extinct species of animals, and which, according to Carl Vogt, are of like antiquity with the Engis and Neanderthal skulls; the human bones which A. Issel states that he found in Pliocene deposits (therefore belonging to the Tertiary period) in the neighborhood of the town of Savona in Liguria, (the find of Colle del Vento), and which bear all the physical signs of very high antiquity, and others. These and a number of similar discoveries of various dates require, however, a more accurate testing and establishment by scientific authorities, before they can be employed as satisfactory scientific evidence.

But even now we have by no means exhausted the proofs of the high antiquity of the human race upon the earth. . There is still a *third* series of proofs, (which, however, must be passed over here in a very rapid sketch), and for these we are almost exclusively indebted to the celebrated and indefatigable French palæontologist, E. Lartet. Although the geologist, who pays attention only to the position of the strata and the possibility of their having undergone disturbances after their original deposition, may still perhaps entertain some doubt upon the subject,* this evidence can leave no doubt on the mind of the zoologist and palæontologist as to the contemporaneity of man and the Diluvial animals. *The proofs in question consist in the traces of the action of man upon the bones of extinct animals.* Even before Lartet, such things were known. Thus in Sweden and Iceland signs of wounds made by the hand of man during the life of the animals had been found upon the osseous remains of an Auroch, (*Bos priscus*), and of an Irish-Deer, and the same fact is said to have been observed in America upon injured bones of the Mastodon. But our first accurate and certain knowledge upon this point was furnished by Lartet, who has made the subject his special study. He indicates, in France, *nine* characteristic Diluvial animals, namely, the Cave Bear, the Cave Lion, the Cave Hyena, the Mammoth, the Rhinoceros with a bony septum to the nostrils, (*R. tichorhinus*), the great Irish-

---

* In fact such doubts have been raised by certain French *savants*, such as Elie de Beaumont, Eugène Robert and others, notwithstanding the extreme improbability of their having any solid foundation from a geological point of view,— and the true diluvial character of the axe-bearing deposits has been questioned. Even if such doubts may be scientifically and geologically well-founded they must vanish before the immense mass of other facts and evidence leading from all sides to the same result. Moreover, at present all the more considerable *savants* of the world, almost without exception, admit that the evidence of the contemporaneity of man with the great Pachyderms of the quaternary epoch and with the diluvial animals in general is complete. A sharp criticism of the objections to the genuineness of the flint-instruments raised by Eugène Robert, Decaisne and others, will be found in a small work by Gabriel de Mortillet; *Les Mystifiés de l'Académie des Sciences*, Paris, 1865.

Deer, the Reindeer, the Aurochs and the Urus. By the occurrence of these species he distinguishes *four* successive periods, of which that of the Cave Bear is the most ancient, that of the Mammoth and Rhinoceros the second, and that of the Urus the most recent. Now Lartet has ascertained that bones of nearly all these animals show unmistakable signs of the operations of man, either during the life of the animals or while the bones were still in a fresh state, the bones being sometimes injured by wounds, sometimes worked upon and sometimes broken or split. The last form of human interference is that most frequently met with, and its object was evidently to enable the marrow to be taken out of the bones, this having been apparently as great a dainty with our earliest ancestors as it still is among both savage and civilized people.* Many bones also exhibit a peculiar striation, as if the flesh had been scraped from them with knives or flint flakes.

But besides all this, there are numerous indications of somewhat artistic work, such as drawings, rough sculptures and the like. These are rude figures or outlines, generally representing animals then living, engraved by means of fragments of flint upon the bones and horns of the great Irish Deer, the Reindeer, etc. With some of these were found fragments or plates of schist with engraved outlines of animals, especially of the Elk and Reindeer, but some also of much more ancient species, such as the Mammoth or long-haired Elephant, etc. Even the rude and imperfect outline of the figure of a man has been dis-

* That this special fondness for marrow persisted long after the times of primeval man is proved by a notice by the Greek writer Procopius, who lived about the year 550. In his Gothic History he describes people, whom he calls the *Scrithifinns*, living in the extreme north of Scandinavia, and states as the principal indication of their savage state, that the children are nourished not with their mother's milk, but with the marrow of animals. As soon as the child was born, the mother wrapped it up in a skin, hung it upon a tree, put some marrow in its mouth, and then went straight off to the chase again. An excellent mode of rearing children, and one that certainly is to be recommended from the point of view of economy of time!

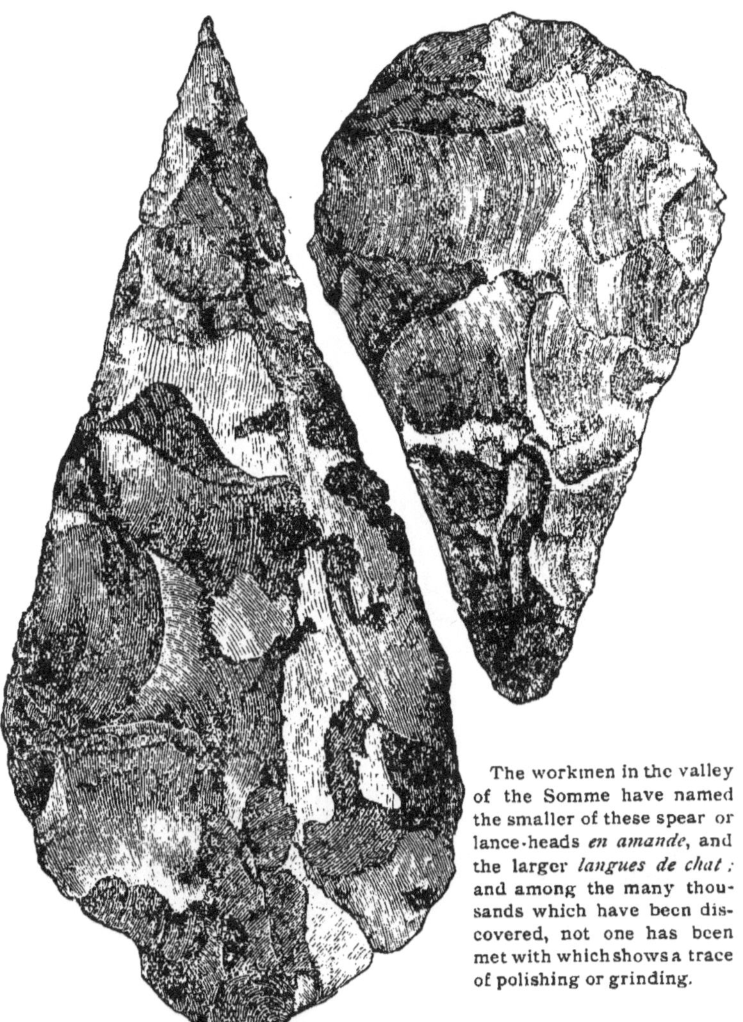

The workmen in the valley of the Somme have named the smaller of these spear or lance-heads *en amande*, and the larger *langues de chat :* and among the many thousands which have been discovered, not one has been met with which shows a trace of polishing or grinding.

FLINT INSTRUMENTS FROM HOXNE — HALF THE ORIGINAL SIZE.

"The presence of implements of this type in gravel drifts," says Hodder M. Westropp, *Introductory Essays on Pre-Historic Archæology*, "which geological evidence assigns to a very remote period, and in conjunction with bones of extinct animals, argue a very remote antiquity for their manufacture, and a very early date for the men who fabricated them. The extreme rudeness of the implements bespeak a corresponding rudeness and barbarous condition of the men who made them, and induce a belief in the inferiority of this primitive race.

"These implements have a deep claim on our interest, as they make known to us the earliest productions of the hand of man — as they mark the first step in human industry, and as they show, in the most unequivocal manner, 'the length of time which must have elapsed since the first appearance of man in Western Europe.'"

covered, engraved upon a fragment of Reindeer horn, between two very characteristic horse's heads. These drawings, which are of course very rough and often very grotesque, display to us the very infancy of art; nevertheless from the unanimous testimony of those who have seen them, they are so characteristic that we may recognize at the first glance the animals or objects which they were intended to represent. The figures of the Reindeer and the Mammoth* are particularly distinct. Thus M. de Lastic found in the cave of Bruniquel, on the banks of the Arveyron, a bone adorned with carvings, on which were engraved a perfectly recognizable horse's head and the head of a Reindeer, the latter easily identified by the form of its antlers. The handles of daggers made of ivory or bone have also been found, on which the above-mentioned animals were represented at full length. Reindeer horn is the substance most frequently engraved upon or worked, and adapted to all sorts of purposes.

In all, Lartet has discovered and enumerated seventeen localities, where these objects have been found and where, according to him, man undoubtedly lived contemporaneously with the animals just referred to. In the year 1864, he and Christy first

---

* A plate of ivory, broken into several pieces which were imbedded separately in ossiferous loam hardened by the infiltration of lime, showed, when put togeth r, (as described by Carl Vogt in an essay published in the *Kölnische Zeitung* for 1866) the outlines of no less than three elephants walking one behind the other, of which however the entire body only of the middle one was visible. By the curvature of his teeth, the long mane flowing down from the withers and the dense hairiness of the lower surface it was at once shown to be a Mammoth drawn from the life. Figures of the Reindeer are extraordinarily frequent; the animal is shown in the most various positions and is readily recognizable by its antlers and hair-tufts. On a piece of slate in the possession of the Marquis de Vibraye the artist has even ventured upon the representation of a group of Reindeer fighting with each other. Usually several animals of the same species or groups of them are represented, a leader preceding them, whilst the others follow represented at half length. "In many groups we seem to recognize a cautious watching with the nose and eye, the scenting of peril."

As regards the representation of a human figure mentioned in the text, this appears to be naked, and in the meagerness of the hips and tighs and the prominence of the belly reminds us rather of the Australian than of the European type.

exhibited to the French Academy a number of such specimens from the numerous bone-caves of the Dordogne ; the inspection of these carried conviction to the most incredulous.*   But a few years later the quantity of these remarkable objects had·become

* Christy deposited in Paris a rich collection of such objects, which furnished a very distinct picture of that distant time.   In 1866 Professor Schaaffhausen of Bonn, laid before the 23d General Meeting of the Natural History Society of the Rhineland and Westphalia, various implements of this kind made of the bones and horns of the Reindeer, such as arrow-heads with barbs, needles and dagger-like knives, together with models of other objects, upon some of which pictures of animals presenting the most striking likeness were cut.   All these objects were imbedded with flint knives and bones and teeth of the Reindeer in a solid calcare-ous concretion.—A whole block of this remarkable breccia had been presented by Lartet at the Professor's request to the Museum at Poppelsdorf.   To this the Proffessor added a description of some similar discoveries in the Todtenfeld at Uelde, not far from Lippstadt in Westphalia, the numerous bone-caves of which promise, when carefully examined, to furnish results no less interesting to the student of prehistoric times than those obtained from the caves of Belgium and the South of France.   At the above-mentioned locality there were found numer-ous broken human bones, with perforated teeth of the Wolf, Dog and Horse, mixed with rude flint knives and an awl made from the metatarsal bone of a stag. The mode in which the human bones were broken leaves scarcely any doubt, according to Schaaffhausen, that here the remains of a meal of cannibals have been preserved, the same thing having already been proved by Spring with regards to the discoveries in the cave of Chauvaux in Belgium.

In 1865, Professor July of Toulouse, when lecturing upon fossil man in the Rue de la Paix at Paris, laid before his auditors some still more interesting objects :—
" Here," he said, "are two lower jaws of the Cave-Bear, which have very proba-bly been fractured by man in the living animal, and in which union has taken place in the normal way.   Here is a skull of the same species (skull from Nabrigas) which has been pierced in its frontal part by a flint arrow. It is also a flint arrow that we see still adhering to this vertebra of a young Reindeer found in the cave of Les Eyzies by MM. Lartet and Christy.   Lastly I must tell you that Major Wanchope has found a flint hammer buried in the skull of a gigantic Deer (*Megaceros hibernicus.*)

"This tooth of *Ursus spelaeus* (the Cave Bear) which has served to make a knife of which the enamel forms the edge,—this phalange of the same animal, pierced with a hole which traverses it from side to side,—these barbed arrow-heads made of the bones of the Stag and Reindeer, and the grooves in which seem still ready to receive the poison which formerly rendered them so dangerous,—these antlers on which the flint saw has so clearly left its mark,—and these bones of lost species, fashioned into knives, polishers, awls, pins, needles, and even into whistles or objects of ornament,—will not so many combined proofs gain you over to the cause of M. Boucher de Perthes, which is also ours ?   It is very evident that the bones thus worked could only be so treated in the fresh state, &c."

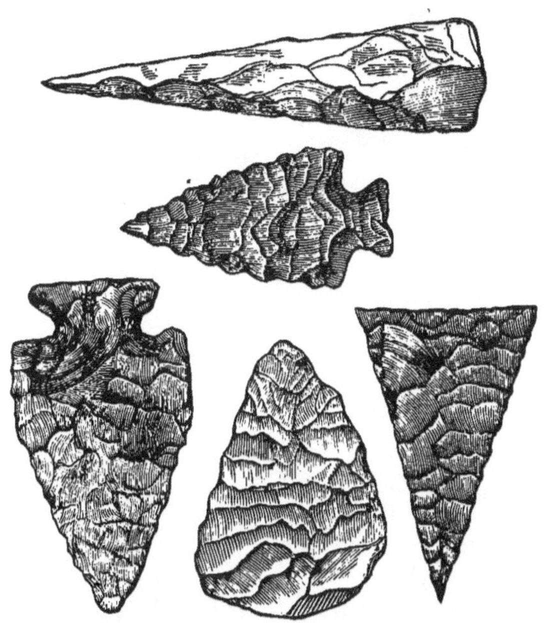

IMPLEMENTS OF CHIPPED STONE.   EUROPE.

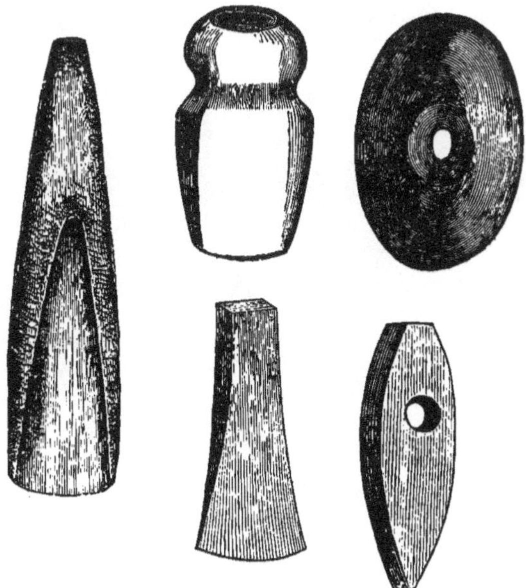

IMPLEMENTS OF POLISHED STONE.   EUROPE.

so great, that in the Paris Exhibition of the year 1867, whole glass cases were filled with these and the other material proofs of the prehistoric existence of man. Gabriel de Mortillet, the celebrated French archæogeologist, concluded a report upon this portion of the Exhibition in these memorable words: "The contemporaneity of man with those species of animals which last became extinct, his contemporaneity with the Reindeer as an indigenous animal in France, is amply, positively and irrevocably proved by the discovery of the products of human industry abundantly mixed with the remains of these animals, which have now become extinct or have emigrated, in undisturbed quaternary beds and in the midst of cave deposits which have never been *disturbed*. Upon this point the glass-cases, which occupy the left hand side of the first gallery of the history of French industry, can leave no doubt. They are quite sufficient to convince any one, however incredulous or obstinate.

"The glass-case showing the state of art in the Reindeer period furnishes a still more decisive demonstration. The hand of man has perfectly represented not only the Reindeer, an animal which has now emigrated, but also the great Cave-Bear, the Cave-Tiger and the Mammoth, all extinct animals, and this has been done upon the spoils of the Reindeer and the Mammoth themselves. Man was therefore incontestably contemporaneous with the animals of which he employed various parts and which he figured so accurately. It is impossible to have a more convincing demonstration."—(*Revue des cours scientifiques*, 1867, page 703.)

The discoveries of Lartet and his followers relate only to the bones of so-called Diluvial animals. But within the last few year, further discoveries in the same direction have been made known by a French naturalist, M. Desnoyers, and if these prove to be correct, they will carry back the antiquity of the human race upon the earth to a period of which no one hitherto

ventured even to dream, except perhaps upon purely hypo-
thetical grounds.   These consist of the traces of human action
on the bones of animals belonging to the *Tertiary period*, found
in the gravel-beds of St. Prest near Chartres in France.   They
are said to be perfectly analogous to the traces of human action
observed on bones from the Diluvial period.

The Tertiary period forms, as is well-known, the last of the
three great sections, (the Primary, Secondary and Tertiary
periods), under which it is usual to arrange the fossiliferous
strata of the earth, and consequently its geological history.
The Tertiary immediately preceded the Diluvial period.   Sir
Charles Lyell has personally examined the specimens referred
to and regards the conclusions which have been drawn from
them as certainly very probable, although, on the whole, in his
Antiquity of Man, he expresses himself rather doubtfully about
the matter.   On the other hand Carl Vogt, (in his *Vorlesungen
über den Menschen* and in the *Archiv für Anthropologie*),
declares, that the discovery is a genuine one and open to no
doubt.   He also maintains that the formation in which these
bones were found, is decidedly Tertiary and therefore geologically older than the French Diluvial formations.   According to
him it is characterized by the presence of the Southern Elephant, (*Elephas meredionalis*), and belongs to an epoch which
undoubtedly preceded the glacial period and the age of the
Cave Bear, the Mammoth and the Tichorhine Rhinoceros.
The French naturalist Quatrefages also takes the side of
Desnoyers, and declares that his investigations bear the im-
press of the most severe and careful study.   Desnoyers' testimony is the more valuable as, up to the year 1845, he was one
of the most decided opponents of the notion of the existence
of fossil man.

Its value is still further increased by a communication made
by Abbé Bourgeois to the International Congress of Prehistoric
Anthropology and Archæology held at Paris in the year

1867.—In the very same Tertiary strata of St. Prest, in which Desnoyers found worked bones, M. Bourgeois discovered implements of stone. He afterwards stated that he had also found numerous worked flints in strata likewise of Tertiary age in the commune of Thenay near Pontlevoy, and from this and some other discoveries he concluded, that the existence of man reached a very high antiquity, extending even into the Tertiary period. He added that Abbé Delaunay had found near Pouancé, (Maine et Loire), fossil bones of a *Halitherium*, (a herbivorous cetacean of the Miocene or Middle Tertiary period), with evident signs of having been operated upon with cutting instruments.

Lastly, M. A. Issel communicated to the same congress a notice of several human bones which, as he stated, he had found in beds of the Pliocene age, (i. e., belonging to the last section of the Tertiary period), in the neighborhood of the town of Savona in Liguria, and which presented all the physical tokens of very high antiquity. (See the *Compte rendu du Congrès international d' Anthropologie et d' Archéologie préhistorique.* Paris, 1868).

As a matter of course we can only hope that these remarkable discoveries will be confirmed in course of time, and after they have been submitted to a careful, critical examination. But, if they prove to be well founded, they are doubtless strongly in favor of the conjectures of those naturalists who, upon theoretical grounds alone, have held that the earliest appearance of man upon the earth must be referred back at all events to the last and perhaps even to the middle or the earliest section of the great Tertiary period.

In this summary the evidences in favor of the great antiquity of the existence of man are exhausted, at all events in their principal outlines. But we could not mention in it those evidences which, leaving geological times out of consideration altogether, are derived from the present epoch — from the period of the earth's formation which is now passing. And yet the *alluvium* or so-called recent formations furnish evidence of a very high antiquity of the human race upon the earth—an antiquity indeed which leaves far behind it not only the truly historical periods, but even the times of Biblical tradition. For whilst the latter can only be calculated backwards to five or seven thousand years at the utmost, the duration of the alluvial period according to the calculations of Geologists was at least a hundred thousand years, and perhaps still more, so that this alone gives a very wide range in time for the so-called *prehistoric* existence of man. ·

Moreover, the evidence derived from this source has one great advantage over the earlier proofs ; it does not rest upon argument, but, at least in part, upon direct calculation and observation. The discoveries made in the alluvial deposits are now, as might be expected, very numerous and varied; only a few of the best known will be cited here as examples.

In the years 1851 to 1854, experimental borings were made in the Delta of the Nile in Lower Egypt, and objects of human handiwork or fragments of pottery were found at depths of sixty to seventy feet. Reckoning the thickness of the alluvial deposits in the Delta of the Nile at five inches in a century, we obtain for these relics of human activity an antiquity of 14,400 to 17,300 years. But if we follow M. Rosière in estimating the rate of deposition at only two and one-half inches in a century, we obtain for a fragment of red brick found by Linant Bey, at a depth of seventy-two feet, an antiquity of thirty thousand years. Burmeister who assumes that the addition to the thickness of the soil in Lower Egypt is three and one-half inches in the century, and that since the appearance of man in that region two hundred feet have been deposited, extends his calculation of the antiquity of man to no less than seventy-two thousand years. (See his *Geologische Briefe.*)

In Sweden a fisherman's hut was excavated, the age of which

is to be reckoned at ten thousand years or even more. Another similar discovery was made in the same country, during the digging of a canal between Stockholm and Gothenburg, when a hearth built of stones, with fragments of wood charcoal, was found beneath an accumulation of "Osars" or erratic blocks in the deepest layer of the subsoil, proving that man must have dwelt on that spot during and even before the so-called glacial period.

In Florida, (North America), portions of human skeletons were found in a bank composed of coral-rock, the age of which is calculated by Agassiz to be *at least* ten thousand years. On the same continent, in the Mississippi delta, during the excavation of the gas works at New Orleans, human bones, (including a skull, exhibiting all the characteristics of the aboriginal South American race,) were found at a depth of sixteen feet, beneath six different alluvial beds. The antiquity of these remains is estimated by Dr. Dowler at from fifty to sixty thousand years. This estimate has been repeatedly attacked with a view to invalidate it, but Carl Vogt, who reproduces the whole calculation in his *Lectures on Man*, says it is impregnable. According to Broca all the endeavors that have been made to diminish the antiquity assigned to this celebrated discovery, have been incapable of reducing it below fifteen thousand years. Sir Charles Lyell, (in his *Antiquity of Man*), cites an old sea-bottom, strewn with fragments of ancient pottery, near Cagliari, (Sardinia), which must have an antiquity of at least seventeen thousand years.

A few years ago, in making a railway near Villeneuve on the Lake of Geneva, the section of a conical hill of alluvium was exposed, and from the contents of this Dr. Morlot inferred an antiquity of from seven to ten thousand years for the existence of Man at that spot.*

Here, also, we must refer to the celebrated *Pile-buildings* or *Lake-dwellings* of Switzerland, Italy, etc., which have attracted

* See Appendix No. 4.

so much attention of late years. These prove beyond the shadow of a doubt the existence of a primeval, prehistoric, semi-aquatic population in Europe, of whose existence history gives us no hint whatever.*

To the same category belong the vast, primeval turf-moors of Denmark and Iceland, which conceal in their bosoms innumerable proofs of the very high antiquity of man in these regions;† the ancient Mounds or Earthworks in the valleys of the Mississippi and Ohio in North America, which also incontestably prove the existence of a very ancient population already considerably advanced in civilization, which possessed and cultivated the land long before its occupation by the red Indian hunters;‡ and lastly the wonderful Danish shell-heaps or *kitchen-*

---

*See Appendix No. 5.   † See Appendix No. 6.

‡ When America was first discovered and for a long time afterwards, that continent was regarded as destitute of all ancient civilization, analogous to that of Europe. Hence people were the more surprised when, by the investigations of Squier and Davis on the *Ancient Monuments of the Mississippi Valley,* the opposite was proved, and it was shown that, long before the times of the Indian Redskin, those plains must have been the seat of a cons'derable civilization. Great walls of earth, ruins of towns, remains of statuary, objects of gold, silver and copper, pottery, ornaments, stone-weapons, &c., prove that the western hemispheres were not always interminable forests and endless prairies, serving no other purpose than that of forming a hunting-ground for the red hunters. The earth-mounds, which are often so large that four of them together exceed the great Egyptian pyramid in cubic contents, may have served in part as temples, in part as burying places, and in part as fortifications. The Europeans who made their way there found the mounds covered with a dense forest in which the red Indian hunter dwelt, without any traditional connection with his civilized predecessors; and from the growth of plants and trees upon the earth-works an approximate antiquity of several thousand years before the European immigration has been assigned to them. The human skulls which have been exhumed in some places belong to a different race of men from those now living.

Quite recently, in South America, mummies with brown hair have been discovered. If this brown-haired race came from Europe this must have happened long before all history; and on the western shores of that continent a civilization must have flourished, of which all traces had already disappeared when the Roman dominion was extended over Britain, Gaul and Spain.

According to Scherzer (*Vortrag auf der Naturforscher-Versammlung in Wien, 1856*), the Toltecs met with by the Spaniards are the architects of the monuments and buildings in the interior of America. They first appear in the seventh century upon the plateau of Mexico, and their remnants still linger in Central America.

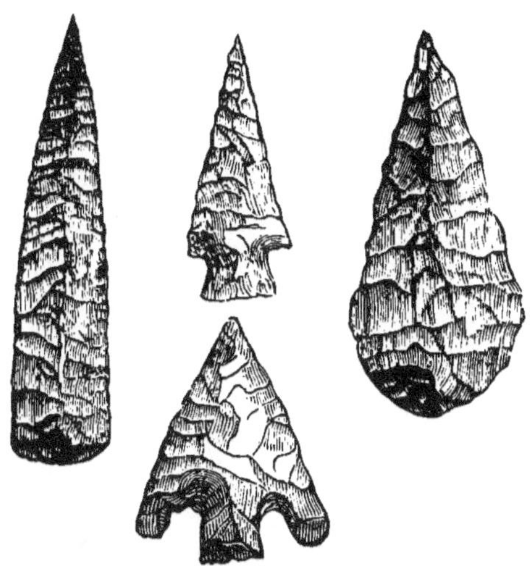

IMPLEMENTS OF CHIPPED STONE.   NORTH AMERICA.

STONE ARROW-HEADS, MODERN.   CANADA.

middens, (Kjökkenmöddings), consisting of enormous heaps of the shells of marine animals, especially Oysters, which have served for the nourishment of primeval men, by whom their shells have thus been accumulated. These heaps, which are placed upon the sea-shore, are often as much as one thousand feet in length, by one hundred to two hundred feet in breadth, and five to ten feet in height. They occur on the coasts of Zealand and Jutland and of the islands of Fünen, Moën, Samsoë, etc., and also on some parts of the Swedish and Genoese coasts, always along the creeks and bays, where the force of the waves is great, and generally at the very edge of the water, except in those places where alluvial deposits or elevations of the land have subsequently removed them to a greater distance. In these shell-heaps direct traces of the existence of man are always found, especially weapons and other instruments of stone, horn and bone, fragments of clumsy pottery, stone-wedges, stone-knives, etc., in great abundance, accompanied by fragments of charcoal and ashes, but no traces of corn, bronze or iron, or of orchard fruits or domestic animals, with the sole exception of the Dog. The numerous bones of animals which have been found, belong chiefly to the Urus, the Aurochs, the Stag, the Roe-deer, the Wild Boar, the Fox, Wolf, Beaver, Otter, etc., and all the bones containing marrow have been split up for the purpose of extracting from them that favorite article of food. Human bones never occur in the kitchen-middens, probably because the people who formed them were accustomed to bury their dead.*

That these shell-mounds or offal-heaps must be of great antiquity, reaching indeed into a period geologically separate

---

* By the exertions of the Danish archaeologist Worsaae, the Museum of Northern antiquities and the geological Museum of the University of Copenhagen, contain an extraordinary abundance of objects from the kitchen-middens brought there and exhibited in their natural state. These shell-heaps have long been known, but they were regarded as natural deposits until, in the year 1847, three distinguished Danish *savants*, Steenstrup, Forchhammer and Worsaae, investigated them thoroughly and ascertained their artificial origin.

from ours, is proved by the circumstance that shells of the marine Mollusca contained in them, (such as the Oyster, *Ostrea edulis*, the Cockle, *Cardium edule*, the Mussel, *Mytilus edulis*, etc.), are still of a size which is never attained by representatives of the same species now living in the Baltic. Living specimens are not more than one-half or even one-third of the size of those in the shell-mounds. The cause of the diminution of size is as follows: The Baltic, being no longer freely in communication with the Ocean and receiving the waters of numerous rivers, does not retain the character of a true sea, but is merely brackish, whilst these Molluscs require to live in the salt-water of the open sea in order that they may attain their full size. This is the case in a particularly remarkable degree with the common Oyster, which, as has been stated, is very abundant in the shell-mounds; this mollusc does not now occur in the Baltic except just at its entrance, where it communicates with the open Ocean. From this we must conclude that, at the time when these heaps were formed, the Baltic had quite a different form from that which it now possesses, and especially that its communication with the Atlantic ocean was much more free and open. Nevertheless, the kitchen-middens, notwithstanding their high antiquity, belong only to the recent or alluvial period, as they contain only the bones of animals still living. The sole exception to this statement is the Wild Bull or Urus, (*Bos primigenius* or *Urus*), which, however, was seen by Cæsar. Quite recently similar shell-mounds have been discovered upon a great extent of the coasts of both North and South America.*

* Shell-mounds and kitchen-refuse have been found in America in great abundance. In South America on the east coast, on the Pacific ocean, in Brazil and Guayaquil and on the east coast of North America, near Halifax in Nova Scotia and on Margaret's Bay. These last contain only implements of the stone-age; and with these are found bones of the Moose, Bear, Beaver, Porcupine, &c. The shells found belong to the species, *Venus mercenaria*, *Pecten islandicus*, *Crepedula formicata and Mytilus edulis*, the last in so fragile or soft a condition,

To the pile-dwellings, kitchen-middens and the like, we must add as the last and latest term in the series of traces of his existence left by prehistoric man in the alluvial soils, the tumuli or "giant's graves," as they are sometimes called, which were formerly supposed to contain the bones of a race of giants who lived before man, and also the remarkable objects known as *Dolmens* or "stone tables." But although the grave-mounds and stone monuments themselves are gigantic, the men who built them were nothing of the kind, but rather of smaller stature than the men of the present day.* They were probably supplanted by the taller, more powerful and more civilized race of the *Celts*, with whose appearance on the scene the first dawn of history in central Europe commences.

With these, therefore, we have arrived at the close of that series of facts fitted to throw some light upon the prehistoric existence and high antiquity of man upon the earth, and consequently at the end of our description of the whole matter before us. This subject can only be sketched here in its most general outlines and so as to show its most prominent points, just as an Alpine traveler standing in the centre of a mountain-panorama is usually told the names only of the most prominent and striking of the infinite chain of peaks and mountains surrounding him, whilst the hundreds of smaller peaks, though in their own way perhaps equally remarkable, are passed over in silence. Certainly the questions which naturally arise from the consideration of these facts as to the antiquity and origin of our

as to fall to pieces when touched. A traveler, Clement Markham, has recently given a more accurate account of the shell-mounds found on the coast of Ecuador, not far from Guayaquil; they consist of fragments of pottery and of four different sea-shells, one of which is extinct in that region. Many cutting instruments made of quartz-crystals were also found.

As regards the absence of human bones in the shell-mounds mentioned in the text, the rule appears to be not without exceptions. At least it is stated in the *Anthropological Review*, (February, 1865, page XXIX.), that human bones have been found in the shell-mounds of Caithness, in the same state as the bones of animals associated with them.

* See Appendix No. 7.

race, or the consequences which we are justified in deducing from them, are of more importance and significance than the facts themselves.

Thus, what is truly the antiquity of the human race upon the earth reckoned in years? What is the relation of this antiquity to the antiquity of the earth itself? And what is its relation to the periods of history and popular tradition? How is it that we have no historical traditions of this earliest period? And what is the relation between the primitive time and the primitive condition of our race in prehistoric periods? Are we to suppose that man has gradually struggled from a low and rude state into civilization? or that he fell from a primitive state of high cultivation, only to work his way again to the same condition at a later period? and if the former be the case, how has his gradual advance to his present state of civilization been effected? All these questions, which are almost immediately connected with the highest interests of humanity, we shall now endeavor to answer to the best of our power, and so far as the present state of knowledge will permit. But before doing so we may remark that these questions and conclusions do not merely occupy our intelligence, but must also appeal to our emotions, when we consider the immense series of races which have disappeared before our time, and the immeasurable grandeur of that Creation in the midst of which we live.

As regards the first question, or that of the determination by years of the antiquity of the human race, any such calculation is excessively difficult except in the case of the alluvial deposits. With respect to these we know pretty nearly the depth of deposit produced in a certain time, and then according to the depth at which human remains or objects of human workmanship have been found, we may calculate the time which must have elapsed since those objects were deposited there. But as soon as we pass from the Recent period to the so-called geological periods, we no longer possess any such standard of

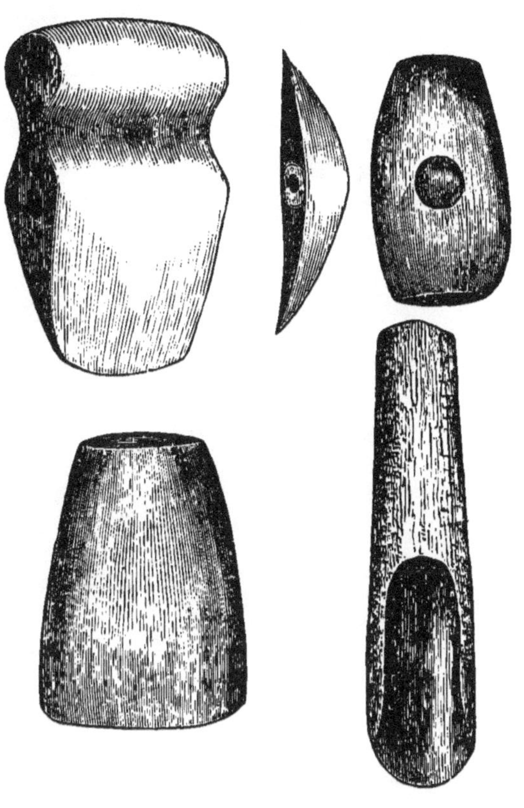

IMPLEMENTS OF POLISHED STONE.   NORTH AMERICA.

measurement and have to depend solely upon approximate data. Hence this question has been answered in the most different ways. In Geology we know no *absolute* numbers, but only such as are *relative* or proportional. We do not even know exactly the total length of the Alluvial period which separates us from antediluvian times, but have to depend upon calculations which are different in different places, and which indeed indicate an actual difference in the length of this period at different parts of the earth's surface. And as no definite line of demarcation exists between the Alluvium and Diluvium of the older geologists, and as the two pass gradually one into the other, we do not even know how long the existence of the antediluvian animals, upon which, however, the whole question turns, may have extended into the alluvial period at particular places; and we know nothing certain as to the time either of their first appearance or of their extinction. Nevertheless this much is certain, that since the time when those deposits, in which we find the remains of man and of Diluvial animals intermixed were produced, considerable geological changes must have taken place in the surface of the earth.* Thus, to cite only a few of these changes as examples of the rest, nearly all the European rivers had at that time, at least in part, a different and more elevated course; England and France were not yet separated by the Channel, but formed a single, continuous mass of land, so that the men of that period might have gone on foot from London to Paris, if those cities had then been in existence; and the proud Thames, upon whose bosom nowadays the ships of all nations rest, still formed only a humble affluent of the German Rhine. The beautiful Switzerland, so favored by all tourists and lovers of Nature, was then inaccessible to human foot;—from the summit of the Alps to beyond the Jura, down to Geneva and even to far distant Soleure, it was buried beneath

* This is a point which has been demonstrated by Lyell in his *Antiquity of Man from a geological point of view*, in great detail and with great scientific knowledge.

the chilling pressure of an enormous mass of ice, which bore upon its mighty back gigantic fragments of rock, and rolled them along to places where they now look as if they had been transported by the hands of giants. The great desert of the Sahara was still overflowed by the waves of the sea ; its desert and burning sands were not yet exposed so as to produce that glowing wind, which, nowadays, after traversing the Mediterranean, melts away the winter-snows on the summits of the Alps as if by magic, and converts the plain of Switzerland, formerly buried under everlasting ice, into a blooming country covered with towns and villages.   Lastly, the animals and plants then living were essentially different, in accordance with this different state of things, from those of the present day.

Such important changes as these, in the structure of the earth's surface, in climate, in the distribution of land and water, and in the organic world, necessarily imply the lapse of a very long period of time, that is to say, long in comparison to the standards which the shortness of our own lives has led us to accept as our rules ; for in the history and development of the earth a thousand years count as little more than a moment in our own existence.

The traces of the Diluvial period itself, the duration and extent of which of course are of the highest importance in this question, are not, as was formerly supposed, the results of one or several sudden catastrophes, but of a very gradual course of development and of multifarious and distinct natural processes. For their production they would certainly have required far more time than the formation of the Alluvium. We possess sufficient evidence that man must have lived* even during and before the glacial epoch, a subdivision of the quaternary or Diluvial period, probably extending very far back in it.

From this it follows, that his existence did not merely coincide with the conclusion of the period of the Diluvium, but that it

* See Appendix No. 8.

extended far into that period, perhaps even to its commencement, a fact which is further proved by the deposition of the
diluvial flint axes in the very lowest bed of the Diluvium, quite
close to the underlying chalk.   But if the discoveries of MM.
Desnoyers, Bourgeois, etc., above referred to, prove to be
correct, the existence of man extends far beyond even the
Diluvial period and far into the great Tertiary epoch, and in
this case his presence on the earth can only be calculated by
hundreds of thousands of years!

You are doubtless startled, honored reader, by the magnitude of this number; and yet in comparison with the enormous
periods of time which the earth has seen pass away during its
gradual devolopment and formation, it is a mere nothing.   In
the attempt to calculate the time required for the building up
only of the stratified portion of the earth's crust, geologists have
reached a period of from six to seven hundred millions of
years!   Other geologists make a rather smaller calculation,
but in this case a hundred million years more or less is of little
consequence.

Thus we see that, great as may be the antiquity of man in
comparison with the periods of history or tradition, he is nevertheless very young upon the earth itself, and under any circumstances, is one of its last and most recent productions.   For
even supposing that man was in existence as early as the close
or even the middle of the Tertiary period, he still reaches but
a little way up in the great scale of the history of the earth.
This scale, so far as it relates to the fossiliferous strata, has been
divided by Lyell into thirty-six members, but this number now
appears to be too small, as still older strata have recently been
found to contain organic remains.   In this scale then, the man
of the Tertiary period would extend to No. 3 or No. 4, or at
the outside to No. 5 or No. 6!   Innumerable races of plants
and animals preceded him in series long drawn out, and during
almost infinite periods of time, and man himself plays, as it

were, only in the last act of a colossal Drama, the first scenes of which are concealed from us by impenetrable darkness.

Upon theoretical grounds Sir Charles Lyell regards it as very probable, that man lived as long ago as the Pliocene or last subdivision of the Tertiary period ; but he considers it improbable, that the existence of the human race dates back to the Miocene or middle division of the same period.   This latter opinion he founds upon the fact that about this time the general character of the organized world, (animals and plants), was still too different from that of the living forms.   On the other hand, Sir John Lubbock asserts, that in his earliest beginnings man must have lived in the Miocene period, but that we can hope to meet with his bones or other remains from that epoch only in the tropical regions which have as yet been so imperfectly explored !   Wallace even thinks that we must refer the first appearance of man upon the earth still farther back, to the *Eocene* or first subdivision of the great Tertiary period.

From this we may see, that philosophers are still much divided in opinion as to the real antiquity of our race upon the earth, and that it is still quite impossible to estimate it definitely in years.   All that we can regard as perfectly certain is, *that the known historical period is a mere nothing in point of time when compared with the periods during which our race has actually inhabited the earth*, or as Lyell significantly expresses it, this historical period is comparatively ·only a *creation of yesterday*.   In this opinion all students of the subject now agree, even those who were formerly the most obstinate of its opponents.

In point of fact, true history, that is, such history as we may consider authentic, from its being transmitted to us by credible written or traditional evidence, by no means attains so high an antiquity as is commonly believed.   It only commences with the institution of the Greek Olympiads or with the year 776 B. C. The famous Trojan war is certainly a good deal older and carries us back to 1100 or 1200 years B. C.; but the account of it is well known to be only a mixture of fiction and truth. That the Greeks themselves did not venture to date their history very far back, appears from the circumstance that Hecatæus of Miletus, who lived 500 years B. C., expresses the opinion, that for some 900 years the Gods had no longer taken women for their wives. This, therefore, would indicate a date of 1400 years before our era.

Beyond this earliest dawn of history we have nothing but myths and traditions, oral communications transmitted from generation to generation, or isolated data derived from old documents; or a history has been artificially compiled from monuments, buildings, old inscriptions, etc. Thus the traditions of the Aryan race of mankind reach to two thousand years B. C. The Semitic writings place the birth of Abraham, the progenitor of the Jews, at about 2000 years B. C.,* and throw back the Deluge into the fortieth century before our era. From the creation to the Deluge the Bible reckons from one to two thousand years, and from this we get a total of from five to six thousand years before Christ.

The very ancient history of the Chinese contains two isolated dates as the oldest. According to their writings the Deluge admitted by them took place in the time of the emperor Yao, or in the year 2357 B. C., and the art of writing was invented by Huangti as early as the year 2698 B. C. About this time, and whilst the Jews still led a nomadic life under the patriarchs, the Chinese must have already attained a very high degree of civilization. The mythical or legendary history of that people indeed reaches the enormous antiquity of 129,600 years, a lapse of time which, according to their traditions, was composed of twelve great divisions, (each of 10,800 years), and embraced

* According to calculations made upon the authority of the inscriptions upon some Assyrian tablets now in the British Museum, the time of Abraham would fall about the year 2290 B. C.

three great periods, namely: the reign of *darkness*, the reign of *the earth*, and the reign of *man*. Professor Spiegel gives a somewhat similar account of the Babylonians, who ascribed to their ten most ancient patriarchs lives amounting altogether to 432,000 years.   According to Alex. von Humboldt, Strabo says of the aborigines of Spain, (the Turduli and Turdetani), "they make use of the art of writing and have books containing memorials of ancient times and also poems and precepts in verse, for which they claim an antiquity of six thousand years."

As regards the derivation of history from Monuments and Inscriptions, the first place is due to the most anciently civilized land in the world, Egypt.   We all know what grand and interesting results the observations and excavations of the learned, aided by the deciphering of the hieroglyphical writings, have brought to light in that primitive land of marvels, the source of all the arts and sciences; and I will therefore only mention that all these results have been thrown into the shade by the recent discoveries of M. Mariette, who has found sculptures, inscriptions and statues dating back to no less than from 4000 to 4500 years B. C.   He also discovered pictures and inscriptions upon the walls of the tombs of that time, which leave no doubt, that even at that far distant period a comparatively high state of civilization must have existed in Egypt.

We may judge of the high idea the Greeks must have had of the civilization and power of Egypt, when we find Homer, (800 B. C.), in the Iliad speaking with great admiration of the Egyptian Thebes with its hundred gates, from each of which two hundred chariots went forth to battle, (and Memphis was much more ancient); and Achilles cries: "Not if you offered me the wealth of the Egyptian Thebes with its hundred doors, would I stir from this place!"   Consider also the pyramids of Egypt, forty and more in number, which could only be the result of the industry of a thousand years, and must be regarded as the monuments of a long line of royal races which have sunk one by one into the tomb. And this agrees perfectly with the mythical history of the Egyptians, which commences many thousands of years before their historical era, the latter beginning only with Menes, the first historical king of Egypt, five thousand years B. C.* These traditions of the most ancient civilized peoples, reaching as they do so far back in time, consequently agree perfectly with the teachings of modern science, and show that some recollection, however obscure, of a far distant past must have been retained in the memory of these peoples. Thus even if all the geological and palæontological evidence which has been brought forward to prove the high antiquity of the human race should be denied credence, this circumstance alone, in conjunction with the perfectly demonstrated high degree of civilization of the ancient Egyptians at least six thousand years ago, must convince us that the opinion hitherto prevalent and founded upon biblical authority, namely, that the human race is not more than six thousand years old, cannot possibly be correct. The adoption of such an opinion can only be explained by the profound ignorance which formerly prevailed as to the prehistoric periods of the human race. These were enveloped in complete and impenetrable darkness, illuminated by no single ray of light; but nowadays this is all changed, and a new science, called *archæogeology* by Boucher de Perthes, (a combination of geology and palæontology with archæology), has already thrown a satisfactory light upon those periods, and in course of time will illuminate them still more. Probably many of my readers will ask here : But how is it that there is no historical evidence of this long period which we call *prehistoric?* Why is this subject enveloped in an obscurity so complete that we have no direct information upon it? The answer to these questions is not difficult.

It is evident that the state of prehistoric man was one of primitive and natural barbarism, in which he neither felt the

* See Appendix No. 9.

necessity, nor possessed the means of handing down historical traditions. These means could only be furnished by the invention of the art of writing, which took place at a very late period, and is in itself very complicated. Until then, only oral tradition was known, and this indeed has existed from very ancient times. But even this could only prevail to a very limited extent, hampered as it would be by the deficiencies of an imperfectly developed language and by the want of materials worthy of transmission. The life of the primitive man was no doubt of the greatest simplicity and uniformity, and, according to our ideas, most wretchedly tedious. It was an uninterrupted and miserable strife with savage animals and with innumerable hardships of the external world! The combats of primeval man with the large animals of the Diluvial or the Tertiary period may certainly have had in them much that was striking and worthy of being handed down to posterity, and we know that in fact, contests with animals play a very prominent part in the earliest legendary chronicles of all anciently civilized peoples. It has therefore often been supposed, and probably with justice, that these legends may not be wholly poetical and imaginative, but that they may be founded at all events partially in truth, and especially that the well-known terrible narrations of fearful battles with Dragons, monsters and wonderfully formed animals of enormous size, may in part have originated in the fact that man really saw and fought with the large and sometimes curiously constructed animals of the Diluvium or Tertiary period.

Be this as it may, it is nevertheless certain that man in his rude, primitive and natural state was quite incapable of having a history, and that he must have struggled up to a certain and not very low degree of civilization, before he would experience the desire and obtain the means of communicating his experiences to posterity in a durable form. That this is not a mere theory, but the actual fact, may be seen clearly from the condition of existing savages, who have lived from time immemorial in nearly the same state, and at any rate without any real or written history. There can be no doubt that this condition of our existing savages furnishes the best picture we can have of the primitive condition of man, and that there is an almost perfect analogy between the two conditions. All the narratives of travelers show that there is a wonderful resemblance in the weapons and other implements, the customs, and the mode of life of the savage peoples visited by them, to those of primeval man, so far as we can make out the state of the latter from his scanty remains.*

This leads us quite naturally to the second and last part of this section—to those questions as to the primitive state and primitive times of the human race, which follow immediately from our investigations into its antiquity. How was our oldest ancestor—the primitive man—constituted both physically and morally? what did he do? how did he live? wherewith did he clothe and feed himself? How did he make his gradual progress towards civilization? And what can we deduce from these re-

---

* In speaking of certain prehistoric discoveries made in Britain, Bernard Owen expressed himself as follows to the Anthropological Society of London? "In the spear and arrow-heads from Caithness, the resemblance to the American weapons in material, form and size, and especially in the mode of attachment to the shaft, is so great, that the two are scarcely distinguishable."

Of the Mexican Indians we know that they still bleed themselves with lancets of obsidian, (Brasseur); and eye-witnesses describe how the existing Tasmanians select a suitable flat stone from the ground, strike fragments from it, and employ it at once as an implement.

We are acquainted with stone-implements from America which are even very similar to the most ancient Drift-implements. Indeed the working of stone is so simple that we cannot wonder that stone-implements from almost all countries, (Europe, Asia, America and Australia,) should be strikingly similar in appearance. The stone age has prevailed in every great region of the inhabited world, and still partially persists in America, Australia, &c.; for there are races enough who have never been acquainted with the use of metals. Nay, plenty of savage tribes have been found who had no knowledge even of the use of fire; and until the arrival of Europeans, the Australians knew nothing about cooking or boiling food. Their nourishment consisted principally of marine animals which were devoured raw, just as was the case with the ancient builders of the kitchen-middens or shell-mounds. In Tierra del Fuego and in Brazil, moreover, extensive and perfectly *fresh* shell-heaps of the kind above described are still to be found.

searches into the primitive existence of man, which upset everything previously regarded as true, and open to us a view into an immensely distant past hitherto completely enveloped in obscurity,—what can we deduce from these with regard to our proper subject, namely, the position of man in nature and the important question, Whence do we come?

It true that to enter upon this field is so far an uncertain and dangerous course, that with regard to most points we have to depend rather on assumptions, conclusions from analogy and the like, than on direct knowledge, and thus fancy must more or less lend its aid to reason in testing and arranging the evidence. Nevertheless, we possess a series of certain data which may furnish us with a tolerably perfect notion of the condition of primitive man, and of his excessively slow progress through the lapse of thousands of years to his gradual perfection and ennoblement. And this is especially the case when we call in to our assistance the numerous observations which have been made on existing savage tribes, in which, as already indicated, we have before us a very distinct and instructive prototype or representation for enabling us to judge of the condition of our most ancient human ancestors. In all probability, however, the general condition of primeval man was still lower and more imperfect than even that of our most barbarous savages. From the earliest period of his existence known to us, he has left behind him nothing in the shape of weapons or implements, except those rough stone wedges already described, which were produced by merely striking together nodules of flint in their fresh and readily cleavable state. At that early period he was unacquainted even with that first and most primitive of all arts, the art of making *pottery*, the indestructible remains of which are met with so abundantly at a somewhat later period; nor had he then any of those implements made of wood, horn and bone, which are also found in such plenty among the remains of a latter date. The difference between the man of the Diluvial and Tertiary period and the civilized man of the present day, must therefore have been still greater than that between the Australian savage and the cultivated European of our own time,—a difference so great that it is only with difficulty and inward reluctance that the uninstructed mind can resolve to admit a logical connection between that period and the present, and takes refuge in the most improbable theories of the creation of man, rather than accept the truth which lies so evidently before it. For upon this point at least, our observations leave no doubt whatever. Man has not, as the old conception of the universe represents him, descended upon the earth from heaven as a child of paradise, a finished and to a certain extent perfect being, but, like all the rest of the organic world, he has gradually been developed in the course of many thousands of years and of innumerable generations, commencing his existence as a rude savage, scarcely above the grade of animality, and almost crushed by the forces of external nature. Naked, or poorly clad in the skins of animals or the bark of trees, living singly, or in isolated families in forests, caverns and clefts of the rocks, or on the banks of rivers, *and armed only with his wretched stone-wedges*, this savage or primitive man had to maintain an almost unceasing struggle with the overpowering forces of nature which surrounded him, and with the powerful animals of the Diluvial or Tertiary period.* Out of this contest he certainly would not have come as a conqueror, (perhaps,

---

* It has often been considered impossible or inconceivable that the most ancient men, with their wretched weapons, could have held their ground before the gigantic animals of the past. But a glance at the still existing savages of America, Africa and Australia, who likewise venture, with their simple and imperfect weapons, to attack the most formidable animals, and even combat them victoriously, may teach us better. "Those must be blind," says J. P. Lesley "who cannot recognize the traces of this long, hard, desperate, bloody and diabolically cruel contest between the first men and all the adverse forces of the air and the earth, a contest in which all the advantages were on the side of Nature, and in which, nevertheless, man conquered, because the powers of mind and reason came to his assistance. When we consider what the weapons and implements of the primitive man were, our astonishment that civilization ever found a time and a starting point must be increased."

indeed, he would never have begun it), if he had not been supported by his comparatively great intellectual power. For, as regards his bodily powers, these were scarcely greater and probably less than those of men of the present day.

The widely spread belief in the former existence of a race of human giants is perfectly erroneous, and, as already stated, depends solely upon the discovery of the bones of gigantic animals which were confounded with those of men. It is true that some very ancient human skeletons or parts of skeletons have been found, which must have belonged to comparatively large and very muscular men, such, for example, as the skeleton of the famous Neanderthal man, and the human bones recently found by M. Louis Lartet in one of the caverns of Perigord, (Les Eyzies), and probably belonging to the period of the Mammoth, which seem to indicate a rude, but strong and muscular race of men, with an approximation in the structure of the bones to the type of the apes, and with prognathous jaws, but nevertheless with a comparatively good development of the brain. On the other hand, most of the discoveries of the so-called Quaternary period indicate a small race, with a narrow skull and prognathous jaws, and therefore of a type resembling that of the Negroes or Mongols. In the most ancient period of the Mammoth and Cave Bear, the men, according to Brocca, (*Rapport de 1865—67*), were not of large stature, had a narrow head with a retreating forehead, and oblique, (prognathous), jaws, in fact a general conformation of the body such as is now approximately met with in the lowest races of Australia and New Caledonia. This is proved particularly by the ape-like human jaw from La Naulette which will be described hereafter, and by the analogous bones found by the Marquis de Vibraye in the cave of Arcis-sur-Aube. But the existence of this rude and small type of man lasted until a much later period of prehistoric time, namely into the so-called *Reindeer period*, as is proved especially by the discoveries made in the numerous

caves of the Belgian province of Namur, which were examined by
a special scientific commission by the orders and at the expense of
the Belgian government.   The report of this commission, dated
March 26, 1865, states that besides great quantities of partially
worked Reindeer horns and bones, flint instruments, black
pottery, shell ornaments, etc., etc., there were found a great
number of human bones, all of which must have belonged to
men of small stature, in this respect most closely agreeing with
the existing Laplanders.   The remains of fourteen individuals
found in the Trou de Frontal, as already mentioned, like the
human bones in the cave of Aurignac, indicate a smaller race
than that now in existence.   The report prepared by M. E.
Dupont describes the Belgian cave-man as ''petit, bien musclé,
vif et maladif.''

That a similar small race must have continued to exist even
during the *Bronze-period*, which followed the Stone-age, and in
which man had already learnt the arts of alloying and working
in metals, is proved by the well-known small size of the handles
of the bronze weapons.   This fact had struck archæologists
generally, long before anything was known of Diluvial man.

If the primitive man was thus so inferior even in corporeal
attributes to the men of the present day,* this was still more
strikingly the case with regard to his intellectual capacities.
Although his mental powers enabled the primitive man, notwithstanding his comparative bodily weakness, to come off
victorious in his contests with animals which exceeded him
greatly in size and strength, these faculties can nevertheless
only have been of the most imperfect and undeveloped kind
when compared with the general intellectual culture of the
existing generation.   This indeed is demonstrated by numerous discoveries of ancient and primeval human skulls in the
most various parts of the world, as these, almost without exception, when they belong to a tolerably high antiquity, show a

* See Appendix No. 10.

rude or undeveloped form, and, in accordance therewith, a comparatively small development of the brain.   In some respects they remarkably approach the type of the lowest of existing races of men, that of the barbarous aborigines of Africa or Australia.   Among such the following may be cited :

The numerous negro-like skulls from the Belgian caves found by Spring and Schmerling;* the so-called Borreby skull from Denmark ;† the skull which was discovered by Link among those collected by Schlotheim from the gypsum-caves near Köstritz and which was remarkable for the singular flattening of its forehead ; the skulls of similar form discovered by Lund in a Brazilian bone cave mixed with the remains of extinct animals; that found by Castelnau under the same conditions in the rocky caverns of the Peruvian Andes, which had a similar form and was much elongated behind;‡ the skull, already mentioned, resembling that of a Caffre in form and having a low, narrow, receding forehead and very prominent superciliary ridges, which was found in company with Mammoth bones near Canstatt in the year 1700, and is now preserved in the Museum of Stuttgart.   The very ancient skull found in the Isle of Portland and presented a few years ago by J. W. Smart to the Anthropological Society of London, also belongs to this category ; it had its bones very thick, exhibited very prominent orbits and was altogether of so low a type that it resembled the

---

* See Appendix No. 11.

† These skulls, found in the tumuli of Borreby and belonging to the stone age of Denmark, are small, round, and brachycephalic ; they have a retreating forehead, a declivous occiput, a depressed vertex and projecting supraorbital arches. They resemble no other European race, except perhaps the Lapps or Finns.

‡ A strongly receding forehead always indicates a small or low development of the brain, as is shown by the configuration of the skull among the lowest races of mankind. Frère, whose rich collection of skulls of all centuries of our era has been incorporated with the new Anthropological Museum at Paris, cites as the principal result of the comparison of such skulls, that the more ancient the type the more developed is the skull in the occipital region and the flatter is the forehead, so that the transition of barbarous peoples towards civilization is revealed by the increasing elevation of the frontal region.

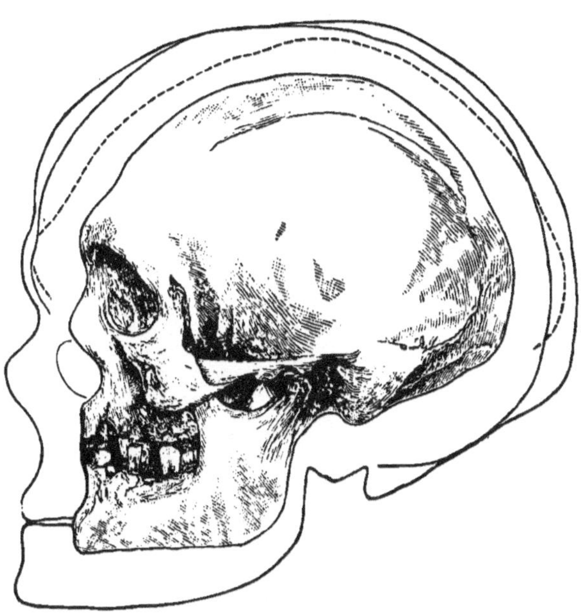

OUTLINES OF THREE PRE-HISTORIC EUROPEAN SKULLS COMPARED WITH ONE
FROM HOCHELAGA.

Outer outline, Cro-magnon skull; second outline, Engis skull; third outline
(dotted), Neanderthal skull; inner figure, Hochelagan skull on a smaller scale.

very lowest of Negro skulls (see *Anthrop. Review* for October, 1865.) We may also mention the human skulls of very low type found in an old grave in Caithness, among which there was one which was declared by several scientific authorities to be the very worst-formed European skull that they had seen, with the sole exception of that from Neanderthal,*—the skulls found on the Cotteswold hills and reported on by Dr. Bird† in the periodical above quoted, (February, 1865); the skull with a depressed forehead, a greatly developed occiput and Negro-like

* In an ancient grave near Caithness in the north of Scotland, a number of human skeletons and skulls of very low formation were recently found. The worst-formed of the skulls is very prognathous, (oblique-toothed, snoutlike); its forehead is very narrow and low, the skull itself depressed and rooflike in the middle; the brain very scanty. With it there were six other skulls more or less approaching the type just described, and all showing in the middle the rooflike projection. Probably these primitive men were cannibals, as would appear from the judgment of Professor Owen upon one of the human bones found, which was split up. The skulls themselves, according to Laing, approach most nearly to the African type.

Similar low-formed skulls were also found on the Shetland islands. (See the details in the *Anthropological Review*, February, 1865, page XXXIV).

Professor Wilson, who, as already stated, has made a thorough study of the prehistoric times of Scotland, and has proved that before the immigration of the Celts, two or three generations of aborigines must have preceded them there, describes the Scotch primeval man from his investigations as follows : "Intellectua'ly, he seems to have occupied the lowest grade to which an intelligent being can possibly sink ; morally, he was the slave of superstitious ideas ; and lastly, corporeally, he did not differ much from the present inhabitants of the same country, with the exception of the miserable development of his brain." Nevertheless the stone weapons found in the Scotch graves of this period, rough as they may be, are still far beyond those of the Diluvium, which are larger and ruder and indicate a race of men which may indeed have been stronger, but which occupied a lower position.

† One of the graves on the Cotteswold Hills near Cheltenham contained, according to Bird's report, the bones of several individuals with long oval heads and narrow foreheads. These skulls were strongly developed behind, but narrow and low in front, and contracted in the forehead. The frontal sinuses and eyebrows project and present above a wide and deep depression of the forehead. The jaws are strongly developed and the teeth very much worn away. The frontal suture did not occur in many skulls of children !

Another grave contained the bones of eight human beings, (adults and children), with well-developed heads. With them were found implements of stone and bone and old pottery.

type, described by Professor Cocchi, from the Valley of the Arno near Florence, (see note, page 46,) etc., etc.

. All these discoveries, together with a great many others which could not be particularized here, are, however, surpassed in interest and importance by the celebrated Neanderthal skull which has already been referred to. This was found in 1856, associated with an undoubtedly fossil skeleton in a limestone cavern of the Neanderthal near Hochdal, (between Düsseldorf and Elberfeld), and has been carefully examined and described by Drs. Fuhlrott and Schaaffhausen.

It has a very narrow, flat and surprisingly depressed forehead, whilst the orbits and surpraciliary ridges are developed and prominent to a degree such as has never been observed in any other human skull. This particular conformation must have given the face of the Neanderthal man a frightfully bestial and savage, or ape-like expression. The rest of the skeleton to which the skull belonged also presented many resemblances in its structure to the osseous framework of the lower races of men. The ridges and crests especially, which served as points of insertion for the muscles, are very strongly developed, so that we may conclude that their possessor was a very strong and muscular, if a very savage man. This remarkable discovery naturally created much sensation in the learned world beyond Germany, especially in England and France, where many plaster casts of the skull were distributed. In England the distinguished Professor Huxley, after careful examination, declared the Neanderthal skull to be the most bestial and ape-like in existence, corresponding most nearly with the skulls of the Australians. Professor Schaaffhausen expresses himself in the same fashion. In 1864, at the Congress of Naturalists at Giessen he declared, in opposition to other interpretations, that the Neanderthal skull represented a race-type, and that the entire and undoubtedly fossil skeleton, which precluded the supposition of idiocy, exhibited a number of characteristics such as have been of late years observed in the skeletons of very low races of men. He maintained finally, that the skull and skeleton must undoubtedly have belonged to one of the Autochthones, or primitive inhabitants of Europe, living before the Indo-Germanic immigration.* As a matter of course many objections were raised to this interpretation of the remains, on the part of those who had an interest in invalidating this important piece of evidence, but these produced no result. The chief objection raised by those who were not accurately informed upon the subject, was founded on the supposition that the discovery in the Neanderthal was an isolated one, and that the peculiar and unexampled form of the skull was to be explained away as abnormal or exceptional. But in reality this is so far from being the case that Professor Huxley was quite justified in declaring that the Neanderthal skull is by no means so isolated as it

* The first account of the Neanderthal skull was given by Dr. Schaaffhausen at the Meeting of the Natural History Society of the Lower Rhine on February 4, 1857, from a plaster cast prepared in Elberfeld. He even then stated that it bore no traces of artificial deformation, but was to be regarded as a natural formation, which in the strong prominence of the upper supraciliary region, caused by the extension of the frontal sinuses, showed the human type in such a low stage of development as could hardly be found among the rudest of living races of men.

Dr. Fuhlrott of Elberfeld, to whom we are indebted for the preservation of these bones, (which were at first regarded as those of some animal), afterwards brought them to Bonn for the purpose of being accurately examined anatomically, and on June 2, 1857, he gave a detailed description of the place where they were found and of the discovery itself before the general meeting of the Natural History Society of Rhenish Prussia and Westphalia. The details, together with a comparative summary of all that had been previously published in books and journals upon the Neanderthal Skull, will be found in Dr. Fuhlrott's Memoir already cited: *Der fossile Mensch aus dem Neanderthal, &c.*, (Duisburg, 1865). All the attempts that have been made, (by Meyer, Wagner, Blake, Pruner-Bey, Davis and others,) to diminish or bring in question the value of this discovery with respect to the primeval history of man, by giving it a different interpretation, must from this and from the explanations given by Prof. Schaaffhausen in his memoir, *Zur Kenntniss der ältesten Rassenschädel*, be regarded as completely unsuccessful. Schaaffhausen says: " To regard the unusual development of the frontal sinuses in the remarkable skull from the Neanderthal as only an individual or pathological (morbid) deviation, there is not the slightest reason; it is unmistakably a race-type, and stands in physiological agreement with the remarkable strength of the bones of the rest of the skeleton."

might appear to be at the first glance, but *that it truly forms only the extreme member of a series leading by slow degrees to the highest and best developed forms of human skulls.*

The Borreby skulls belonging to the stone-age of Denmark are especially considered by Huxley to show a great resemblance to the Neanderthal skull, a resemblance which is manifested in the depression of the cranium, the receding forehead, the contracted occiput and the prominent supraciliary ridges. The same may be said, more or less, of the other remains of skulls mentioned in our preceding enumeration, as well as of a great number of skulls and fragments of skulls found, (with bones), chiefly in the north of Europe, which are cited in detail by Professor Schaaffhausen in his important memoir, *Towards the knowledge of the skulls of the most ancient races.* In all these, similar characters were observable, although in a less ·degree. In nearly all these crania the strong projection of the supraciliary ridges and the low, flat, receding forehead are expressly noticed as characteristic peculiarities.* But if we

* "It is worthy of notice," says Prof. Schaaffhausen in the memoir cited in the text, "that a similar, although smaller projection of the supraciliary arches has generally been found in the skulls of savage races, as well as in very ancient skulls." Then follows a long enumeration of such cases from which we select the following as the most noteworthy: "The remarkably small skull from the graves on the island of Moën, examined by Prof. Eschricht; the two human skulls, described by Dr. Kutorga, from the government of Minsk, (Russia), one of which, especially, shows a great resemblance to the Neanderthal skull; the human skeleton found near Plau in Mecklenburg in a very ancient grave in a *squatting* position, and associated with implements manufactured of bone, with regard to which Dr. Lisch remarks, that "the formation of the skull indicates a very distant period, when man stood on a very low grade of development;" and a similar discovery in another ancient grave in Mecklenburg (the Kegelgrab of Schwaan), in which the remains of no fewer than eight bodies were found together in a *squatting* position in the original soil, and their skulls likewise presented short, retreating foreheads and projecting eyebrows."

A number of further proofs of the low development of the skull and brain in the primeval man are cited by the same author in a quite recent memoir: *On the primitive form of the human skull*, (1868), which he concludes with the following words:

"From what has just been under consideration we may regard it as beyond doubt that a skull, which does not bear the signs of a low organization, cannot be regarded as derived from primeval man, even though it may have been found among the bones of extinct animals. But it is further clear that we must now place the man of the primeval time a step lower than the rudest savages of the actual world."

leave out of the account the last mentioned character of the prominent supraciliary ridges, we have in the Peruvian skull of one of the Titicaca race obtained by Baron von Bibra from an ancient tomb at Algodon Bay in Bolivia, and brought by him to Europe, a form which, in its excessively small size, the narrowness and lowness of its forehead, which indeed is almost entirely deficient, and its elongated occipital region, exceeds even the Neanderthal skull in animality and inferiority of conformation. Bibra says that it has more analogy with the skull of a monkey than with that of a man, and the chemical examination that he made of its bones indicates that it is of a very high antiquity.*

From all these facts, and from many other discoveries of human bones, including a great number of lower jaws of very bestial form, which will be more particularly referred to hereafter, we may conclude with certainty, that our most ancient European ancestor, or the primitive man in all countries, must have been almost infinitely inferior to our existing race of men both corporeally and intellectually,—in other words, he must have been an extremely barbarous and perhaps almost dumb savage, who worked his way up to a certain degree of civilization and made actual intellectual progress by extremely slow degrees and by means of almost inconceivable efforts, impelled thereto either by his own faculties or by influences from without. Nay, from the observations now before us, it would almost seem, that for thousands of years scarcely any progress of this kind was made. At least according to the calculations of Lyell

---

* Even this skull is not isolated, but it resembles many skulls from the neighborhood of the Titicaca lake in Peru, which all, according to Bibra, have a greater resemblance to the skull of an ape than to other human skulls. They usually have in the middle a blunt, comb-like elevation along the whole length of the skull, and are so badly formed that they were long regarded as artificially deformed, which, however, is certainly not the case with the skull brought home by Bibra. In Algodon Bay, Bibra found thirty to forty tumuli in which human bodies of a small race were put together in a *squatting* posture. They belonged to an old Peruvian race, or to a people who chi fly inhabited the region of the lake of Titicaca. Most of the mummies found in Peru and Bolivia resemble this race (See von Bibra, *Die Algodon-Bay in Bolivia*, Vienna, 1852).

and others, (see Appendix No. 8,) a very long period must have elapsed between the deposition of the upper and lower gravel beds containing flint axes in the Valley of the Somme which are of considerable thickness.   And yet no considerable, readily perceptible difference can be pointed out between the axes from the upper and lower beds, so that the industrial condition of primitive man must have remained nearly unchanged during a very long period of time.   There is indeed some difference between the axes, but it is so slight as to be recognizable, according to Lyell, only by the eye of the practised observer, whilst the uninitiated can see nothing of it.   It has, however, been observed that the so-called *oval* forms predominate over the *elongated* ones in the deeper beds.*   With more accurate knowledge and more abundant material we shall no

* At the anthropological congress in Paris in 1867, M. Reboux stated that he had examined more than a thousand flint axes collected in the evirons of Paris near the Seine (at Perret, Clichy, Batignolles and Neuilly), and distinguished among them *three kinds*, namely, *split off*, *chipped* and *polished*.   According to him the split-off axes or chips lay lowest down and the polished ones uppermost, and they were never mixed together.   All this, however, was received with doubt by the Congress.   On the other hand, Professor Broca in his Report of 1867, which has been so often mentioned, stated that the gradual improvement of the flint axes of Abbeville, (in the Valley of the Somme,) had been clearly shown by Gabriel de Mortillet.   In the lowest beds they are lance-shaped and of large size.   In the gravelly sand which covers the Diluvium and in which no Mammoth bones are to be found, they are elliptical, elongated and of smaller size.   Finally, in the light, superficial soil of the declivities, they are polished and sharpened, like those which have been found in the dolmens.   The question whether this improvement was effected by internal progress or by the arrival of new peoples, is left in doubt by Broca; but according to him, the latter is rendered probable by the observations of Lartet and Christy.   The inhabitants of the caverns of Perigord in the south of France had already, according to Broca, attained a high degree of dexterity and made a great number of instruments of bone, ivory and Reindeer horn.   Their drawings even indicate an artistic feeling which leaves far behind the rude sketches on many Celtic monuments, (and consequently of much later date) They must have led a quiet, contemplative life, and were probably destroyed by a stronger, but ruder people.

Broca regards these advanced men of the so-called Reindeer period as probably the more cultivated descendants of the rude savages of the diluvial time.   But notwithstanding the progress they had made they still fabricated their stone implements merely by the process of *striking* and without grinding them, as was subsequently done with the smoothed or polished stones.

doubt eventually succeed in obtaining more delicate distinctions, and may thus arrive at a better notion of the gradual course of the development of civilization.

At a somewhat latter period the differences in the stone weapons become so considerable, and the gradual progress in industrial skill of the primitive peoples shows itself so distinctly, that in accordance therewith the so-called *stone-age* has been divided into three distinct, consecutive periods or sections, characterized chiefly by the form and the greater or less perfection of the stone weapons and other instruments. These are the *ancient*, *middle* and *recent* stone-ages, and they certainly embrace an enormous lapse of time, as the ancient stone-age is undoubtedly intimately connected with the first appearance of man upon the earth, and the most recent age of stone was prolonged far into the historical period, and even continues to the present day among many savage tribes.

But in order that this expression, "the stone-age," may be rightly understood, it must be borne in mind that of late the prehistoric periods of the human race and its development in civilization have been generally divided, after the example of Northern *savants*, into the *ages of stone, bronze* and *iron*, and that this division although often attacked and doubted, has by degrees been fully established in archæological science. It is true that the periods are united by the most gradual transitions from one to the other, and that they frequently seem to invade one another's territories, but on the whole they indicate quite correctly the gradual progress of civilization, the true civilized periods commencing only with the introduction of iron.* *Bronze*, an alloy or mixture of copper and tin, was evidently a much less perfect material than *iron*, the use of which alone

---

* According to M. Gabriel de Mortillet, a recognized authority, the first appearance of iron is completely prehistoric, and the three periods of Stone, Bronze and Iron have very gradually followed one another, a all events in Switzerland and Italy.

could have rendered possible that advance in civilization which has landed us at our present stage of development.

Of course *stone* was the most imperfect material, and its displacement by bronze or brass was a greater step in advance *at the time it occurred*, than that subsequently caused by the introduction of iron.

From this mode of division, which now serves us as a measure for determining the most ancient periods of the human race, we see at once that in reality the course of development of human society has been the very opposite of that imagined by the poets of classical antiquity, and pictured by them in their writings. For while they represent a golden, a silver and an iron age following one another, and accompanied by a constantly increasing deterioration in the condition of human society, in reality the very reverse has taken place. "A life of perfect indolence and perpetual serenity was not the lot of the oldest human inhabitants of our country, but a life full of severe and heavy labor, of great and ceaseless cares. And when at last the bronze, and after it the iron age came in, this last did not indicate a growing deterioration in the conditions of human existence, but the greatest improvement, and the most rapid progress that has been or could have been made towards the freedom of man."— *Virchow.*

However, as we have already said, it must not be supposed that well-marked boundaries exist beween these three periods; on the contrary, gradual transitions are everywhere perceptible. A transitional period of this kind must have occurred especially between the ages of Stone and Bronze. It is indicated by numerous tombs and other places in which implements made of stone and bronze are found *together*. Implements of pure copper are also found in this transition period, so that many people have been inclined to intercalate here a special *copper-age*. Objects of bronze and iron are also found together in many places ; but whilst the bronze was speedily and completely superseded by iron, the stone-weapons held their ground much longer, and their use extends, as has already been stated, far down into historic times.* Perhaps the last stone weapons may have been manufactured with iron instruments, and it is said that the English actually fought with stone implements against William the Conqueror.† A circumstance of great significance in the history of human development, observed in this transition from stone to bronze and from bronze to iron, is that *the first bronze weapons were made exactly after the pattern of the old stone implements*, and in the same way also the earliest implements of iron after the pattern of the bronze implements which preceded them, although without such models before them no one would have thought of bringing the malleable and ductile metal into the rough and inconvenient forms of the productions of the stone age. From this instance we see most distinctly

* In countries out of Europe, according to the researches of Rougemont, (*L'âge du Bronze*, *&c.*), copper seems often to have preceded iron. The art of smelting iron appears to be of very ancient date in Africa. In America, (Mexico, Peru, &c.), scarcely anything but copper or bronze was worked; iron was very rarely or not at all employed. In China and Japan, however, as in Europe, we can distinguish the ages of stone, bronze and iron. On the other hand, in the north of Tartary and in Finland we may almost say that there was an iron age without any copper or bronze.

† " The use of stone weapons, leaving out of consideration certain savage tribes of recent times, was much in vogue during historical antiquity. According to Herodotus, the Ethiopian archers whom Xerxes brought with him in his army against Greece, made use of short reed arrows which had stone tips. During the researches made not long since by Francois Lenormant in ancient Attica, an enormous quantity of lance-heads, made of flint and of very rude manufacture, was found in a small mound. On the battle-field of Marathon, in the mound which the Athenians raised over the bodies of those who had fallen for their fatherland, a number of stone (and bronze) arrow-heads were discovered." (*Thomassen, Enthüllungen aus der Urgeschichte*, page 36 Neuwied, 1869).

Tacitus also, (*Germania*, Cap. 47), relates of a people inhabiting the northwest of ancient Germany, whom he denominates the *Fenni*, that in war they made use of arrows which were furnished with bone tips. It is extremely probable therefore that this people also possessed stone weapons. Indeed the difficulty of obtaining iron in sufficient quantities even after it was known, and the want of knowledge of the mode of working it, may have induced or compelled many of the peoples of later periods still to continue the employment of stone weapons and implements.

that the human mind cannot produce anything at once and directly from itself, but that it is everywhere confined strictly to the laws of its gradual, sensualistic development, and to the nourishment furnished to it by impressions from without. Most certainly we have no right to compassionate the limited capacity of·our oldest ancestor, who was incapable of his own powers to rise to the idea of a true metallic implement, and could only by degrees observe how the new material was capable of taking improved forms, as we ourselves are every moment guilty of the same fault, but on a larger scale, and both in material and intellectual matters can break loose from the old and antiquated only with the greatest trouble. Take as an instance the defective construction of our railways and railway carriages, which are still made on the pattern of the old and inconvenient post-roads and stage-coaches, although, with the materials now at our command, if only these models were thrown aside, the whole arrangement might be infinitely better adapted to its purposes and rendered less dangerous, more convenient, and cheaper.*

After all these digressions we must return to our main subject, the stone-age, which in its three consecutive phases or divisions of the *ancient, middle* and *recent* period, is best of all fitted to furnish us with a picture of the gradually ascending course of

---

* For this purpose the breadth (*Spurbreite*), of the iron rails and the width of the railroad in general must above all be made much greater; the carriages, constructed in two stories, must run not *over*, but *between* the wheels, with the lower story reaching nearly to the ground; at the same time their interior must not be divided into little cells for the imprisonment of martyrs, but arranged in the form of large and small saloons fitted up with all conveniences, and so as to facilitate communication throughout the whole train. The ingress and egress of passen· gers to and from the train must be facilitated and hastened by means of movable platforms standing at the same height as the person; the ticket offices and any others that may be necessary must be placed in the train itself, &c. With such an arrangement, running off the line would become an impossibility, the detestable rocking of the carriages would cease and their motion become scarcely perceptible, a far greater number of passengers might be conveyed, (notwithstanding the greatly increased convenience,) more rapidly, more safely, and cheaper, without any injury to health or personal comfort, even on the longest journeys, &c.

civilization. ⸜ The *ancient* stone-period is characterized by those stone axes of rude form on the pattern of those of Amiens, Abbeville, Hoxne, etc., which are found chiefly in the gravelly or sandy deposits of former river beds, but sometimes also in caves of the most ancient kind. They show no traces of fine work, and were produced merely by blows or taps; they are not smoothed or polished and have no holes for the handle, no ornamentation, or anything of the kind. Associated with them we find no traces of metal, no pottery and no remains of domestic animals; on the other hand, they are accompanied by numerous bones of extinct animals of the Diluvial period, such as the Cave Bear, the Mammoth, the Woolly Rhinoceros, etc. Sir John Lubbock, (*Prehistoric Times*, London, 1865,) calls this the *Palæolithic period*, to distinguish it from the second or *Neolithic period*, and according to him, as already mentioned, about three thousand flint implements of this age have probably been found in the North of France and South of England. M. E. Lartet thinks that we should distinguish in the Palæolithic age an ancient period of the Cave Bear, and a more modern one of the Elephant and Rhinoceros, but this distinction has been regarded as superfluous by other writers, especially by Carl Vogt.*

According to Carl Vogt, (*Archiv für Anthropologie*, 1866, Part I,) the man of the oldest stone age, who must be regarded,

---

* Lartet's *four* epochs of the Stone-age are therefore the period of the *Cave-Bear*, that of the *Elephant* and *Rhinoceros*, that of the *Reindeer* and that of the *Aurochs*, a mode of division to which MM. Troyon and d'Archiac adhere in essential points. A somewhat different scheme, founded upon the epochs of Swiss Glaciation, has been proposed by Professor Renevier of Lousanne; it is as follows:

1. *Preglacial epoch*, in which man lived contemporaneously with *Elephas antiquus, Rhinoceros homitœchus* and the Cave-Bear.

2. *Glacial epoch*, in which man lived contemporaneously with the Mammoth, Tichorhine Rhinoceros, Cave-Bear, &c.

3. *Postglacial epoch*, in which man lived contemporaneously with the Mammoth and Reindeer.

4. *Last epoch*, or epoch of the *Pile-buildings*, in which man lived contemporaneously with the Gigantic Deer, the Aurochs, &c.

however, only as the descendant or successor of a still older and more barbarous race belonging to the Tertiary period, was of large stature, powerful and longheaded, (dolichocephalic,) judging from the skulls of Engis and the Neanderthal. He paid honor to the dead, was acquainted with the use of fire, made hearths, split the hollow bones and skulls of animals in order to extract the marrow and brains from them, adorned himself with corals and the teeth of wild animals, and clothed himself in skins or in the bark of trees softened by beating. He possessed rude axes and knives split off from blocks of stone, and implements of bone adapted for various purposes. And judging from the great abundance of flint instruments found in the European caves, he was spread over the whole of central Europe north of the Alps.

This description does not exactly apply to the barbarous primeval man of the earliest diluvial times, and it would appear that the describer must have had in his mind at the same time a series of cave-discoveries belonging to a somewhat later date. Westropp who distinguishes *four* stages of civilization, names this earliest stage of humanity that of *savagery*, and supposes it to be followed by the stages of *hunters*, *herdsmen*, and *agriculturists*.

The ancient stone age is immediately followed by the *middle stone age*, characterized by stone weapons and flint implements of finer workmanship and greater finish.

We might also call it the period of *flint knives*, as these are found in enormous quantities, whilst the axes are far less numerous in proportion. But it is generally indicated as the *Reindeer period*, and the man then living as the *Reindeer-man*, on account of the immense quantity of worked and chiselled bones and antlers of the Reindeer, (or Stag,) which we find in localities belonging to this time. This manufacture of the bones of Mammals and fishes, shells, etc., was carried on partly for purposes of domestic utility and partly for the production of ornamental objects. But the extremely imperfect civilization of the man of this period is shown by the circumstance that he still possessed no domestic animals, with the exception, perhaps of the dog, and that the remains of a very rude, blackish pottery are only found here and there. The bones of animals found belong partly to extinct forms and partly to species which are still in existence, but which, like the Reindeer, retreated to high northern latitudes before the period of history or tradition. The whole period of the Reindeer-man is completely pre-historic, as according to the unanimous opinion of naturalists the Reindeer emigrated from our regions in pre-historic times.

To this period belong the greater part of the objects discovered in caves, especially in the numerous caves of the South of France and Belgium, which have furnished such abundant materials for the primeval history of man. It would appear from this, that the Reindeer-man lived chiefly or almost exclusively in caverns, which, indeed, not only at that period, but long before and long after it, served mankind as places of residence or of refuge.* The cave of Aurignac described at the beginning of this section, in which flint knives, ornaments, instruments of bone, etc., were found, must be placed in this series. It is also characteristic of this period that in the localities belonging to it numerous remains of man himself have been found, whilst this has hitherto been the case to a very limited extent in localities of the earliest stone age. According to Carl Vogt the skulls of this, (second,) period exhibit a flatness of the frontal region, with a considerable development of the occipital part and a rooflike form of the cranial arch (as in Australian skulls.) With this structure is usually combined strong prognathism or obliquity of the teeth, a short form of the head, (brachycephalism,) and a feeble structure of the body, so that the general picture of the man of the Reindeer time

* See Appendix No. 12.

corresponds most closely with that of the existing Laplanders. The great artistic sense which is displayed in the drawings and carvings of the Reindeer-man, as previously described, is very remarkable, and the progress towards civilization which was made by him in the finer finishing of his weapons and implements and by the invention of pottery was very considerable. As Vogt says, the Reindeer-man excelled particularly in the art of working in bone. He evidently lived only by the chase and by fishing, and thus represented the second or hunter-stage of the four degrees of civilization established by Westropp. To the same stage this author also refers the kitchen-middens or heaps of culinary refuse, as we find in them only chipped stone implements, but none polished or smoothed by grinding.

An exceedingly brilliant light has been thrown upon the Reindeer period and the Reindeer-man by the very careful investigation of the Belgian caves which has been made during the last few years, as also by the celebrated discovery at the source of the Schussen near Schussenried in Swabia.*

The middle stone-age is followed by the *recent* stone-age, or Lubbock's *Neolithic period*. It is characterized by the profuse occurrence of stone weapons and implements of fine workmanship,† and especially by the circumstance that these implements are not, as previously, prepared by chipping or tapping, but

* See Appendix No. 13.

† According to an admirable article by Sir John Lubbock on the use of stone in ancient times (*Revue Littéraire*, 1865-66, No. 1), there are in the great Museum of Antiquities in Copenhagen alone about eleven to twelve thousand articles in stone, and the number of all the specimens contained in private and public collections in Denmark is estimated by Mr. Herbst at 30000! The Museum of the Royal Irish Academy contains nearly 700 flint flakes, 512 celts, more than 400 arrow heads and 50 lance heads, besides 75 of the so-called scrapers, and many other articles made of stone, such as sling-stones, hammers, whetstones, millstones, &c. In the same way the number of specimens in the Museum at Stockholm is estimated at between fifteen and sixteen thousand. "From this," says Lubbock, "we may conclude that there was a time during which human society was in so rude a state, that stocks and stones, horns and bones were the only instruments that man was able to procure."

polished or smoothed by a process of grinding and cutting; they are also engraved or furnished with scratched ornaments and provided with holes for the reception of the handle. These cut or polished stone implements have long been known, and all Museums swarm with them. On account of their generally chisel-like form they are commonly known as *Celts*, (from the Latin *celtis*, a chisel.) The celts are found most abundantly in the North, especially in Denmark.

What especially distinguishes this third and most recent stone-age from its two predecessors, is the greater development attained in it by the art of pottery, which is of such great importance in the progress of civilization. Numerous remains of earthenware made by hand occur in the localities of this period.*

A no less important advance in civilization is indicated by the presence of the bones of tamed or domesticated animals, and by the signs of the commencement of agricultural pursuits, including the keeping of cattle. The man of that time, whose intellectual and bodily nature was more and more approaching to the present condition, may therefore have been not merely a hunter, but also partly a herdsman and agriculturist. Subsequently also he understood the arts of spinning, of weaving coarse stuffs, and of building permanent huts and dwelling places. The traces of this age are spread over nearly the whole earth. In general all discoveries made in the so-called *alluvial soil* are referred to it, as also the turbaries and shell-heaps

---

*The first appearance and gradual progress of the art of pottery is very characteristic in the primeval periods of the human race. During the most ancient cave period it is probable that nothing of the kind was used except rude lumps of clay with a hollow in the middle for keeping water to drink in the interior of the caves. Subsequently the vessel was dried in the sun to make it harder. But it was only in the Reindeer period that man seems first to have employed fire for hardening vessels. In order to make the clay resist the fire better, it was probably mixed with quartz-sand. These most ancient vessels are, however, very rude, and were manufactured solely by hand, as may still be seen distinctly by the impressions of fingers upon them. They are usually of a blackish color. The use of the potter's wheel was introduced much later.

already described, the Swiss pile-buildings, and the Irish lake-dwellings, the tumuli or grave mounds, the Dolmens, &c. The most ancient remains of the so-called *Celtic* age must also be referred to this period, which indeed, as already stated, sends its last offshoots far into the historical period. Scattered through the whole of Europe there is a great number of graves, the contents of which show them to belong to one of the two last mentioned periods of the stone-age. By the increasing delicacy and perfection of the weapons and implements, as well as by their greater adaptation for the most varied purposes both of peace and war, these graves display in a remarkable manner the gradual progress of the people of the stone age. But this progress must have required an enormous lapse of time, and the advance itself must have taken place slowly in proportion to the antiquity of the men and their poverty in the means of progress. How many thousands of years may have elapsed before the transition from the oldest to the middle stone-age could have taken place? before man succeeded in giving a rather more delicate or improved form to the rough flint hammers of the oldest period, or in adapting the material at his command to more multifarious purposes? This remarkably slow progress cannot astonish us if we only bear in mind the picture of the condition of this period which has already been sketched, and consider on the one hand the enormous difficulties with which the primitive man had to contend, and on the other the absence of all impulse, whether from within or from without, to any such progress. For *stability* or tendency to invariability or immobility may be regarded as the fundamental character of the savage and primitive state of man, a character which of itself and without the accession of external impulses possesses essentially a tendency to almost infinite duration. This indeed may be observed in the case of existing savages, who remain almost stationary for thousands of years without making any essential progress. With regard to this, Lyell says very appropriately: "The extent to which even a considerably advanced state of civilization may become fixed and stereotyped for ages, is the wonder of Europeans who travel in the East. One of my friends declared to me, that whenever the natives expressed to him a wish 'that he might live a thousand years,' the idea struck him as by no means extravagant, seeing that, if he were doomed to sojourn forever among them, he could only hope to exchange in ten centuries as many ideas, and to witness as much progress, as he could do at home in half a century."

As may easily be imagined it is precisely the *first* step in the path of civilization that must have been the most difficult and therefore the slowest. On the contrary, with every fresh advance, both the means and the desire to overcome the difficulties or obstacles in the way must have been increased. With regard to the external obstacles to progress no doubt the large and powerful animals of the Diluvial period must have disappeared and the mighty geological catastrophes of that age must have run their course, before man could obtain sufficient space and opportunity for the development of his powers and the wider diffusion of his race upon the earth. And even after all this had taken place, impulses of some particular kind would be required to rouse the primeval savage from that sluggish, inactive and unintellectual state in which one generation after another had sunk into the grave like the beasts surrounding them, and to force upon him, as it were, the necessity of advancing in civilization.

Among impulses of this kind I reckon prominent natural phenomena, geographical or climatic changes, the immigration of old or irruption of foreign races, wars, famines, expulsions from dwelling places, migrations, the commencement of relations of traffic and commerce, the gradual improvement of language, etc., and especially the rise of certain highly endowed individuals who possessed themselves of a political or spiritual sovereignty.

Without any such impulses it is possible that the savage state in which our oldest ancestor lived, might have persisted to the present day. It is true that many people talk about the existence of an innate and necessary instinct of progress in human nature, and believe that this instinct must always and necessarily produce its due effect. But in the presence of so many eloquent facts which testify to the contrary, it will be difficult for any one with an unprejudiced judgment to believe in such a necessity. Thus not only are there people who have remained stationary at the same degree of culture from the very dawn of history, but there are others, such as the Chinese, who have certainly attained a certain stage of progress, but have then remained without alteration, whilst we can only find one comparatively small group of nations which has hitherto been constantly engaged in a course of progress and improvement. But even this progress in them has not always proceeded spontaneously from within, but the impulse towards it has come in historic times only from without. We also see those nations which were formerly the greatest and most powerful and endowed with the most advanced civilization, such as the Egyptians, Assyrians, Jews, Greeks, Romans, &c., now in a state of almost complete decay, whilst their place in the scale of progress has been taken by quite different peoples in other lands. Thus it is quite conceivable that the European primitive man would perhaps never have emancipated himself from his state of rude servitude to nature, if impulses from without, and especially the occasional immigration of foreign races of a higher degree of culture, had not been brought to bear upon him. Whether a complete displacement or destruction of the aborigines by the new-comers took place under these circumstances, or only a mixture and consequent ennoblement of the native race, is a question which can hardly be answered directly, but the second case is certainly by far the most probable.*

*See Appendix No. 14.

With this we may consider that we have touched upon all the essential points in our knowledge of primeval man and his rude condition, scanty as this is at present. It is remarkable that a certain reminiscence of this early condition must have been preserved among the most ancient men and in the earliest recollections of peoples, for among very many of the latter, unmistakable traditions of the first rude commencements of culture and civilization are to be found. Thus, for example, the Chinese possess a complete picture of the progress of their civilization, which in its main features agrees perfectly with the results of our scientific investigation. This picture commences with the time when men lived naked upon the trees and were still unacquainted with the use of fire. Afterwards they clothed themselves with leaves and bark, later still with skins, &c., &c. In the same way, according to Prof. Spiegel, (*Genesis und Avesta*,) the most ancient traditions and legends of the Hebrews, Phœnicians, Hindoos, Babylonians, &c., all point to a primitive savage state from which the human race rose to a higher condition only by the help of the Gods, or of specially endowed men, (the so-called patriarchs.) According to the legends of the Babylonians their ten most ancient patriarchs lived altogether 432,000 years! The Iranian heroic legend endeavors to show a gradual development of the human race from a state of complete savagery to a regular state of social life, and this it does by the same steps of development that are accepted in the Semitic legends. Its first king, Gaiumard, taught men to clothe themselves in the skins of animals and to eat the fruits of trees, whilst an accidentally ignited tree taught a subsequent king, (Huscheng,) the use of fire. In this a divine nature was immediately supposed to reside, and the worship of fire commenced.

By the Phœnicians also the first use of fire and the discovery of the art of producing it by friction, are placed in the second generation of the human race. According to the Bundehesch, a very ancient Iranian document, the first men lived only on fruits and water. It was only at a later period that they made use of milk and flesh, acquired the knowledge of fire, clad themselves in the skins of animals, built themselves huts, &c.

If we leave out of consideration the merely poetical ideas of the gold and silver ages, throughout the whole period of classical antiquity, no other notion than the above prevailed as to the primitive state of our race upon the earth and the slow and gradual course of its development. As a proof of this we may cite the celebrated passage in Horace, (*Satires*, Book I. 3,99,) which, moreover, seems to have been founded upon the well-known dissertation on the Epicurean philosophy of the history of Creation in the fifth book of the didactic poem of Lucretius Carus. "When animals," says Horace, "first crawled forth from the new formed earth, a stupid and filthy flock, they fought for acorns and places of refuge with their nails and fists, then with cudgels, and finally with weapons which, guided by experience, they had made for themselves. Then they invented names for things and words to express their thoughts, after which they began to abstain from war, to fortify their towns, to establish laws, &c."

After the period of classical antiquity had passed away, and by means of influences of an unscientific kind which I will not characterize more particularly, a conception quite opposite to that just described was brought forth, and gradually arrived at almost universal acceptance. This is the notion that the primitive man was not a barbarous savage, but on the contrary, a being as perfect as possible and endowed with the highest and best qualities, and that we ourselves are only the degenerate descendants of a better and more noble race, corrupted and ruined by sin and labor. A consequence of the adoption of this opinion is that even scientific men are fond of representing the existing savages as the degraded and degenerate posterity

of more highly endowed forefathers.* In this sense the Count
de Salles says: "Man, created by God, passed from the hands
of the Creator as a perfect work, complete in body and spirit.
Whatever may be the actual degradation of many men, civilization is their final goal, as it was their original state.†

"It is difficult to conceive," says Quatrefages after citing this
passage, "upon what facts this author relies." In point of
fact, such an opinion as this having sprung solely from theoretical considerations can only appeal to theoretical grounds,
whilst it is in the plainest contradiction to every known fact.
If the men now living were really only the degenerate and
partially corrupted descendants of a former higher and better
race, it would be difficult to understand how the human race
could still exist, as it is a law generally recognized and proved
by experience, that degenerate or degraded tribes and individuals are never of long duration, but that they gradually
disappear.

Lyell argues admirably against this view in the following
words: "But had the original stock of mankind been really endowed with such superior intellectual powers and with inspired
knowledge, and had they possessed the same improvable nature
as their posterity, the point of advancement to which they
would have reached ere this would have been immeasurably
higher. We cannot ascertain at present the limits, whether of
the beginning or the end, of the first stone period, when Man
co-existed with the extinct Mammalia, but that it was of great
duration we cannot doubt. During those ages there would
have been time for progress of which we can scarcely form a
conception, and very different would have been the character

---

*In the case of many, or at all events of some savage tribes, this view may un-
doubtedly be to a certain extent correct, but as a general rule it is certainly quite
false.

†The great poet Milton also was, as is well known, a supporter of this hypothesis of the perfection of the primitive man, and sings of Adam as the most perfect
of men and of Eve as the loveliest of women.

of the works of art which we should now be endeavoring to interpret,—those relics which we are now disinterring from the old gravel-pits of St. Acheul, or from the Liége caves. In them, or in the upraised bed of the Mediterranean, on the south coast of Sardinia, instead of the rudest pottery or flint tools so irregular in form as to cause the unpractised eye to doubt whether they afford unmistakable evidence of design, we should now be finding sculptured forms, surpassing in beauty the master-pieces of Phidias or Praxiteles; lines of buried railways or electric telegraphs, from which the best engineers of our day might gain invaluable hints; astronomical instruments and microscopes of more advanced construction than any known in Europe, and other indications of perfection in the arts and sciences, such as the nineteenth century has not yet witnessed. Still farther would the triumph of inventive genius be found to have been carried, when the later deposits, now assigned to the ages of bronze and iron were formed. Vainly should we be straining our imaginations to guess the possible uses and meaning of such relics—machines, perhaps, for navigating the air or exploring the depths of the ocean, or for calculating arithmetical problems, beyond the wants or even the conception of living mathematicians.''

Now we do not find in the depths of the earth such things as are here described by Lyell, but in all cases just the reverse, and we must therefore feel convinced that man did not, in accordance with this opinion which we find coming to the surface from time to time,* commence with great things to end with small, but that beginning with small things he has ended with great, as indeed is the rule in almost all human affairs!

Which of the opinions here described is not merely the most probable but the most encouraging and satisfactory, the author may confidently leave to the judgment of the reader. It is only

See Appendix No. 15.

by a complete misapprehension of the truth and of right sentiments that so many men can have been induced to reject the view
here developed of the antiquity and origin of our race upon the
earth as being repulsive and discouraging, and to imagine that
if it be adopted the elevated sentiment of the dignity of human
nature must be endangered. We do not know how to combat
this false pride which regards a lowly origin as something contemptible and degrading better than in the admirable words of
Professor Huxley, who speaks as follows in his remarkable
memoir on the *Place of Man in Nature:* "Thoughtful men,
once escaped from the blinding influence of traditional prejudice, will find in the lowly stock whence man has sprung the
best evidence of the splendor of his capacities ; and will discern
in his long progress through the Past a reasonable ground of
faith in his attainment of a nobler Future."

In reality the humbler our origin, the more elevated is our
present position in Nature! the smaller the commencement, the
greater is the termination! the harder the struggle, the more
brilliant the victory! the more painful and tedious the course by
which our civilization has been attained, the more valuable is
this civilization itself, and the more powerful the endeavor not
merely to retain it but to still further develop it! It is not hu-
miliation and discouragement, but incitement to something still
greater, that the thinking and right-feeling man must derive from
the knowledge of the antiquity and primitive state of his race
upon the earth! Probably everything that we possess in the
way of culture, civilization, art, science, morality and progress,
is nothing but the product of an infinitely slow and difficult development and self-education, starting from a rude and brutal
state, advancing step by step from knowledge to knowledge,
and rendered possible by an enormous lapse of time, in comparison with which the duration of our own existence is like
that of a flash of lightning. In the light of such knowledge as
this, our present state of culture must appear doubly important,

precious and grand, as it is the final result of an immense elevation, the production of which has consumed and exhausted the powers of so many generations of men. Those who laid the first foundations of this great edifice could have had no suspicion of its future grandeur!

"Certainly," cried Professor Joly of Toulouse, equally poetically and truthfully, at the close of his lecture upon fossil man, endeavoring to bring clearly before his auditors the enormous progress made by science and the arts in the long lapse of ages, "certainly, the little flint hammers of the first inhabitants of Gaul cannot be compared with those heavy blocks of iron which are set in motion in our manufactories by the force of falling water or of steam. There is a wide interval between their frail skiffs, their canoes hollowed out by the axe and the action of fire, and our immense armor-plated ships of war. There is also a wide interval between the coarse stuffs manufactured at Wangen and 'Robenhausen, and those supple, delicate and splendid tissues which are produced by our Jacquard looms. The men of the ages of stone and bronze most certainly never suspected that one day the most ingenious machines would take the place of handiwork, increasing the products a hundredfold, and at the same time improving them. They could never have imagined that steam would transport our vessels in a few days from one hemisphere to another; that the golden Phœbus and the pale Phœbe would depict their own visages in the *camera obscura;* that the master of the thunder, the black-eyebrowed Jupiter, as he was afterwards called, would be reduced in our days to play the part of a mere postman; or that man, armed with Volta's pile, would introduce a light more brilliant than that of the sun into places where the sun had never penetrated. Especially, we may say, they could never have suspected that their own existence would be contested and even denied by the *savants* of the Institute." (*Revue des Cours Scientifiques*, 2ᵐᵉ *Année, No. 16.*)

In reality the subject of our book is anticipated by the preceding considerations and general details, as the view of the position of man in nature maintained in it is proved not merely by the results of archæogeological studies or investigations upon the geological antiquity of man upon the earth and his primitive condition, but equally, or perhaps even still more by the results of systematic zoology, comparative anatomy, physiology, ethnography, psychology and the allied sciences, but above all by the study of the developmental history of the organism of man and animals, which has become so important of late. These results, brought together from such numerous and diverse scientific sources, all agree in so unmistakable and surprising a manner, and all point so completely in one direction, that I hope the careful reader will no longer have any doubt as to the true place of man in nature when he has reached the end of the following section, which will treat of the points relating to the second of the three great questions proposed by us, — the question: "What are we?"

This section will also contain an exposition and discussion of the theories which have lately been proposed with regard to the infinitely important question of the origin and descent of the human race from the world of animals most nearly connected with it.

END OF THE FIRST PART.

WHAT ARE WE?

"It is dangerous to let man perceive too distinctly how closely he approaches the animals, without at the same time showing him his greatness.—It is also dangerous to let him see his greatness too much, without at the same time indicating his lowliness.—Still more dangerous is it to leave him in ignorance upon both subjects.—On the contrary, it is of the greatest advantage to give him a clear notion of both."—PASCAL.

"Like the Roman emperors, who, intoxicated by their power, at length regarded themselves as demigods, the ruler of our Planet believes that the brute animal subjected to his will has nothing in common with his own nature The affinity of the ape disturbs and humbles him; it is not enough for him to be the king of animals, but he will also have it that an impassable gulf separates him from his subjects, and, turning his back upon the earth, he flies with his threatened majesty into the cloudy sphere of a special "Human kingdom." But anatomy, like those slaves who followed the conqueror's car crying out 'remember that thou art a Man!' disturbs him in his self-admiration, and reminds him of that visible and tangible reality which unites him with the animal world."—BROCA.

"For it is indeed the true characteristic of science, that she casts her net in search of results on every side, seizes upon every perceptible property of things, and subjects it to the hardest tests, no matter what finally comes of it."—GRIMM.

IN the first section of this book, after giving a general exposition of the position of man in nature and showing the great importance of the investigations relating to it, we went into the details of the question, and by referring especially to the researches which have been made upon the antiquity of the human race, and the rude, brutal state of our oldest ancestors, the so-called *primeval men*, furnished evidence of the natural position of man and of his gradual and painful upward development to a more cultivated and truly human condition.

But in this second section this earliest ancestor of ours will be traced in another direction ; and in the first place the question will be discussed of the true position which our race occupies in the zoological system and with regard to the animal world which is so nearly related to it, but especially with regard to the highest representatives of the Quadrumana, and at the same time of the Vertebrate type in general, which come nearest to man in form and structure.

And here again the known facts speak a language so clear and incapable of misinterpretation that, when once we are in possession of accurate information on the subject, we can only ask with no small astonishment how it was possible that this matter, at least in its main outlines, could ever have been misunderstood or erroneously conceived by men who could both see and think. For even at the first superficial glance it must be clear to every man who is moderately well educated, that, on all sides of his bodily structure, man is most intimately allied and bound to the organic world surrounding him, that he throughout obeys the same organic laws of form, structure, adaptation and reproduction,—and that he must therefore necessarily be arranged as an integral constituent of one zoological system. It was and is possible to overlook this simple and important truth only by reason of the immense influence of human subjectivity or self esteem, which regards it as degrading that we should be placed on the same grade as the animals, or arranged with them in the same system. But as a matter of course, *in scientific matters*, this subjectivity must be put in the background, and truth can only recognize a perfectly objective consideration, to a certain extent abandoning the personally human standpoint, or indeed rising above it. This is well explained by Professor Huxley in the following manner. ''To see this rightly,'' he says, ''let us for a moment emancipate or disconnect our thinking selves from the mask of humanity; let us imagine ourselves scientific inhabitants of the planet Saturn and well acquainted with the animated creatures which inhabit the earth, their anatomical and zoological characters, etc. Now suppose that some enterprising traveller, whom the difficulties of space and gravitation had not prevented from visiting other planets, had brought back with him from the earth, among other things, a specimen of the genus *Homo*, preserved may be in a cask of rum, and that we have been called together to examine this specimen of a creature previously unknown to us, of a peculiar 'erect, featherless biped,' and determine scientifically its position in the system. What would be the result of such an investigation? All the Saturnian philosophers would agree without the least hesitation, that the new creature was to be arranged in the well known group or sub-kingdom *Vertebrata*, and among these was to be referred specially to the class *Mammalia*, as all the anatomical and zoological characters presented by it agree precisely with those of that group and class. If we were further to inquire in what particular subdivision or order of the Mammalia the creature in question was to be placed, there could be no more room to doubt that it could belong only to one of these orders, namely, that of the *Simiae* or *Apes*, (using that word in the broadest sense.)

The structure of the bones, of the skull, and of the brain, the formation of the hands and feet, the teeth, the muscles, the viscera, etc., are all founded in the ape and in Man upon precisely the same principles, and Huxley, himself an anatomist of great reputation, in his *Memoir on the relations of primeval man to the animals immediately below him*, takes the trouble, (which was hardly necessary for educated readers,) of proving in detail and by the comparison of every more important organ, that all the differences of bodily structure that we can find between man and the most highly organized apes, (*i. e.*, the so-called *anthropoid* or man-like apes,) *are not so great in degree* as the differences between the higher and lower species or families of the Simiae.

"Thus," says our author in summing up the results of his

investigations, "whatever system of organs be studied, the comparison of their modifications in the ape series leads to one and the same result—that the structural differences which separate Man from the Gorilla and the Chimpanzee are not so great as those which separate the Gorilla from the lower apes." From all these considerations Huxley draws the important conclusion that, from a systematico-zoological point of view, we have not even the right to separate Man as a distinct order of Mammalia from the order of the Simiae, or as they have hitherto been erroneously called, Quadrumana or four-handed animals, and certainly not to sever him (as was formerly pretty generally done) entirely from the rest of the world and relegate him to a particular kingdom of nature, the so-called human kingdom, standing on the same footing as the animal and vegetable kingdoms. On the contrary, man, considered scientifically, can only be regarded as a distinct family of the highest order of Mammalia, an order which embraces in addition the true apes as well as the so-called Prosimiæ, (*Lemurs*, etc.) Following the example of the celebrated lawgiver of systematic zoology, Linné,* we may most appropriately designate this order by the name of "Primates," that is to say, pre-eminent or noble forms.† This highest order of the Primates is divisible according to Huxley into seven families of nearly equal systematic value. The lowest grade is formed by the *Galeopithecini* or flying Lemurs,—the highest by man or the family of the *Anthropini*.‡

Immediately below man come the great man-like apes and the monkeys of the Old world, and the monkeys of the New world, as the second and third families in descending order.

First, the true Apes and Monkeys of the Old world, (Africa and Asia,) forming the family of the *Catarrhini* or "narrow-

*See Appendix No. 16.   ‡See Appendix No. 17.

† The usual mode of grouping of the animal world proceeding in order from below upwards, or from the individual to the more general, embraces the following ideas : the *species*, the *genus*, the *family*, the *order*, the *class*, the *group* or *sub-kingdom*, and the *kingdom*.

nosed Simiae;" after these the monkeys of the New world or America, called *Platyrrhini* or broad-nosed Simiae."

"Perhaps," says Huxley in concluding his remarkable exposition of this subject, "perhaps no order of Mammals presents us with so extraordinary a series of gradations as this— leading us insensibly from the crown and summit of the animal creation down to creatures, from which there is but a step, as it seems, to the lowest, smallest, and least intelligent of the placental Mammalia.* It is as if nature herself had foreseen the arrogance of man, and with Roman severity had provided that his intellect, by its very triumphs, should call into prominence the slaves, admonishing the conqueror that he is but dust.— These are the chief facts, this is the immediate conclusion from them to which I adverted at the commencement of this Essay. The facts I believe cannot be disputed; and if so, the conclusion appears to me to be inevitable."

The grouping is arranged somewhat differently by Professor E. Haeckel, of Jena, who has lately written upon this subject in a very thoroughgoing manner.† He separates Huxley's last three families, the Prosimiae in the wider sense of the word, entirely from the order Primates, so that in this order there remain only man and the so-called true apes and monkeys of the old and new worlds. The Prosimiae or Lemures, on the other hand, are regarded by Haeckel, as the common trunk-group from which the other orders of the so-called Discoplacentalia, or Mammalia with a disk-like placenta,‡ have very

---

* Placental mammals are those whose young during the period of pregnancy are nourished by means of a *placenta* within the uterus itself. They form the highest grade of the Mammalia in opposition to marsupials or pouched Mammals, which carry their young in a pouch or bag of the abdomen and nourish them there by suckling, and probably originated from the latter in geological times, (at the end of the Secondary or the commencement of the Tertiary epoch.)

† *Ueber die Entstehung und den Stammbaum des Menschengeschlechts.*— (On the origin and genealogy of the human race.)— Two lectures.— Berlin, 1868.

‡ The Discoplacentalia, or Mammalia with a disk, or cake-like placenta, form the highest grade of the placental Mammalia, the latter including besides these the lower developmental forms of the *Zonoplacentalia*, or Mammals with a zone-like placenta, and the *Sparsiplacentalia*, or Mammals with a placenta formed of scattered lobes or cotyledons. The Zonoplacentalia and Discoplacentalia are further united more closely to each other, inasmuch as both possess a *decidua* or deciduous membrane, which is deficient in the Sparsiplacentalia.

probably been developed as four divergent branches, namely the *Rodentia* or gnawing mammals, the *Insectivora*, the *Chiroptera* or Bats, and the true *Simiae*.*

"Man, however," according to Haeckel, "cannot be separated from the order of the Simiae or true apes, as he stands nearer in every respect to the higher apes than these to the lower true apes." He therefore forms with these animals the highest order of the Discoplacentalia under the common and long known name of the *Primates*, whilst the four other orders of this group of Mammals are formed by the Prosimiae, Rodentia, Insectivora and Chiroptera. Of the true apes the Catarrhini or narrow-nosed forms, the apes of the old world as they are called, approach nearest to man, as is shown by the formation of the nose, which is characterized by a narrow septum and by having the nostrils directed downwards, and also by the dentition, which is exactly the same as in man, the number of teeth being thirty-two, whilst in the Platyrrhini or broad-nosed apes there are thirty-six teeth;† even leaving out of consideration

---

* According to Haeckel, the Prosimiæ are very remarkable animals. While probably numerous genera and species were living in the early Tertiary period, they are represented at present by only a few living forms which have retired into the wildest regions of Asia and Africa. The various genera of the Prosimiæ exhibit striking forms of transition to the other orders of Discoplacentalia; and for these as well as other reasons the now living Prosimiæ may be regarded as the last remnant of a very ancient and for the most part long since extinct ancestral group, from which the remaining orders of the Discoplacentalia have branched off, and in which, so to speak, like four sisters, they had their common root or ancestress. Consequently the human race also has to seek its primeval ancestors in the Prosimiæ, separated from which it is by the intermediate form of the true apes. From them Haeckel traces the genealogy of the human race further backwards, through the Marsupial, Ornithorhynchian, Amphibian and Piscine stages, to the so-called *Leptocardia*, which appear to be the lowest stage of the vertebrate type, (being without head, heart or limbs, &c.), and are themselves the product of a very long process of development out of the still lower *worms*, and finally out of the most simple conceivable primitive organism (monad).

† The dentition, as is well known, furnishes a very characteristic indication of affinity among the Mammalia, and is therefore of high systematic value. But it is not merely by the *number*, but also by the kind and general structure of the teeth, and by their earliest development, that man and the true apes, especially the Gorilla, are brought so near together.

all other similarities or agreements in structure. Only a low
and small section of this order, the Marmosets of America,
differ rather widely from man in having the fingers and toes
armed with *claws*, instead of *nails*, such as are possessed by man
and the other apes. The Marmosets are placed by Huxley as
the fourth of the seven families established by him in his highest
order, and Haeckel also leaves them in the order Primates,
regarding them as a peculiarly developed lateral branch of the
Platyrrhini.. Among the Catarrhini themselves the *Lipocerci*
or tail-less forms approach most nearly to man and are therefore
called Anthropoid or man-like apes.   Under any circumstances,
according to Haeckel, the anatomical and structural differences
between man and the man-like Catarrhini are less than those
between the latter and the lowest representatives of the
Catarrhini group, such as the Baboon for example.*

Of the Anthropoid apes there are now existing only four
genera, with about a dozen distinct species; these are the well
known Gorilla, Chimpanzee, and Orang-Outan and the Gibbons,
the last also named long-armed apes. Each of these animals
has certain peculiarities in which it approaches nearest to man:
thus the Orang approaches·nearer than all the rest by the structure of the brain and the number of its convolutions ; the Chimpanzee by the structure of its skull and its dentition; the Gorilla
by the formation of its limbs or extremities, and the Gibbon finally
by the structure of its thorax. In perfect accordance with this
peculiar condition of things, the Simian resemblances of the
lower races of man are in like manner by no means concentrated
in any one tribe, but are distributed among different peoples in
such a manner that each tribe is endowed with some inheritance
from this relationship, some more, others less, as Dr. Weissbach

---

* The Catarrhini in general may be divided into two great sections,—the *tailed*
and the *tail-less*. The first of these sections includes the Baboons, Macaques,
true Monkeys, (*Cercopithecus*,) Slender Monkeys, (*Semnopithecus*,) Thumbless
Monkeys, (*Colobus*,) and Proboscis Monkeys; the second includes the Gibbons,
Chimpanzees, Orang-Outans, and Gorilla.

has ascertained by the comparison of the measurements of various parts of the body in different races of man collected by Scherzer and Schwarz on the voyage of the Novara Frigate, (Vienna, 1867,) with corresponding measurements of the Orang.

According to this writer the Australian has the most resemblance to the apes in the length and breadth of his foot, the slenderness of his legs, his broad nose and wide mouth, and the length of his arms ; whilst other anthropologists consider that in the lateral compression of his skull, the greater number of his teeth, the later ossification of the intermaxillary bone, his smaller brain and the greater symmetry of its convolutions, as also in his long arms and narrow pelvis, the negro presents the greatest anatomical resemblance to the apes.   Some of the Platyrrhini or flat-nosed American .Monkeys also possess man-like characters.   We find among them skulls of a fine, rounded form, with considerable development of the brain-case and comparatively small projection of the muzzle, and in strict accordance with all this frequently a very man-like countenance.   Thus the Saïmiri has a facial angle* of 65 to 66 degrees, whilst in man this angle averages from 70 to 80 degrees, (in the Caucasians 80 to 85, in the Negroes 65 to 70,) and in the true Anthropoids never amounts to more than 50 degrees,† and thus the Saïmiri agrees in this respect completely with the Neanderthal skull described in the first part of this book, the facial angle of which was also estimated at 65 to 66 degrees.   According to Giebel, indeed, it is only their size that gives the three first-

---

* The facial angle of Camper is formed by two lines, one of which touches the most projecting points of the frontal bone and upper jaw, whilst the second is drawn from the orifice of the ear to the bottom of the nasal cavity. The more acute the angle thus formed, the more bestial in general is the face, whilst it becomes more elevated and human in character in proportion as the angle approaches a right angle, (90 degrees,) because under these circumstances the capsule of the skull, which contains the brain, acquires a preponderance over the essential parts of the face or muzzle.

† The young of the Anthropoid apes however constitute an exception to this rule. Thus in the young Orang, which possesses a very beautifully arched, well formed and man-like skull, the facial angle rises to 67 degrees.

mentioned Anthropoid apes their man-like character, whilst, as regards corporeal structure, some American Monkeys, and the Gibbons of which several distinct species exist in southern Asia, are decidedly more anthropomorphous. The anthropoid apes, two forms of which, (Gorilla and Chimpanzee,) live in Africa, and two, (Orang and Gibbon,) in Asia, have only been accurately known in recent times, so that even the great Cuvier, (who died in 1832,) could regard them as creations of the imagination of his colleague Buffon. Now, however, all the considerable zoological gardens and museums of Europe possess living or dead examples of them. It was only by report that early fabulous accounts of the existence of such animals in distant regions of the earth had penetrated to Europe, and upon these Professor Huxley gives us interesting information,* together with a sketch of the natural history of the anthropoid apes, in the first of the three memoirs which he has published under the title of *Evidence as to man's place in nature.*

His statements, however, although made only about six years ago, have already in some respects become antiquated, at least with regard to the Gorilla, (*Troglodytes Gorilla* or *Gorilla Gina*,) the last discovered and at the same time the most remarkable of the four anthropoid forms. This animal is very large, has very man-like limbs, and, when moving upon level ground, takes a half erect posture. Du Chaillu's narratives of his extraordinary strength and savage nature seem to be exaggerated. It is possible that the Gorilla was seen by the Carthaginian sailor, Hanno, who, in the year 510 B. C., sailed with a fleet round the west coast of Africa, and found wild, hairy men which he named Gorillas upon an island in a gulf.

The Gorilla is at any rate of the four anthropoid apes the one which, notwithstanding certain very bestial characters, never-

* See Appendix No. 18.

theless shows the most striking approximations in his structure to the human form, and partly for this reason, partly on account of the strange stories related of him, he has attracted a remarkable amount of general attention during the last few years. Of all the anthropoid apes he is especially characterized by the fact that in consequence of the structure of his foot and of the muscles of his leg he is able with the least comparative effort to stand and walk upright, and at the same time possesses the most human forms of hand, although in other respects, especially in the formation of the skull and brain, he is exceeded in resemblance to man by some other apes.*

All this shows clearly enough that the separation of man from the Mammalia which approach him most closely as a distinct order or class, or even as forming a distinct human kingdom, can no longer be maintained in the present position of science, and that the entire conception which lies at the foundation of this separation must be rejected even from the points of view opened to us by systematic zoology. But in order to advance as securely as possible with regard to this important point we add to the evidence of English and German naturalists already cited, the no less clearly expressed opinion of a French zoologist of the most modern school. In an excellent book upon the *Plurality of Human Races*, (Paris, 1864.) M. Georges Pouchet, rejecting the notion of the existence of a distinct human kingdom as set up by Geoffroy Saint-Hilaire and De Quatrefages, declares that in his physical or corporeal structure man stands in the closest juxtaposition to the anthropomorphous apes, and that this is a fact which no one can seriously dispute. And this resemblance, according to him, does not exist merely in external form, but we find it to be much greater when we resort to the careful examination of the internal parts and most essential organs, or to the microscopic investigation of the anatomical constituents of the body. We

* See Appendix No. 19.

can only come to the establishment of a distinct "human kingdom" when we compare the two extremes,—the highly cultivated European, elevated and ennobled by inherited qualities
from generation to generation through thousands of years, with
the brute animal,—overlooking the innumerable intermediate
grades which unite them.   Even the ideas of *good* and *evil* or
of *God* and *immortality*, upon which, in the absence of essential ·
corporeal differential characters, M. de Quatrefages thought
he might found his human kingdom, do not exist among all
peoples, but are either entirely wanting or in the highest degree
discrepant.   From the animal to man there is only an uninterrupted gradation or chain of allied links, and the same scientific
method must be applied to both.   The order *Bimana*, (as dis-
tinguishing man from the ape,) is, according to Pouchet, only
a creation of the writing table, and could only have been invented . in a country in which the covering of the feet is
universal, for the uncovered foot of man, when not spoiled by
the customs of civilized life, in reality forms an admirable pre-
hensile organ and is employed as such by nearly half the tribes
on the face of the earth.*   Hence man might be described as
quadrumanous with quite as much justice as the apes, and
most certainly he cannot be regarded as forming a distinct
order, but only a distinct family of the group of Mammals
hitherto characterized as Quadrumana.

So much for the consideration of man and his relationship to

* E. Goeffroy saw how the artificers in the bazaars at Cairo made use of their
great toe for a thousand purposes of grasping or seizing.—A Nubian, or negro,
on horse-back prefers to take the reins between the great toe and the other toes;
and all Abyssinian horsemen ride in this manner.—The negroes on the dahabiehs
or passenger-boats that navigate the Nile, climb the main-sail yard by seizing the
sail-rope with their foot.—Modera narrates that one day three naturalists in the
north of New Guinea beheld the trees full of natives of both sexes, who, with their
arms behind them, were leaping from branch to branch, gesticulating like apes,
screaming and laughing.—G. POUCHET.

Further examples of the use of the human foot as an organ for grasping may
be seen in my *Vorlesungen über die Darwin'sche Theorie*, pp. 197, 198, and how
very common this use appears to be among wild races in general who live partly
in trees.   In the same direction points the peculiar circumstance that among these
people the great toe is, as a rule, much further removed from the other toes than
among Europeans, who by constantly clothing and squeezing the foot have more
or less alienated it from its original destination.

the animal world from the standpoint of systematic zoology. As a matter of course the result thus attained is perfectly in accordance with that furnished by general and comparative anatomy, or the study of the general and special anatomical structure of the body in the different classes of animals, a science which, since Cuvier's time, has become so amalgamated with systematic zoology that it is no longer possible to separate them.   As the principal parts or organs of the human body agree most perfectly in all essential particulars both of external form and internal composition with the corresponding parts of animals, especially the Mammalia and their highest representatives.   Indeed, so much is this the case, that, as is pretty generally known, for thousands of years men had no means of getting a knowledge of the human body, except by the dissection of the bodies of animals.   Before men ventured, in opposition to the general prejudice, to dissect human bodies, the sole aid to the knowledge of human anatomy was the dissection of Mammalia, and by this means they were as well instructed as to the *essential* parts of the human frame, as we are at the present day.   The celebrated surgeon, Galen, of Pergamos, who lived in the second century of our era and set up a system of medicine which maintained its predominance for nearly fourteen centuries, studied the structure of the body only on the carcasses of apes, which he had at once recognized as the most man-like in form of all animals ; and as late as the sixteenth century anatomy was taught and studied only from the skeleton of a Monkey, (the Magot or *Innuus sylvanus.*) Vesal or Vesalius, the body-surgeon of the Emperor Charles the Fifth and of Philip the Second of Spain, was the first who ventured to dissect human bodies, and in so doing was so unfortunate that during his dissection of the body of a young Spanish nobleman who had been under his treatment, the heart began to beat.   In accordance with the imperfect physiological notions of that age it was believed that Vesalius had dissected a *living man*, and in order to expiate this great crime the celebrated anatomist was obliged to make a pilgrimage to the Holy Land, on his return from which he perished by ship-wreck.

How great the anatomical similarity between man and ape must be, may be seen from the words of the celebrated anato-mist, Professor Owen, who has studied the subject the most carefully of all living anatomists, and whose opinion bears the more weight, because he has taken his stand on the side opposed to the view here maintained, and places man and the apes in distinct sub-classes, although not upon purely anato-mical grounds.

In a paper, *On the characters of Mammalia*, (Journal of the Proceedings of the Linnean Society of London for 1857,) Owen says :—"Not being able to appreciate or conceive of the dis-tinction between the psychical phenomena of a Chimpanzee and of a Boschisman or of an Aztec, with arrested brain-growth, as being of a nature so essential as to preclude a comparison between them, or as being other than a difference of degree, I cannot shut my eyes to the significance of that all-pervading similitude of structure—every tooth, every bone, strictly ho-mologous—which makes the determination of the difference between *Homo* and *Pithecus* the anatomist's difficulty. And therefore . . . I follow Linnæus and Cuvier in regarding mankind as a legitimate subject of zoological comparison and classification."*

Of course all this cannot make the anatomical difference between man and his nearest allies in the series of Mammalia any less than it really is, and it is indeed so great that the first glance generally suffices to enable the practised anatomist to recognise any characteristic part of the body, especially of the

* "Surely it is a little singular," says Huxley, after citing the above passage, "that the 'anatomist' who finds it 'difficult' to 'determine the difference' between *Homo* and *Pithecus*, should yet range them, on anatomical grounds, in distinct sub-classes!"

skeleton or bony framework, as belonging either to man or to an animal. But the distinction does not affect the systems or organs themselves, such as the bones, muscles, nerves, blood-vessels, viscera, etc., which both in their coarser parts and in their more minute chemical and microscopic constitution pre-sent pecisely the same kinds of form and arrangement; it is rather a difference of degree, size and development. Some-times it is in a greater delicacy of details, a higher and better development of particular parts or organs, that the human structure exceeds the animal; or the special arrangement of the entire structure acquires a peculiar or divergent formation, as is especially seen in the structure of the osseous and muscular systems, in that of the trachea, the brain, etc.* But even these peculiarities of structure in man often indicate most definitely his animal relationships. Thus in dissecting the human body we not unfrequently find in the muscular system, (which, as is well known, has a greater tendency to individual variation than any other part,) peculiarities of arrangement in certain bodies closely resembling those occurring in the apes; and according to Dr. Duncan, (*Transactions of the Anthropo-logical Society of London, 1869,*) this condition of things may even go so far, that he regards it as an indisputable fact, that the anomalies or abnormal variations in the origin and insertion of the muscles in man constitute the normal or regular condi-tion in the apes. Professor Hyrtl, in his *Human Anatomy*, also particularly cites a number of such variations in the muscles, presenting an analogy or correspondence either with animal structure in general or with that of the apes in particular, and indeed some of these variations are actually described by him as "Ape-structures." Precisely in the same manner, the first or milk-dentition of man possesses a remarkable similarity to that of the apes, and it is only the second dentition that ac-quires the true human form. The structure of the three noblest

* See Appendix No. 20.

organs of sense, (those of sight, hearing and touch,) also shows an agreement between man and the apes which is wanting to all other Mammalia; this is treated in more detail in the author's *Lectures on Darwin*, (page 185.)

It is scarcely necessary to add that the results obtained by means of comparative anatomy are completed and confirmed by the revelations of comparative physiology or the study of the functions of the body in the different classes of animals, and in man himself. As the structure and function of an organ or living part of the body are known by observation to be always necessarily in accordance so long as there is no disturbance of equilibrium by illness or defective development, the above-mentioned result seems to be a matter of course even upon theoretical grounds; and although man is somewhat or even very superior to animals physiologically, this is only to this extent, that his physical or corporeal organization is distinguished from that of animals by its higher and finer development, its more complicated structure, by an increase in the division of labor, by better adaptation, or by the greater development of certain particularly important organs, and thus is enabled to perform operations which are impossible to animals. Nevertheless, just as in the case of the bodily structure, there is nothing more than difference of degree or of development, and this development commences even with the lowest forms of all, and from these ascends gradually, but always under the strict observance of the the same universally prevalent laws of life. Hence, investigators of these laws of life, physiologists as they are called, like the anatomists of former days, have never possessed any means of obtaining information as to the physiological processes which occur in the human body of more importance than investigations and experiments on animals. We may indeed say that three-fourths of our knowledge of human physiology or of the laws of human life have been acquired in this way, and that this knowledge is no less accurate than it would have been had the observations been made upon man himself. So far as observations of this later kind are possible they have always confirmed the results obtained by the study of animals and the conclusions derived from them, either entirely or with very slight modifications due to the difference of human structure; they have shown that the fundamental laws of life are the same and unalterable in all living creatures. For instance when the cut nerve in the thigh of a frog, (certainly a low form of animal,) contracts or reacts when irritated, it does this in exactly or almost exactly the same way as the nerve of a man would have done if similarly treated; and when the chest of an animal is laid open and the beating of the heart, or the working of the lungs is observed, we have before us, with only a very slight difference, precisely the same spectacle that would have been presented to us if we saw the opened chest of a living man. In the animal, as in man, the eye serves for vision, the ear for hearing, the tongue for tasting, the stomach for digestion, and the liver for the secretion of bile ; the feet serve for locomotion, the lungs for breathing, the kidneys for the separation of water, etc. By means of chloroform the animal is stupefied just like the man; they live, sicken and die by the same processes and causes. Hence the objection that we so often meet with in anti-materialistic controversial writings, that the knowledge gained from the study of animals cannot be applied to man, who is not an animal but something quite different, namely, *a man*, only betrays the grossest and most absurd ignorance of physiological science or of the laws of life. Even so-called *savants*, especially out of the philosophical camp, are in the habit of pluming themselves upon wisdom of this kind, which reminds us of the time of Moses or of the land of the Phæacians.*

The particular bodily organ or system, by which chiefly man is man, which together with his other advantages, (such as the structure of his hand, his erect attitude, his articulate speech,

* See Appendix No. 21.

etc.,) gives him his principal superiority over the animal, and which is therefore characterized in man by a strength of development not witnessed elsewhere, is the *brain* in combination with the *nervous system*. This noblest and most important of all organs, with which all the mental or intellectual activities known to us both in man and animals are indissolubly connected, is constructed in the Vertebrata in accordance with a grand and general fundamental plan, which commences in the fishes and from these animals upwards becomes further developed, constantly increasing in distinctness and power, probably under the influence of such momenta or causes as Darwin has described in his immortal work on *Natural Selection*. The greatest step in this upward development and advance towards perfection of structure is not, however, made by the brain at the point where we might perhaps have expected it, namely, between the animals and man, but in a much lower position, between the marsupial and placental Mammals; for here a perfectly new structure, the great commissure, makes its appearance and unites the two halves of the cerebrum which were previously separate. From this point onwards the two great hemispheres of the brain, the most important portions, intellectually, of the whole organ, constantly increase in size and in the complication of their structure, and arch over the cerebellum more and more, until finally, by a complete series of gradual modifications, they attain their highest development in the apes and in man, in which they are exactly alike in all essential parts. For different as the brains of man and of the apes may be in size and development, it has nevertheless been demonstrated by numerous anatomical investigations of the most careful kind, that all the essential parts and relations of the human brain are perfectly prefigured in animals, and that the superiority of man is due solely to the comparatively high development of these parts, combined with a considerably increased size of the whole organ. This important truth cannot be better illustrated than by the recent attempt of one of the greatest of living anatomists, Professor Owen, to establish upon the brain and its structure a specifically distinctive character between man and animals.   He affirmed that the complete over-arching and concealment of the cerebellum by the cerebral hemispheres, the existence of the hinder horn of the great lateral cavity of the brain and the presence of the so-called *pes Hippocampi minor*, an elongated white swelling on the floor of this hinder horn, are all peculiarities of the human brain which do not occur in animals, and with which, therefore, peculiar and high intellectual powers must also be united.   Taking his stand upon these assertions Owen thought that he had a right, from a systematic zoological point of view, to regard man as forming a distinct sub-class of Mammalia, which he called *Archencephala* or "brain-rulers."

This remarkable statement at once gave rise to a whole series of anatomical investigations upon the brain of the apes and to a philosophical dispute of which the details may be found in Huxley's well-known *Essay on Man's Place in Nature*, and also in the author's *Lectures on Darwin*, (2nd edition, pp. 182, et seq).   This dispute ended in the demonstration of the exact contrary of Owen's assertions in so evident a manner, that finally their author himself found it necessary to retract them publicly, although at the same time he declared his adherence to his classificational views already indicated, supporting them by the consideration of the general high development of the different parts of the brain.* Now it is true that, not merely in size, but also in the comparatively higher development of its individual parts, and especially in the number, depth and want of symmetry of the superficial convolutions, and in correspondence therewith in the comparatively stronger development of the *gray substance*, (which, as is well-known, must be regarded as the true seat of mental or intellectual activity,)

* See Appendix No. 22.

the human brain far exceeds that of the Mammalia most nearly allied to him; but all these superiorities are *relative* and not *absolute*, and in their details are already indicated or prefigured in the brains of the apes in such a manner that the ape's brain may to a certain extent be regarded as a sort of sketch or model, which has merely been more accurately worked out in man.*

"The surface of the brain of a monkey," says Huxley, "exhibits a sort of skeleton map of man's, and in the man-like apes the details become more and more filled in, until it is only in minor characters, such as the greater excavation of the anterior lobes, the constant presence of fissures usually absent in man, and the different disposition and proportions of some convolutions that the Chimpanzee's or the Orang's brain can be structurally distinguished from Man's."†

Now as the brain is the sole and exclusive organ of thought, and as all intellectual power goes parallel with its size, its development and its grade of structure in general, just as every physiological function depends upon the size, form and composition of the organ which subserves it, it cannot be doubtful,

---

* On this affair of Professor Owen, and on the general question of man's place in nature, Prof. Broca, in his Report for 1863, (Report on the Transactions of the Anthropological Society of Paris), expresses himself as follows :—

" From the zoological or anatomical point of view, man differs less from the four higher Apes than they do from the rest of the apes. With them he constitutes a natural group, the *Anthropomorpha*, of which he forms only the first subdivision; and our learned colleague, Prof. Charles Martins, of Montpellier, has made us acquainted with two new osteological characters which are met with in this group alone. . . . . Man is man through his intellect; and if he be distinct from the lower animals, he must be so by virtue of his brain, which is the organ of intelligence. Nevertheless anatomy finds between the brain of the chimpanzee and that of the lord of the earth only slight differences of form and constitution, which have been pointed out by M. Auburtin. The distinctive marks asserted by Prof. Owen have been repeatedly recognized as inaccurate. The higher apes, like ourselves, possess a posterior lobe of the cerebrum, a posterior cornu of the large lateral ventricle of the brain, and a hippocampus minor; and nothing in the order of things, except the very considerable difference of volume and the unequal abundance of the secondary convolutions, entitles us to assume a decided, absolute difference between the brain of the lowest man and that of the highest ape."

† See Appendix No. 23.

that from the standpoint of the materialistic or realistic philosophy the intellectual life of man must be regarded only as a
higher stage of development of the faculties which are dormant
in the animal world. This proposition is demonstrated not
only by the above theoretical consideration, but also by direct
comparison of the minds of man and animals and by a thoroughgoing examination of the intellectual and moral faculties
characteristic of man, both in the civilized and in the savage
state.   However, before going further into this matter, we
must, in order to be able to judge quite correctly of the position
of man in nature, first of all take counsel of another science,
which stands in such intimate connection with those to which
we have hitherto appealed, (zoology, anatomy and physiology,)
that it cannot be treated separately from them. I mean the
equally modern and interesting science of *Developmental
History*.

This comparatively modern science has brought to light a
number of extremely remarkable facts, which can leave no
doubts in the minds of those acquainted with its results as to
the close and intimate relationship of man to the animal world.
These facts, however, notwithstanding their great importance
and significance, are unfortunately still entirely or almost unknown in many circles; nay, even some naturalists, zoologists
and anatomists sometimes show a most lamentable ignorance
of these facts in their writings and statements, to say nothing
of the speculative philosophers and theologians, who think that
they can attain to the understanding of man and his place in
nature by pure thought, or by Divine inspiration, whilst in
general they have scarcely a suspicion of these facts, or of the
true laws of nature.   "Ignorance and superstition," says
Haeckel with equal pungency and truth, "are the foundations
upon which most men build up their knowledge of their own
organism and of its relations to the totality of things ; and those
plain facts of the history of development, which might throw

over it the light of truth, are ignored." Indeed, since Darwin indicated what has given a perfectly new direction to the study of organic nature, namely, that in it every thing depends upon development, proper attention has been paid to these facts, at least on the part of the younger and more active naturalists, and their great significance in a philosophical consideration of nature, (which indeed cannot be too highly appreciated,) has been recognized. This significance cannot be better indicated than in the following words of Professor Huxley: "The facts," he says, "to which I would first direct the reader's attention, though ignored by many of the professed instructors of the public mind, are easy of demonstration and are universally agreed to by men of science; while their significance is so great that whoso hath duly pondered over them will, I think, find little to startle him in the other revelations of Biology."— Let us now pass to these facts themselves and give an account of them in as condensed a form as possible.

Every living creature whether large or small, high or low, simple or complex, commences its earthly existence in a very simple form, infinitely different from its fully developed or perfect state, and from this first stage to its final development passes through a whole series of successive changes or developmental stages. These stages or steps have now become perfectly well-known, by the investigations of embryology or the study of the evolution of the germ. In all those living beings, Plants or animals,) which may be called highly organized, the first of these stages is the formation of an egg or germ-cell, whilst in the lowest forms increase or propagation is usually effected by simple division of the general substance of the body into two or more separate creatures, or by budding, (*gemmation*,) sprouting and the like.*

This ovum is the same in its fundamental structure throughout the organic world, only differing in slight variations of

* See Appendix No. 24.

form, size, color, &c.* We are here specially interested only in the ovum of the Mammalia or at all events of the Vertebrata in general, and this appears every where to be almost the same structure, including even that of man, whose ovum differs so little from that of the higher Mammalia, that no essential distinction can be demonstrated between them, any more than between the ova of different Mammalia. "There is not much resemblance," says Professor Huxley in his luminous manner, "between a barn-door fowl and the dog who protects the farm-yard. Nevertheless the student of development finds, not only that the chick commences its existence as an egg, primarily identical in all essential respects, with that of the Dog, but that the yelk of this egg undergoes division—that the primitive groove arises, and that the contiguous parts of the germ are fashioned, by precisely similar methods, into a young chick, which, at one stage of its existence, is so like the nascent Dog, that ordinary inspection would hardly distinguish between the two."

Here, however, we must not have the ordinary fowl's egg in our minds, as this, like the eggs of Birds in general, or of the true Reptiles, is distinguishable at the first glance from the egg of the mammalia, because in it the true egg, which is not larger than the mammalian egg and in all respects behaves in precisely the same manner, has been surrounded by a *nutritive yelk*, (the well-known yelk of the egg,) which is easily distinguished from the *formative yelk* of the egg, and also by the albumen and shell as external additions.

By means of these additions the bird's egg brings with it into the world ready prepared all the materials necessary for the formation of the young bird, whilst the egg of the Mammal or of man carries with it from the ovary into the womb only the supply necessary for the first foundation of

* For further details upon this subject see the author's " *Physiologische Bilder*," in the chapter on the cell, (pages 261 to 270.)

the young animal, and receives all subsequent supplies from the maternal organism.*

The same facts as in the case of the Fowl and Dog are revealed to us by the developmental history of every other Vertebrate animal, whether it be a Mammal, a bird, a lizard, a snake or a fish, and in a broad sense the same may be said of every organic being. Always at the outset and at the moment of first formation we find a structure which we call an egg, and which consists of a small, round, very delicate body, one-eighth to one-tenth of a line in diameter, enclosed by a firm membrane and filled with a viscid fluid with numerous scattered granules which is called the *yelk*, (*vitellus*.) In the midst of this yelk lies the beautiful vesicular *nucleus*, one-fiftieth of a line in

---

*Just that portion of the fowl's egg which from its minuteness escapes the observation of the novice and of the housewife who uses the egg for cooking purposes, is in reality the most important, because from it the development of the young being begins. It is only after this ovule or proper ovum is formed in the ovary that the other substances which complete the egg (yelk, white, and shell) gradually take their places around it. These substances contain all the materials necessary for the formation of the young chick, as fat, albumen, salts of lime, &c., out of which muscles, nerves, bones, and feathers can be developed ; while the calcareous shell enclosing the whole, permits by its porousness the entrance and exit of the necessary gasses. Now, in order to bring about the development of this crude amorphous mass, which contains within so small a space all the elements and dispositions necessary for the formation of a living organic being, nothing is required but warmth and a comparatively short time, during which the simple germ contained in the yelk undergoes a whole series of well-known stages of development or formative changes, as the last result of which the finished chick appears. A more striking proof of the spontaneous activity and creative force of Nature, excluding all not material or not natural influences, cannot be found !

With many animals, as with the frog, the whole of this metamorphoses proceeds outside of the body of the mother, and not within a closed shell, but openly, so that the development can be the more easily observed of the tadpole into the proper frog.

It is well known that the insect world also presents numerous examples of this gradual change of form —a change which is often so considerable that only scientific investigation could demonstrate that animal forms so widely different in appearance belonged to each other. Everywhere, however, whether we contemplate the highest or the lowest grades of the animal world, the nature and the course of the transformation are fundamentally the same and follow the same immutable laws. Hence, infinitely various as nature appears in her innumerable modes of manifestation she remains fundamentally ever the same, single and uniform !

diameter, with its clear contents; it is also known as the *germinal vesicle*. In this vesicle again a still smaller body, (only one-five-hundredth of a line,) is enclosed; this is the *germinal spot* or *nucleolar corpuscle*. This, as well as the egg itself, consists of an albuminoid mass.

This same simple and similar structure then is exhibited by the egg in all the higher animals, especially the Vertebrata, *before* their fertilization by the semen or male reproductive material. The remarkable discovery of the egg of the Mammalia and of man in its place of origin, (the *ovary*,) was made not much more than forty years ago by the celebrated embryologists von Baer. The detached egg on its migration had however been previously seen in the oviduct.

When once the existence of the egg was discovered the next thing of course was to ascertain the further course of its development, and to observe how the *embryo* or *fœtus* was gradually developed from the fertilized egg. The first step in this progress is, that the contents of the egg-cell undergo the remarkable process called *segmentation*, in which the originally amorphous mass of the yelk, by continual division and subdivision, in which the germinal vesicle and its nucleus take part, becomes broken up into an aggregation of elementary parts called *embryonal-cells*. These cells in their turn are capable of all possible further changes of form, and from them the future organism is built up by a constantly increasing formation of new cells. As Huxley admirably expresses it: "Nature, by this process, has attained much the same result as that at which a human artificer arrives by his operations in a brickfield. She takes the rough plastic material of the yelk and breaks it up into well-shaped tolerably even-sized masses — handy for building up into any part of the living edifice. . . . Every part, every organ is at first, as it were, pinched up rudely and sketched out in the rough; then shaped more accurately; and, only, at last, receives the touches which stamp its final character."

At the commencement and even through a considerable period of embryonic life* this goes on in the different animals and groups of animals in so uniform a fashion, that the young of all animals are almost exactly alike, or at all events are very similar, not only in external form but also in all the essentials of their structure, however different may be the form of the animal subsequently to be produced from them. In this respect, therefore, the embryos behave exactly like the egg itself, which is found almost everywhere to present at first the same form and size. From a certain period of embryonic life, however, the differences of the individual forms gradually make their appearance and become more and more distinct as the creature under observation approaches its permanent structure and the time of its birth. But even here it is remarkable that the more closely individual animals resemble each other in the mature state, the longer and more closely do their embryos also resemble each other; whilst the embryos become earlier and more distinctly dissimilar in proportion as the animals to be produced from them differ from each other later in life. Thus, for example, the embryos of a Snake and a Lizard, two forms of animals which are comparatively speaking nearly allied, resemble each other in appearance longer than those of a Snake and a Bird, two animals which are very far removed from each other.

* The exceedingly important facts of embryology, or the science of the gradual development of the embryo from the ovum, were first established about the middle of the last century, by the great German naturalist Caspar Friedrich Wolf, in his celebrated *Generations Theorie*. Till that time the altogether false belief had prevailed that in the ovum was contained from the first an exceedingly minute but yet perfect organic being in the form of the future animal, which required nothing more than to grow larger by incorporating the nutriment supplied by the media surrounding it. The ancients, indeed, were generally acquainted with the embryo only in a pretty far advanced stage of development, at which the form of the future animal may be recognized with some distinctness; and certainly this gave rise to the theory of *evolution*, which for a long time dominated science. Now-a-days this theory is completely displaced by Wolf's theory of *epigenesis*, which shared the fate of nearly all great discoveries; for it remained unacknowledged for half a century, until Oken, Meckel, Baer and others brought it into credit.

In the same way, and for the same reason, the embryos of a Dog and a Cat continue longer to present a resemblance, than those of a Dog and a Bird, or a Dog and a Marsupial animal. But at the first beginning and during the first period of embryonic life the embryos even of the most different animals or groups of animals, such as Mammalia, Birds, Lizards, Snakes, Tortoises, &c., are so similar in appearance that, according to the definite assertion of von Baer, they can generally be distinguished, from their external aspect, only by difference of size. There are also some characters of form and external outline, which sometimes, but not always, render it possible to distinguish them, but these are exceedingly insignificant. Professor Agassiz found this to his cost; for having one day neglected to furnish an embryo in his collection with a ticket, he was afterwards unable to determine whether it belonged to a Mammal, a Bird, or a Reptile.*

Thus the study of developmental history furnishes us with clear and incontrovertible evidence of the close relationship of all living creatures with respect to their first production and formation, and in connection with our special subject we have now only to ascertain whether this natural evidence possesses the same validity in the case of our own species. "One burns with impatience," says Huxley, "to inquire what results are yielded by the study of the development of Man.—Is he something apart? Does he originate in a totally different way from Dog, Bird, Frog and Fish, thus justifying those who assert him to have no place in nature and no real affinity with the lower world of animal life? or does he originate in a similar germ, pass through the same slow and gradually progressive

* It must not be supposed, however, that no differences exist between the various embryos. On the contrary, there must be such differences of a very definite and marked kind as regards both molecular and chemical constitution ; but they are so delicate that they cannot be detected either from external appearances, or by any ordinary means of investigation at our command. It is to these differences of the most minute constitution, therefore, that we must ascribe the foundation of those differences of structure which afterwards diverge so widely.

modifications,—depend on the same contrivances for protection and nutrition, and finally enter the world by the help of the same mechanism? The reply is not doubtful for a moment, and has not been doubtful any time these thirty years. Without question, the mode of origin and the early stages of the development of Man are identical with those of the animals immediately below him in the scale, &c." As regards the human ovum, it is in all essential particulars like that of any other Mammal, differing, at the utmost, only a little in size. Its diameter is one-tenth or one-twelfth of a line, and it is consequently so small that with the naked eye it can only be perceived as a little point. But when suitably magnified it is seen to be a spherical vesicle containing in its interior a slimy protoplasm or *yelk*, and in this the *cell-nucleus* or *germinal vesicle* with its *nucleolar corpuscle* or *germinal spot*. Externally the entire structure, which is also called the *ovicell*, is enclosed by a thick, translucent membrane, the *cell-membrane*, or *vitelline membrane*.

It seems unnecessary to give any further description of this simple and yet complicated structure, with which every man, whether born in a palace or in a hovel, commences his existence, as it would require to be made in precisely the same terms that have already been used in describing the egg of the Mammalia. There is no visible difference between them except that of size. Nevertheless such differences do exist, and indeed must exist in a very definite and characteristic manner. But they do not lie in the external form, although even here subtle variations not recognizable by our instruments of research, may and indeed must exist, but rather in the inner chemical and molecular constitution and in the tendency, caused by this, to a peculiar systematic and individual further development. "These delicate individual differences of all eggs which depend upon indirect or potential adaptation, are indeed not directly perceptible with the extraordinarily coarse means of investigation possessed by man, but they are recognizable by indirect inferences as the first causes of the difference of all individuals."— *Haeckel.*

What is the subsequent destiny of this vesicle or ovicell? It quits the organ, the *ovary*, in which it was formed and matured, (in the human subject every four weeks, in animals only at the so-called *rutting* season,) and passes thence by mechanical causes into the *oviduct.* If the egg-cell is not fecundated here it is lost and disappears without leaving any traces. If, on the contrary, it is fertilized by the male semen, it becomes developed in the womb, (*uterus*,) into an *embryo*, and, as a rule, does not quit that organ until its perfect evolution into a young creature capable of life.* And all this takes place exactly in the same way as in any other Mammal. Even the changes of form or transformations which the human embryo undergoes from this period are exactly the same as have been already described in the case of animals. First of all the process of segmentation of the yelk or cell-division occurs, commencing by the division of the germinal spot and then of the germinal vesicle itself into two separate cells. These then divide again, and this process is continued until, finally, a spherical mass of cells, called glob-

---

* The vital movement and further development of the egg commences at the moment when it is fertilized by the male seminal cell, and then up to the close of individual life it follows rigidly the direction which has been impressed upon it both by its own constitution and by that of the male reproductive material. As to the purely mechanical and material nature of this process there can be no doubt, and yet the two reproductive elements which meet in it are so minute and so slightly distinguishable from other elements of the same nature, that there is nothing but an infinitesimal and inconceivable delicacy and difference of these materials in their intimate chemical and molecular constitution that can be regarded as the cause of the innumerable (systematic and individual) differences of the subsequent development.—"We must stand," says Haeckel, "in wonder and admiration before the infinite and to us inconceivable delicacy of the albuminoid material. We cannot but be astonished at the undeniable fact, that the simple egg-cell of the mother and a single seminal filament of the father transfer the individual vital movement of these two individuals to the child so exactly, that afterwards the most subtle bodily and mental peculiarities of the two parents reappear in it." Who can venture, in the presence of such facts, to speak of "brute" matter or to deny its ability to produce mental phenomena ?

ules of segmentation, is produced. This aggregation of cells now becomes converted into a spherical vesicle, the *blastoderm*, on one side of which a disciform thickening, (the *embryonal spot,*) is produced by continual increase or growth of cells from the globules of segmentation which are more strongly accumulated at this point. Soon afterwards this embryonal spot acquires an elongated or biscuit-like shape and forms the first definitive foundation of the true body of the embryo, whilst the blastoderm itself is only employed for nutritive purposes. The embryonal spot consists of three superimposed and closely united leaves, the three *germ-lamellae*, produced in this way,— the cells formed by the process of segmentation arrange themselves in accordance with a plan common to all Vertebrata, in three membranous layers, each of which has a perfectly definite share in the subsequent building up of the tissues. From the *outermost* or superior leaf are produced the external skin with its folds and appendages, (such as the sebaceous glands, sudorific glands, hairs, nails, &c.,) and also the active central nervous system, the brain and spinal cord. The *innermost* or inferior germ-lamella furnishes the material for the formation of the mucous membranes which line the entire alimentary apparatus from the mouth to the anal aperture with all its enlargements or appendages, such as the lungs, liver, intestinal glands, &c. Lastly, the *middle* lamella gives origin to all the other organs, namely, the bones, muscles, nerves, &c.

As the first *visible* rudiment of the young organism, an elongated, shield-shaped elevation of darker color makes its appearance in the middle of the embryonal spot ; it is surrounded by a lighter colored pear-shaped part of the spot, and along it the three germ lamellae are intimately united. In the middle line or longitudinal axis of this shield-shaped prominence a straight shallow furrow or groove now makes its appearance ; this is the *primitive groove*, (also called the primitive band or axial plate,) which, as Huxley says, "marks the central line of the edifice which is to be raised, or, in other words, indicates the position of the middle line of the body'' of the future animal.   On each side of the groove the superior or outer germ-lamella then rises in the form of a long fold or ridge; these two ridges finally unite above and form the so-called *medullary tube*, an elongated cavity for the brain and spinal cord, which are to be produced from the walls of this tube. The cavity itself becomes the central canal of the spinal cord and the brain cavity.   In the lowest forms of Vertebrated animals, (*Amphioxus*,) it remains through life a simple tube pointed at each end; whilst, in all other Vertebrata, the anterior extremity of the medullary tube becomes enlarged into a rounded vesicle, the first rudiment of the brain, and only the posterior extremity, forming the tail, remains pointed.

Simultaneous with these processes is the formation at the bottom of the primitive groove, or in the middle germ-lamella, of a solid cellular thread or cartilaginous rod, the *notochord*, (or *chorda dorsalis*,) on each side of which the middle lamella becomes developed into quadrangular dark spots, arranged in pairs, the *primitive vertebræ*, which, with the notochord, constitute the first rudiment of the vertebral column.   The latter is produced by the growth, from the dorsal surface of the notochord, of certain arched processes, which springing upwards finally unite to form a tube embracing the spinal cord.   Many fishes retain this dorsal chord, (which in all Mammalia, and in Man, is entirely absorbed,) throughout their whole existence,— indeed all the grades of development which the human embryo gradually passes through, are permanently represented in the great series of the Vertebrata when we pass from the lowest forms upwards.   The most ancient Vertebrata which we find buried in a petrified state in the depths of the earth and which opened the great procession of the Vertebrate type in the organic history of the world millions of years ago, also possessed, instead of a vertebral column, only a cartilaginous rod or gelatinous cord to which we have given the name of *chorda*, and it was only at a later period that this was replaced by the true vertebral column composed of biconcave vertebræ.

In this stage *the embryos* of *all Vertebrata, including man, are still perfectly similar.* "In the earliest rudiment of the embryo," says Giebel,* "when it consists only of the primitive groove and notochord, it is impossible for us by the most minute observation to distinguish the human individuality from that of any other Vertebrate,—of a Mammal or a Bird,—a Lizard or a Carp."

But even at a still later period the greatest similarity of development persists, and it is only by degrees that the differences become more prominent by the stronger growth of particular parts. Thus the four extremities of the Vertebrata, which at first grow out of the downward processes of the walls surrounding the primitive groove in the form of little buds, and by degrees acquire the true structure of the limbs, are so much alike during the first weeks or days of their production that the delicate hand of Man, the coarse paw of the Dog, the elegant wing of the Bird and the stumpy fore-leg of the Tortoise can hardly be distinguished from one another. Nor is there any more distinction between the leg of Man and of the Bird, or the hind leg of the Dog and Tortoise. And yet there are scarcely any parts of the body which, when fully developed, are more variously formed than the limbs of the Vertebrate animals. In a somewhat earlier stage, when even the rudiments of the fingers or toes are not yet formed and the limbs only form simple rounded processes shooting forth from the sides of the trunk, it is not even possible to distinguish between the fore and hind limbs. With regard to the fingers and toes themselves it is a very remarkable circumstance that their presence to the number of five is the rule throughout nearly all the Mammalia. This applies even to the so-called Solipedes, (*e. g.*

* *Der Mensch, 1861.*

the Horse,) which, in the embryo-state, exhibit five toes ; these however are afterwards fused together into the *hoof-bone*, but in individual cases, (deformities,) the whole or a part of them are retained.

What is true of the limbs, is true in exactly the same manner of all other parts or organs, which all at first have the same form and gradually develop their specific and permanent differences. The difference however consists very often merely in the fact that certain parts or organs, which in the lower series of animals attain a permanent development and a corresponding importance, lose this importance in higher groups, become retrograde, and are either entirely lost or retained in a very aborted state. As an example of such organs we way take the tail in man. In the earliest period of his embryonic existence man possesses this part in just the same state of development as the embryos of tailed and tailless Mammals. It is only towards the sixth or seventh week of embryonic life that the tail begins to retrograde and finally disappears, leaving only a small rudiment, consisting of from three to five aborted vertebræ, which form the lower extremity of the vertebral column even in the adult and fully developed man, but remain concealed beneath the skin. They are immediately connected with the sacrum and bear the name of the *os coccygis*.

The theme of tailed men has already often been treated in a burlesque fashion, and the absence of a tail in man has always been regarded as an essential prerogative of his and as an important distinction from the animal world.

In all this it was indeed forgotten that in the first months of his embryonic existence man is not destitute of this animal appendage,—nay that he even bears it about with him, (although in a very rudimentary form,) throughout the whole of his life. Nor was it taken into consideration that the large apes, which are so nearly allied to man, (Orang, Chimpanzee, Gorilla,) are also tailless, of course in precisely the same sense as man. According to Haeckel the aborted tail of man is "an incontrovertible proof of the undeniable fact that he has descended from tailed ancestors." He says indeed that in the tail of man rudimentary muscles are still present,—the remains of those muscles which in earlier days served to move the tail of his ancient progenitors.

But even amongst those ancestors of man which are much further removed from him in the great series of organic development, some have impressed their striking and unmistakable seal upon the human embryo. In the first weeks, (or days,) of their embryonic life all Vertebrata possess an extremely important external structure, which is common to all, but subsequently becomes converted into organs of the most different kinds. These are three or four fissures on each side of the neck, with intervening processes or arches, which in Fishes become the *branchial arches* and are destined to bear the respiratory organs or *gills, (branchiae.)* These branchial or visceral arches, also called *bronchial arches*, with their intervening branchial or visceral fissures are originally present in Man or in the Dog as well as in other Vertebrata. But it is only in the Fishes that they remain as they were in the embryo, and become converted into respiratory organs,—in the other Vertebrata, on the contrary, they find a different employment and serve as the rudiments of the different parts of the face and neck.

Similar legacies from the animal world to man, or so-called *rudimentary organs*, are very numerous. We may indicate, for example, the so-called *intermaxillary bone*, which was so long supposed to be wanting in man and yet was at last discovered by Goethe ;* the rudimentary *muscles* for the movement of the ear, which by long practice some individuals are actually able to use in moving that organ ; *the male milk-glands,*

* See Appendix No. 25.

which in many men have even been seen to the number of four, (the two lower ones in a very rudimentary state ;) the human milk-dentition and its resemblance to that of the lower Mammalia in form ; the traces of ribs on the cervical, (or neck-) vertebræ in man, &c., &c.

Rudimentary or aborted organs, which may be detected in great abundance throughout both the animal and vegetable kingdoms, are among the strongest supports of the theory of derivation, as indeed of the monistic or unitarian conception of the Universe generally. "If the opponents of this conception," says Professor Haeckel, "understood the enormous importance of these facts, they must be reduced to despair. None of these opponents has been able to throw even a faint glimmer of light upon these extremely remarkable and important phenomena. There is scarcely a single one of the more highly developed forms of plants or animals that has not some rudimentary organs. . . . It is the reverse of the formative process, in which by adaptation to peculiar conditions of existence and by the use of a still undeveloped part new organs are produced, &c."

These remarkable facts of inheritance and of the existence of rudimentary organs, like the previously described embryological and comparative anatomical resemblances in general, stand in immediate connection with another, no less remarkable discovery, which shows that there is not merely a complete parallelism of the *individual* and *systematic* development, but also a parallelism of these two with the *palæontological* development, —that is to say the laws, in accordance with which the first development of the individual creature takes place, may be recognized not merely in the present world, but also in the history of the past. It is the well known relation of *juxtaposition*, *cause and effect and succession* that is unmistakably presented to us in this triple developmental series, and demonstrates to us with a distinctness which cannot be misunderstood, the great affinity of all organic beings to and their derivation from each other.   Thus, in the great series of the Vertebrata we find permanently represented all the grades of development which the human embryo successively passes through ; and, on the other hand, the human embryo passes through a graduated series of metamorphoses which closely approximate it at each stage of its development to the lower grades of development of the Vertebrate type,—that is to say, man (after representing in the egg-state the lowest stage of life, the cell or Protozoon,) resembles a *Fish* in the earliest stage of its embryological development, then an Amphibian, and only at a later period a Mammal. Moreover the different steps, which it surmounts in this last or Mammalian stage, correspond to the different stages of development through which the Mammalian type gradually rises from the lowest to the higher orders and families.*   But this is not all ; all these stages or grades of development again precisely resemble the steps by which the Vertebrate type has risen gradually during geological times and in the course of many millions of years to its present state of perfection, and the remains and representatives of which we find buried in the depths of the earth.   This great truth cannot be better expressed than in the admirable words of one of the greatest of living Naturalists, Professor Agassiz, who says : "It is a fact which I can now assert as universal that the embryos and young of all actually existing animals, to whatever class they may belong, are *the living miniatures of the fossil representatives of the same families.*"   Exactly the same idea is expressed by Professor Haeckel in the following words :—"The series of multifarious forms which any individual of any series of animals passes through from the commencement of its existence, from the egg to the grave, is an abridged and condensed repetition

* "The different animals," says Professor Schaffhausen, "are the forms of animal life fixed at different stages, and the higher animal advances during its development through the lower forms, but never perfectly reproducing them, since the incessant formative impulse is constantly tending to remove the similarity again immediately."

of that series of different specific forms through which the ancestors and primitive progenitors of that species have passed during the enormously long periods of geological history."

Consequently the development of the individual during and even after its embryonic existence is nothing more than a short and rapid repetition of the course of development of the type to which it belongs, or in other words the miniature, enclosed in a narrow frame, of the sequence of those ancestors which form the entire ancestral chain of the individual in question and which in its most essential features is still represented by the systematic sequence of the living types of animals. There can be no more striking proof of the close relationship and connection of man with the totality of organized nature, and especially with the animals immediately below him. This fact at once throws an equally bright and astonishing light upon the important question of the origin and derivation of the human race itself, a question which as a matter of course is most intimately and necessarily connected with our subject, or the question of the position of man in nature. Since the celebrated Darwinian theory has brought the doctrine of the derivative nature and conversion of organic beings into more general acceptance, and at the same time general attention has been attracted directly to the relation of man to that doctrine, this equally important and interesting question has excited the minds of men in a most remarkable manner, and its answer in a Darwinian sense has given rise to a very wide spread emotion. We may remark in passing that this emotion, which has often been accompanied or followed by the drollest outbreaks of virtuous indignation, is a striking proof how little the great results of natural history have become generally diffused, notwithstanding the innumerable attempts that have been made to popularize them, and that it is precisely the most important results of these investigations and the conclusions founded upon them that are still the greatest mysteries to the majority of men.

It is true that at the root of this emotion lies the just conviction, which is productive of uneasiness to many minds, that all investigations into the position of man in nature and his relation to the rest of the organic world must finally lead up to the question of the origin and derivation of the human race, and certainly these researches, which are in part of a very difficult and subtle kind, and *in themselves* possess interest chiefly for those who make a special study of them, would scarcely have interested the public so much, if there were not always in the background the necessary and unavoidable tendency to this very question. As I stated in my third lecture on Darwin, the whole question is to a certain extent an *affair of the heart* for us, and no doubt it requires the most thoroughgoing examination and investigation. Professor Huxley, who was the first to come boldly before the general public with opinions as to the natural origin and animal derivation of man founded upon anatomical considerations, expresses himself in the same terms. It is true that similar views had often been expressed before Huxley, but they were supported less upon particular facts than upon general philosophy, or upon reflections derived from a general view of natural phenomena. Since Huxley came forward, however, numerous voices have been raised in other countries on the same side,—in Germany, especially those of Professor Ernst Haeckel of Jena and Hermann Schaaffhausen of Bonn, the latter as I shall speedily show, having really a claim to priority over Huxley, in so far that he definitely asserted the animal derivation of man ten years previously. It is a very wide spread notion that Professor Carl Vogt, the celebrated naturalist and writer, is the true originator of the idea of the natural and especially of the Simian origin of man. This opinion, probably a consequence of Vogt's lectures delivered in all the great towns of Germany, is in fact erroneous. Vogt was even for a long time a very decided and energetic champion of the doctrine of the *immutability of species*, which necessarily excludes the theory in question, and it is only since Darwin and by Darwin's means that he has become of a different opinion. But even since this conversion he has never, so far as I know, expressed himself publicly upon the point in question so distinctly and decidedly as the naturalists just mentioned.

In his well known *Lectures on Man*, (Giessen, 1863,) the intimate relationship between Man and animals is certainly recognized and supported by facts, and the systematic position of man is discussed in exactly the same manner as by Huxley, —and finally at the conclusion of the work and in the last lecture the animal and especially the Simian origin* of man is represented as the necessary consequence of the whole theory. Vogt has also subsequently published a series of investigations upon the so-called *Microcephali*, (not indeed intended for the general public,) in which he treats this human deformity as a kind of intermediate form between man and animals produced by *atavism* or *retrogression*, and gives to the Microcephali the characteristic name of "ape-men."† But how far Carl Vogt

---

* When the term "Simian origin" is employed it is always to be understood in the Darwinian sense, as signifying derivation from an antediluvian, extinct and still unknown progenitor, holding a middle place between the Human and the Simian types. A derivation of man from one of the existing anthropoid apes has, so far as I am aware, never been seriously maintained by any one.

† Vogt regards microcephaly as an arrested formation of the brain, especially of the anterior hemispheres; and he believes that it corresponds to a lower stage in the developmental history of man, and therefore has a *typical* significance; while other investigators see in it only a morbid *malformation* brought about by various causes, and deny that it has any meaning in favor of the derivation of man from a lower animal. According to Vogt, moreover, there is a great analogy between the microcephalic brain and that of the ape as regards the laws of their growth, in that both are distinguished from the normal human brain by their increase of volume after birth proceeding only very gradually and to a small degree, while the brain of a healthy human child during the first year after birth makes a vast advance, increasing proportionally nearly as much in that time as it does during the rest of its life. Now as arrested growths are in a manner the mile-stones on the path which leads back to the point of origin of man, microcephali are, according to Vogt, nearer to the ape and so to the common ancestor of the latter and man, than is an ordinary man. A description of two *living* microcephali is given, by the author of the present work in No. 44 of the *Gartenlaube* for 1869.

has gone upon this point in his public lectures on the primitive
history of man, or how far he has gone into its details, we are
unable to judge precisely, as these lectures are as yet only
known from newspaper reports.   In any case Vogt cannot be
regarded as the originator of the entire theory, merely because
he was the first to lecture upon it in public.   Huxley's work so
often cited, which marks an epoch in the history of the subject,
appeared in the same year as Vogt's *Lectures on Man* and
treats the question in a far more thoroughgoing and definite
manner; it has therefore in any case the priority over Vogt's.
But at a much earlier period than either of them, and indeed at
a period when, considering the prevalent prejudices in opposition to it, greater scientific courage was necessary, Professor
Hermann Schaaffhausen ventured to lay down the outlines of
the theory of organic development and to establish as its necessary consequence the doctrine of the animal derivation of man.
This he did in three memoirs printed in the years 1853, 1854
and 1858:   *On the color of the skin in the Negro, and the
approximation of the human figure to the animal form*, (1854,)
— *On the persistency and transformation of species*, (1853,) and
On the connection of the phenomena of nature and life, (1858.)
As evidence of this I may here cite a passage from the first
mentioned of these three memoirs, in which the author demonstrates by striking examples that not only the color of the skin,
but also the different form of the head, upon which the distinction of the various races of men has been founded, varies in the
most essential manner with climate, soil, civilization, mode of
life, &c., and that from this, in conjunction with the circumstance that the diminution of intelligence in races causes animal
forms to become more and more prominent, the question must
arise *whether the human form has not been produced from the
animal, and whether the increase of intelligence has not brought
about this development?*   He then continues in the following
terms:—"There is nothing in the least lowering to man in our

regarding his creation as a natural development, nor is the human intellect thereby placed upon the same level with the intelligence of the animal. We may regard the highest intellectual and moral interests of the human race as an undoubted fact and nevertheless admit the possibility that the human mind has risen from a state of animal rudeness to the highest intellectual development. It will of course be objected that man and animal are essentially different. But if we had never witnessed the development of the chicken from the egg, should we not with still more reason regard these as two essentially different things? Why should not the outlines of the moral world of man exist in the sentiments of an animal mind? If organic bodies have been constantly advancing towards greater perfection, why should not a gradual unfolding of the intellectual powers also be possible? It is a more elevated and worthy view of the plan of creation to regard all nature as a whole, coherent by its development, than to imagine the Creator repeatedly destroying his creation, in order to set another in its place.''

Unfortunately these three admirable memoirs remained too little known for them to have exercised any great influence in favor of the theory of evolution which was destined soon afterwards to make such great progress. And yet they must be regarded as having already established that theory and its application to Man in all essential points !* But if we leave out of consideration all more profound scientific evidence and merely attend to the question of the origin of man, Dr. H. P. D. Reichenbach, of Altona, has a greater claim to priority than any of the naturalists just mentioned.—On September, 24, 1851, that gentleman delivered before the Twenty-eighth Meeting of German Surgeons and Naturalists in Gotha, a discourse *On the Origin of Man*, printed at Altona, in 1854, in which the doctrine of the animal-derivation of Man was most

* See Appendix No. 26.

definitely laid down and defended. "But where was the soil," he says in this little work, (pages 7 and 8,) which is written in a rather grandiloquent style, "where was the soil on which the first man was formed and rested, and where the maternal bosom from which he derived his nourishment? To these questions, however the pride of man may struggle against it, we can only answer : *The soil on which the first man was produced was an animal,— his first mother an animal,— and the first nourishment of his mouth the milk of an animal.*" *

From all this it is sufficiently clear that the theory of the animal origin of man is not, as so many people in their ingnorance suppose, a discovery of Vogt's, but that it is a theory founded upon the progress of development of Science, which in some way or another would sooner or later have been brought to light. Essentially, as has already frequently been stated, it is completely included in the theory of derivation and change, and is a necessary and inevitable consequence of this. Hence even Lamarck, the celebrated predecessor of Darwin, did not hesitate, at the commencement of the present century, to apply the theory of transformation established by him to man and to

* In the further course of his treatise, which starts from palæontological facts, Reichenbach relies chiefly on the knowledge which has been gained among savage races, and on the points of animal resemblance of the Negro, the New Hollander, the Bushman, the Pescherä, the savages of the interior of Borneo and Sumatra, &c., as well as on their lower grade of mental culture. Also, towards the end of his pamphlet he distinctly expresses the idea of the gradual rise of the whole animal and vegetable kingdoms from a cell-formation intermediate between plant and animal; and he concludes with the words : "But what is the most incomprehensible of all is, that a great natural philosopher of our time should say that man is only a modification of the Deity, when we know from nature that he is only a modified animality."

That these views, so openly expressed at that time, in opposition to the general prejudice, did little more than draw upon their originator ill-will and scorn, and, after they were printed, passed away without leaving a trace, is easily understood.

The writer had an opportunity, at a subsequent assembly of naturalists, of becoming acquainted with the old gentleman who had such an acute presentiment of the scientific future ; and certainly the triumphant development of his views which has followed must have been a joy and satisfaction to him, even though he himself remained forgotten.

assert the gradual production of man from a man-like species of Ape. Lorenz Oken, the head of the Natural Philosophical School in Germany, which embraced similar ideas, also expressed himself in the same manner, (1809 to 1819.)

Darwin himself, the true father of the evolutionary theory now prevalent, proceeded more cautiously than Lamarck, and for some reason not yet explained, left the question whether and how far this theory is to be applied to man, untouched.* This, however, did not prevent its being perceived that the animal origin of man is equally a necessary consequence of the Darwinian as of any other theory of evolution, and it is undoubtedly recognized as such by all the serious adherents of Darwin. But even if this were not the case it would not alter matters in the least, for without Darwin and the Darwinian theory Anthropology would of itself in course of time have arrived at this necessary result,—indeed even before Darwin it had already been attained, although only in the minds of certain individual students. If we accept only one great law of organic development, leaving out of consideration Darwin and his theory, its correctness or incorrectness, we can form no other hypothesis of the production of man. For it is impossible to conceive that this law of development has suddenly been broken at a particular point, and that by supernatural intervention a new member of such importance as man has been inserted in the natural series of beings and provided with all those animal resemblances, indications of relationship, etc., which should belong to him in accordance with that law.† Such considerations as these had led the author of this book, long before anything was known of the Darwinian theory, to the idea of the natural origin of man

* This was written before the publication of Darwin's celebrated work, *The Descent of Man.*—*E.*

† "If the theory of derivation," says Professor Haeckel (two lectures on *The Origin and Genealogy of the Human Race*, 1868,) be a necessary and general law of induction, its application to man is only an equally necessary special law of deduction,—a theory which follows from the former by inevitable necessity."

and especially of his animal descent, an idea he expressed openly
and without circumlocution as long ago as the year 1855 in the
first edition of his work on *Force and Matter*, *without at that
time*, having the least suspicion how soon positive observation
and the advancing knowledge of nature would lend efficient aid
to this idea.   At present (but already fifteen years have elapsed)
the theory of the animal origin of man is an undeniable requirement not merely of a rational theory but of positive investigation
and of science itself.   It is supported above all things by the
common plan of development in the organization of the entire
living world, which as already stated is most clearly and indis-
putably revealed in three directions (geologically, systematico-
anatomically and embryologically.)   Then we have all the positive arguments which arise from direct comparison, and which
were first laid down connectedly and with distinct reference to
this object by Professor Huxley in his three celebrated essays
on *The Position of Man in Nature*.   After furnishing in the
first of these memoirs a detailed description of the four most
man-like apes, the Gibbon, Chimpanzee, Orang and Gorilla (an
abstract of which is given in Appendix No. 18, of the present
book,) Professor Huxley passes, in his second memoir, to his
well known anatomical comparison of the structure of the body
of man with that of the large apes, especially the Gorilla, and
arrives at the important conclusion, which has already been
mentioned, that the anatomical differences between man and
the most highly organized apes are not so great or so important, as the differences of the various families of apes.   In
his mind and in that of every thinking person, this result leads
to the further question,—if we admit the mutual derivation of
animals: is this principle also to be applied to man and to the
equally interesting and important question of his first origin?
Huxley of course answers this question with a decided affirmative and adds that in such case either the origin of man must
be explained by the gradual transformation of a man-like ape,

or man must be regarded as a special branch of the same fundamental animal stock as the apes.   This necessarily leads Huxley
further to the Lamarckio-Darwinian theory of the transformation
of species, of which he confesses himself to be an adherent, at
least in general.   Hence also he naturally becomes a decided
supporter of the animal origin of man.   "But," adds Huxley,
after this declaration of opinion, "even leaving Mr. Darwin's
views aside, the whole analogy of natural operations furnishes
so complete and crushing an argument against the intervention
of any but what are termed *secondary* causes, in the production
of all the phenomena of the Universe, that, in view of the
intimate relations between Man and the rest of the living world,
and between the forces exerted by the latter and all other
forces, *I can see no excuse for doubting that all are co-ordinated
terms of Nature's great progression, from the formless to the
formed—from the inorganic to the organic—from blind force
to conscious intellect and will.*"

It would be impossible to express more distinctly and decidedly the fundamental idea of the materialistic conception of
the universe and nature, and the developmental theory which
stands in necessary connection therewith.*

At the conclusion of this essay Huxley also speaks in admirable terms which we cannot take too much to heart, upon the
absurd fears entertained by the general public and their unfounded horror of any such theory.   For this I must refer the
reader to the work itself.

The third and last of Huxley's memoirs relates to some
recently discovered fossil remains of Man, which appear fitted
to a certain extent to fill up or at least diminish the structural
interval which separates Man from the animals, and thus to
add palæontological arguments to those hitherto obtained from
systematic, anatomical and embryological investigations as to
the position of man in nature and his animal origin.   The most

* See Appendix No. 27.

important of these remains is the celebrated *Neanderthal skull* already mentioned and described in the first section of this work, (page 76,) which Huxley describes as the most ape-like of all the human skulls that he has ever seen, and of which he says that in its examination we meet with ape-like characters in all parts, and also that it has the greatest similarity with the existing Australian skulls and with the ancient Borreby skulls. Huxley also states expressly that this skull is by no means an *isolated* phenomenon, but that it is only the extreme term of a long series of bestial or at least very lowly developed human skulls of the past and present periods. A detailed account of the discoveries relating to this subject has already been given in the first section of this book.

Since Huxley wrote as above cited, a great number of similar discoveries confirming the idea of the relationship of man to the animal world have been made, and amongst these the most remarkable is the discovery of the celebrated human jaw of La Naulette.

But before I pass to the detailed description of this discovery I will remark that the *mandible* or *lower jaw* is of all the bones of the body that which in the first place is most readily pre-served, and, in the second, is most frequently met with in a fossil state separated from the rest of the skeleton. The latter circumstance is due to the fact that in consequence of its loose attachment to the upper jaw, (which is effected only by a small and not very firm joint and in other respects by muscles which are subject to decomposition,) it is separated from the rest of the skeleton more readily and quickly than other bones ; the former to the fact, that by reason of its peculiarly solid consistency, which resists destructive agencies, it is able to persist longer than other bones in the soil. To this we may add that when once this bone is separated, from its compara-tively small size and corresponding lightness, it is more readily carried to a distance by external agencies than other parts of the skeleton, and may easily be deposited in any place.   If this applies to the lower jaws of animals, which on account of their solidity and other characters were preferred by the primeval men for the manufacture of weapons, tools, etc.; it applies also and in a still higher degree to the very solid and characteristically formed lower jaw of man ; and the lower jaw has in fact been found more frequently than any other parts of the body in the researches that have been made for the fossil remains of our earliest ancestors.

. Thus, in the year 1866, a fragment of a human jaw with very remarkable and animal characters was found by the indefatigable Belgian Cave-explorer Dr. Edward Dupont in the *Trou de la Naulette*, a bone-cave situated on the bank of the little river Less⌃, not far from the village of Chaleux.   It was in a deposit of river-loam covered with a layer of stalagmite and at a depth of about four metres.   The most remarkable of its characters, besides the comparative thickness and rounded form of the bone and its elliptical dental curve, *is the almost entire absence of the chin*.   The projecting or prominent chin is so distinctive a character of man, that Linné, the great law-giver of systematic zoology, could name no better bodily distinctions between man and animals than the upright position and the prominent chin of the former.   In animals, instead of projecting, the chin retreats, and the jaw of La Naulette holds an intermediate position between the two; where the projection of the chin ought to be, it exhibits a line descending perpendicularly.

Moreover, the cavities destined for the reception of the canine teeth are remarkably wide and large, as in animals, although the canines themselves are closely contiguous to the incisors and molars, and the jaw is thus shown to be undoubtedly of human origin.   But what is still more remarkable than this is the circumstance that the three hinder or persistent molars present exactly the same relative sizes as is usual in the anthropomorphous apes. Thus, whilst in the higher races of Man the three true molars are so arranged that the first is the largest and the last or hindermost the smallest, we find in the dentition of the lower races, such as the Malays and Negroes, that all the three molars are of equal size, and throughout larger than usual. But in the Anthropoid apes the first true molar is the smallest and the last the largest, and this is the case also in this fossil human jaw, the last or hindermost molar of which even appears to have possessed five roots. (The large size of the hindermost molar certainly indicates a low grade of organization.) To all this may be added that the inner surface of the jaw at the. point of the so-called suture or symphysis, behind the incisor teeth, forms a line obliquely directed upwards and consequently leaves no doubt as to the prognathism, (a very characteristic mark of the animals and lower races of man,) of its former possessor.

All these characters in conjunction with the general aspect of the bone indicate that it is a human lower jaw of very animal formation, and especially that it is the most ape-like jaw hitherto discovered. It was found associated with the bones of extinct animals, principally the Mammoth and woolly Rhinoceros, so that there can be no doubt as to the fact that this man must have been a contemporary of those animals, and must therefore have lived in the so called *Mammoth period*. The implements or flints found with it also correspond to that period and present the same type as those of St. Acheul, (Valley of the Somme.)*

The lower jaw of La Naulette is, however, no more a peculiar and isolated bone of its kind, than the Neanderthal skull in its way, but it is supported in its evidence by a complete series of similar or allied bones. Such is the celebrated human jaw of Moulin-Quignon, already described, (page 43,) which displays a tendency towards animal structure in the shortness

* See Appendix No. 28.

and breadth of the ascending ramus, the equal height of the two apophyses, the indication of prognathism furnished by the very obtuse angle at which the ramus joins the body of the bone, etc.; and also the human jaw belonging almost exactly to the same type, (according to Pruner Bey,) which was found near Hyères, But above all we must mention the jaw found in the cave of Arcis-sur-Aube, (Burgundy,) associated with bones of extinct animals, which possesses all the essential characters of the jaw of La Naulette, although in a somewhat less degree; and that discovered in a fissure of the tertiary limestone near Grevenbrück and described by Schaaffhausen, (*Sitzungsber. der niederrhein. Gesellsch.*, 1864, page 30,) which indicates a low structure by its elliptical dental curve and inlying dentary bone; whilst the human lower jaw found in the cave of Frontal associated with reindeer bones is remarkable for the size of the molars and the extraordinary thickness of the bone in the molar region. Finally, we have to notice the fossil human jaw already referred to, (page 46,) from the gravel-pits of Ipswich, which was exhibited in April, 1863, to the Ethnological Society of London, and exhibits, with all the signs of very high antiquity, the characteristics of a low conformation.

We may look forward with confidence to further discoveries of the same kind, although the conditions are peculiarly un-favorable for the preservation of human bones from the reindeer period and from a period preceding that of the cave-inhabitants, and although their preservation can as a rule be anticipated only in particular cases and by a combination of peculiarly favorable circumstances. It must be remembered, however, that the traces of those innumerable generations of animals, which peopled the surface of the earth from its earliest existence, and whose bones in general possessed a much greater power of resisting destructive agencies than those of man, have nearly all disappeared with the exception of a comparatively few relics, which a happy chance has buried in the interior of protected caves, in the depths of peat-mosses or in the sand and gravel of former rivers!

But this very difficulty of preservation, and the small number of very ancient human remains render it all the more significant that these remains almost without exception bear upon them the evident signs of an inferior conformation, and that among them there are some which exceed in their animality of character the lowest and most animal of existing races of men! To this we must add that these discoveries have hitherto been made almost exclusively in regions now inhabited by civilized nations, and in which we certainly cannot place the so-called *cradle* of mankind. Under any circumstances the discoveries hitherto made by no means point upwards, as ought to be the case in accordance with the old opinions, but downwards, and indicate the existence of a ruder, more animal and more lowly developed human race, which formed to a certain extent an intermediate form between the existing men and the highest known forms of animals, and of which the remains still remain buried in the depths of the earth. Moreover we must not forget that the common character of all these lower structures consists in a tendency towards that fœtal conformation or towards that early stage in the development of man, which has already been described in its chief outlines, and that in this again the general harmony of organic nature, a condition of the law of development which we have seen to be its fundamental law, is most distinctly manifested. Why, we cannot help asking, why has not a single discovery or a single fact been made known, which contradicts this fundamental law or proves the former existence of a more perfect, more highly organized or more highly developed race of men?

Significant as all these discoveries are in themselves it is, however, unnecessary for the theory of evolution that we should find directly intermediate stages between the forms of men and animals living in the present day, as it is now almost universally admitted by all adherents of Darwin or of the doctrine of derivation, that man is not directly derived from the Anthropoid or Man-like apes with which we are acquainted, but from an unknown and long since extinct intermediate or ancestral form, or perhaps from several such forms, in exactly the same way that, in accordance with the Darwinian theory, we assume the former existence of similar extinct stocks for nearly all living forms of animals.   We should thus have to assume one or more ancestors of this kind for man and animals, and to suppose that the existing forms of man and of the higher apes are only the last offshoots of developmental series ramifying at an early period from common fundamental stocks.

This opinion is also essentially supported by the fact already cited that the truly human characters or resemblances are not combined in any single genus of Anthropoid apes with which we are acquainted, but distributed among them in various ways.   Indeed, particular human characters, such as the formation of the skull and face, are more highly developed in the group of the Platyrrhini, notwithstanding its distance from man, than in the Catarrhini, or even in the true Anthropoid apes themselves.   This remarkable fact leaves scarcely any doubt that a separation of originally combined characters and a ramification in various directions during further evolution, such as the theory of derivation compels us to accept for most of the higher existing forms of animals, must have coöperated also in the production of man and in his branching off from the common fundamental stock of the Primates ; and according to this theory the living forms of Anthropoid apes are to be regarded not indeed as the ancestors or progenitors of man, but as his near relations or cousins.

This view finds further efficient support in the well known circumstance that quite recently some fossil remains of apes have been discovered, which seem to indicate the actual former existence of such primitive stock-forms.   Of these a short account has already been given in the author's *Lectures upon the Darwinian Theory*, (pages 204 and 205.) These discoveries have hitherto been made only in Europe, (France and Switzerland,) but similar ones may fairly be expected in those tropical or equatorial regions which are now the true home of the Anthropoid apes, and especially in their tertiary formations, most probably those of southern Asia.* There, or in Africa, or in the Islands of the Malay archipelago, we shall probably some day meet with that Man-Ape or Ape-Man, with that immediate intermediate form between man and animal, which certainly has not yet been found, but whose former existence is indicated by so many convincing proofs.† That this intermediate or transitional form is no longer in existence need not surprise us, as it is well known that all the non-persistent intermediate forms become extinct with greater facility and rapidity than other types, and the chief cause of the comparatively large gaps which we now detect throughout the plan of creation is to be found in this rapid extinction of the intermediate forms.

Hence, although the gap or interval between man and animal, which nowadays certainly exists and is of great width, seems to be one which can scarcely be filled up, we do not hesitate to regard such a condition of things as founded upon the natural plan of development, and consider that this apparently immense gap has not always exhibited the same void that it does at present. Already the great apes are in course of extinction, and they become rarer from year to year by the

---

* The existence of fossil apes was formerly regarded as impossible, but we are now acquainted with no fewer than fourteen species, of which Europe has furnished six or more; whilst the great continent of Africa, the special habitation of ape-like men and man-like apes, has not yet offered a single example of this kind. Africa, however, has been but little investigated.

† Even if this palæontological intermediate form should never be discovered, we must, in estimating the importance of this fact, bear in mind the extreme imperfection and incompleteness of the geological record of creation, interrupted as it is by sunken or submerged lands. "Geology is a magnificent inscription, but forever disfigured ; we can certainly decipher some fragments of lines relating to those long past times, but we shall never read the whole."—*G. Pouchet.*

advance and competition of man. In a short time they will have entirely disappeared. The lower races of man, which exhibit so much animality of structure, likewise die out year by year, and the savants of future ages would therefore have to regard the interval between man and the animals as still deeper and more impassable than it appears to us, if they did not possess in writings, pictures and collections such evidences of the past as may enable them to arrive at a sound judgment.

Now that these results have been established in a general way, and the animal origin of man has been shown to be most probable, especially upon natural History grounds, we have to ascertain how such a process of the production of man from animal or animal-like beginnings may also be possible or conceivable in its details, in other words, the *when? where?* and *how?* of his first production. We have also in an especial manner to decide whether a *unity* or a *plurality* of origin is to be regarded as probable or certain

This last important question coincides with or forms part of the question as to the *unity or plurality of mankind* in general, which has been so often treated and already answered in the most various fashions,—a question which has constantly given rise to innumerable and continuous disputes among naturalists, and has divided them into two great parties—the so-called *monogenists* and *polygenists*. Essentially these disputes only reproduce the old obscurity, removed by Darwin, as to the signification and origin of the idea of the species; hence the whole question has lost most of its former importance, since Darwin's appearance. For if we once accept the possibility of the conversion of the ape-type into the human-type, (whether gradually or by sudden changes,) it is of little consequence to the argument, whether this conversion has taken place one or several times and in one or several places, or whether the existing differences among the individual races of men are due to gradual transformations of an originally uniform type or to original differences of derivation. As a matter of science, therefore, it is quite indifferent whether the old, equivocal idea of species is or is not applied to man with all his variations and aberrations; the whole dispute retains a fundamental significance only for the theologians and theological naturalists, who still, quite erroneously, invoke the mythical narratives of the Bible in proof of the specific unity of the human race.

But even if we place ourselves at the former standpoint of science and apply the antiquated idea of species to Man, the facts are but little in favor of the Biblical, (or philosophical,) unity of the human species. For the African Negroes, the Chinese and the Aryans are certainly in the sense of biological science as well characterized species at the best-founded of those which zoology has ever distinguished among animals, although all these forms have hitherto been regarded only as races or varieties of a single human species.* And among these which we may call *good* species, we have then no small number of *bad* or doubtful species to intercalate. In this respect *philology* furnishes the same result as biology and shows it to be scarcely conceivable or possible that all the tribes of the earth can have originated from a single pair, at all events at a not very distant period. A distinguished historian and philologist in comparing the languages of the extreme east with those of the Aryan group says that, "if the planets whose physical constitution resembles that of the earth are inhabited by organized beings like ourselves, we may assert that the history and languages of those planets will not differ more from ours than do the history and language of the Chinese." According to the celebrated linguist A. Schleicher, also, it is "positively impossible to refer back all languages to a single primitive tongue. An unprejudiced investigation rather indicates as many primitive languages as there are distinguishable stock-languages.

* See Appendix No. 29.

We must, consequently, suppose a large but indeterminate number of primitive languages."* (See *Schleicher on the significance of language in the natural history of man*, 1865.)

To return now to the matter immediately before us. Looking at it from the standpoint of the derivative theory, many observers have been struck by the fact that there is a remarkable agreement in *the color of the skin* and also in the *formation of the skull* between the extreme human races and those anthropoid apes which even now inhabit the same regions of the earth with them. For the Orang or Orang-Outan which inhabits the Asiatic Archipelago, is of a *yellowish red* color and *brachycephalous* or short-headed like the Malays; whilst the Chimpanzee and the Gorilla, both of which are indigenous to Africa, are black and *dolichocephalous* or long-headed like the Negroes.

This peculiar relation would seem to indicate a common origin for both, so that it is possible the yellow or short-headed man might have originated from a stock-form resembling the Orang, and the black or long-headed man from one resembling the Gorilla or the Chimpanzee. This supposition has been chiefly put forward by Professor Schaaffhausen, who calls

* According to Schleicher, certain language-provinces may be distinguished on the earth's surface, just as botanical and zoological provinces have been. This holds good, for example, of all the languages of the aborigines of America, which, notwithstanding all their variety, exhibit such an agreement that a special original source, common to them all, may be imagined. Most confusedly intermingled are the civilized languages of Asia and Europe.

Consequently, we have every reason to suppose that, in essentially homogeneous and neighboring districts, similar types of language were developed independently, just as, it may according to all probability be supposed, was the case with man himself.

The origin and development of language as such, of course, falls far anterior to all *history*, and accordingly in the *second* of the three periods distinguished by Schleicher for the development of man generally : 1, of physical development ; 2, of the development of language ; 3, of historical life. Indeed, many organisms on the way to becoming man may not have been developed up to the stage of speech-formation, but have fallen into a stationary condition and then become retrograde. "The remains of these beings that have continued speechless, become arrested and never become human, and are presented to us in the anthropoid apes of the present time."

attention to the fact that southern Asia and equatorial Africa are precisely those parts of the earth's surface which have given origin to the two extremes of human structure, between which all the other forms may be arranged. These two crude and original types of the long-headed and short-headed man, the Ethiopian and the Mongol, the African and the Asiatic, which as we have said, even at the present day form the two extremities or opposite poles of the long series of Men, may be recognized in all their distinctness in the oldest trace or remains of our race upon the earth, and thus indicate a probable difference of origin. It is true that in Europe we find both forms mixed together even at the most ancient part of the human period known to us, but, according to Schaaffhausen, this may possibly be due to an alternate immigration of both races from Asia and Africa in primeval times. The circumstance that the most ancient civilization had two starting points, (India and Egypt,) of which one is in Asia and the other in Africa, is also in accordance with this view.

However, Schaaffhausen admits, (as indeed he cannot help doing,) that, in accordance with the Darwinian theory, which presupposes the unlimited variability of all organic beings, it must be *possible* that the human race originated from a single pair, but he regards such an assumption as *improbable*. "The Gorilla and the Orang," says Schaaffhausen, "are also both Anthropoid or man-like apes of very similar structure, but what is there to prove their common origin? "In the same way there may have been for man several developmental series, starting from primitive forms separated from each other in space."

The most decided of the polygenists is Carl Vogt, who, even before his acceptance of the Darwinian theory, was one of the most zealous supporters of the plurality of the human species and also of their multiplicity of origin. According to him the facts do not indicate a common stock or a single intermediate form between man and ape, but lead us to assume "several parallel series, more or less limited locally, which may have been developed from the different parallel series of the apes." Even the American man may, according to Vogt, have originated separately from American apes.

The theory of the animal or more specially the simian origin of man has received its widest and most consistent development at the hands of Professor Haeckel, who has followed it out strictly in accordance with the Darwinian theory, and from a point of view standing intermediate to those of the polygenists and monogenists.*

According to him this doctrine is of such importance, "that hereafter men will celebrate this vast advance in knowledge as the commencement of a new period in human development." From zoological comparisons Haeckel concludes that all the apes of the old World must be descended from a single stock-form which possessed the same nasal structure and dentition as all the living Catarrhini or narrow-nosed apes; and from this he draws the further conclusion, that man has also been developed from it, or that the human species is a branch of the Catarrhine group and must have been developed in the old World at a period of hoary antiquity from Apes belonging to this group which have long since disappeared. Haeckel regards the notion that the American man had a special origin from apes living on that continent, as perfectly erroneous; in his opinion the primitive inhabitants of America migrated there from Asia, and perhaps in part also from Polynesia.

"As regards the genealogy of Man," says Haeckel, "it is quite certain that he must seek his immediate animal ancestors among the Catarrhini. Of course no single one of all the living apes is to be reckoned among these ancestors, which have long since become extinct, and at the present day man is separated from the Gorilla by a gulf almost as deep as that

* See his two addresses *On the Origin and Genealogy of the Human Race*, Berlin, 1868, and his *Natural History of Creation*, Berlin, 1868.

between the Gorilla and the Orang.   But this does not furnish
the least evidence against the well-founded supposition that
the most ancient Catarrhine, (or narrow-nosed,) form developed
from the Prosimiæ was the common primitive stock of all the
the rest of the Catarrhini, including man.   It was only a single
branch of the multifarious group of the Catarrhini, a branch
long since extinct and still unknown to us, that under favorable
circumstances became transformed, by means of natural selection, into the primary progenitor of the human race.   At any
rate this process of metamorphosis was of very long duration,
and the fossil apes have hitherto revealed to us neither its time
nor its locality.   In all probability, however, it occurred in
Southern Asia, which is indicated by so many signs as the
common primeval home of the different species of man.   Perhaps it was not Southern Asia itself, but a continent situated to
the south of it which afterwards sank beneath the surface of the
Indian ocean, that was the cradle of humanity.   The epoch at
which the transformation of the most man-like apes into the
most ape-like men took place was probably the last section of
the true Tertiary period, the so-called Pliocene epoch, or perhaps even the preceding Miocene epoch.

Hence we must expect the discovery of the fossilized remains
or bones of the ape-like ancestors of the human race, (if any
such still exist,) in the Tertiary formations of Southern Asia,
whilst it is regarded by Haeckel as a matter of absolute certainty, that no existing species of ape can be the progenitor
of man.

The first step in the production of man, the immediate
transitional form from the most man-like apes to man and the
common stock-form of all the species of man, was, according
to Haeckel, the supposititious, (and long since extinct,) creature which he names the primitive or ape-man, (*Homo primigenius, Pithecanthropus, Alalus.*)   This was produced from the

Anthropoid apes by complete habituation to an erect gait, and the stronger differentiation thus caused between the extremities by the development of the fore-limb into the true hand, and of the hind-limb into the true foot. He was still destitute of the essential characteristic of the true man, namely, articulate speech, and the conscious thought which is associated with it. There are many reasons, according to Haeckel, which justify us in supposing that this primitive man must have been a woolly-haired, prognathous, long-headed being, of a dark brown or blackish color The hairy covering of his body may have been stronger and thicker than in any other species of Man ; his arms were probably longer and stronger in proportion, and his legs shorter and thinner, with undeveloped calves. His gait would be half erect, with inbent knees. His home may have been southern Asia or eastern Africa, or perhaps a continent now submerged.

From this primitive man, by natural selection in the struggle for existence, there was developed as a last and topmost branch, the true or speaking Man, (*Homo*,) distinguished from his predecessor, by many advantages, but chiefly by the greater differentiation or better development of the limbs, the larynx and the cerebrum, and by the possession of articulate speech. It is probable, however, that the corporeal changes were completed long before the production of an articulate language, "and that the human species with its erect gait, and the peculiar form of body superinduced thereby, existed before the true development of human speech, therewith the second and more important part of the production of man, was completed."

This last process, the production of articulate language, in combination with the higher development or perfection of the larynx, which again must have been accompanied by a corresponding improvement in the brain, probably did not take place until a period when the speechless primitive man had already become divided or sub-divided into a number of species or sub-species. For, according to Haeckel, the various languages show so great a difference among themselves that it is impossible to believe that they could have had a common origin, and we must therefore assume the existence of as many primitive languages as there are families of languages. Hence the sub-division of the primitive man into the various species of man must have occurred before the time of the origin of language. "Nevertheless, even these must converge at their origin at a higher or lower point, and therefore all must finally be derivable from a common primitive stock."

In all probability, according to Haeckel, this process of the formation of species of man from the primitive stock took place in the following manner. In the first place, there were developed from the speechless primitive man a number of different species long since extinct and quite unknown to us, of which the two most divergent prevailed over the rest in the struggle for existence, and in their turn became the stock-forms of all other human species. These constituted a *woolly-haired* and a *smooth-haired* species. The woolly-haired species spread especially to the south of the equator, whilst the smooth-haired branch turned towards the north, and in the first place peopled Asia. A portion of it may have been driven towards Australia. Perhaps the existing Papuans and Hottentots are remains of the first, and the Alfurus and a part of the Malays of the second stock. However, the descendants of the woolly-haired stock, (the Papuans or Negritos, the Hottentots, the Negroes, Tasmanians, etc.,) have remained at a much lower stage than most of the descendants of the smooth-haired stock, to which, according to Haeckel, we must refer the Australians, the Malays, the Mongols, the Americans, etc., but above all the white or Caucasian race of man. "This species," he says, "has become more highly and beautifully developed than any other, chiefly by adaptation to the favorable conditions of existence presented by Europe, with its temperate climate and exceedingly advantageous geographical conformation.'' In Haeckel's opinion this species was produced in southern Asia from a branch of the Malayan and Polynesian species, or perhaps from a ramification of the Mongolian. From southern Asia the white man has spread westwards and become diffused over western Asia, northern Africa and the whole of Europe. His skull is most frequently of an oval form and holds a middle place between the long- and short-headed types,—the two extremes and rudest forms of cranial structure. This species, however, is considered to have divided at a very early period into two divergent branches, — namely, the *Semitic* stock, which spread in the south, and from which originated the Jews, Arabs, Phœnicians, Abyssinians, etc.; and the *Indo-Germanic* stock, which migrated more towards the west and north and gave origin to the most highly developed civilized races, the Hindoos, Persians, Greeks, Romans, Germans, Sclaves, etc.* The white or Caucasian species of man is destined to hold the sovereignty of the earth, whilst the inferior races, such as the Americans, Australians, Alfurus, Hottentots, etc., are advancing with gigantic strides to their destruction. On the contrary it is to be expected that the three other species of man, namely, the Ethiopian in Central Africa, the so-called Arctic or Polar man in the polar regions and the Mongolian man in Asia, will still for a long time be successful in the struggle for existence with the Caucasian species, because they are better adapted than the latter to the peculiar conditions and especially to the climate of their native countries !

---

* The Semitic form of language is so essentially different from the Aryan or Indo-Germanic, that we cannot believe in their having had a common origin, although, *anthropologically*, the two stocks approach each other so nearly. From this we must conclude, either that the descendants of the same ancestors, when geographically separated, developed among themselves totally different languages, or that they were separated before they possessed any language at all !

Haeckel's theory, of which we have here given the principal outlines, consequently to a certain extent combines the views of the polygenists and monogenists. Thus it assumes the existence of a number of species or races of men very early separated from one another and sharply defined, (especially from a linguistic point of view,) but at the same time regards all these only as branches or offshoots of a single primitive stock-form which became extinct at a very ancient period. A perfectly analogous position is taken by Georges Pouchet, although in other respects he is one of the most decided adherents and defenders of polygenism. In his thoughtful book on the *Plurality of Human Races*, (Paris, 1864, second edition,) he says :—" In the night of time there existed a certain species, less perfect than the most imperfect man, and itself ascending by a certain number of intermediate species the nature of which it is impossible for us at present to suspect, to that primordial Vertebrate which we assume. This species, a mere rough sketch of what man now is, gave birth, after the lapse of a considerable time, to several other species, the parallel and unequal evolution of which, in accordance with what we have said of animals, has nowadays for its contemporary, (but not its final,) expression the different human *species* commonly designated as *races*. Thus the whole of humanity would be related, if we may be permitted to use this expression, not in the *serial direction*, as the monogenists suppose, but in a *collateral direction*, and in a degree which we are unable to determine ; the prognathous races having probably deviated less from the antecedent type, whilst the others are further removed from this type and more perfect."

The diversity of opinion here indicated as existing in observers who are perfectly in unison upon the main question itself, and especially the opinion of a decided polygenist just cited, show, at any rate, that, as has already been stated, the question of the *unity* or *plurality* of the human race and its origin has lost the greater part of its former importance, having found its solution in the higher unity of the general theory of descendence. Whether the humanizing of the animal has taken place once or several times, at a single definite place or at several places, simultaneously or at different times, in the Pliocene, Miocene or Eocene period or even earlier, are subsidiary questions which have only a subordinate significance with regard to the main point. Perhaps science will never be able to give us any satisfactory information upon them, but even then she will be in no worse position with regard to these questions, than the adherents of the Biblical history of Creation when *they* are asked whether Adam and Eve were or were not provided with a navel.* With regard to the precise manner of production of a more man-like creature from an ape-like Mammal we can as yet of course only raise general suppositions and hypotheses, to which, however, we may hope that future investigations and discoveries will some day furnish a more solid base, As Rolle says, (*Der Mensch, etc.*, Frankfurt a. M., 1866 :) "It is a justifiable hypothesis, that certain conditions of existence may in some way have mitigated the commencement of that retrograde metamorphosis of body and mind leading back towards the bestial form, which attacks the existing large apes at the period of the second dentition, and thus have given to the antediluvian anthropoids a character, the

* This oft-repeated question is generally treated as only a jest and like the similar one : Which existed first, the egg or the hen? And yet, as soon as Adam and Eve are regarded as another designation for the first human beings generally, there is in it the deepest wisdom and the whole mystery of the origin of man. Every placental animal (including man) that is born living from a mother's womb bears externally the distinct sign of its former physical connexion with the maternal organism in the form of a navel ; and the absence of this would signify a substantial creation not dependent on parents. Scientifically such a thing is impossible or inconceivable. Hence the first human beings also must have borne this sign of their natural origin ; and from this simple consideration the logical necessity of the whole descendence-theory follows. It also follows from the relation of hen and egg ; for no hen can be produced without an egg, and no egg without a hen. Hence each of them can only be the last result of a long preceding transmutation of forms and ultimately of a spontaneous origination of the first and simplest element of organic form !

human expression of which still strikes us in the little round-headed monkeys of South America." This conjecture is evidently founded upon the well-known observation that the young of most animals, but especially of the large apes, display a *comparatively* better and less animal development both of their corporeal and intellectual qualities, and particularly a better conformation of the skull, than the adults, and that this advantage, the effects of which have even been observed in negro children, is only lost at the commencement of perfect maturity, when the rude nature of the animal, (or of the savage man,) acquires its full force. This observation is remarkably in accordance with the fact recently disclosed by Welcker, Vogt and others, that the young ape comes into the world with a brain of much greater size in comparison with that which it is subsequently to attain than that of man, whilst the human child, by a great advance during the first period of life, quickly approaches the goal which it is ultimately destined to attain. Hence the infant ape brings with him into the world the foundation of a higher development, which, however, becomes abortive in the further course of his simian existence, but which in one or more of the Anthropoid apes of antediluvian times may nevertheless have been capable of becoming developed into human characters. This development may have taken place equally well, (in accordance with the Darwinian theory,) either *very gradually* by the influence of natural selection and the processes associated with it, or *more suddenly* by the birth in one place or another of an individual variety or aberrant form characterized by the peculiarly favorable development of some important parts or characters, (such as the size and capability of evolution of the brain,) which by the help of this quality triumphed over its competitors in the struggle for existence. Similar phenomena, which, according to Owen, can properly only be reckoned amongst those of the formation of *monsters*, (abnormal productions with a monstrous or excessive

development of particular parts,) have been often enough observed in both the animal and vegetable kingdoms. That such
a process as this, so far as it relates to man, is no longer observable, need not surprise us, because, as has already frequently
been remarked, the existing species of apes can only be regarded
as being more or less nearly related to man, but by no means
connected with him by a direct genealogical tie. In fact the
living Anthropoid apes can only be considered the terminal
members of a distinct vital branch which is already in course of
extinction and therefore has for the most part lost its former
vitality and reproductive power. The close and powerful competition of man, which has been acting incessantly during so
many thousand years, must of itself cause the retrogression and
final disappearance of this lateral branch of the great stock of
the Discoplacentalia. Thus man himself, with every step he
takes forward on the great ladder of progress and civilization,
breaks down behind him a portion of the bridge which formerly
united him with the animal world. Widely separated from all
other creatures he feels himself to be the ruler of the world, and
in his pride forgets that his first cradle, like that of the founder
of Christianity, stood in a stable or in a still humbler place.
Nevertheless, or perhaps for this very reason, there can scarcely
be a better means of recognizing our own nature or the true
position of man in Nature, than the careful study of those of
our animal cousins and relations which had the misfortune, (or
the happiness,) to strike into a path of progress which leads
their race to its destruction after a comparatively short period of
existence. And in this study nothing surprises us more than
the wonderful traits of far-reaching intelligence and extraordinary habituation to human circumstances and wants that we
meet with in these animals, and especially in their young.
With it disappears, at least partially, that feeling of disgust and
repugnance with which, (unjustifiable as it is from a scientific
point of view,) we have hitherto been in the habit of regarding

these creatures,—casting them from us, as it were, as carica-
tures or distorted pictures of ourselves. This feeling, which
originated in a period of ignorance, and was nourished by false
philosophical theories having no foundation in a true knowledge of nature, resembles that sentiment which impels savage
tribes to regard their near relatives with greater repugnance
and hatred than their *white* enemies and oppressors, or so
frequently produces a fiercer enmity between the nearest blood-
relations than between perfect strangers. We look at a *Lion*
with admiration, nay, with a certain sentiment of respect, and
regard him as the king of beasts, although in this respect he
stands far below the *Ape*, who, even if he were not our nearest
animal relation, would still have a much greater claim than
any other animal to our sympathy and interest on account of
his intelligence, his docility, his address, his pathetic attach-
ments, his approach to humanity in form and behavior, etc.
The reports and narrations of trustworthy travellers and observers, which prove this, are innumerable, and quite lately
the celebrated traveller and naturalist A. R. Wallace has published an extremely interesting and instructive account of a
young Orang, which he had the opportunity of observing very
closely.*

Indeed it is sufficiently well-known, that the intellectual life
of animals has hitherto been greatly underestimated or falsely
interpreted, simply because our closet-philosophers always
started, not from an impartial and unprejudiced observation
and appreciation of nature, but from philosophical theories in
which the true position both of man and animals was entirely
misunderstood. But as soon as we began to strike into a new
path it was seen that intellectually, morally and artistically the
animal must be placed in a far higher position than was formerly
supposed, and that the germs and first rudiments even of the
highest intellectual faculties of man are existent and easily de-

* See Appendix No. 30.

monstrable in much lower regions.* The pre-eminence of man over the animal is therefore rather *relative* than *absolute*, that is to say it consists chiefly in the greater perfection and more advantageous development of those characters which he possesses in common with animals, all the faculties of man being as it were prophetically foreshadowed in the animal world, but in him more highly developed by means of natural selection. On closer consideration all the supposed *specific* distinctive characters between man and animals fall away, and even those attributes of humanity which are regarded as most characteristic, such as the intellectual and moral qualities, the upright gait and free use of the hands, the human physiognomy and articulate language, social existence and religious feeling, etc., lose their value or become merely relative as soon as we have recourse to a thoroughgoing comparison founded upon facts. In this, however, we must not, as is usual, confine our attention to the most highly cultivated Europeans, but must also take into the account those types of man which approach most nearly to the animals, and which have had no opportunity of

---

* If space would permit it would be easy for the author to support this assertion by innumerable proofs.   But as this cannot be done he begs to refer the reader to the numerous recently published essays and observations upon this subject, as also to the dissertations upon it given by himself in previous works.   The second volume of his *Physiological Pictures*, which is not yet published, will also contain an essay upon the mind of animals.   In this essay it will be shown by numerous well authenticated examples and facts, that the intellectual activities faculties, feelings and tendencies of man are foreshadowed in an almost incredible degree in the animal mind.   Love, fidelity, gratitude, sense of duty, religious feeling, friendship, conscientiousness and the highest self-sacrifice, pity and the sense of justice or injustice, as also pride, jealousy, hatred, malice, cunning, and desire of revenge are known to the animal, as well as reflection, prudence, the highest craft, precaution, care for the future, etc.,—nay, even gormandizing, which is usually ascribed to man exclusively, exerts its sway also over the animal.   Animals know and practice the fundamental laws, and arrangements of the state and of society, of slavery and caste, of domestic economy, education and sick-nursing; they make the most wonderful structures in the way of houses, caves, nests, paths and dams; they hold assemblies and public deliberations and even courts of justice upon offenders; and by means of a complicated language of sounds, signs and gestures, they are able to concert their mutual action in the most accurate manner.   In short the majority of mankind have no knowledge or even suspicion what sort of creature an animal is.

raising themselves from the rude, primitive, natural state to the grade of the civilized man.

In such a study as this, just as in the investigation of the animal mind, we at once arrive at the knowledge of quite different things from what the closet-philosophers in their pretentious but hollow wisdom have hitherto endeavored to make us believe, and we ascertain immediately that the human being in his deepest degradation or in his rudest primitive state approaches the animal world so closely that we involuntary ask ourselves, where the true boundary line is to be drawn?   Whoever then wishes to form a judgment as to the true nature of man or his true position in nature must not, as our philosophers and *soidisant* "great-thinkers" usually do,* leave out of consideration the primeval origin and developmental history of man, and looking merely at his own little self in the delusive mirror of self-esteem, abstract therefrom a pitiable portrait of a man after the philosophical pattern.   He must on the contrary, grasp at nature itself with both hands and draw his knowledge from the innumerable springs which flow there in the richest abundance.

Nowhere do we find these springs richer and more copious than in the reports of travellers in distant lands as to the savage men and tribes which they have met with, and especially in those simple narratives which often in a few words give us a deeper insight into human nature and its near relationship to the great outer world than the study of the thickest volumes produced by our closet-philosophers.   All the definitions of these learned gentlemen, all their tenets and arguments, all the deductions from the so-called "highest principles of science" which they profess to have discovered, are broken by the force

---

*They derive the name of "thinkers," like *lucus a non lucendo*, not from thinking but very frequently from *not thinking*, but are nevertheless arrogant enough to denounce those who disclose their threadbare nonsense, and are not satisfied with their empty verbiage, as "ignorant materialists." May all thinking men arise and chase these paid dealers in wisdom, these profaners of the temple, out of the sanctuary of true science!

of these simple facts, like soap-bubbles against the objects which they strike. There are men and tribes and conditions of human life upon the surface of the earth characterized by such an absence of every thing that the cultivated European is accustomed to regard as the eternal and indispensable attribute of humanity, that in reading the accounts of them we are inclined to think that we have fables rather than truth before us. Those who believe that the distinctive attribute of man is to be found in his *moral sense*, or in his higher *intellectual activity*, will find on forming a closer acquaintance with man and the conditions of human existence, that the facts are no more in favor of their views,* than of those who think to find the absolute pre-eminence of man over the animals in his family life and the establishment of marriage,† in his social organiza-

* See Appendix No. 31.

† Of the institution of marriage many of the savage tribes which have been depicted in Australia, Africa, Asia, &c., have as good as no conception; and with them family life is at the lowest stage — nay, almost lower than with the beasts. Amo g the *East-Africans* there subsists, as Burton states, no attachment between father and child; but, on the contrary, there prevails, after the time of childhood, a natural enmity between father and son, as among wild beasts. The children are sold, the wife is driven out of doors at pleasure. Sir S. W. Baker says : The *Sudan negro* knows not love; the wife is only a domestic animal and a beast of burden; polygamy prevails everywhere. Among the *Australians*, according to Duboc, it is only at the beginning that the mother concerns herself about her child; afterwards the original connection is entirely forgotten. They, like most of the South-Sea Islanders, have no knowledge of genuine marriage, and hence have not even the idea of *paternity.* Hence among such tribes the heirs are often not the father's own children, but his sister's children. Nay, there is even a tribe, (the Wanyamwezi,) among whom the children born *out of* their so-called wedlock, the illegitimate, are made heirs, to the exclusion of the legitimate ! Similar facts, as Sir John Lubbock, (*On the Primitive Condition of Mankind,*) informs us, are found among the ancient Jews, Greeks and Romans; while respect for woman has only very slowly made its way with the advance of civilization. According to the same author, many peoples, (for example the Egyptians, the Chinese, the Greeks, the Indians,) have even traditions concerning the *introduction of wedlock and marriage* — which at any rate proves that the id a of it cannot be innate and founded in human nature as such !

Finally, the most savage of the savages, the Dokos, the savages of Borneo, &c , have no notion whatever of marriage, wedlock or family, and live promiscuously with one another like the brutes. Indeed, as before mentioned, Otto Schmitz says of the Apaches, who are much superior to the Dokos, &c., that they know no marriage, but only a longer or shorter co-habitation of the sexes, and that the children are very soon lost in the horde.

tion,* in his sense of shame,† in his belief in God,‡ in his possession of the art of counting,§ or in the facts that he alone makes use of instruments,|| and knows the use of fire and employs it

* Even this is only a result of a certain degree of social development and among the wildest peoples is so imperfect that they run about pell-mell in troops or hordes, like wild beasts, without any chief or any other arrangements that might remind us of our own social condition.   On the other hand, the principle of association is developed to an almost incredible degree among many of the *Articulate* animals.   Think of the *bees, wasps, termits* and *ants* and their wonderful social economy, which is carried out so far that the last mentioned, according to the well-known observations of Huber and others, engage in set battles with each other, undertake plundering expeditions, bring home other ants as *slaves* and employ them in service, aud keep in their extensive and well-managed social dwellings other animals as "milch-cows," &c.   The *termites* or white ants have a perfectly organized state, with king, queen, workers, soldiers, servants, &c., and construct a building, ten and more feet high, with domes, towers, myriads of chambers, corridors, subterraneous passages, stone bridges and vaults, store rooms, &c., with which in strength and boldness, as well as judiciousness of arrangement, a human edifice can scarcely be compared.   In its interior is situated a so-called royal residence, with chambers and galleries around for the attendants, and with special breeding-rooms and nurseries, and, lastly, a public place of assembly.   To carry off the rain there are numerous gutters and tubes, with under-ground draining-channels.   There is no doubt, also, that the termites have a language, by the help of which they mutually explain very detailed affairs.   Not less remarkable are the celebrated *dog-communities* in the North American prairies, with regular semi-subterraneous cities which sometimes extend to a circumference of thirty English miles, and contain a hundred thousand inhabitants. According to the most credible assertions of eye-witnesses the prairie-dog frequently lives in his house together with a species of small owl and the rattle-snake — which strange social confederacy appears to be entered into for the sake of procuring food and of defence against danger.

† The natives of Australia are destitute of all sense of shame and never think of covering their pudenda.   As G. Pouchet informs us, the Australians in the towns of the English colony, if not prevented by the police, would daily violate public decency after the manner of monkeys in a menagerie.   "The Australians," say Lesson and Garnot, (*Annales des Sc ences Naturales*, 1867,) "have never felt the need of a woolen covering otherwise than to protect their chest ; no idea of shame has ever caused them to think of veiling their sexual parts."   More or less the same is found in all savage or uneducated peoples, who in this point are quite like European children.   Even highly civilized nations, (*e. g.* the Japanese,) have, as is as well known, quite different ideas of modesty from ours; and the highly cultivated nations of antiquity, the Greeks, Romans, Egyptians, Phœnicians, &c., even consecrated in relation to sexual matters a lasciviousness of manners of which we can now scarcely form a conception.   (For particulars see Rosenbaum's interesting pamphlet : *Geschichte der Lustseuche.*)   The delicate consideration with which modern cust m has regulated the mutual relations of the sexes and has covered them with a veil of sweet secrecy, is not any thing innate or original, but a consequence of the development which forms the history of civilization, the gradual raising of human nature above that of the brutes.   Nevertheless, from time to time the old barbarism again breaks out with violence, either in isolated shocking outbreaks of the repressed or forcibly restrained impulses or in certain nudities or effronteries of society itself, tolerated though not sanctioned by custom.   As a rule, however, such in some measure morbid excrescences of society belong to an age that is dying out or already morally submerged, while they are almost banished by the breath of a new political or social spirit.

‡ See Appendix No. 32.   § See Appendix No. 33. | See Appendix No. 34.

for cooking his food,* that he alone wears clothing,† commits suicide,‡ cultivates the ground,§ etc., etc.

Articulate language may certainly be regarded as the most characteristic attribute of man, and by virtue of this, in connection with the better development of the larynx, vocal organs and brain, and in association with his erect posture and the increased usefulness of the hands, he really first became a man; yet it is only the result of a whole series of long-continued and tedious processes of development, and occurs among some

* There are still peoples such as the Dokos, the Andamans, &c., who know not the use of fire and devour all their food raw. Moreover, that the use of fire cannot be an attribute of humanity as such is shown by the circumstance that so many peoples have been *fire-worshippers*, and in part are so still, that, therefore, they considered fire something extra- and supernatural. In like manner, when Magellan set fire to the huts of the Marian-Islanders, to whom fire was unknown, they looked upon it as a kind of living monster which devoured wood. Also in the Ladrone Islands the Spaniards found the natives unacquainted with the use of fire. Finally, there are sufficient traces from antiquity that in the oldest times the use of fire was still unknown, in the traditions of the Egyptians, Phœnicians, Persians, Chinese, Greeks, &c., about its introduction and the gradual spread of the knowledge of it.

† See Appendix No. 35.

‡ There is said to be a well authenticated case of the suicide of an ape. But even should this not be the case, sufficient instances are known of animals, (horses, dogs, &c.,) from excessive attachment to their dead or slain masters, refusing food and so killing themselves. On the other hand, self-slaughter is, from intrinsic moral reasons, exceedingly rare among children and savages.

§ Although M. Rochet, (in the *Bulletin of the Paris Anthropological Society,*) has endeavored to establish that agriculture, as well as the mental and moral qualities and the above-mentioned characteristics, is a sign of the difference between man and beast, yet it is well known to be only the result of a pretty far advanced state of civilization, while the savage and primitive man lives merely on the spontaneous productions of nature and what he can get by hunting; and from this condition he passes first through the pastoral to reach the agricultural stage. Besides, animals at times practise agriculture, as is proved by the example of the *Agricultural ant* in Texas, observed during ten years by Dr. Lincecum and described by him in the *Journal of the Linnean Society,* (quoted in the *Ausland,* 1862, No. 10.) On ground with a stony substratum, they build a store-house in the soil and plant round it a sort of grass which bears a small white seed. This seed is gathered, dried and carried into the storehouse. After wet weather it is sometimes brought out, dried and sorted.

This animal therefore stands in *one* respect higher than the above-mentioned negroes of Ky'schland, (Africa,) whom the traveller Baker, (*l. c.,*) designated as apes, who depend for subsistence solely on what nature produces, therefore neither sow nor plant, and consequently are frequently on the verge of starvation.

savage tribes in such a rude and imperfect condition that it can hardly be called language in the human sense of that word.* Formerly language was regarded as something innate and in-herent in man, existent, even at his first origin in a certain degree of development; but the recent investigations of phi-lologists have taught us quite the contrary of this, and shown us that languages, like species, have grown up and been produced from simple beginnings by a slow and gradual process during the lapse of thousands of years.† Most certainly the zeal with which at the present day the *savants* of all countries study the important problem of the origin of language and propose their theories upon this difficult question, furnishes the best proof that they have escaped from the above mentioned prejudice. With an instinctive knowledge that language must have been developed in man gradually from the rudest commencements, they long for information as to the mode of this evolution and as to the first efforts of speaking man to give his thoughts and sentiments regular expression in connected speech. For un-doubtedly the earliest man was just as incapable of any such regular speech, as the animals and even some savage tribes at the present day.

According to Westropp, (*Origin of Language,*) the earliest man can only be regarded as a dumb or speechless creature, which only by degrees learnt to give definite expression to his feelings and necessities, just as children do nowadays, and a very long time must have elapsed during which man was able to express his wants only by gestures and inarticulate sounds. But in all this there is nothing more degrading than in the circumstance that we ourselves were once infants, "mewling and puking in the nurse's arms." Articulate speech is only a gradual acquisition which has risen by degrees from the rudest commencement to its present perfection; like every thing else it has its beginning, its growth, its development, its progress, its

* See Appendix No. 36.   † See Appendix No. 37.

maturity and finally also its decline.   Its development has been as much a necessity and as much in accordance with fixed laws, as that of the body and mind of man himself, and it first arose from those inarticulate sounds or cries of joy, pain, grief, pleasure, etc., which are also known to animals.*   Everything else belongs at once to the grade of development.   Now as regards the course of this development, it probably commenced only. by the formation of what may be called *sounds of feeling*, followed soon afterwards by *imitative sounds*, (onomatopœia,) in which the sounds of external nature were imitated.   These would increase the scanty treasury of words.   Hence in all languages, numerous and different as they are, (the number on the whole earth is reckoned at about three thousand,) there is a considerable number of words of similar meaning and more or less similar in sound.   Thus according to William Bell, (*On the origin of language*,) the word *loh*, for example, is a monosyllabic root for the designation of *light*, *flame*, etc., which occurs in many languages and was originated from the simple exclamation : *oh !* with an *L* or vibration of the tongue placed before it.   For a long time language consisted only of such monosyllabic words, whilst by degrees the polysyllabic words were formed either by doubling the simple sounds, as in the words *marmor*, *papa*, *purpur*, etc., or by what is called *agglutination*.

* The animal cry was, according to Clémence Royer, the first commencement of speech.   There were different cries for the different sensations, as hate, love, terror, joy, anger, fear, &c.   These tones or primitive sounds were the first roots of all languages; and to them the imitative sounds from external nature were afterwards joined.   This *tone-language* is as much the property of the brute as of man ; and, in the widest sense of the term, every animal has a language — that is a means of mutual understanding with his fellows, whether it be a cry or a song, a gesture or a look, &c.   Longing, fear, hunger, love, &c., each of these sensations had its special expression with the brute ; *verbal language* only is peculiar to man ; but even this was at first merely a brutish stammering.

The gap between our modern developed languages and this earliest primitive condition of language was filled by the whole long series of prehistoric peoples, with whom thousands of original forms of language may have become extinct. But even now our languages are still very imperfect, and this imperfection presents great obstacles to our minds and their mutual intelligence.   Hence the fate of humanity hangs on the future perfecting of languages.

Examples of imitative sounds are the words "baa" for sheep, "moo" for cow and the like; or such words as "wind," "whist," "rash," etc.

The simple exclamation also was imitated by companions, and thus gradually became a fixed sign representing the sentiment or feeling expressed by it. Thus whist, the exclamation was at first only an involuntary *accompaniment* of the sensation, it afterwards became independent of this, and from being an expression, was converted into a sign of feeling, which, instead of being called forth by the feeling, was rather fitted to call it forth. "The origin of the consciousness of the distinction between the sound and the sensation," says J. Bleek, "this establishment of the sound as a peculiar entity which being seized by the will is thus converted into its instrument, is the first foundation of humanity."—(*On the origin of language*, Weimar, 1868.)

But as in most cases the life of the feelings is silent, and in general only a very small portion of it makes itself heard, it is easy to see with what tardiness and difficulty the reciprocal action between word and sensation must have produced the gradual rise of speech and of the consciousness which belongs to it. The first stage of mutual communication by word or speech therefore consisted, according to Bleek, in a person who experienced a certain condition of mind for which a word was known, uttering that word; and the first phase of the existence of the word as such occurred, when the simple exclamation of feeling was not uttered as an exclamation, but employed *voluntarily* in order to call forth the feeling associated with it or that supposed by the companions of the utterer to correspond to it. In the second phase the individual sound established itself by frequent employment as the conventional expression for the sentiment or feeling indicated by it, and gradually departed more and more from its primitive signification. At the same time the necessity of expressing mixed sentiments also produced mixed or composite sounds or words and mixtures of entire complex sounds.

In the third and last stage of the first or initial period of the formation of speech, expressions were already formed in this manner by the combination of known words for a great number of mutual conditions unassociated with any emotional sounds, and which therefore were not expressible by words in the previous stages. The reciprocal amalgamation of distinct and previously separated sounds or words then carried on the formation of new words, which gradually departed more and more from the primitive expressions of mere emotional life, and gave rise to the further development of true language. This further development, as Bleek remarks, belongs to the history of language, rather than to the problem of its origin, the latter being already solved by the formation of words and their separation both in sound and sense from the primitive emotional sounds.

The well-known zoologist, Dr. Gustav Jäger, also essentially adopts this mode of explanation, but he looks at the question chiefly from the zoological point of view and endeavors to demonstrate a close connection between the vocal utterances of man and animals.

According to him this connection is so intimate, that it is impossible to elucidate the question of the origin of speech without a careful study of the language of animals. Speech in the widest sense of the word was discovered, according to Jäger, long before there were any men ; for the pairing call, which is so general among animals, is a language. But still higher than this is the call produced from the pairing call by imitation, which is susceptible of various modifications, and capable of expressing both joy and terror, satisfaction and alarm. Beneath these is the simple emotional cry, which usually occurs in animals only under the influence of strong emotions, such as fear of death, anger, great pain, etc. Many have the command only of these two or three sounds, whilst others possess comparatively a very rich language. The most complex is the language of Birds, which have very probably served as the preceptors of man.

According to Jäger, therefore, the primitive speech of the human race was merely a *natural language*, analogous to those of animals, and also analogous to the gesture-language of savages, deaf-mutes and pantomimists; whilst our present conventional languages rest solely upon a further development of the primitive natural language.

But according to this author, the production of the true human language was preceded by an aphonic or dumb period of receptivity,—just as the Apes, which approach man so closely, are remarkably voiceless, but very receptive or inquisitive, and many ages of the employment of a mere gesture-language may have elapsed before the speechless primitive man, (Haeckel's *Alalus,*) has brought his conceptions of the outer world so far that by means of the differentiation of the organs, which had taken place in the meanwhile, and under the influence of social progress, he was able to add sounds or words to his gestures. By custom, inheritance, etc., a language was then at last formed; and this, in some favored races, became constantly enlarged with the growth of the idealistic power and the increasing stock of ideas caused thereby, whilst in other races it either remained stationary, or even entered upon a retrograde course.

How impossible it is to establish an *absolute* separation between the language of men and animals, is shown by the fact that so many of those general ideas which have become quite familiar to civilized nations by the richness and continued development of their speech, are so strange to many savage tribes that they do not even possess expressions for them. How then can we make it a reproach to the animal that he is destitute of certain other ideas expressing simpler relations, whilst even among men so great a difference is to be found in the development of ideas and language?

Writing, also, like language, arose quite gradually, and by the contemplation of external objects.   Thus, according to d'Assier, (*Histoire naturelle du Langage*, Paris, 1868,) the first Chinese alphabet represented all ideas by definitive pictures.   A large circle denoted the *sun;* a smaller one conveyed the idea of a *star;* a cross represented the *moon*.   The earliest Chinese hieroglyphs also agree almost entirely with the Egyptian; because the first sensuous perception of external nature was everywhere the same.   The Peruvians represented the arrival of the Spaniards in America by means of a Swan swimming towards the shore and spitting forth fire, in which the color of the animal was intended to denote that of the strangers, its swimming body the ship, and its fire the guns of the Spaniards.   From this sort of *rebus* or hieroglyphic writing, in which the idea of *night*, for example, is expressed by an owl or by a darkened cross, the transition to the true alphabet took place very slowly, and has indeed never been completely effected by many peoples, (such as the Chinese and Mexicans.) Between them there is the intermediate stage known as *syllabism*, so that *hieroglyphics*, *sallabism* and *letters* constitute the three successive stages of writing, the interchanges and intermixture of which are very easily recognized in the inscriptions and manuscripts of the Egyptians

Thus we have shown by the evidence of well-informed men of science, and in part even by direct observation, that even the human speech, that most important attribute of man and of his humanity, that chief aid to his intellectual progress, that most striking distinction between man and the animals, is after all the product of gradual and slow development.   We have seen that even this can only be regarded as a higher stage of development of aptitudes and faculties already existing in the animal world; and this being the case it seems to the author that the last difficulty is removed which still stood in the way of the application of the great organic law of development and progress to man and of the admission of his animal origin.

Thus then the light of science is broadly thrown upon a question which formerly seemed to mock all the efforts of investigators, and we have made the first step in an intellectual revolution destined to move the world in the direction of a philosophical realism. In consequence of this the position of man in nature and his relation to the world around him, in other words the response to the great question, "What are we?" will be conceived in a totally different spirit, and in one infinitely more in accordance with truth and reality, than has hitherto been the case. There may still be some who, in the face of such a result as this, cannot break free from the prejudices of the past; and who would rather consider themselves the descendants of a lump of earth into which God in old time breathed the breath of life, than as the final products of a natural process of organic development and progress. Such people may console themselves with the words of Claparède, who says: "It is better to be a perfectionated ape, than a degenerate Adam," or with those of Bernhard Cotta, who expresses himself as follows in his *Geologie der Gegenwart:* "Our ancestors may certainly do us much honor. But it is much better when we do them honor." Lastly they may consider that human progress, which is desired by all, if regarded in the light of the theory of development, is in accordance with natural laws and therefore incessant and eternal, always supposing that man does not allow the powers and faculties conferred upon him by nature to lie fallow or become abortive, but makes full use of them for the constant amelioration of his condition and of his position with respect to nature, materially as well as intellectually,—physically as well as politically, socially and morally.

To elucidate this progress and development of the future, at least in its broad outlines, and both in its natural and artificial relations in accordance with the indications of the past, will be the object of the third and last section of this book.   It will as far as possible, set before us the future of man and of the human race, its physiological and moral prognosis! "For," as J. Bleek says, "the course which we have already traversed, and the comparison of what we have attained with what we have left behind and started from, justifies us in forming the highest hopes with regard to what our race may possibly attain."

END OF THE SECOND PART.

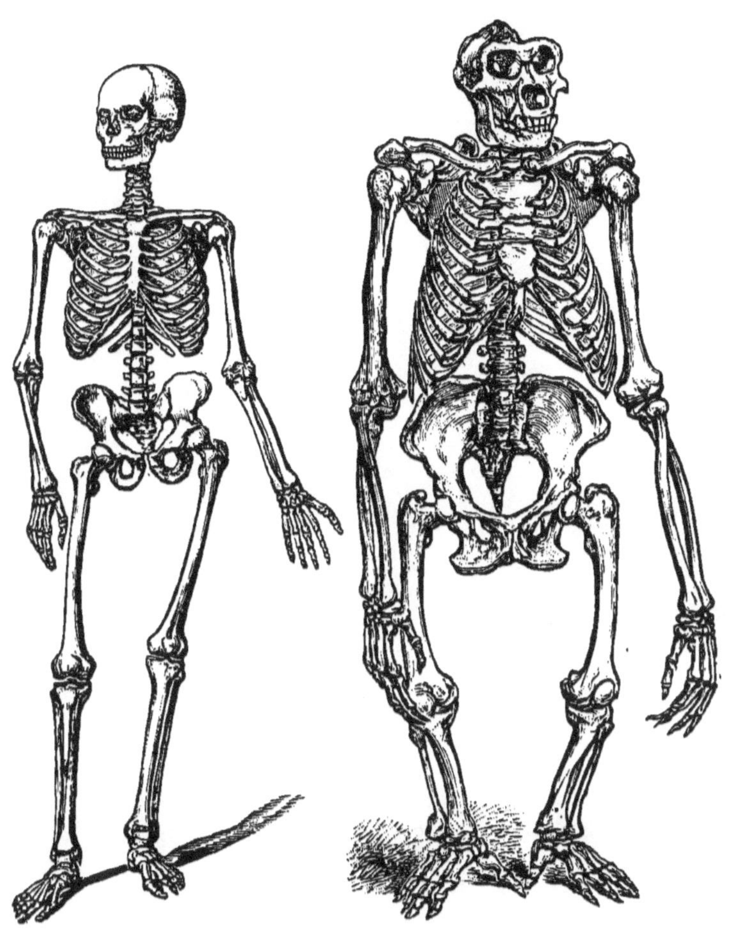

SKELETON — MAN.   SKELETON — GORILLA.

WHERE ARE WE GOING?

THE FUTURE OF MAN AND OF THE HUMAN RACE.

"The sovereignty of man consists in his conviction that there can be no higher purpose than that of humanity, in which the development of the earth is consummated."—RADENHAUSEN.

"As long as the animal nature predominates in man, climate and local conditions will exert their influence unrestrictedly, and as in the vegetable and animal worlds, produce the greatest multiplicity of structures. But with the awakening of the intellect, an activity commences which strives to free man from the constraint of nature in the same way in the most different countries, until at last in the highest stages of civilization, the better forms of human society not only acquire concordant customs in the matter of food, clothing, and habitations, but also, by a similarity of thought, feeling and endeavor, demonstrate that higher unity of the human nature which, although not present at the origin of our race, shines upon us as the brilliant goal of·human development, which is a matter of more importance."—SCHAAFFHAUSEN.

"For as soon as we have once clearly understood that individual life and action form only a small fragment of the great, eternal life of mankind, and that it is only by partaking in the latter that the individual man really lives, and as we may hope, lives forever,—striving for the general good no longer appears a duty hard of fulfilment, but a necessity of our nature which we are the less able to resist the more we have recognized the true essence of things. And in truth it is the sentiment of such a relation that is the great source of all noble and good efforts. Neither the fear of eternal damnation, nor the hope of individual happiness, can really serve as truly saving ideas to raise man to a higher existence, even when we leave out of consideration that each of these two fundamental doctrines of the vulgar dogmatism really places only a refined selfishness as the lever of its ethics."—J. BLEEK.

THE great mystery of the existence and origin of man, on which so many generations have in vain exhausted their strength, is, it seems to the author, *solved* by the statements with regard to the position of man in nature and his natural relations to the universe, given in the first two sections of this book. What farther explanations can be required upon these subjects? An insight into the process of the formation of man, into the natural *how?* of his origin and development in the past as in the present, is all that we can rationally expect from human science.   For the question *how?* or *whence?* is the only one which, in accordance with the laws of cause and effect, we can expect to be answered by nature and the essence of things; whilst the *why?* is a foolish question, which goes far above us and never can be answered by us.   If we were to ask *why* man is here, it would be equivalent to the question why all other things exist, why the Universe exists, why there is any existence at all?   That we can never expect a satisfactory answer to such questions as these is self-evident.   Existence, whether individual or general, is simply a fact which we must accept as such, and at the same time admit that, as, both in accordance with the laws of logic and from experience, it must be regarded as without beginning and without end, both in space and time, it is useless to talk about a definite cause for it,—about the *why?* of its being.

It is, however, quite a different matter when we take the *how?* into consideration, and set before us the question of the manner in which the individual consecutive phenomena of nature and of existence are bound or held together in accordance with the inviolable laws of cause and effect.   In this department, as we have said, modern science has furnished us with the grandest and most unexpected results, and has shown us that the whole great mystery of being, but especially that of organic existence, *depends upon gradual evolution.*   In the process of evolution, so simple in itself, dwells the simple solution of all those complicated mysteries which man has hitherto believed could not be solved without the aid of supernatural powers.   To trace this process in its details and in all its phases both in time and space, and in this way gradually to acquire a more exact knowledge of those indestructible threads which unite man with nature and the totality of extra-human existence, is the task of modern science.   All appeals to supernatural or unnatural or even merely forced modes of explanation must in this case be most stringently rejected.   Simple, natural suppositions, in accordance with the known laws of nature or at all events not contradicting them, can alone claim acceptance, but these only until they are replaced by better ones, approximating still more closely to the truth and the real state of the case. When no explanation is possible with the existing means of Science, the case must remain as an open one, requiring elucidation ; but it must not be covered up and concealed from the public eye by imaginary theories after the well-known and convenient fashion of the speculative philosophers, or by the use of obscure terms which require an explanation of their own, or may even be incapable of interpretation.   But as such explanations can only relate to the mode or to the simple proceeding of a later entity from an earlier one and to their casual connection, and, as, moreover, with all our knowledge, we move constantly in a circle, in which the beginning and the end are nowhere or at every point, it becomes clear to us why we must be satisfied with these explanations of natural connection, and why the question as to a first or supreme cause of all being or as to the *why?* of existence is one which in a philosophical sense cannot be raised.*   "Whatever is absolutely incapable

* " The mystery of existence " as the author wrote years ago in a friend's album, " dwells in the figure of a circle.   Without beginning, without end, and without cause, eternity can only revert into itself, and begins and ceases at every point of the immeasurable universe.   But the human intellect, accustomed to see everything that exists pass before it in space and time, and in accordance with the laws of cause and effect, shrinks the more from this simple solution of the great worldmystery, the less it has freed itself from these barriers by reflection and knowledge."

The speculative philosophers or metaphysicians indeed will be just as averse to such a simple solution as the great mass of the ignorant, or of those who are captive in theological bonds, because by it their whole striving after the discovery of supernatural causes of the world and of the order existing in it must at once be wrecked, and their comfortable mode of philosophizing would immediately sink to the level of a useless clash of words in the eyes of every clear-thinking person.

"It is easy to see," as James Hunt admirably says in connexion with this, " why so many philosophers still cling so strongly to philosophy in order to solve the problems of the world.   The reason is that the method of philosophy in the treatment of all questions is so much easier than that of the direct observation of nature and careful accumulation of facts, which must be used systematically and patiently in drawing conclusions, that there will always be men who will prefer a philosophy founded on brilliant sophisms and fluent dialectics to the toils of a true scientific method."

of comparison," says Buffon, "is also absolutely incomprehensible ; we only know mutual relations."

In connection with this generally recognized truth, the third or last of the great questions proposed by us, the question : *where are we going ?* can only be answered with regard to this earthly life, with respect to the earthly future and perfectibility of man.   For even if we admit that it is due only to the limitation of our knowledge, or the imperfection of our means of knowledge, that the destiny of the individual man or of mankind beyond this earthly life must ever remain hidden from us, or that we can never attain a clear insight into the true essence of things,* even this admission would not do the least injury. Our efforts, (whether theoretical or practical,) can only be directed to that which we are able to grasp with our perceptions and judgment, and more than a thousand years of experience has taught us that our scientific knowledge constantly brings us into closer connection with nature and earthly existence the more it increases in depth and compass, whilst on the other hand it removes us in the same proportion from the spiritualistic hypotheses and chimeras of the past.

The researches into the antiquity and origin of man and his normal connection with the organized world in general, which formed the subject of the first and second sections of this book, furnish the best proof in confirmation of the above assertion. Man did not come upon the earth spontaneously, but by the mediation of the same natural forces and causes to which all life owes its origin.   He did not descend from above or from the ether, but he has sprung up from below by the same processes which lie at the foundation of all terrestrial development.   In accordance with the present state of our knowledge, he can be regarded as nothing more than the last and highest product of that slow process of development and evolution by which our planet, the earth, in the course of enormous periods of time

*See Appendix No. 38.

completes its natural cycle of life, which in turn is only a single phase of eternity. What higher or more perfect structures than ourselves may still slumber in the womb of time, to come forth hereafter by the same process, we know not. But upon one point our science leaves no doubt, namely, that hitherto nothing higher or more perfect than man has been produced by Nature, and that it is not only the right, but the duty of man to regard himself as the ruler over all existences accessible to him, and to guide and change them as much as possible for his own necessities and purposes.

It is easy to see that by this a perfectly new and previously unknown principle was introduced into nature and the world in general, a principle which is essentially distinct from any thing that preceded it. For it is only in man that the world becomes conscious to such a degree that it rises out of its previous dream-like natural existence and allows dominion over nature to take the place of a nearly involuntary subjection to it. Nevertheless this did not take place suddenly or all at once, but very gradually and only a long time after the birth of those creatures which we may regard as the earliest representatives of the human type, for only the gradual evolution and inheritance from generation to generation of the faculties awakened in those creatures by their more perfect organization could originate that advance or continual improvement of mankind which we must at present regard as the final and highest object of all earthly existence. But whilst, in those earliest periods of his development, man was subjected to precisely the same natural laws or conditions as the forms of the vegetable and animal worlds which had preceded him in a long series of influences, whether injurious or beneficial, to which he could oppose but a feeble resistance, he has subsequently, in the lapse of time, by the further development of his mental faculties, emancipated himself more and more from those influences, and has finally attained a point at which he may say to himself with no little pride that his present and future fate has become more or less independent of nature, that is to say, *it is in his own hands.* Nature has, as it were, recognized herself in him,—has consciously advanced in opposition to herself,—and has thus undertaken a peculiar task, the fulfillment of which will remove both nature and man further and further from the rude and imperfect states of the past.

By Darwin's admirable investigations we have been taught to recognize as the principal cause of the transmutation and evolution of the organic world in its natural state that *struggle for existence*, which has now become so celebrated, in combination with the influences of *variability*, *natural selection*, *inheritance*, *&c.* All these influences, (perhaps with the exception of inheritance), must act with the more intensity, the greater the power of nature over the organic being. This applies also to the momentum of *migration*, upon which much stress has lately been laid, and to the influence of alterations in the external conditions of life, which Darwin, as is well-known, did not sufficiently estimate. For the less the individual being was able to resist these influences by intelligence or independency, or by the extreme simplicity of its conditions of existence, the more strongly must they have made their dominion over it felt. If the perfectly purposeless co-operation of all these causes, in themselves purely mechanical, has produced not merely a transmutation but at the same time a general advance in the organic world, so as finally to lead to the birth of a being destined to put its own spontaneity in the place of the mechanical forces of nature, this is due neither to any preconceived plan, nor to any personal merit, but it is merely the necessary consequence of definite natural conditions coinciding precisely in a particular manner and no other. Man has therefore no one to thank for his existence, and must seek the purpose of his existence only in himself and in his own welfare and that of his race. This welfare, however, is synonymous with the greatest possible emancipation from the influence of, and do-minion over those natural forces which originally called him and the whole organic world into existence.* If the struggle for existence be the vital phenomenon which most *closely* unites man with animality, then this must be strongest and fiercest in the primitive or natural state, and at first so occupy the whole of life that no opportunity is left for intellectual development, such as we now regard as the task of mankind. On the other hand, however, the unfavorable position of man in the natural state and his natural defencelessness face to face with the animal world, must have forced him all the more to the greatest pos-sible exertion of his mental and bodily powers in the struggle with the nature which hemmed him in and overpowered him, thus becoming a main incitement to human advance in the matters of weapons, dwellings, clothing, food, &c. The diffi-culty of the struggle also impelled him to mutual assistance and

* Every answer to the question so often discussed as to the destiny of man or the purpose of his existence derived from points of view different from those here supported, appears absurd or untenable as soon as we confront it with the facts and with the results actually attained in life and history by the individual man or by the human race. Existence is everywhere and in every condition or moment of its happening *its own object!* Man is here not to prepare himself (as the Theologian says) for a better world, or to inhabit and people the earth (as the teleologists will have it), or (as the philosophers suppose) to bring about a recon-ciliation between being and thinking, between God and the world,—but, simply, *to be here!*—One might add " and to be happy or comfortable here," if this pur-pose did not for the most part disappear under the mass of miseries and horrors which the struggle for existence and for the good things of the earth brings with it. The free spontaneity of man with reference to the general weal which may be attained in the future, will alone be able to raise him above this difficulty, and consequently to make him the creator of his own happiness. But until then let us give up amusing him with delusive phantasms of a something invisible or un-attainable to be striven for by him, and drawing him away by them from the care for his own weal and that of his race! If, then, we wish to find the true destiny of man we must turn away from the general notion implied in the word " des-tiny," which always presupposed the unproven existence of a destinator, and seek the purpose of his existence in himself and in his relations to his surroundings, just in the same way that existence *in general* also cannot be conceived with ref-erence to any purpose lying outside it, but is merely existence for its own sake, and therefore at every moment fulfills its destiny or purpose,—that is to say, if we choose to make use of the essentially unphilosophical notion of destiny or purpose at all.

social union, and this union again became a mainspring of progress. It was only when the struggle with the animal world had been brought to a successful issue, that the contests of man with man commenced, leading to those perpetual sanguinary wars which constitute the history of all tribes and nations in a backward state of civilization.

But what more than any thing else assisted man in his struggle for existence, was the circumstance that the knowledge or experience gained by the individual did not die with him as in the case of animals, but by the agency of education and tradition each successive generation was enabled to develop a greater power of resistance than its predecessor in its struggle for existence. This influence may have been very imperfect in its action in those earliest periods of humanity when man approached most closely to the animals, and thus the advance during those periods may have been excessively difficult and slow (as indeed has already been indicated in the first section); but the conditions must have become more and more favorable the further man departed from his animal origin and brought into use the innumerable aids of advancing civilization.

In the present state of our knowledge there can be no doubt that corporeal peculiarities or advantages of organized beings (whether congenital or acquired during life) are inherited by their progeny, to which, when they are useful in the struggle for existence, they communicate an impulse towards a more perfect development. Experience leaves no doubt that this is the case also with *intellectual* peculiarities, advantages, &c., in an equal, if not in a higher degree. The material reason for this may lie in the extraordinary delicacy and flexibility of the organ of intellectual activity, the brain, the gradual improvement of which, both in the animal and the human species, admits of no serious doubt. By means of this organ and by the aid of its activity man has easily compensated for all the disadvantages of his bodily organization in comparison with animals, and has gradually elevated himself to the position of the undisputed lord of creation. Even the powers of Nature he has conquered and forced into his service to such an extent, that in his case the original relations of Nature to the organized being are exactly reversed. The struggle for existence itself, which was at first, as in the animals, almost entirely a struggle for the external conditions of existence, has become changed in its whole nature by the progress of the human intellect,—from the domain of mere material life, it has passed to the region of the mind,—to the political, social and scientific domain. At all events this is the case in the civilized nations, but it is true that among savage tribes and on the more unfavorably situated parts of the earth's surface the struggle for mere existence still rages here and there in its rudest form.

It is clear that man's independence of the determining influences of external nature increases in proportion to the advance of civilization, and that therefore the transforming effects of climate, soil, food, locality, &c., which make themselves felt so unrestrainedly by the world of animals and plants, must remain more or less without action upon the civilized man. And in fact we see how the civilized European or American by means of his improved arrangements and knowledge is enabled to maintain his existence under all latitudes and circumstances, and even to compete successfully in their own countries with the aboriginal tribes who may be regarded as best adapted to the localities and climate. All backward branches of the great human family will by degrees disappear with but few exceptions under the pressure of civilized man, and we can even now easily foresee the time when a certain uniformity of culture and material conditions or a true cosmopolitism of civilized man will be diffused over the greater part of the inhabited and habitable part of our planet. Even those natural influences which act most determinately upon our race in the natural state, such as climate, nature of the soil, distribution of land and water, &c.,

have become to a certain and not inconsiderable extent serviceable to civilized man ; whilst he has found such efficacious means of protection against those actions of nature which he cannot directly govern, that they are incapable of troubling him except in a very diminished degree.* It need scarcely be added that the dominion of man over the organic world of animals and plants is now so great and permanent that, as Alfred Wallace, Darwin's associate in his studies and opinions, has already well shown,† we may foresee a time when there will only be cultivated plants and animals, and when human selection will have replaced natural selection everywhere except in the sea.

From these points of view we must also answer the question which, since the promulgation of the Darwinian theory, has so frequently been raised, whether it is possible that in the future, other and higher races or branches of the great human family will be developed from those now existing, as might be expected from the example of the past. In the various attempts that have been made to answer this interesting question, which is of such importance in connection with the future of the human race,‡ there has been ample room for fancy and the rage for

* On the great Pacific railroad, man now traverses in a few days, surrounded by all the conveniences of the highest luxury and without the least personal fatigue, the greatest breadth of the greatest continent of the earth, rushing now over boundless prairies and now between the dreadful precipices of snow-capped mountains, which formerly kept thousands of unlucky wanderers for months on the road and cost them life and health. And at the same time he knows that at the moment of his departure his arrival at his destination which will take place a week later, has already been communicated there by means of the railway telegraph, and has been made known in the local journals the day afterwards!

† On this subject see my *Six Lectures on the Darwinian Theory*, Leipzig, 1868.

‡ According to an English writer, J. W. Jackson, (see *Anthropological Review*, 1867,) the existing man in the view of the developmental theory is only the commencement of a new Zoological order or of the biped and bird-type of the Mammalia. He will, therefore hereafter, become more covered with hair or feathers, divide into different species and genera, and in his perfected state will only inhabit *suns*, of which the planets are merely the embryos. In his moral nature man is not the fulfillment of the Divine idea of manhood, but only a divine preparation for this. "There is method in this madness!"

hypothesis to make themselves felt, although as yet they have produced nothing tenable.   If the question be conceived merely from the standpoint of the theory of evolution, this being accepted as an incontestable natural law, we can scarcely find any but an affirmative answer for it.   But, on the other hand, when we recognize the fact that the activity of man himself has introduced an entirely new order into the world of living beings and, partially at least, substituted rational spontaneity for the blind force of nature, we shall be inclined to doubt whether man in his present condition can be regarded as unconditionally governed by the above-mentioned law or condition of things. The causes which in early times of the human race drove certain tribes or branches to quit their dwelling places for distant regions, where they sometimes subjugated the people living there and sometimes intermingled with them, in conjunction with their greater rudeness and the stronger influences of the forces of nature, may in those days have given many opportunities for the breaking off of new races or varieties of man, even though we can scarcely believe, (with Wallace,) in the primitive unity of the human race or assume that the many and great diversities of the human type are all mere ramifications of a single fundamental stock, produced by the struggle for existence.   On the contrary it has already been shown in the second part of this book, how many important reasons there are in favor of the opinion that, even at his first development from the world of animals, man made his appearance as a number of different species.   These species may certainly have subsequently become extraordinarily multiplied and increased and may sometimes also have intermixed, but nevertheless we must not suppose that this process will continue without limit when opposed by the mighty and equalizing influences of civilization.   It seems rather to be probable that under the influence of this momentum a *reducing* movement will be opposed to the *differentiating* one, thus tending to superinduce a greater uniformity or similarity of mankind in all parts of the earth, and this by the destruction of the weaker and a constant increase of the stronger or more intelligent races.

By all this the *possibility* of the formation of a new and higher race in some particularly favored locality and from a stock characterized by remarkable adaptability is by no means excluded, but considering the equalizing tendencies of the present day and especially the rapidity of communication and the consequent diffusion of every advance in civilization, such a possibility does not seem probable. In the present aspect of the struggle for existence bodily influences or external influences in general come but little into the account,—the battle is now fought, as has previously been stated, chiefly upon intellectual and moral fields, and these now-a-days are readily and quickly equalized over the whole civilized surface of the earth.

Thus, if what has just been said is correct, there is no great room to expect the formation of new and more highly endowed races of men, but nevertheless this need not impair the prospect of a progressive development of humanity and of the human race itself. The progress remains the same or becomes still more considerable, but the mode or the means by which it is attained are different. Whilst the struggle between peoples was formerly a contest of weapons, strength of body, courage and ferocity, it now consists in an emulation in good and useful arts, in discoveries, contrivances and sciences. The time is past in which one people subjugated another or exterminated it to take its place; it is not by destruction but by peaceful competition that one can attain a superiority over the other. But by this means that uniformity of culture and that intermixture of races are brought about, which so powerfully oppose the separation of new species. The advancing development of the human race will not therefore in future occur solely or chiefly in particular races destined eventually to subject or displace the others, as has hitherto been the case, but it will

constitute an uniform acquisition of the whole species.   How
far humanity itself will at the same time undergo development
may be difficult to determine beforehand ; but, in harmony
with the change in the nature of the struggle for existence,
this development will certainly be rather intellectual than corporeal, or in other words it will advance *pari passu* with a
greater evolution of the tendencies and faculties now slumbering
in the *brain* of man.   For as man now-a-days carries on his
struggle for existence chiefly by means of this organ, and this
will be the case more and more hereafter, so the beneficial and
propulsive consequences of this struggle will also be favorable
to this organ and its activity, as indeed we know from experience it has been in the past.*   Even backward peoples or
races when, favored by their small personal requirements, they
come into competition with civilized man, (as in the case of the
Chinese and Africans in America,) can only stand this competition permanently when they at the same time adopt all the
existing aids of civilization and follow the same general course
by which humanity is at present striving to reach its ideal of
civilization.   But by this means they also are carried away,
perhaps unwillingly or at least unconsciously, by the general
movement of civilization which has been set going by the more
highly developed brain of the Europeans, and thus sink more
or less as specially characterized races.

So far it would appear that all the momenta which are connected with the progress and dissemination of civilization over
the earth's surface are less in favor of the formation of new
races of man, than of the diffusion of a more or less uniform
type of high human culture,—and this would also be the issue
of human development which, in accordance with the general
principles of humanity and justice, must appear most desirable.
The suppression of a lowly race or people by a higher or more
powerful one has always produced such a mass of misery and

* See Appendix No. 39.

injustice, that the repetition of such a process can only evoke
the most disagreeable sensations in every friend of humanity.
In the present state of the human conscience such suppressions
as this would appear to be doubly cruel and lamentable, even
though the replacement of the inferior by a higher or better
type must in itself be regarded as just.   But inasmuch as this
displacement or replacement may take place under present
circumstances without acts of violence and merely by the irresistible power of conviction, the common and uniform progress
of humanity has become a more probable course than that of
the suppression of races.   At present, indeed, mere example
generally suffices among the civilized nations of the earth to
render every progress, every improvement, every increase of
knowledge common property!

Thus in the lapse of time and by the progress of civilization
the struggle for the means of existence, such as we witness in
all its unmitigated violence in the life of animals and in the
lower stages of human development, has become rather a
struggle for existence itself and a contention both of individuals
and of peoples for the acquisition of the highest earthly benefits,
in which we have to do less with mutual suppression, than with
mutual competition or overreaching.

It must not, however, be concluded from this that the
struggle itself has therefore become weaker or easier.   On the
contrary it rages on the domain of morals, to which it has
been transferred, as violently and inexorably, as it formerly
did on the physical field.   Moreover it has become more
complicated and multifarious than the rude struggle with
nature, as it no longer relates merely to the simple support of
existence, but to a great number of advantages of political,
social or material position which are united therewith.   On one
hand this has produced the advantage that the struggle has
called forth in man a whole series of impulses and faculties,
which are scarcely, if at all, developed in the animal, and in

this way has become a principal cause of both general and individual progress,—whilst on the other hand it has given rise on the moral domain to horrors and barbarities without number, of just the same kind as those which formerly existed in physical life.* In comparison with the mere struggle with nature, the social struggle of man has the further great disadvantage that the effects of the natural laws are more or less prejudiced by the will and the contrivances of man, and that in this case therefore it is by no means always the best, the strongest or the best fitted individual that may expect to be victorious over his competitors. On the contrary the rule is rather the suppression of individual intellectual greatness by the influence of family, position, race, wealth, &c., in the interests of personal preferences. Nevertheless the impulse of human nature towards movement and progress is so considerable that it attains its object even under the most unfavorable circumstances; but how much more would this be the case if these obstacles and inequalities were as far as possible removed, leaving a free stage, unaffected by injustice and oppression, for the action of the natural law! The struggle of man

* In a social point of view, F. A. Lange (Die Arbeiterfrage, 1865,) has added to the struggle for existence the *struggle for an advantageous position*, the fundamental law of which, however, is the same as that of the struggle for existence, inasmuch as the germs of the capacity and inclination for advantageous position are scattered through the masses, but destined in the great majority to be aborted. Take away or diminish the pressure which the struggle for existence opposes to the aspiring powers, and forms and performances of an advantageous kind shoot up in unexpected abundance; whilst by an increased pressure the finest talents become aborted, and this with the heavy consciousness of abortion. It is nothing but a deeply rooted error to suppose that every talent or genius will work its way under any circumstances. We forget. especially in this to take into account the effect of higher position upon the development of the fundamental powers, and over-estimate the performances of those who are accidentally highly placed in accordance with their value to the whole. This evil can only be operated against by lightening as much as possible the struggle for existence by means of such arrangements as will present space and the possibility of development to every aspiring talent, and prevent *in future the weal of millions from being sacrificed to the glory of a few!* In the greatest possible equalization of the means by which the struggle for existence is fought out by each individual, lies the problem of the whole future of the human race !

for existence is also far more full of suffering than that of the animal, inasmuch as man, whether as a class or an individual, generally feels the consequences of neglect, oppression or conquest very heavily and painfully, whilst the animal only sees a blind natural destiny in his lot and bows before it unresistingly. This sentiment in man becomes especially painful when the general consciousness of the good or better is more or less in advance of the actually existing arrangements. It is in such a critical period that we now find ourselves, for there has probably never been a period in which there existed so great a disproportion between requirement and fulfillment, between idea and actuality, between thought and being, as at present.

All arrangements in the state, in society, in the church, in education, in work, &c., in consequence of a most prominent law of inertia, have remained far behind what is required by the general human consciousness, elevated as it is by scientific knowledge, reflection and material progress. If the forces opposed to progress had not so great and powerful a reserve in the indolence and immobility of the great and ignorant masses, a very different state of things would long since have taken the place of that which has hitherto prevailed.

In such a position of affairs as this there can be no greater or more elevating task for the philanthropist, than the investigation of those points in which this disproportion makes itself most strongly felt, and in which the struggle for existence may be rendered easier and more advantageous both for the individual man and for mankind in general. These are at the same time the very points at which man is best able to show his dominion over the rude natural conditions, and thus to raise himself furthest above his lowly past. The farther he departs from the point of his animal origin and relationship and replaces the force of nature, which formerly exerted an unlimited influence over him, by his own free and rational spontaneity, the more does he become *man* in the true sense of the word, and

the more does he approach that goal which we must regard as
the future of man and of the human race.   But for this purpose
it is above all things necessary for him to recognize that his
natural destiny can never be attained by him so long as he, like
the animals, feels only as an individual being and carries on his
struggle for existence upon his own account alone, and guided
by mere personal or egotistic motives.   Man is a sociable or
social being and can evidently attain his destiny, and consequently also happiness, only in conjunction with his like, or in
other words, in the midst of human society.   The individual is
all that he can be only in and with humanity at large, or by its
means, and his endeavors after personal happiness are therefore .
most intimately connected with the striving of mankind in general after prosperity and progress.

This great and evident truth has unfortunately been too much
misunderstood or overlooked hitherto.   It is true that civilized man has long since overcome the rudest and most primitive form of the struggle for existence by means of regular
political and social institutions, and invented a multitude o
arrangements which are intended or adapted to protect individuals at least from the most injurious consequences of this contest, and also to secure the possibility of existence to the weak
and defenceless.   Personal benevolence derived from the principles of general philanthropy also accomplishes much that
serves to soften the hardships and terrors of the contest, or at
all events to shelter those who are overcome in it from being
pitilessly trodden down.   But that this is the case is rather the
result of chance than of necessity, and we cannot deny that the
essential principles, upon which even now human society is
founded, are still the old principles of the rough struggle with
nature which have only acquired a milder form by their transfer
to the moral or intellectual region.   That these principles are
not every where applied to their fullest extent, is due to the
amelioration superinduced by the general goodness of human

arrangements, and by the greater diffusion of the principles of humanity among mankind ; but as a general rule these principles only make themselves felt where the good or the interest of the individual as such is not in question, whilst, wherever this is the case, social egotism has no bounds and recoils before no deeds. Even now-a-days those who are stronger, richer, more highly placed in society, or more knowing than the rest, exercise an almost undisputed dominion over the weak, the ignorant and the lowly, and think it quite proper to exert their powers to the utmost in their own interests.

In such a state of things the collective body cannot well feel as such ; it must perceive that it is better that all should strive with united forces and mutual support towards the same goal, towards liberation from the trammels of the forces of nature, than that the best powers should destroy each other by mutual contests. Competition, which in itself is so beneficial, may and will continue, but it must be transformed from the old and rude form of contest and destruction in the struggle for existence into the nobler and essentially human form of competition for the highest general well-being. In other words the struggle for the means of existence will be replaced by the struggle for existence, man by humanity at large, mutual conflict by universal harmony, personal misfortune by general happiness, and general hatred by universal love ! With every step in this path man will depart more and more widely from his past animal condition, from his subjugation to the forces of nature and their inexorable laws, and approach more and more to the ideal of human development. On this course he will find again that Paradise, the ideal of which floated before the fancy of the most ancient nations, and which, according to tradition, was lost by the sin of the first man. The only difference will be that this Paradise of the future will be not imaginary but real, that it will come not at the beginning but at the close of our development, and that it will not be the gift of a Deity, but the result of the labors and merits of man and of the human intellect.

After having established the general principles from which, in accordance with the materialistic or naturalistic conception of the Universe, we must regard and predict the future development of man and of the human race, we have now to apply the general views thus obtained to particulars, and enquire how the different forms of human thought and sociality will have to be moulded in future in accordance with these principles.

GOVERNMENT.

THE purpose of government is the attainment of the greatest possible welfare for all. As this is conceivable only under the existence of the greatest possible freedom for all, the free spontaneity of all nations and the legal equality of every citizen of a state must be the highest principles of every constitution of the future. That this requirement *a priori* excludes every monarchical or hierarchical principle is a matter of course. In a political relation no one should be the subject or the lord of another! The introduction of a *republican* form of Government in the civilized states of Europe, America, &c., can therefore only be regarded as a question of time. The existing monarchies are nothing more than the remains of the former feudal state and of the military conquests of past times, or perishing ruins of a period when, in politics, man only recognized the relations of Lord and Subject, of conqueror and conquered. The sentiment of the present day is agitated to its inmost depths by the thought that *one* should be the ruler or to a certain extent the possessor of many, or that many should be the subjects of a single individual, and this condition would long since have been got rid of if the upholders of the old system could not calculate upon the support of the inert and indolent masses, who have been so long accustomed to obedience, in opposition to the knowledge of the more cultivated classes, and if a certain dread of change and of the uncertainty of the future were not more powerful even among a section of the latter than their insight into better things.

The defenders of such a state of affairs usually assert that the people are not *ripe* for a republican form of government; but in this they apply an idea, good in itself, to a false argument, as even the best-formed fruit will never attain maturity in the absence of the vital conditions necessary for it, such as air, light, heat and nourishment. But for the maturation of freedom, the best agent is freedom itself. A man whose limbs are tied will never learn to move freely, whilst when he is allowed to make free use of them he may perhaps fall once or twice but will always stand up again.

Moreover political freedom is in itself a thing so simple and easy of comprehension that even some of the most ancient civilized nations, and amongst these such as were most noted for intellectuality, possessed it to a very considerable extent; and it would truly be a remarkable circumstance if men at their present stage of culture are not ripe for a state for which their civilized predecessors were well-prepared thousands of years ago. If we are to wait until, under the pressure of a monarchical form of government *all men* without exception shall pronounce in favor of a change to the republican form from their own judgment and conviction, we may probably wait for ever. But in all times the better understanding of the few has outstripped the want of intelligence of the many and formed the leaders of the ignorant masses to the greatest revolutions. This will be the case also in the politics of the future, and the more inasmuch as the example of grandest political development known in history is extant in the present day under a republican form of Government. It is quite inconceivable that the United States of America could ever have taken that un-exampled flight of political and material development that it actually has taken, under a monarchical form of Government, however much there may be to blame in their political management.

Many, indeed, reply, and with justice, that in politics less depends on the *form* than on *the substance*, and that, as history proves, men may live with much less freedom under a republican form of government, than under some others. But the misuse of a thing does not justify the heaping of blame upon it, and if a monarchy leaves the liberty of the subject unmolested, this is more or less a matter of accident or good will; whilst if freedom suffers in a republic, the mass of the citizens are themselves to blame, but are at the same time in a position to correct their errors. But even if all these advantages did not exist, the mere pride of the freeborn and freethinking man must reject with indignation every thought of personal subordination in a political point of view, and put in for himself a claim to the right of free spontaneity and to the benefit of legal equality.

Among the republicans of the present day there exists a rather profound diversity of opinion as to the comparative advantages of *federalism* and *centralism* — of a confederate or united republic. The latter, being the simpler and more natural, would probably not have met with so many opponents if the minds of politicians had not been unnecessarily prejudiced against its principles by the disagreeable results which have been experienced in France from the excessive extension of centralization. On the other hand, the experience neither of Switzerland, nor of North America, (both federal republics,) is at all in favor of federalism, the consequence of which has been in the former the proverbial cantonish spirit and the Sonderbund war, and in the latter the great American civil war which spread so much misery and unhappiness over the great republic of the west. In federal republics we have to fear the breaking up and the self-will of the individual states; whilst in the united republics the infringement of liberty by the central power, and an unnecessary subordination of political or local peculiarities under the general will, are to be dreaded. Both these difficulties, it seems to the author, may be easily got rid of by the combination of the principle of *unity*, which is essential to good government with the widest possible extension of the autonomy or self-government of the *communities*.

In the government of free communities, such as our German ancestors possessed, there is the surest foundation for the individual liberty of the citizen, and it is also adapted to allow free play to all justifiable peculiarities of particular races or districts without injury to the necessary unity of the entire state and its government. Even in the animal organism, which may furnish us with the best type of the organism of the state, each individual part, nay even every individual cell or cell-complex, possesses its own individuality, and yet by its activity contributes its full share to the existence of the whole. This wonderful interweaving of the life of the separate parts with that of the whole which is presented to our view by the animal organism, depends upon the same principle which is constantly becoming more and more predominant in our present political and social conditions, namely, the principle of the *division of labor*. We find that this principle is the more distinctly developed, and that the activity of the different parts is the more thoroughly employed for the benefit of the whole organism, the higher we ascend in the animal kingdom, whilst, on the contrary, in Plants and in the lowest animals, the different parts usually possess so much individuality that very commonly the whole organism may be divided into two or more independent organisms without any injury to life. This comparison may furnish us with the best possible indication of the direction in which our political development must ascend, and show us that the object of the political organism will be better attained the more we succeed in combining a high degree of division of labor, and the greatest possible independence of the individuals and communities forming the state, with the co-operation of all for the welfare and existence of the whole.*

* See Appendix No. 40.

NATIONALITIES.

PRECISELY the same principle which we have found to be involved in the natural progress of the mutual relations of individuals, must also hereafter become the guiding principle in the intercourse of peoples and nations. In the place of a mutually destructive struggle, we shall have a competition in all useful things, and a more or less general endeavor to overcome the obstacles which stand in the way of human happiness. Even under present conditions this principle has already become so powerful and important, that our existing systems of government, which in their nature still depend entirely upon the old principles of mutual diplomatic and military enmity and suppression, have not quite succeeded in escaping its influence, and in modern times the endeavors of the individual states are unmistakably directed towards putting out of the way as much as possible all causes of warlike complications, and cultivating instead of these the arts of peace and the blessings of mutual good understanding. It is true that this state of things is only a provisional one, and one that may be upset at any moment by the desire of fame on the part of misguided sovereigns or the combatativeness of the enormous armies kept on foot by them. But as soon as we have left this stage of barbarism behind us, wars between different nations will hardly be posssible, as every one will see that every war carried on by one state against its neighbor is at the same time a war against itself and its own dearest interests. Moreover, all sufficient inducement to war will be wanting, as no one will think of subjugating or destroying a justly independent people or nation for the benefit of another, and any disputes that may occur will easily be settled by an arbitration of nations or a national Areopagus.

A chief difficulty in this mutual unification of peoples will consist in the definition and limitation of *nationalities*. Important as are the arguments that may be urged against the strict carrying out of what is called the Principle of Nationality (which at present forms the guiding spring of all political popular movements,) it is and must be the only principle upon which a permanent and just separation of nations can be effected. Every people possessing in itself so much vitality, as to have developed in itself a language, literature and history of its own, and which cannot be regarded as a mere appendage of a larger race or a branch from such a race incapable of independent life, has a right to independent existence and must be protected and sustained therein. Doubtful cases and disputes as to the limitation of the different nationalities at those points where they are partially intermixed, will have to be submitted to the judgment of a well-informed and impartial national tribunal, always supposing that the parties interested are unable to come to a mutual understanding. And this at all events under such circumstances as are to be anticipated, will not be difficult, as in this case there will be no question of mutual oppression or forcible extirpation of national peculiarities, but the only purpose in view will be the attainment of peaceable cohabitation. That absurd national hatred of former times, which has produced so much mischief, has already really disappeared from the minds of the larger and more powerful civilized nations, to make room for a mutual esteem and for a general desire for peaceful relations or peaceful competition, as for example, between the Germans and the French, the French and the English, the Germans and the Italians, &c. No doubt this sentiment will by degrees be diffused throughout the masses and render great national wars no longer possible. The immense and indeed incalculable gain that national well-being will derive from the cessation of those enormous and exhaustive military preparations which the European states still think necessary for their safety, is too well known and generally recognized to require special notice here.

SOCIETY.

F AR more important than any political or national reforms, is the reformation of Society in the direction of the view of civilizatory progress here described by us. For of what use to the individual are political liberties or the satisfaction of his national pride, of what advantage to him are theories of national prosperity, if the enjoyment of these things is embittered or rendered impossible to him by social oppression? All political progress is and must remain a chimera so long as society feels itself uneasy and uncomfortable in its very heart, and the people will not attain to quietness and the cheerful enjoyment of their existence until *political* liberation has found its necessary complement in *social* freedom. In no department of human being has the struggle for existence raged more violently or left behind it deeper traces of its destructive action, than in the social field, since it passed from the natural to the intellectual field of action. Unfortunately by daily custom and constant familiarity our nerves have become so blunted to the presence of much misery that we seem scarcely any longer to notice the boundless inequalities and injustices which have been the consequences of the social struggle for existence,—we find the whole thing just as natural as the terrible and remorseless nature-struggle itself. But in this we forget the immense difference that exists between the natural law, which admits of no exceptions and usually destroys its sacrifices quickly and without their ever coming to a consciousness of their condition, and the conscious struggle of man which is carried on under the pressure of regulations and conditions which, being human, are capable of improvement. It is true that the origin of these regulations and conditions is due to a historical development which presents a great similarity to the course of natural development, and which could only to a certain extent be influenced by the arbitrary action of man. But in proportion as mankind advance towards the height which they are destined to reach ; in proportion as they find themselves more and more in a position to replace the rude conditions of nature by free and rational spontaneity, the more must the question press itself upon them whether the state of inequality and injustice which we see extending almost without bounds through human society is *necessary*, or more or less *accidental*, and whether we are in a position to counteract the injurious consequences of this condition of things both to the individual and to the community by the arrangements of society itself.

We have just seen that the great principles of liberty and equality are the determining and almost undisputed principles of the future from a political point of view, and we can by no means see why these same principles should not also be recognized as the determining principles of social progress. At present, indeed, there are very few men who see the necessity of *social* so clearly as that of political reform, and it is, in fact, among the most freethinking of politicians that we frequently find the most inveterate enemies of the endeavor after social improvement. Nevertheless, we shall hardly find any one to assert that oppression and plunder are not as bad socially as politically ; and no one will give a negative answer to the question whether any individual man, at the moment of his birth, does not bring with him into the world an equal claim upon the entire (material and intellectual) property of humanity, and especially of his people or nation. On the other hand, no one will be any more inclined to deny that in reality and in the present state of society this claim is a horrible mockery. For one is born with the crown upon his head ; another rolls in countless gold even in his cradle ; another with his first breath may call his own a great part of that soil upon which we all are born, and which should justly be the common property of us all ; and another, before he begins to think, is destined to hold rank, riches, position, consideration, and lordship over his fellows ; whilst another comes naked and bare into the world like the beasts, and, like the "Son of Man," hath no place whereon to lay his head.   The earth itself, which has produced him, regards him to a certain extent as an outcast, or as coming into the field too late, and he can only make good his right to his miserable existence by appropriating the forces bestowed upon him by nature (whether corporeal or intellectual) to the service of others.   But even under this condition and when he voluntarily sacrifices his life and health to this service, society usually prolongs his life only in the most miserable fashion, and leaves him, in the midst of a national prosperity never before realized, to suffer all the pangs of that mythical Tantalus who saw all sorts of food constantly before him, but which he could never reach.   Boundless poverty side by side with boundless riches ; boundless power side by side with boundless weakness ; boundless happiness side by side with boundless misery ; boundless slavery side by side with boundless will ; boundless excess side by side with boundless want ; fabulous knowledge side by side with fabulous ignorance ; the most strenuous labor side by side with careless enjoyment ; beautiful and glorious things side by side with the deepest depression of human existence,—such is the character of our existing society, which in the magnitude of these contrasts exceeds even the worst times of political oppression and slavery.   Daily we are forced to allow the most moving tragedies, arising from these contrasts, to pass before our eyes without being in a position to prevent their terrible recurrence,—constantly we are forced to confess to ourselves that daily and hourly men perish quickly or slowly by the want of the merest necessaries of life, whilst close beside them the more favorably placed section of society is swallowed up in excess and luxury, and the national welfare improves in an unheard of manner.

When we wander through our large towns or great industrial districts, we have, at almost every step, the opportunity of observing how the dens of want and misery are hidden behind the mansions of riches and happiness,—how in view of groaning tables and overloaded stomachs, hollow-eyed hunger may be seen bearing its pangs in silence,—and how, side by side with luxury and arrogance of all kinds, hopeless want creeps shyly and anxiously into the darkest corners, or sits in gloomy despair hatching deeds of horror. How often could the poor laborer rescue his starving children from the most terrible death by means of the crumbs which fall from the rich man's table and which even his dogs disdain! and what the palled palate of the epicure rejects with disgust, would be a delicacy for him who eats only to satisfy his hunger! Even intellectual food or intellectual enjoyment is so unequally distributed that often the smallest portion of what is offered to those standing in good positions and perhaps rejected by them as quite contemptible, might suffice to make the happiness of the poor but longing mind or to guide it to better purposes. How much talent, how much genius may slumber in the masses who can never attain the circle of action suitable to them, but are constantly yoked to the plough of trivial avocations, whilst incapacity and weakness spread themselves out upon the seats of power and learning. How much hunger (intellectual or physical) could be satisfied without any trouble, if means and cultivation were more equally distributed! How satisfied might every one be, either with food or with learning, if all were active. and so many had not to work for one or for a few!*

* See Appendix No. 41.

It is, as we have said, the social struggle for existence, not yet regulated by the principles of reason and justice, that has gradually called forth all these inequalities and monstrosities of society. In this it has been most essentially supported by those innumerable political oppressions, acts of violence, robberies, conquests, &c., with which the past history of nations is filled, and of which the mournful effects are still regarded by uninstructed reason as the necessary consequences of social movement.

Thus the present state of society and the distribution of property in society is by no means, as many think, the mere consequence of a natural development, but of a concatenation of circumstances and causes, among which the legitimate gain and personal industry of the individual, important as they are, play on the whole only a secondary part. The place of the old political violence has been taken by the rage of social oppression and plunder, which recognizes no other object than that of becoming rich and prosperous as quickly as possible at the expense of others, and for the attainment of this purpose leaves no means of mutual competition or overreaching untried. It is a matter of course that those who have been beaten in competition, or have been overreached, endeavor to make good their loss by every means offered to them by cunning or power, although owing to the inequality of the contest they usually meet but little success in this. Of forbearance or pity there is no more in this social war, in which every one's hand is against his neighbor (at least as far as it is carried on between individuals,) than in the rude natural struggle already described. It is as it were a general flight or race of fear before the troubles and wants of life, in which the majority in their flight have scarcely a glance of pity, let alone a helping hand, to bestow upon those who are sinking to the ground beside them, and strike down those who stand in their way without hesitation. Unceasingly the stream roars onwards over those unfortunates who fall, and the universal war cry runs as follows :—*Save himself who can! succumb who must!*

There can be no doubt that this state of things must bring with it the greatest disadvantages to the nobler impulses and tendencies, or to the moral nature of man, and that it must cause a boundless egotism to be the main-spring of human affairs. Every deviation from the prescriptions laid down by social egotism avenges itself in the most grievous manner upon the individual, and compels him, if he will not be untrue to the cogent commands of the principle of self-preservation, immediately to return into the beaten track. Even the most devoted philanthropist could not withdraw himself from these commands of social egotism, unless he is willing to find himself immediately affected by the greatest personal disadvantages.*

There will not be many men who will venture to dispute the above propositions, which are merely derived from daily experience, or to deny the simple principle of natural justice, that all men at their birth bring with them into the world an equal right to all the (material or intellectual) possessions of mankind existing at that moment. But after admitting these and similar truths, they will immediately add with a compassionate shrug, that there is no rational or available means of improving this state of things,— that there have always been riches and poverty, and that inequality of position and property, differences of station, culture and the like, are necessary and indispensable attributes of human society, without which it could not subsist. To this they will add that if even now, in disregard of all existing rights which have been generally well-acquired, we were to undertake a general distribution of goods amongst all the living, the old inequality would very soon return. Lastly, they will picture in the liveliest colors the (real and imaginary) dangers of *communism* and then show that all attempts of this nature have failed most ignominiously

* See Appendix No. 42.

and must always fail on account of the weakness and insufficiency of human nature.   The last statement certainly
need not be admitted, and to the former ones we may reply as
follows :   That the existing egotism of human nature, which
rules society, is principally the consequence of the egotistical
state of human feeling and society, which has prevailed for
many thousand years and hardened in the constant struggle
for existence, and that a better guidance and education of the
human mind, and especially of the spirit of Society in the
direction of reciprocity and fraternity, would produce astonish-
ingly different results.   Further, that all the communistic
attempts that have been made have not failed, and that, where
they fell through, they were often destroyed rather by external
than by internal difficulties.*   And finally we may justly call
attention to the fact that the advantages of a community of
goods are extraordinarily great both economically and morally,†
and that we may easily imagine a state of Society in which
without any danger to the objects of Society itself or to the
individuality of the persons composing it,‡ labor would acquire
a perfectly unconstrained and spontaneous character, serving
only the purposes of the community.   But although all this
may be urged against the opponents of communism, yet for
the present and for a long time to come there is so little chance
of any practical realization of such ideas or propositions, that
all further reference to the subject seems superfluous.   The
general and quite insuperable aversion of men to all kinds of
communistic propositions or systems is opposed to it, as also
the still actually existing weakness and insufficiency of human
nature itself, which can only be conducted to and rendered

*See Appendix No. 43.   † See Appendix No. 44.

‡ " Obliteration of individuality," is the watchword that our philosophers and
political economists have given out against communistic systems of all kinds,
although it is perfectly unjust, and although there are so many individualities
whose obliteration would really be of no consequence.   Moreover our present
form of society, I think, does quite enough for the obliteration of individuality,
and for the production of a general personal insignificance.

capable of better things by many years' education in the spirit of community and general philanthropy.

We have nothing for it, therefore, but to look about for some other means which may serve, at least to some extent, to weaken the frightful contrasts and monstrosities of the present condition of society and thus gradually lead to a better state of things. Here again science, and especially natural science gives the right clue. For if, as has already been shown, the true task of humanity, or of human progress in opposition to the rude natural state, consists in the struggle *against* the struggle for existence, or in *the replacement of the power of nature by the power of reason*, it is clear that this object must above all be attained by the greatest possible equalization of the circumstances and means under which and with which each individual has to fight out his struggle for existence, and to carry on the competition for the preservation of his life. Nature knows no such equalization, or admits it only in an exceedingly imperfect fashion, and the weaker or less favored party saves itself in Nature rather by evasion or flight from the stronger or from unfavorable influences, than by direct opposition. Even in man this was formerly the case to a great extent, if we leave out of consideration the immediate natural influences which man opposed more or less directly by the aid of his power of reflection and knowledge. But just as he has successfully carried on this contest with the external world and still continues to fight it out victoriously, he must also fight out the much more difficult internal contest against his own animal nature, and, as we have said, put the law of reason in place of the law of nature. If in politics we have long since come to replace the old system of oppression and domination by the now generally recognized principle of *equal rights* and *equal duties*, we must likewise socially replace the system of mutual plunder, which has hitherto prevailed, by the principle of *equal means* or *equal circumstances*. What sort of combat would it be in which one of the combatants made his appearance naked and armed with a wooden sword, whilst the other advanced to battle cased in steel from head to foot, and with sabres and guns? What sort of race would it be in which one of the runners had to trust only to the powers of his naked feet, whilst the other had the aid of all the means of locomotion which the progress of the arts had rendered possible? And what sort of competition for existence is that in which one party appears furnished with all those innumerable advantages which rank, riches, culture, position, &c., are able to confer upon him, whilst the other has nothing to depend upon but the force of his naked arms or of his uncultivated understanding?—force which, moreover, has probably been checked in its development even in his earliest youth by bodily or spiritual destitution. Such a state of things cannot really deserve the name of a struggle or competition for existence, as its issue in by far the greater number of cases is decided beforehand, and the whole merely represents a state of permanent social slavery sanctified by age, and inherited from generation to generation. Of course such a state greatly paralyzes the desire to struggle or the endeavor for personal improvement in the depressed portion of society, as any one from whom nearly every prospect of success or victory is taken will find no particular pleasure in the struggle, but will only think how he may scantily support his life, destined as it is to the service of others. Fortunately most of these Pariah's of society, whilst possessing no distinct consciousness of their position or knowledge of the causes which lead to it, have likewise no feeling of its horrors. If they had such a feeling and consciousness, that social revolution which has been so often prophesied and which is so much dreaded by the proprietary classes, would long since have become a fact.*

It must indeed be admitted that a complete equalization of

* See Appendix No. 45.

the means with which each individual carries on his struggle for existence can scarcely ever become a matter of possibility; but even a *partial* equalization would be attended with the most beneficial consequences to the state of society and would sharpen, instead of weakening the desirable spur of competition. For when it is assigned to everyone to enjoy only the fruits of his own industry or of his own exertions, and not to loll upon the bed of idleness while the fruits of the industry or good fortune of others are poured into his lap, he will find himself from the first impelled, in the interest of self-preservation, to industry and activity, whilst at present even those who feel in themselves the impulse to work are often enough condemned by their social position to an involuntary inaction. Even the natural inequalities of society and the necessary difference of occupations in society will not suffer under such an equalization. Birth, family, residence, talents, personal desires, bodily strength or weakness, intellectual advantages, &c., superinduce a multitude of differences of human nature which are quite incapable of equalization by external means, and which in the further course of each individual life will make themselves felt with the same or probably, (when the external means of existence are equalized,) with far greater force than hitherto.

In order to bring about the desiderated equalization to a certain extent, and place the individual in a position in which he may be able to develop his natural talents satisfactorily, and find no obstacles to applying his industry and his faculties in any direction of social life, far greater means must be furnished to the community or the state than has hitherto been the case. This object may be attained in part by giving up the so-called ground-rents, (especially that which arises from simple increase of the population,) or by bringing back the property in land and soil, which of right belongs to all in common, out of the possession of private individuals into that of the community,*

* See Appendix No. 46.

and in part by a perfectly feasible and gradually increasing limitation in favor of the community of the right of leaving private
property to descendants.*   These proposals have nothing to do
with communism, although to many they may at the first
glance appear to be connected with it, as nothing is contained
in them which is in contradiction to the principle of private
property as such, or which could hinder the individual from
enjoying or employing in the fullest degree the produce of his
own industry and endeavors.   The care of his descendants also
would not be taken from him so long as no complete abolition
of the right of inheritance is proposed ; but this care will weigh
upon him with infinitely less pressure than hitherto, as the
community would under all circumstances take charge of the
education and culture of children until they attained an age to
earn their own living, and must always take charge of those
descendants who are incapable of earning anything, whenever
these were not sufficiently provided for by private means.†
But the consciousness that the individual by his industry is
working and caring not merely for himself and for his heirs,
(who are often very undeserving or who do not require his
aid,) but also for the community at large, would act most
beneficially in opposition to those egotistical impulses or tendencies which, as we have seen, at present unfortunately constitute the mainspring of all social activity, and have as their
consequence a fundamental corruption of the social nature of
man.   The individual will also perceive that, whilst he works
and cares for the community, he is doing the same for himself
and his household, inasmuch as all are merely individual constituents of the whole, and must prosper as the community
prospers.   The so-called Manchester men, who see in government only a sort of police establishment for the security of life
and property, will not find this easily intelligible ; they wish to
know as little as possible of government and only require that

*See Appendix No. 47.   †See Appendix No. 48.

social murder and slavery should go on with as little hindrance as possible under its protection.　In this, indeed, they are strongly supported by a reference to our present conditions of state, which really make all governmental interference in private and social relations appear most undesirable, and represent only a political plundering of the entire body of the people on a large scale by a dominant minority.　A very different thing from this government of force, which must be regarded as a remnant of the middle ages, is the true *popular government*, in which the community is only the expression of all, and in which all are only the expression of the community.　Such a state as this really resembles an organism, in which all the juices flow constantly and in uninterrupted streams from the circumference to the centre, to flow back again immediately from the centre to the different parts, and furnish them with strength and health. In this uninterrrupted ebb and flow, in this ceaseless interchange of juices between the individual parts and the great central points, lies the best guarantee of health, whilst every interruption of this movement, every stoppage or accumulation of the blood in the different parts has illness or discomfort as its consequence.　Just so is it also in the body of the state, which must be less comfortable in proportion as the interchange between the whole and the individual parts is less, and as property and riches accumulate in an unnatural manner at particular parts of the periphery and fix themselves there without any free circulation with the general body.　Hence the enormous private fortunes which have been gradually accumulated, chiefly in consequence of inheritance and marriage, in the hands of individuals or families, and the employment of which is left entirely to the will of individuals, cause just the same danger to the community or to the state as the excessive possession of land by private individuals.　By the immense influence which property and riches have acquired in our present social and political condition, these fortunes have arrived at the formation of a state in the state; and, in time to come, and in proportion as the theory of the Manchester men makes way, they will do this still more, and finally things will come to such a pass that no regular government can any longer exist. Money or the god Mammon will in the end remain the sole ruler of states, and we even now use a very characteristic expression when we call the millionaires, "Money princes," as if to intimate that in their hands property and riches are combined with exorbitant political influence.

The measures proposed by us will of course operate most effectually against this unnatural accumulation of such large private fortunes as are injurious to the community,—they will constantly carry back the national riches from the hands of individuals to the place where they naturally and justly belong, namely, the lap of the nation itself. Like a beneficent rain they will there distribute themselves among the individual members, and awaken life and health where before there was only desolation and misery. In this way, without the detested communistic division and without any infringement of private interests, a certain amount of division will be taking place continually and at every moment, and a constant, normal and legitimate equalization between the whole and the parts, as also between the parts themselves, will be established.

A method which accomplishes so much and yet affects or injures no one in his personal rights, should not be rejected without consideration, (as it probably will be by many who read these lines,) but should be carefully examined so that an impartial and unprejudiced opinion may be formed upon it. Even those practical scruples or doubts as to the possibility of carrying it out, which, as in the case of everything new, will here make themselves felt with great energy, may all be removed without much difficulty, as a little consideration will make plain to any one who desires to arrive at a clear judgment on the subject. It will not be difficult by legislative processes to prevent unlimited donations in case of death, and to render fraudulent evasions of the law impossible. The limitation of the power of bequest also will not, as many think, excessively injure the impulse to acquisition among individuals. Innumerable examples prove that the desire of acquiring property is not in the least altered or affected by the want of direct or needy heirs of the body ; and if here and there an individual should be induced by the want of direct inheritors to spend more upon himself or upon others than he would otherwise have done, we can find no injury to the community in this. On the contrary, a counterpoise to that avaricious and useless spirit of hoarding, which at present rules the minds of most men of property, would be of the greatest service, and at any rate useful and necessary expenditure of the moment would no longer be limited to the same extent as hitherto from considerations of the future and to the injury of the present. The thirst for money and riches has the peculiarity that it is not, like any other thirst, stopped by being satisfied, but in general increases in the same proportion that food is offered to it. Every rich man is inspired by the wish to become still richer in order that he may rival or excel those who already exceed him in riches and in external display,—and the cases are comparatively rare in which great private wealth is employed in carrying out generally useful plans for the furtherance of the common weal, arrangements for the assistance of struggling talent, and so forth.

It is clear that in this way only tendencies and impulses are cultivated which are useless or injurious to the common weal, such as avarice, jealousy, envy, ostentation, dishonesty, &c., whilst philanthropy, furtherance of the common weal, the support of suffering or needy people, sacrifices for great purposes, furthering the well-being of man in material or intellectual matters, &c., must stand behind these egotistical motives or tendencies.

This entire condition of things must, however, be reversed as soon as the individual is brought by the arrangements of society itself, into a different and more intimate connection with it, and with the community in general. The tendency to employ his wealth not merely for himself but for purposes of public utility will increase to an unexpected extent, and in place of that absurd desire of personal ostentation which prevails at present among nearly all wealthy people and impels them to lavish unhesitatingly uncounted sums upon the gratification of the smallest and pettiest personal desires and vanities, whilst an equally petty avarice prevails in opposition to all non-ego-tistical objects, we shall have love of the community, assistance to others, furtherance of great and general purposes, &c. But even should this action upon the spirit of individuals and this improvement of human nature be wanting, the state or the community will take that care upon itself, and employ the wealth constantly flowing to it from the private property of the dead, not only for the advancement of the common weal, but also for the furtherance of all general objects beneficial to mankind as such, and to its advancement. Thus, while at present the wealth of the nation is to a certain extent held in private hands and is in general employed in a manner either use-less or positively injurious to the community, the very opposite must then be the case to the blessing of all. All this necessarily leads to the *question of capital*, which has become so important and been so often discussed in our day, and upon which, un-fortunately, infinite obscurity still prevails in most minds.

CAPITAL.

CAPITAL, in the most general sense, is another denomination for work already done and completed, or, more correctly expressed, it is the collected and stored up bodily and intellectual work of our ancestors and contemporaries, converted into possessions or useful property of all kinds,* (such as money, arable lands, houses, goods, means of transport, tools, knowledge, &c.)

From this definition it appears at once how brainless and senseless is the cry against capital as such which is now the fashion among the working classes. The battle-cry of the workman should not be: Down with capital! but: Long live capital! Were we in a position at present with a single blow to cause all capital to disappear from the world, we should voluntarily throw ourselves back into that rude and miserable state, in which our earliest ancestors led their half-animal lives in a most imperfect manner, as indeed the progress of civilization consists chiefly in the gradual accumulation of those innumerable appliances and knowledges by which alone a civilized life, freed from the rude bonds of the force of nature, is rendered

---

* Many define capital as the excess of the produce of labor over its wages, or as the increased value of the work perfomed by the capitalistic method of production, which the capitalist or speculator puts in his pocket. It is clear that this is no definition nor even an explanation of the mode of origin of capital, but only an expression of one of those multifarious processes by which capital accumulates in individual hands. By such definitions nothing is explained, but only an unnecessary agitation is produced. Even F. A. Lange (*Die Arbeiterfrage, &c.*) gives no explanation of the mode of origin of capital, but only explains the causes or *one* of the causes of its unfair distribution, when he says that capital on the whole originates in part directly and in part indirectly from the lordly possessions and the privileges of the feudal ages.

possible.   The greater, the more extensive and the more valuable that enormous treasure of physical and intellectual property which mankind accumulates in its gradual course of development, and bequeaths onwards from generation to generation, the more does it approach the fulfillment of its true destiny, and the greater will also be the general proportion of its happiness.   The evil of which we have to complain is not due to the fact that this treasure or capital, (in the widest sense,) exists at all, but to the circumstance *that it is not in the same measure or in the same manner at the command of every individual.*   If all had capital, no one would have occasion to complain of it, but in all probability every one would tell of its advantageous effects.   It is only the interest on capital that converts capital into that detested instrument of the rich against the poor, by which the former are always sure that, without any exertions of their own, the labor of others will always be performed for them and for their support.

Thus if we examine the affair to the bottom, it is clear that the whole misconception which attaches to the so-called power of capital has its foundation not in the existence of capital as such, but solely in its unequal *distribution*, which contradicts the principles not only of justice, but also those of sound national economy.   All the reproaches and curses that have been cast upon capital seem to be unjust so long as we speak of capital in itself, and probably become more or less just when we substitute for it the expression, "private capital."   In fact we can by no means see why the labor of the past and of the community in the present should benefit, not the community, but only individuals, and why what belongs to mankind is withheld by individual interests.   Even without considering what has been left us by our ancestors and the universal right of all in the soil, the enormous increase of value which all existing property experiences by the simple increase of population, by the increase of credit, and by the rise of all industrial, mercantile and other conditions, is so much the direct consequence of the common activity of all, that it must appear to be the greatest injustice that the chief benefit of this increase of value accrues almost exclusively to individual persons who are accidentally in possession of this or that property, and who perhaps have contributed least of all by their own activity to bring about the result. No one will be inclined to assert that those in whose hands capital or the results of the industry, the skill, the thought and the exertions of the generations which lived before us and of those still living, is now chiefly to be found, have earned it by their own activity and industry, or that the poverty and want of property of the lower and working classes are the consequences of misfortunes which they have brought upon themselves. There is therefore no other means to level these irregularities so as to satisfy justice and the needs of national economy, except the partly permanent and partly temporary restoration of capital,—the wealth of the people,—the property of mankind,—to the hands of those to whom they naturally and justly belong, namely, into the possession of the community or of mankind as such.

Whilst these goods then stand once more at the disposal of the individual so far as he requires them for the development and utilization of his powers, they make him independent of the dominion of private capital and enable him, without sacrificing his powers in the service of others, to serve both himself and the community or humanity at large by his activity. But the former power of private capital itself will lose almost all its importance in the presence of the enormous concentration of the wealth of the people in the hands of the state or of the community, and the diminution or perhaps total cessation of the interest accruing from it under competition with the capital of the state, will render it impossible for idlers any longer to live without exertions or deserts of their own at the cost of the community or of others. The chief benefit will however consist in the fact that the wealth of the nation will be taken from under the influence of the arbitrary will, the stupidity, the malevolence, or the avarice of private individuals, and will no longer be applied to unproductive or even injurious purposes, but solely to the benefit and welfare of all.   The boundless and most pernicious rage of speculation will come to an end, and in place of incalculable national debts we shall have an inexhaustible national wealth.   Even the private individual who has worked so long and successfully as to be able to take his ease, as the phrase goes, will probably in most cases prefer to hand over the wealth acquired by him, in whole or in part, to the community and in return for it to stipulate for a corresponding maintenance for life.   Lastly, one part of what we now denominate capital and the part to which the disagreeable accessory notion of capital principally clings, namely, *money*, will scarcely be necessary to the state, as it will probably in most cases be possible to attain all the purposes of society by organization and mutual equalization of work.

LABOR AND LABORERS.

O NE of the greatest follies which the present age has committed and is still committing is the creation of a special
laborer's question and its separation from the great or general
social questions. In this case, also, as in the question of capital, the root of the matter does not lie in work itself but only in
its unjust distribution. Fundamentally, all men are laborers
with the exception of the comparatively few who live upon the
stored up fat of their predecessors, or upon the labor of others;
and if work, as is certainly the case, is very differently paid for,
this generally stands in a not unjustifiable relation to the kind
and difficulty of the work, and to the dangers and expenses
connected with its acquisition or performance. It is therefore
only an unnatural revivification of that class-opposition, which
is in opposition to all the principles of modern times, to place
the laborer *par excellence* (that is to say the industrial or factory
workman) in contradistinction to all the other classes of society,
as Lassalle has done, and to require for him special privileges
within a society which has elevated political equality into its
leading principle. *Labor* is depressed, not the *laborer* as such.
If we recognize as just the principles upon which existing society is built up, we must also accept all their consequences, and
not make it a ground of complaint that the inexorable struggle
for existence gives unequal results, when the means with which
it has to be fought are themselves unequal. The ignorant
workman excited by all sorts of demonstrations has now-a-days
accustomed himself to regard his master as the real cause of his

miseries and wrongs, but this is just as unwise or foolish as for him to regard capital in itself as his enemy. ˉWithout capital and without a master he might at any moment die of hunger, and as a *work-taker* he is very often in a comparatively much more favorable position than his *work-giver*, who on his part, if he is not himself à capitalist, depends upon other capitalists, and in general has to struggle with a multitude of galling cares and dangers of which his workmen have no conception. The workman, all whose aspirations are directed merely to the increase of the wages paid to him, does not consider that the work-giver, however rich or prosperous he may be, does not pay him out of his own pocket, but only out of the pockets of the public, and that this as well as the competition which hems him in on every side, lay upon him certain limits which he cannot overstep without bringing himself to ruin. The existing relations between work-givers and work-takers or the so-called capitalistic mode of production is only a necessary and inevitable result of our given social relations, and those who, whilst acknowledging these relations, declaim against this mode of production and its consequences, which are certainly often very grievous,* act in just as wise a manner as a surgeon who should take a symptom or external manifestation of a disease for the disease itself. Moreover the reproaches cast upon the capitalistic mode of production and the so-called *wages-system* generally apply only to very large industrial undertakings and to those trades in which *only* working hands and capital are

---

* "The capitalistic mode of production," says J. G Eccarius, (*Eines Arbeiters Widerlegung der national-ökonomischen Lehren;* J. S. Mill, Berlin, 1869,) "is under the most favorable circumstances a social war without interruption. The improvement of the machinery of production goes about like a roaring Lion and seeks whom it may devour. It is a barbarous war,—the artillery and the victories are all on one side, the killed and wounded on the other. It is an abominable ard contemptible war produced by avarice,—undisguised avarice,—which is the more hateful because the accumulation of wealth for wealth's sake is represented as an ennobling principle, and proclaimed by its worshippers a divine ordinance or an eternal law of nature bringing health to humanity. Those who perish in this struggle have not even the comfort of dying for a good or glorious cause,—they are inspired by no fanaticism, by no illusion. They are mere sacrifices to Plutus, who are acquainted with their fate and see their destruction before them at every step."

employed, whilst wherever a business or a factory depends upon the creative activity, the inventive genius, the industry or any other special faculty of its undertaker, or even upon the particular goodness of its whole organization, the increased gain, falsely called the premium on capital of the undertaker or organizer, *is very well earned.**

In order to get rid of the wages-system and give the workman the actual produce of his labor instead of the mere wages, Lassalle and his adherents have, as is well known, proposed the establishment of *productive associations* as they are called, that is to say, independent associations of workmen for productive purposes, and this by the aid of state credit or by the help of the state.   This proposition is subject to a considerable number of both external and internal difficulties which render its being carried out under existing circumstances exceedingly questionable.   But even if this were not the case, and if we could suc-

* In an essay on the premium on capital in his *Pioneer*, Karl Heinzen expresses himself upon this point very well as follows:

"But what measure shall be applied when the works necessary for carrying on a business are of completely different kinds and the capitalist is not merely its undertaker but also, by special qualification, its creator and maintainer? It is true that without the aid of the workmen the business can no more exist than without capital; but shall the capitalist have no preference over those who help him in his business? shall they have an equal claim with him to profit? shall the greater share which he appropriates to himself be regarded as an objectionable 'premium on capital,' when he alone is the soul of the business, when it only exists by his creative activity, when its nature requires special faculties which he alone possesses, and perhaps he only attained them by the greatest sacrifices?

"Even in the most everyday business we are perplexed by the question of the right mode of division. Take a merchant's business:— To carry it on we require, besides the undertaking capitalist, book-keeper, clerks, messengers, carters, servants, &c. Shall all these assistants have an equal right to the profits with the capitalist? Shall his right to a greater share be disputed as 'premium on capital?'

"Let us take another example. An author who possesses the necessary capital sets up a newspaper. Notwithstanding his intellectual and pecuniary capital, he is unable to bring it out without the assistance of a book-keeper, a manager, a set of printers and even a printer's devil. The Journal, however, prospers by the industry and talent of its founder, and by this talent and industry alone. His capital would be less powerful without his talent, than his talent without his capital. Now does justice require that he should divide the whole profit of his undertaking with his assistant workers down even to the printer's devil? Does he not do enough if he pays each of them the highest price for his work, which cannot by any means be brought into the same category with his own? Is he to be condemned as a capitalist if he estimates the product of his activity which decides the prosperity and even the very existence of the business, at a higher value than that of his workmen?"

ceed by means of the universal suffrage advocated by Lassalle, in securing the acceptance and coöperation of the state for his proposals (which, however, is very improbable without some previous social reforms), it would very soon appear that these state-factories would be by no means in a position to attain the object expected from them, namely, the liberation of the workman from his depressed social position, or would attain it in a very imperfect degree. For in the first place the average net profit of a particular factory or business, which may certainly appear very large in the hands of an individual, is comparatively very small as soon as it comes to be divided among all the partakers and co-laborers in the business or among a great number, and in times of crisis, of want of business or of greatly increased competition it may even fall far below the level of what is generally paid to the individual workman as wages.

In the second place the factories guaranteed by the state, (assuming their practicability and greater profit to be permanent,) will still benefit only a part and probably a comparatively small part of the working population, as no one will be inclined to assert that all the occupations of daily life could be carried on by means of such organized factories or associations, (in which, moreover, the want of unity between the individual partakers would form an essential stumbling-block.) Consider for example the very large class of domestic servants and many other branches of human activity!

Thus even if we presuppose the establishment and the anticipated result of such associations established by the aid of the state, there will always remain a great residue of workers not engaged in these associations. The necessary consequence of this is the formation of an aristocracy of laborers and of a *fifth state* besides the existing four. Within this fifth state and among these true *prolétaires* the whole movement will then begin again from the commencement, and indeed more violent-

ly, threateningly and bitterly than before, as the hatred of the
poor will be excited against their better situated or more
favored *confrères* not merely on account of their social inferiority, but also on account of their political inferiority.

Not only this physical but also the intellectual proletariate,
and indeed every other class of society, will immediately lay
claim to the assistance of the state, and with the same right as
the industrial or factory workmen, and it can no more be
denied to them than to the latter.   And at last where is the state,
great as its credit may still be, to obtain all the means to satisfy
such numerous claims?   It is true that state-aid in itself and as
a principle is by no means so objectionable as Lassalle's opponents assert, and the arguments against it, which it has been
attempted to derive from the accepted nature of the state, are
entirely untenable.*   But without a previous reformation of the
law of property, and without the state being furnished with
enormous means, it is simply an impossibility, and it is therefore quite natural that under the actually existing state of things
self-help in accordance with the proposals of the celebrated political economist, Schulze-Delitzsch, is preferred to it among really
intelligent workmen.   Indeed this self-help in which so many
at present pride themselves with mistaken vanity, is in itself
only a very poor expedient, and as a principle just as inefficient
as state assistance is efficient.   For self-help without means
merely signifies simple failure or gradual languishing.   If we
throw a man who cannot swim, without any means of keeping
himself above water, into a rushing stream, (and life is just such
a stream,) he will certainly sink in it.   But if we previously
teach him to swim or to sail and give him a boat or put an oar
into his hand, he will struggle successfully with the waves.
But the blindness that exists as to the present state of society is
so great, that those who possess all the resources for the
struggle or for onward movement in the greatest superfluity,

* See Appendix No. 49.

furnish none of them to their poor or struggling brother, but refer him scornfully to that self-help which in most cases has not been practised by themselves, and rather suffocate in their own fatness, than yield to others something out of their super-fluity, which, perhaps, is even a trouble to themselves. The throwing of an oar or plank from the ship of the rich or high-placed man as it sails proudly by, would often suffice to save the poor one from certain destruction ; but the principle of self-help forbids it, and the poor man must sink with a last despairing glance at those treasures which are often only an annoyance to others, and to him would be synonymous with salvation and happiness.*

All this proves that self-help without aid from the state is just as much an impossibility as state assistance without the aid of society, and also that the root of the whole evil lies not in the position of the laboring class as such, but in the false and insufficient organization of society. The position of the workman is only a simple necessary consequence of our general and economic state and of the false and unjust distribution of labor in social life. Mutual equalization and distribution of the possessions which have become useless to individuals through the community with the assistance of the state, at the same time securing to the individual those means and conditions which he absolutely requires in his struggle for existence, is here also the only means of salvation.

When the working men and the present leaders of their movement have once clearly realized this truth with all its

---

*Schultze-Delitzsch, with his self-help, has, however, the advantage over all his opponents, over all socialistic or economistic systems, *that he takes his stand upon the ground of existing conditions* and from this evolves a directly beneficial activity, whilst all others hope in the future and require considerable political revolutions as a necessary preliminary condition for their practical activity. One may therefore very well be a decided socialist and nevertheless, so long as political conditions remain the same, be active in the direction of Schultz's system. However, it is now a generally admitted fact that this system is almost solely beneficial to small operations, small masters, &c., whilst the actual workman derives very little if any benefit from it, necessary consequences, they will save themselves many useless words and efforts and, what is of more consequence, much self-deception. An evil is not cured by counteracting its symptoms or external phenomena, but by attacking it at the root. In this respect Lassalle has done much mischief by raising a special workman's question when he should have disclosed and attacked the social defects; with his universal suffrage and state-associations he has held out a bait to the workmen, at which they certainly bit with avidity, but which, in the hour of danger, will leave them miserably in the lurch. Lassalle, however, was no socialist, as so many in their ignorance suppose, but an economist; at least his proposals have nothing of a socialistic character about them. Almost at the moment of the first appearance of Lassalle the author publicly expressed the opinion here maintained of him and his system in a report upon Lassalle's Labor-programme, made on April 19, 1863, at Rœdelheim,* and although now seven years' experience lies behind us, he can still subscribe to nearly every word contained in it. The crude communism, into which Lassalle's labor-movement has since degenerated, is, however, the best proof of its intrinsic untenability. But for the workmen themselves and their cause it is a bad sign that names such as those of Lassalle and Schulze-Delitsch could become a sort of Shiboleth or battle-cry to divide them into two hostile camps contending with each other with great fury; this shows a frightful want of consideration and judgment and instead of these a blind imitation or idolatry. But man should have no idols, whether religious, political, scientific or social. Let us leave idolatry to the middle ages, to the hypocrites, the blockheads and the sluggards !

* Herr Lassalle und die Arbeiter. — Bericht und Vortrag, etc., von Dr. Louis Büchner, R. Baist, Frankfort on the Maine.

THE FAMILY.

AS often as proposals have been made for the improvement or reformation of the state of society, an unanimous cry rises from the mouths of opponents that it is intended to undermine the eternal and indestructible chief pillars of law, morals and the family. The family, especially, is regarded in this case as the indispensable foundation of society, as the nursery of every thing good and noble, and as the firmest support of the so-called Christian state,—and every one who ventures to say a word against this institution, sanctified as it is by age, is branded as half a criminal. It is therefore well worth the trouble to examine once for all how far this assertion, which is so generally accepted as incontestible, is or is not correct, and to see whether such terrible consequences, as are generally set before us, are really to be anticipated from a limitation of family rights for the benefit of the community. We then ascertain in the first place that in its present form the family also is closely and necessarily connected with that condition of social egotism which we have found to be the consequence of the unlimited struggle for existence when not yet bridled by the power of reason, and that the family represents on a larger scale in society very nearly what the individual is in the community. We know from history that the striving for family lustre, family power and family wealth has at all times been one of the principal objects of human endeavors, and that to this striving all higher human objects, all considerations of the common-weal have been sacrificed in innumerable instances without hesitation or scruple. Although the great French revolution has effected a great improvement in this respect and, by the principle of individual liberty and equality introduced by it, broken the direct political power of the great families, still the system continues to exist as such in the social domain and by direct means even in the political; and what is called *nepotism*, or the favoring of certain families and their individual members to the injury of the rest and of the community, forms, as is well known, one of the most hateful and at the same time injurious features of our political and social state.

If we leave this out of consideration and consider only the family as such, no one, of course, will deny that in itself it forms a truly human institution, and that in its ideal form it is capable or even destined to exert the most beneficial influence upon human development and manners. But if we enquire further where and how often this ideal family is really to be met with, the answer to this question is very lamentable. Here, as everywhere, the struggle for existence in its wildest form has raged fearfully and most unrestrainedly, and left the happiness and the infinite tendernesses of the true family life to be enjoyed by very few. The family in its true form exists only for the rich and prosperous; whilst the poor man or the *prolétaire* know the family only in a form which in general constitutes the direct opposite of what it should be.

If we consider first of all the lowest strata of society, as those who belong to it are usually destitute of the means of founding a true family, they often enough replace it by vicious courses or illicit cohabitation. Where this is not the case, the family-life of the lower and lowest classes is unfortunately as a rule rather a nursery of evil than of good, and it fulfills its essential purpose only in a very imperfect manner. For during by far the greater part of the day both parents are absent from home seeking their livelihood,—and as to the children, when under the most defective care and domestic bringing up they have attained a certain age, they are regarded by their parents rather as working instruments than as human beings entrusted to their care. The father who, in common life, leads a dependent and servile or uniform, unintellectual existence, sees in his wife and children the only beings in the world over whom he is justified in exerting a certain personal authority, and in the few moments of his being at home or of his family-life, revenges himself for his social depression by the rough treatment or maltreatment of these beings. If to this, as is so frequently the case, drunkenness be added, the matter becomes still worse. The poor children grow up in constant anxiety, in want, under the most unfavorable conditions for life and health, and misguided by the constant spectacle of coarseness and evil.* Thus even in earliest youth the germ of intellectual and corporeal crippling is laid, and whatever of good Nature has still presevered in them is utterly lost when they are forced upon toilsome and wearing labor at an age when the children of the rich just begin really to enjoy their existence. Animal impulses, restrained by no moral counterpoise, and want of insight or of true family sentiment, also allow the families of the poor to become generally much more numerous than those of the rich, and thus the wretchedness of the rising generation is incalculably increased. But our existing system of police, which employs such great means to manifest a hypocritical care for the bare life of those under it, and which sends a poor girl, who in her shame and despair has got rid of her illegitimate child, to the house of correction for many years, makes no enquiry whether and how a great, perhaps the greater part of its future citizens are maltreated both corporeally and intellectually in their childish days, and regards them merely as the property of

---

*Suicides, as is well known, are very rare among children. Nevertheless Dūrand-Fardel has ascertained that between the years 1835 and 1844 no fewer than 192 suicides took place in France, and of these *132 were on account of ill treatment by parents.*

their parents, who are just as likely to rear their child into a monster as into a good citizen. But if the monster is there against our will, the christian state, raised upon the foundations of true morality, is also at hand, to punish the unfortunate victim with chains and dungeon — with sword and rack — for its own guilt !

No one who is acquainted with these circumstances and who has had the opportunity of seeing with his own eyes what a cradle of misery and despair, of abomination and present and future crime the family in its bad form frequently if not generally conceals within it, will be inclined to deny that, at all events for the lowest strata of society, social education is far preferable to domestic, and that an infringement or limitation of this sort of family for the benefit of an education of youth, arranged and supervised by the state, can do no more to injure the principles of morality than those of sound reason.

But not only in the lowest classes of society, but also in its middle and even at its highest point the family is unfortunately only too often a school of despotism or of evil, and rather the tomb than the cradle of good ; and this is especially the case when the chief of the family has a defective character or a bad disposition, or when by misfortunes, disappointments and so forth he is driven to desperate courses, or finally when the harmony between husband and wife, which is so necessary for the existence of a good family, is wanting. It is true that in what is called good society one does not generally have much experience of these things, but the frightful family-tragedies, which from time to time are brought to the light of publicity by peculiar circumstances, allow us to conclude that much is concealed and kept secret. But even where there is nothing of this kind in the case, and in what are regarded as good families, family life does not always exert a strengthening influence upon the nervous system and upon the character, and the numerous hysterical, anæmic and nervous ladies, and the great number of men with no energy and with feeble characters, furnish evidence by no means in favor of our family-education. Taken for all in all a good, prosperous, rightly and rationally conducted family may cause all other systems of bringing up to appear superfluous for its members ; but in the same degree that such families are rare, the value of the family-principle as such is depressed, and in opposition to it the value of a social or governmental system of education rises.   Even if the state were to leave out of account all high moral considerations and entirely neglect the principle of political humanity, it must merely from economical or selfish grounds turn its greatest attention to that which will form the subject of the following section, namely, education.

EDUCATION.

BOTH duty and interest prescribe to the government of the future to turn its chief attention to a general, uniform system of popular education, such as may satisfy the claims of the present state of knowledge. *Duty*, because as we have seen, every man brings with him an equal right not merely to the material but also to the intellectual possessions of mankind or *in specie* of his people, and because he can victoriously support his struggle for existence only when he treads the stage of life furnished with the most necessary means of cultivation of his time; *Interest*, because nothing can be better for the state than if by giving a good education to the people and by leading them to what is good, its enormous expenditure for barracks, prisons, police, and the administration of criminal law, may be rendered for the most part unnecessary.

The theory of the Manchester men would withdraw every thing which does not relate to the protection of person and property from the charge of the state, and leave it to private activity; but how little it has proved itself in respect to the important matter of popular education is shown by England, the classic land of personal liberty, where the rudeness and want of culture of the lower ranks of the people have reached such a frightful pass, that at present the agitation for the introduction of general and compulsory school-education, after the continental and especially the German pattern, has become universal there. On the peoples' school depends the whole future of the state and of humanity; and whoever, in a given state, could make sure of holding firmly in his hand the Ministry of education for twenty or thirty years, might answer for every possible change in that state in the direction of culture, freedom and progress. By education everything good may be made of man and especially of the average man; by the want of it every thing bad. That crimes against the laws of the state or of society are for the most part just as much the result of defective culture or perverted education, as necessary consequences of the general distresses of society, is a fact too well known and recognized to need more than a brief indication. Criminals are therefore as a rule rather unfortunate than detestable, and a future, better time will look back upon the criminal processes of our day with the same feelings with which we now regard the political trials or witchcraft processes of the past. In the same proportion as culture, prosperity and morals advance, we know by experience that crime decreases; it will probably disappear in time altogether, with the exception of a scanty residue, just like the former great epidemic diseases. Crime in political life, is nothing more than disease in physical life; and just as in medicine and in public sanitary administration we have gradually come to see that it is better and more advantageous to prevent diseases than to oppose them after they have broken out, so in the life of the state we shall learn that it is better to prevent crime by rational arrangements or to suppress it at its origin, than to fight against it with fire and sword when it has been produced. Make your arrangements good and wise, O ye rulers of the state, and then men will become also good and wise!

As regards the education or instruction itself, it need scarcely be remarked, in the face of the requirements so often and so pressingly made by all liberal parties and in accordance with the principles established by us, that general, obligatory and gratuitous instruction in national schools until the attainment of a certain age is the least that can be demanded in this respect, whilst the higher educational institutions must at least be open gratuitously for all those who are willing to make use of them. That the fostering of science as such must also form one of the principal tasks of the state, and especially of the state of the future, is a matter of course, although this must be effected in a different way than by our existing Universities and higher educational institutions, which have gradually fallen from their former elevation as nurseries of free science, and become more or less mere training institutions for the learned professions, and especially for future compliant tools of the mechanism of government.*

Moreover, it is not sufficient merely to care for education during the period of youth ; time and opportunity must also be given to the grown-up man to continue his intellectual development and to take part, at least to a certain extent, in the great intellectual acquisitions of his time. This applies especially to the true working classes, who after the termination of their school-time under present circumstances usually escape entirely from the course of culture of their time, and allow the man to rise or sink almost completely into the workman. But in a humanely organized state every one should be and remain a man ; and this can be effected for the working classes only by a legal diminution of the hours of labor and the establishment of a normal working day by the state.† The hours thus daily set free for the workman would give him the opportunity to cultivate his knowledge, to learn to understand the time in which he lives, to enjoy suitable and intellectual pleasures,— in a word to live as a man and not as a mere working machine or beast of burden.

The attention of the state ought to be devoted not only to the intellectual but also to the bodily education of those who belong to it, and to the protection of the rising generation from premature crippling of the body. The sins that are still com-

* See Appendix No. 50.   † See Appendix No. 51.

mitted in this particular, partly by action, partly by neglect, are so indescribably numerous and great that we might fill volumes with their description. Here, again, nothing but social education and governmental supervision can help us. It is a statistically proved and truly horrible fact that the duration of life in the lower ranks of society, especially the working classes, is generally only half or two-thirds of that which the higher ranks enjoy, so that by the present condition of society the former are cheated out of nearly half their normal life. The cause of this sad phenomenon lies in the infinite deficiencies both of public and private sanitary measures, in the neglect of corporeal education during youth, and in the disregard of the bodily welfare of the working classes during their subsequent life. In improving these conditions, the legal abridgment of the time of labor and the alternation of work and recreation thereby afforded, will have the most beneficial consequences.

WOMAN.

IT is a fact historically proved that the estimation of and respect for woman in human society have increased in the
same proportion that the degree of general culture and good
manners has been elevated. In like manner in the present day
we find that the position of woman is the more creditable the
higher the degree of culture in the nation, whilst among savage
tribes she still occupies that lowest grade as the slave and beast
of burden of the stronger sex, which was quite universally assigned to her at the dawn of civilization, and among half-civilized
peoples (for example, in the East) she occupies only the somewhat better position of a half-slave. Even this single fact
might suffice to indicate the way on which the position of
woman has to advance in the future, and to show how a man
belonging to a civilized nation and himself laying claim to culture, has to act towards her. "We men," as Radenhausen
well says (*Isis*, Band III. p. 100), "must accustom ourselves
to regard and treat the female half of mankind not as agents
for the service and gratification of the men, but as our equals."

There is indeed not the slightest visible reason why the principle of equal legal rights, which is at present so generally recognized, should not also be extended to the female half of the
human race. The duties and performances that woman has to
fulfill in the organism of human society do not yield either in
importance or in difficulty to those of the men, and these performances might be increased far beyond their present measure
if only a larger and freer field were opened to the activity of

women.   Even if women, as many suppose, cannot in general compete with men in the force and elevation of their performances, this is no reason from cutting them off from competition, and thus injuring them in the general struggle for existence more than they are already injured by their weaker nature. Moreover, even after the removal of all barriers, this very struggle for existence will furnish the best security that woman shall not overstep the range of activity assigned to her by nature, and all-powerful custom will do more than any police-regulations to keep sensitive women aloof from such things or spheres to which they are not equal or fitted.   There are indeed many branches of human activity for which women are as well fitted as men, if not better, such as agriculture, cattle-farming, gardening, watchmaking, weaving, needlework and the like, also setting up type, post office work, book-keeping, management of money, authorship, etc., etc.   All kinds of arts and even sciences, teaching, medicine, care of the poor and sick, the bringing up of children and so forth, also very frequently find their most distinguished representatives in women.   That they do not always perform so much as men is due not merely to their weaker nature or to their smaller capability of work, but equally, or perhaps even more, to their defective education and depressed social position.   Free women from this depressed position, give them the education and culture necessary for life, and we shall see what they are able to perform when placed on an equality with men politically and socially.— Whether this be much or little, it can only be for the advantage of the community if by increased rivalry the zeal of competition is increased on both sides, and so great an amount of working power, hitherto lying idle, is supplied to Society.   But the least that woman, as such, can demand for herself is, that the course may at least be left free to her on which to try competition with the stronger sex.

"At any rate," as Radenhausen well says, "the female half

has a right to demand permission to try its capabilities for the advancement of humanity in every branch of activity, and that the path to culture which stands open to the male half, should also be opened to it." If this male half or the so-called stronger sex *fears* this competition and seeks to get rid of it by despotic regulations, this is the best proof that in reality woman and her capabilities of performance are more highly estimated than would generally appear, and that this sex cannot resolve to resign the cherished habit of ruling and oppressing.

The position of mitigated slavery which woman even now generally occupies with respect to man, is merely a residue from that barbarous period when the stronger man harnessed the weaker woman to the plough, in spite of her less bodily powers, and set her to perform all labors of the most difficult and humiliating kind, whilst he himself reposed upon his bear-skin; and when the Europeans of the present day exclude women from so many branches of useful activity on the plea that their nature is not adapted for them, this logic resembles the well-known slave-law, which denies to slaves and oppressed people generally the capacity for freedom, and in accordance with this also (in the interest of the oppressor) freedom itself. If it be really true that woman does not possess the capabilities which would entitle her to a position in life equal to that of man, and that she is not able to acquire it, her social position would not be essentially altered in spite of all emancipation. Thus it would only depend upon an experiment, quite free from danger in itself, to ascertain whether the above-mentioned supposition is correct or not.

The objections which have been raised to the so-called emancipation of women, or in other words to their political and social equalization with men, are generally of so untenable a kind that it requires some little self-command on the part of a candid author to argue against them. The commonest and most frequent objection is that woman in her whole nature is intended for domestic life, for the family, for bringing up children and so forth, and that this true destination of woman must be prejudiced by her partaking in public or social affairs or in any other kind of activity. This objection overlooks the essential point on which the whole question turns, and presupposes, quite erroneously, that the object of the emancipation of woman is to tear her from her natural sphere of action or her household duties and to fling her unnecessarily into the business of the great world. No woman who possesses a family and a domestic sphere of action and finds in this activity satisfaction for her mental or moral faculties, will allow herself to be disturbed in this activity or kept away from it by emancipation, whilst that very great number of women who do not possess such a sphere of action or do not find their lives fully occupied by it, suffer the heaviest privation in the want of this freedom, and find themselves condemned *against* their will to a mental or bodily inactivity which often becomes the source of the most serious evils. How many women pine away or deteriorate, sometimes bodily, sometimes intellectually and both in and out of wedlock, under the deadening pressure of a constant idleness which is imposed upon them by an imaginary regard for their position, or by compulsory sloth and inaction! The innate impulse to action then finally breaks out in a love of gossip or dress which ruins the character, and in all sorts of frivolities and absurdities which justly lowers the female sex in the eyes of intelligent men. On the contrary, a woman who has learnt culture and work and is consequently in a position to exert a profitable activity in life, will keep aloof from such follies ; she will not be compelled to speculate only upon marriage and to give her hand to the first comer, often without affection, merely for the sake of being married ; if unmarried she will not feel unhappy through her whole life; and if married she will stand by the side of her husband in quite another fashion than hitherto. Hand in hand with him, not as his servant or as a friend entirely dependent upon him, but as his free and equal companion, she will pass with him through life, and be able in case of need, to take care of herself and her children even without him; whilst, at present, as a general rule, the death of the provider throws the whole family into the always open arms of indigence.

It is an extremely absurd and truly pedantic assertion, that culture and work strip the nimbus of womanhood from woman, and that intellectually developed and independent women are not capable of a true devotion to their husbands. The precise contrary to this is the truth, and there can certainly be no better means of elevating marriage and family-life in general than the emancipation of woman to work, acquisition and culture. The mere consciousness of being unable to support herself, and that she must be all her life long a burden upon her husband or her father, causes a feeling of depression in a woman, which is the greater in proportion as she is sensible and cultivated, and destroys that contentment which is so necessary to happy family-life. "The pure twilight of home," so often referred to, in which alone true womanhood is supposed to thrive and which has been so keenly ridiculed by Fanny Lewald, is merely a great superstition, and is an anachronism in our time of universal striving after freedom and light. If it were not so, "the pure twilight of home" in combination with "true womanhood" would be best found in the harems of Turkish magnates!

With all this indeed it cannot and must not be denied that the majority of women will always and under all circumstances seek and find their true task in life in marriage and domestic cares, although, as has been said, even the wife and mother will essentially improve her own position and that of her family by a greater amount of culture and independence. But because this is the case, shall all those women who do not reach this goal or do not wish to reach it, be forever depressed and condemned to compulsory inactivity? Shall genius and intelligence become of no consequence, merely because they happen to have taken up their abode in a female brain ?   Shall talents and capabilities remain undeveloped merely because a woman possesses them ? and shall the impulse to activity and business be allowed to waste without benefit to mankind merely because they do not appear in the form of a man?   History teaches us incontestibly that there have been among women savants, artists, politicians, &c., as great as among men ; and if their number is small in comparison with the men this is due in part to the natural destination of woman to a more limited sphere of activity, and in part to the want of freedom and equality, as also of the necessary previous cultivation.   Even in the dissimilar education of the two sexes in youth there is an infinite injustice and injury to the woman, to marriage and to the family which cannot afterwards be made good.   A cultivated woman is as great a blessing to the house, as an uncultivated one may be a curse !

It is true that from the scientific or physiological side a weighty objection has been attempted to be raised against the cultivability of woman in comparison to that of man, by reference to the fact that the brain of women is considerably inferior in size to that of man.   This objection sounds curious enough in the mouth of those who in all other things reject the application of materialistic principles, but do not disdain them here, when they can make an advantageous use of them ; but as the fact itself is indubitable, we must accept the consequences deduced from it, if these rest upon correct suppositions.   This, however, is by no means the case.   For in the first place, the smaller stature and weaker muscular development of women, as well as the smaller diameter of the nervous threads which converge in the central parts of the nervous system, quite naturally cause the total mass of the female brain to be comparatively smaller, without necessarily causing the development or energy of the parts of the brain devoted to the intellectual functions to suffer.   In the second place, even if it could be demonstrated that these parts remain in their development behind those of man, this may just as well be ascribed to defective exercise and cultivation, as to an original deficiency. For it is well-known that every organ of the body, and, therefore, also the brain, requires for its full development, and consequently for the development of its complete capability of performance, exercise and persistent effort. That this is and has been the case for thousands of years in a far less degree in woman than in man, in consequence of her defective training and education, will be denied by no one.— Woman, therefore, should not be allowed to suffer under the consequences of a condition of things of which she is entirely innocent,— we should rather seek to cultivate her natural talents to such a degree and in such a manner that she may lose the taste for miserable gossip and finery, and find a pleasure in turning her mind to more serious and useful matters than hitherto. When once this has been effected we shall be in a position, without injury to the community, to confer upon women these political rights which the most advanced among them even now demand for their sex, and their possession of which will place them with regard to their rights on a perfect equality with men. Finally, in confuting this objection a point must not be forgotten to which attention cannot be too often called, namely, that the estimation of the intellectual value of a brain depends not merely upon its size or material bulk, but equally, if not even more, upon its internal constitution and the finer development of its individual parts, and that it is perfectly conceivable that the female brain as regards this fineness and in accordance with the greater fineness and delicacy of the female body generally, may exceed the male brain in the same proportion as the latter exceeds the female brain in its development in size.

The greatest stumbling-block to men has probably been the requirement of equality in political rights on the part of women desirous of emancipation, and in fact *under the circumstances which still prevail* any such experiment must be rather hazardous and extremely dangerous to freedom and progress. Not that we would wish to say that women might not be good politicians! On the contrary, history teaches us most clearly that there have been almost as many *good* politicians among women, as *bad* ones among men.

Even now in political (and other) respects, how many men are more effeminate and greater gossips than the women themselves, and would be more appropriately seated by the hearth or the spinning wheel than in the grave councils of the men! And what comparison can be drawn between the political insight of a cultivated woman, acquainted with the necessities of her time, and that which may perhaps be possessed by a footman or a shoe-black, who has never·looked beyond the narrow circle of his humble daily occupation!

And, nevertheless, this man possesses the suffrage, and by its means takes part in the settlement of the destiny of his nation, whilst the intelligent and highly cultivated woman is esteemed incapable of exercising any such right! But all this applies only in individual cases, and on the whole the still prevalent intellectual immaturity and want of discretion of the female sex, and especially its weakness in respect to *religion*, makes its complete political emancipation appear impracticable, until the indispensably necessary conditions of education and culture, or of uniformity in the advancement of the two sexes, shall have been fulfilled. Almost all experienced politicians agree that the immediate granting of the universal suffrage to women would be equivalent to a political and religious retrogression, which would of course be even much less desired by free-thinking women, and especially by the female leaders of the movement, than by men of democratic opinions. Indeed one of our most prominent authoresses, the equally witty and thoughtful Fanny Lewald, has been led by this circumstance to declare herself against the extension of the suffrage to women at present, and to formulate the requirements of female emancipation as follows :

" Instruction for the ignorant and lowly, and recognition for intellectually matured women !"—a formula to which the author adheres with all his heart !*

* All this of course does not apply to the right of women to the suffrage in *principle*, which we maintain most decidedly, but only regard as practicable when women shall have attained a position of equality with men in life, culture and power of performance. Many opponents of the emancipation of woman have made the absurd objection, that with the exercise of universal suffrage women would also be compelled to do military service like men ; but they have not considered that in consistently following out this principle all weak or crippled men or in general all those not capable of military service ought to be deprived of the suffrage. In her own way and in proportion to her powers woman performs just the same if not greater services to the state than man, and must give up as a sacrifice to the war-god not only the sons whom she has borne and brought up to man's estate, but also her brothers and her husband, and undertake the care of those who are left behind. What unlimited sacrifices women are capable of during times of war, in the care of the sick, providing for the maintenance of the soldier, &c., as also in direct participation in the defence of their country and hearth, are too well-known to render more than this reference to them necessary. But this requirement appears most absurd when we consider that even among healthy men only a comparatively small number usually perform actual military service ; and that those especially who possess and exert the most political influence are precisely those who have never carried a gun ; whilst, on the other hand, the young men capable of bearing arms, who are usually recruited from the rural population, serve at a time when their age denies them any legal participation in the exertion of the general political rights. In time of war, as is well-known, every participation of the armies in the field in political matters entirely ceases.

MARRIAGE.

M ARRIAGE, although it occurs also in animals (*e. g.*, the Storks), is nevertheless in its present form and conception essentially a product of human culture. It is therefore nothing rigid and unalterable, nothing given once for all by nature, but must change and advance with the increase of culture. For our marriage of the present day this is all the more necessary, as in it the old principles of compulsion which formerly ruled in state, church and society, are still fully represented. For the progress of true humanity in the state and society scarcely any thing, however, can be more efficacious than the liberation of marriage from these narrowing bars, and its conversion into a proper relation of the two sexes, brought about by a free and unconstrained choice on both sides and dependent for its permanence upon the continuance of mutual rectitude and affection. In a certain sense it must be admitted that the whole physical and intellectual future of the human race depends more or less upon the future form of marriage. For although the union of the best with the best, as in Plato's ideal State, would not answer, the union of the most suitable with the most suitable will be the right method to produce the best possible race in the future.

Darwin has already recognized what he calls sexual selection as a mainspring of progress in animals, and Prof. Hæckel does not hesitate to declare on the strength of his investigations, that the progress of the human race in history is in great part

the consequence of sexual selection, which is developed to a
far greater extent in man than in animals.   But it cannot well
be disputed that this peculiar element, which has only been
brought to light by Natural History, can unfold its entire and
most important efficacy fully and unobstructedly only when the
union of the sexes is really the consequence of a perfectly free
choice, and of a full mutual agreement with mutual liking and
internal satisfaction.   In contrast to this our present conventional and constrained marriage, as is well known, only too
frequently presents mutual discords and incurable dissatisfac-
tion of the most repulsive character, which is most injurious to
the progress of the race.   Even the emancipation of woman
that we have urged, and her freer and more independent position
with regard to man, will constitute a necessary condition for a
different form of marriage in the future, and the free love-
choice, which has hitherto, contrary to all justice and reason,
been allowed only to the man, must in future form equally a
right of the maiden.   The young woman, having become independent, will no longer find it necessary to allow herself to be
treated like merchandise in the market, or under a half-com-
pulsion to seize upon any marriage that may be offered to her
merely to escape the melancholy state of spinsterhood ; but she
will take the vows only when the married life seems to promise
to her or her advisers greater happiness and greater satisfaction
than the single one.   The number of unhappy marriages,
prejudicial to the progress of the race, which, unfortunately, is
now so great, will then diminish, and that of the happy and beneficial ones will increase.   But where, in spite of this, a disap-
pointment may occur, the necessary facilitation of legal separation will render impossible the repetition of those frightful
domestic dramas, which nowadays, to the shame of humanity,
are so often displayed before our courts of justice.   From the
individual horrors which attain publicity, we may judge of the

many still greater horrors which are borne silently and patiently in concealment, from dread of public shame. Freedom, free-will and perfect reciprocity form the vital air in which alone happy marriages can thrive ; and this leads of necessity to the removal of all artificial obstacles which can be opposed either to the conclusion of marriages, or to the dissolution of those for which a just cause is shown.

Among the most foolish contrivances of political wisdom or political stupidity are the obstacles which in many states are still opposed to marriages in the lower classes, especially the laboring classes, in fear of over-population or the increase of poverty, even leaving quite out of consideration the fact that it implies the greatest and hardest of all injustices to render the unmerited poverty of the individual still harder and more sensible by seeking to shut him off compulsorily from the most natural of human impulses, that of the propagation of his kind. By the increase of its numbers a people becomes not poorer but richer, especially where improved social arrangements make it possible for every one to lead an existence worthy of humanity ; and every new born human-being is a capital which benefits the whole by augmentation of the power both of work and of consumption. The less populated a district is, the poorer it also is and the more miserable is the condition of its inhabitants ; whilst, on the contrary, in the European civilized countries the general degree of prosperity has everywhere risen with a corresponding increase of the population. For there can be no doubt that by the increase of cultivation and its innumerable aids, by increased division of labor and so forth, the general capability of subsistence increases in a much higher degree than the number of people ; and although it must be admitted that under normal conditions a certain limit to the number of the population cannot be overstepped, we are still very far from the attainment of this limit. Great famines occur most readily in thinly peopled regions, or in such as have been depopulated by war, pestilence, &c.; whilst the excess of means of nourishment is nowhere greater than in the enormous capitals of European states, in which millions of men live together upon one spot. When the Spaniards conquered America they found that its population was decimated by frequent famines;—at the present day America furnishes abundant nourishment for a far greater number of inhabitants, and still possesses space and food enough for untold millions !

MORALS.

THE only correct and tenable moral principle depends upon the relation of *reciprocity*. There is therefore no better guide to moral conduct than the old and well-known proverb : "What you would not have done to you, that to others never do." If we complete this proverb with the addition : "Do to others as you would they should do to you," we have the entire code of virtue and morals in hand, and indeed in a better and simpler form than could be furnished us by the thickest manuals of ethics, or the quintessence of all the religious systems in the world.

All other moral instructions whether derived from the conscience, from religion, or from philosophy, are perfectly superfluous in the presence of these simple and practical rules. Of course these rules must become more and more efficacious the higher the condition of reciprocity is developed by the greater advance of the social state, and the more the individual, by intelligence and culture, is rendered capable of comprehending the objects of society and his personal relation thereto, and of arranging his conduct accordingly. It is therefore a generally recognized fact, and moreover sufficiently proved by history, that the idea of morality in general as in particular cases becomes further and more strongly developed in proportion as culture, intelligence and knowledge of the necessary laws of the common weal increase, and that, in accordance with this, greater public order has always gone hand in hand with alleviation of the criminal laws.

(254)

As an individual, or as primitive man, man is entirely unacquainted with morals, and blindly follows the impulses of the passions, the hunger, the cruelty, etc., which he has in common with the animals. His moral properties are only developed by living together with others in a society regulated by certain principles of reciprocity, and by the knowledge of the laws which are necessary for the existence of such a community. The innate conscience or law of morals which so many regard as the true determining principle in the actions of men, is nothing more than a great superstition, an "Infant-school morality," as the philosopher Schopenhauer so significantly expresses it. For the conscience is formed and developed only with the progressive knowledge of the duties which the individual has to fulfill, or thinks he must fulfill towards imaginary supernatural powers (such as Gods, Heroes, etc.), towards his fellow-men, towards society, the state and so forth. This belief, however, is entirely dependent on the grade of general culture or knowledge at which a people or an individual may be at any given time, and is therefore variable according to time, place and circumstances. Moses, the greatest teacher and leader of the Jewish people, felt no stings of conscience when he allowed three thousand of his people to be cut to pieces as a propitiatory offering to the Lord, but only feared that they would not be sufficient, whilst nowadays such a proceeding would be regarded as inexpressibly horrible and brutal ; and the honored David, the darling of all theologians, when he conquered the city of Rabbah (2 *Sam.* XII. 31) "brought forth the people that were therein, and put them under saws, and under harrows of iron, and under axes of iron, and made them pass through the brick-kiln : and thus did he unto all the cities of the children of Ammon"—(cited in Radenhausen, *Isis*, Band II. p. 34). The Phœnicians, Carthaginians, Persians, etc., although belonging to the *civilized* nations of antiquity were not deterred by their conscience from burning their own children alive or burying living innocent men ; and the Inquisitors of the Middle ages and their associates of earlier and later times believed that they were only fulfilling their duty in burning about *nine millions* of people as witches and magicians in the course of eleven centuries, and making so many other innocent people suffer under the most horrible tortures. When the Roman emperors visited the newly formed Christian communities with the bloodiest persecutions, they believed that they were doing good, and that their consciences were clear, just as much as the later Christians themselves when, after their doctrine had become victorious, they revisited all these persecutions and outrages in the most ample measure upon those who thought differently from themselves. The murderous wars of modern times also, arising frequently from the most inconsiderable causes, are generally waged by people who feel not the smallest scruple as to the terrible death and misery of so many thousands caused by them, and who win· by them fame, honor and consideration, whilst in a future and happier time such proceedings will probably be regarded as the gravest moral crimes.

Conscience is therefore nothing established and innate, but rather something variable and acquired, or an expression of human knowledge which advances with knowledge itself. This advancing knowledge has caused the recognition of many things as innocent or permissible which formerly passed as grave sins, and on the other hand has converted many things into sins or crimes which formerly were not so regarded ; and hence also as is well known the ideas of *good* and *evil* present the greatest and most striking differences, nay even complete contradictions, at different times and among different peoples, all of which would be entirely impossible if the innate conscience of man were conferred upon him as an internal prescription binding him for all times. Conscience is also quite independent of the belief in God and of religious conceptions in general ; it changes little, if at all, in accordance with particular creeds, but merely accommodates itself to the knowledge or degree of culture of each individual. Hence also all apprehension that conscience may be lost with some determinate form of faith is entirely unfounded ; on the contrary, it must become sharpened and refined the more the general conscience of mankind is elevated by the advance of culture, and the more independent mankind becomes in thought and being of all merely external rules and dogmas. Indeed the men of the present day, although their attachment to definite rules of faith is far inferior to that of the men of former times, are in general much less inclined than formerly to crimes and acts of violence !—and tolerance, pity, sense of the public good, respect for law, philanthropy, etc., have increased in the same proportion with knowledge, culture and prosperity ! Next to *culture*, happiness and prosperity are the main sources of morality and virtue. Man must be happy in his general condition if he is to be virtuous, and all sins and crimes go hand in hand with starvation, misery, disease or idleness. If we add to this that moral qualities or tendencies are *heritable*, just as much as corporeal and intellectual tendencies in general, it must become clear that the whole moral progress of mankind is founded upon its constant social and intellectual change and advance, and that sin and crime will disappear from the world as soon as the springs of ignorance, want of culture and material misery, which still flow so abundantly, shall be stopped.

Morality may therefore be defined as the law of mutual respect for the general and private equal rights of man, for the purpose of securing general human happiness. Every thing that injures or undermines this happiness and this respect is *evil*,— every thing that advances them is *good*. In accordance with this definition, evil consists only in degeneracy or the encroachment of human and private egotism upon this general happiness and the interests of the fellow man. What is beneficial to the community or to the fellow man is in general good ;

and the notion of good only becomes converted into its opposite by the individual improperly placing the notion of that
which is beneficial or advantageous to himself above the notion
of that which is beneficial to the community or to another person of equal rights with himself.   The greatest sinners therefore
are egotists, or those who place their own *I* higher than the interests and laws of the common weal, and endeavor to satisfy it
at the cost and to the injury of those possessing equal rights.
This egotism in itself is indeed not objectionable, and really
forms the final and highest spring of all our actions whether
bad·or good.*   Moreover we shall never be able to get rid of
the egotism of human nature, and therefore all that we have to
do is to turn it into the right paths or to render it rational and
humane, by seeking to bring its satisfaction into accordance
with the good of all and the interest of the community.   And
for this purpose there can be no better means than the reform
of human society in the interest of the common weal proposed
by us.   For as soon as, by a proper organization of society,
things have been brought to such a pass that the satisfaction
of the personal *I* at the same time satisfies the interests of
the community, and that *vice versa* the satisfaction of the general interests at the same time implies the satisfaction of the
personal *I*, every conflict arising from egotistical motives between the interests of the individual and those of the Society
or of the State will cease, and the principal cause of crime
and sin will be removed.   The individual will then, much
more easily than at present, be able to strive after personal
happiness and agreeable sensations, or to satisfy his personal
I, without injury to the interests of human society ; he will
only advance his own well-being when he furthers that of
the community, and will advance the well-being of the community in advancing his own.

In this accordance of the interests of the individual with the

* See Appendix No. 52.

interests of the community or of all others, therefore, lies the whole, great moral principle of the future. Let this accordance be once established and we have morality, virtue and noble sentiments in profusion. If not, these will be deficient in proportion as society falls short of this goal, and no external or internal means, no religion, no moral preachers, no criminal laws, will be able by any means permanently to make up for this deficiency. *Public conscience is at the same time the conscience of the individual;* this public conscience can only be the consequence of rational political and social conditions and of an education and culture of all, founded on the principles of universal philanthrophy. It is in youth with its capability of education and culture and its ready accessibility to all external and internal impressions that the foundation for the culture of this conscience and therefore of all morality must be laid ; and it must be the highest task of public and general education to waken and strengthen in the young those impulses and talents which are good and beneficial to human society, and to weaken and suppress the bad and injurious ones. In this way a perfectly new race with a different moral organization will gradually be produced ; and crime, sin, vice and the like will disappear in proportion as the soil shall become smaller upon which alone they can thrive !

RELIGION.

THE less man knows of history, of nature, of philosophy and so forth, the more, when he has once begun to meditate upon himself and the phenomena surrounding him, does he feel induced to believe in unknown supernatural and superhuman influences, and to ascribe to them everything that appears to him mysterious in the life of nature and of man. Hence the more religious a man is, the less does he feel in himself the necessity for culture and knowledge; and the ancient Hebrews therefore could not develop among them arts and sciences in the same way as the more free-thinking Greeks, because with them their God Jehovah supplied everything. Nations commenced with the crudest superstitions springing from a deficiency or entire absence of knowledge of the laws of nature, and have risen gradually and slowly from this to that knowledge which is destined hereafter to replace and render unnecessary every kind of religion. Those who see in such an abolition of religion or in a replacement of faith by knowledge, danger to morality and virtue and consequently to the state and to society, must be taught that morals and religion, or faith and virtue, have originally and in principle nothing to do with each other, and have probably been commingled only in the course of history and for reasons of external expediency. For the higher we ascend in the history of religion, the more do we find that the moral law and the priesthood watching over its maintenance disappear from the scene, whilst their place is taken by dogma and external worship, or ceremonies in honor of the Deity.

The most recent investigations of Rénan, Bournouf and others place it beyond a doubt that among the Aryan nations morality never was an integral or necessary ingredient in religion, but that in their ancient religions only two elements are to be met with, namely, *the idea of God* and the *ritual.* This is also the case with the *priesthood* among the Aryans, whose original religious tendency was a decided *pantheism;* whilst in opposition to this the religious tendency of the Semites (from which Christianity has proceeded) was *monotheism*, and was under the charge of a powerful priesthood. In the whole Sanscrit language, the classical primitive language of the Aryan race of men, there is no single word which signifies "to create" in the sense of the Semitic or Christian dogma. Moreover, as Goethe has already shown, the celebrated Mosaic moral precepts, the so-called ten Commandments, were *not* upon the tables upon which Moses wrote the laws of the covenant which God made with his people.

Even the extraordinary diversity of the many religions diffused over the surface of the earth suffices to show that they can stand in no necessary connection with morals, as it is well-known that wherever tolerably well-ordered political and social conditions exist, the moral precepts in their essential principles are the same, whilst when such conditions are wanting, a wild and irregular confusion or even an entire deficiency of moral notions is met with.* History also shows incontrovertibly that religion and morality have by no means gone hand in hand in strength and development, but that even contrariwise the most religious times and countries have produced the greatest number of crimes and sins against the laws of morality, and indeed, as

---

* In China where people are, as is well-known, very indifferent or tolerant in religious matters, this fine proverb is current : — "Religions are various, but reason is one, and we are all brothers."

daily experience teaches, still produce them. The history of nearly all religions is filled with such horrible abominations, massacres and boundless wickedness of every kind that at the mere recollection of them the heart of a philanthropist seems to stand still, and we turn with disgust and horror from a mental aberration which could produce such deeds. If it is urged in vindication of religion that it has advanced and elevated human civilization, even this merit appears very doubtful in presence of the facts of history, and at least as very rarely or isolatedly the case. In general, however, it cannot be denied that most systems of religions have proved rather inimical than friendly to civilization. For religion, as already stated, tolerates no doubt, no discussion, no contradiction, no investigations — those eternal pioneers of the future of science and intellect! Even the simple circumstance, that our present state of culture has already long since left far behind it all and even the highest intellectual ideas established and elaborated by former religions, may show how little intellectual progress is influenced by religion. Mankind is perpetually being thrown to and fro between science and religion, but it advances more intellectually, morally and physically in proportion as it turns away from religion and to science.

It is therefore clear that for our present age and for the future, a foundation must be sought and found for culture and morality different from that which can be furnished to us by religion. It is not the fear of God that acts amelioratingly or ennoblingly upon manners, of which the middle ages furnish us with a striking proof; but the ennobling of the conception of the world in general which goes hand in hand with the advance of civilization. Let us then give up making a show of the profession of hypocritical words of faith, the only purpose of which seems to be that they may be continually shown to be lies by the actions and deeds of their professors! The man of the future will feel far more happy and contented when he has not to contend at every step of his intellectual forward development with those tormenting contradictions between knowledge and faith which plague his youth, and occupy his mature age unnecessarily with the slow renunciation of the notions which he imbibed in his youth. What we sacrifice to God, we take away from mankind, and absorb a great part of his best intellectual powers in the pursuit of an unattainable goal. At any rate, the least that we can expect in this respect from the state and society of the future is a complete separation between ecclesiastical and worldly affairs, or an absolute emancipation of the State and the school from every ecclesiastical influence. Education must be founded upon *knowledge*, not upon *faith ;* and religion itself should be taught in the public schools only as religious history, and as an objective or scientific exposition of the different religious systems prevailing among mankind. Any one who, after such an education, still experiences the need of a definite law or rule of faith may then attach himself to any religious sect that may seem good to him, but cannot claim that the community should bear the cost of this special fancy !

As regards Christianity, or the *Paulinism** which is falsely

---

* Jesus or Jeshua, called Christ, was not and did not desire to be the founder of a new religion and least of all of a world-religion, although millions and millions of men have regarded and still regard him as such. He was merely a Jewish religious reformer, and his original doctrine is neither more nor less than an improved and purified Judaism. His whole efforts were in the direction of the religious sect of the Essenes, from which he arose, and were directed to get rid of, or repress those externals which were then so highly valued and to render religion more internal. Moreover after the death of Jesus the first community of Christians still lived quite in the Jewish fashion, observed the Sabbath and the Jewish laws, practised circumcision and respected Jerusalem and the Temple. It was Saul of Tarsus, afterwards called Paul, originally the most zealous persecutor of the Jewish Christians, but afterwards converted, who first made out of Christianity an opposition to Judaism and gave it great extension by his travels and indefatigable activity. Nevertheless the original pure doctrine was continued among the Jewish Christians as what is called *Petrinism*, which remained strictly faithful to the teachings of the master, but very soon came near its end with the fall of Judaism, and was completely suppressed by the gradually developing *Paulinism* or religion of the *Gentile Christians*, who hated and despised the Jews and their doctrine. This Paulinism speedily ruled the world. Paul is therefore the true founder of Christianity. (See for details the little work by R. W. Kunis: *Vernunft und Offenbarung*, Leipzig, 1870.)

called Christianity, it stands, by its dogmatic portion or contents in such striking and irreconcilable, nay, absolutely absurd contradiction with all the acquisitions and principles of modern science that its future tragical fate can only be a question of time. But even its ethical contents or its moral principles are in no way essentially distinguished above those of other peoples, and were equally well and in part better known to mankind even *before* its appearance. Not only in this respect, but also in its supposed character as the *world-religion** it is excelled by the much older and probably most widely diffused religious system in the world, the celebrated *Buddhism*, which recognizes neither the idea of a personal God, nor that of a personal duration, and nevertheless teaches an extremely pure, amiable and even ascetic morality. The doctrine of Zoroaster or Zarathrustra also, 1800 years B. C., taught the principles of humanity and toleration for those of different modes of thinking in a manner and purity which were unknown to the Semitic religions and especially to Christianity. Christianity originated and spread as is well-known at the time of a general decline of manners, and of very great moral and national corruption ; and its extraordinary success must be partly explained by the prev-

---

* Christianity is not a world-religion, although this is always estimated one of its chief merits. Thus, for example, it does not suit the East and makes no progress there at all, notwithstanding the greatest efforts of the missionaries, presenting in this a striking contrast to Islamism. The latter is constantly diffusing itself through Asia and Africa and is peculiarly a religion for nomadic and seminomadic tribes. Nearly half of Asia has gradually accepted Islamism, although no more can be said in its favor than in favor of Christianity as regards the advancement of civilization. The fathers of Islam themselves, the Arabs, are deeply depressed by it and have exchanged the former bravery, wisdom and noble or knightly sentiments of the pagan times for indolence and stolen enjoyments. Its character as a world-religion and its supposed preëminence over all religions is also belied by Christianity when, as in Persia, it is insinuated in isolated professors among other systems of culture and religion. Thus Count Gobineau reports, (*Les Religions et les Philosophies de l'Asia centrale*, Paris, 1866,) that Christians in Persia, whether Catholics or schismatics and heretics, possess all the vices of the Mussulman and are distinguished from him only by greater ignorance, more superstition and a profound disclination for progress or for any mental effort. On the other hand *freethinkers* are numerous and cultivated in Persia.

alence of a sort of intellectual and moral disease, which had
overpowered the spirits of men after the fall of the ancient civilization and under the demoralizing influence of the gradual
collapse of the great Roman empire.   But even at that time
those who stood intellectually high and looked deeply into
things, recognized the whole danger of this new turn of mind,
and it is very remarkable that the best and most benevolent of
the Roman emperors, such as Marcus Aurelius, Julian, etc.,
were the most zealous persecutors of Christianity, whilst it was
tolerated by the bad ones, such as Commodus, Heliogabalus,
etc.*   When it had gradually attained the superiority, one of
its first sins against the intellectual progress consisted in the
destruction by Christian fanaticism of the celebrated Library of
Alexandria, which contained all the intellectual treasures of antiquity,—an incalculable loss to science, which can never be
replaced.   It is usually asserted in praise of Christianity that in
the middle ages the Christian monasteries were the preservers
of science and literature, but even this is correct only in a very
limited sense, since boundless ignorance and rudeness generally
prevailed in the monasteries, and innumerable ecclesiastics could
not even read.   Valuable literary treasures on parchment contained in the libraries of the monasteries were destroyed, the
monks when they wanted money selling the books as parch-

* To the Romans, with their classical culture, the Jews and Christians appeared
to be *atheists;* for to imagine a simple Deity, incapable of being pictured or felt,
seemed to them to be a denying of God or a dark doctrine deprived of God.
The old idolatry was picturesque, full of life and beautiful, and its feasts were
feasts of joy and sociability.   The monotheistic religions, (Judaism, Christianity,
Islam,) are generally zelotic and intolerant and therefore inimical to progress,
culture and the sciences; whilst in paganism and polytheism there is an infinite
expansiveness and tolerance.   The Greeks and Romans saw in the Deities of
other peoples only their own over again, and therefore never thought of religious
persecution.   Nevertheless it cannot be denied that in a special religious point of
view Christianity must be regarded as an advance upon heathendom with its
absurd sacrificial services, inasmuch as it rendered the belief in God more internal
and intellectual.   But the crude sensualistic conception, which soon overpowered
Christianity in the course of its historical development, renders even this merit
doubtful, and certainly gives its defenders no right to declaim against scientific
materialism.

ment, or tearing out the leaves and writing psalms upon them. Frequently they entirely effaced the ancient classics, to make room for their foolish legends and homilies ; nay, the reading of the classics, such as Aristotle for example, was directly forbidden by papal decrees.

In New Spain christian fanaticism immediately destroyed whatever of arts and civilization existed among the natives, and that this was not inconsiderable is shown by the numerous monuments now in ruins which place beyond a doubt the former existence of a tolerably high degree of culture. But in the place of this not a trace of Christian civilization is now to be observed among the existing Indians, and the resident catholic clergy keep the Indians purposely in a state of the greatest ignorance and stupidity (see Richthofen, *Die Zustænde der Republic Mexico*, Berlin, 1854).

Thus Christianity has always acted consistently in accordance with the principles of one of the fathers of the Church, Tertullian, who says : "Desire of knowledge is no longer necessary since Jesus Christ, nor is investigation necessary since the Gospel." If the civilization of the European and especially of Christian nations has notwithstanding made such enormous progress in the course of centuries, an unprejudiced consideration of history can only tell us that this has taken place not *by means* of Christianity, but in spite of it. And this is a sufficient indication to what an extent this civilization must still be capable of development when once it shall be completely freed from the narrow bounds of old superstitions and religious embarrassments !

PHILOSOPHY.

JUST as the religions of the past have become out of date in
our time, so also in no less degree has the true or speculative philosophy, which has unfortunately, especially in Germany, so long exerted an injurious influence upon the minds
of men, and one prejudicial to the true, free spirit of inquiry.
Its play with half-clear, obscure or perfectly meaningless words
or phrases has gradually caused it to be detested by the educated,* and the belief in its formulas and predictions has disappeared in the same measure that the spirit of inquiry has become
clearer, more thirsty for knowledge and *more candid.* We are
now no longer inclined to take appearance for being, words for
acts, or imagination for reality ; and have perceived that it is
only in scientific observation and in facts that we can seek and
find a firm footing for philosophical theories. ''The empty
twaddle of *Sein* and *Nichts*,'' as B. Suhle (A. Schopenhauer
and the Philosophy of the present day) admirably designates
that so-called dialectic method of the philosophers by profession which was dominant in the first half of the present century,
and attained its climax in the great Hegel, — that ''Deluge of
words poured over a desert of ideas'' as Helvetius so suitably
described the results of the scholastic philosophy of the middle

* Since the times of Scholasticism, nay properly speaking since the times of
Plato and Aristotle, philosophy has been for the most part as Schopenhauer
admirably expresses it *a continual misapplication of general ideas carried too far*,
such as ''substance,'' ''basis,'' ''cause,'' ''the good,'' ''being,'' ''becoming,'' etc.,
etc., and has thus gradually sunk into a mere affair of words.

ages which is still far from being extinct, no longer imposes upon us ; we have looked behind the veil of the mystery and found nothing there except the effete skeleton of philosophical emptiness of spirit and thought, clothed with the motley rags of a philosophical terminology or mode of expression. There is not now and never was or will be a possibility of enlarging human knowledge beyond experience, or human philosophy beyond the conclusions drawn from experience.

The lofty intellectual flights of the professors of Philosophy, which have hitherto been universally esteemed as the highest, are therefore simply absurd, and the air of superiority of the philosophical metaphysicians reminds one of the proverb: "From the sublime to the ridiculous there is but a step" (Suhle). All deductions from the transcendental, or from what flies beyond observation, are illogical ; there is no such thing as the so-called transcendental science nor are there any causeless causes : hence the search of the philosophers after a first or supreme cause is entirely futile. Causal connection or the relation of cause and effect has neither beginning nor end. The necessary consequence of a *First* cause is the irrational assumption, equally contradictory to logic and observation, that the history of existence must consist of *two* different or separated parts, the first of which would be change *without* causality and the second change *with* causality. Every thing in the world is necessarily and normally connected, an opinion, the stability of which, however, we are in a position to demonstrate directly only in a number of cases in the actual world. Hence our knowledge is fragmentary and not only capable of but actually calling for improvement and completion ; whilst the philosophical error seeks to parade before us "unlimited knowledge." We must therefore endeavor to form convictions which are not to stand once and for all, as philosophers and theologians usually do, but such as may change and become improved with the advance of knowledge. Whoever does not recognize this and gives himself up once for all to a belief which he regards as final truth, whether it be of a *theological* or *philosophical* kind, is of course incapable of accepting a conviction supported upon scientific grounds. Unfortunately our whole education is founded upon an early systematic curbing and fettering of the intellect in the direction of dogmatic (philosophical or theological) doctrines of faith, and only a comparatively small number of strong minds succeed in after years in freeing themselves by their own powers from these fetters, whilst the majority remain captive in the accustomed bonds, and form their judgment in accordance with the celebrated saying of Bishop Berkeley: "Few men think; but all will have opinions!" Hence the numerous distorted or condemnatory opinions expressed as to recent advances in science, although the latter may be as clear as the sun and as indisputable as truth itself! Great philosophers have called *death* the fundamental cause of all philosophy. If this be correct, the empirical or experimental philosophy of the present day has solved the greatest of philosophical enigmas, and shown (both logically and empirically) that there is no death, and that the great mystery of existence consists in perpetual and uninterrupted *change*. Every thing is immortal and indestructible,—the smallest worm as well as the most enormous of the celestial bodies,—the sandgrain or the water-drop as well as the highest being in creation — man and his thoughts. Only the forms in which being manifests itself are changing; but Being itself remains eternally the same and imperishable. When we die we do not lose ourselves, but only our personal consciousness or the casual form which our being, in itself eternal and imperishable, had assumed for a short time; we live on in nature, in our race, in our children, in our descendants, in our deeds, in our thoughts,— in short, in the entire material and psychical contribution which, during our short personal existence, we have furnished to the subsistence of mankind and of nature in general. "Humanity," says

Radenhausen (*Isis*, Band III., p. 121), "persists and flows on although the individual disappears after a short course of life; but neither his life, nor that of the water-drop is lost. For just as the latter could not complete its circulation without dissolving or superinducing the combinations of other matters, so every man leaves the traces of his existence behind him in what he separated or brought into new combinations, in the contribution to the culture treasure of humanity, which is furnished by every human life, from the least to the greatest."

Where are the dead? asks Schopenhauer; and he answers: They are with us! In spite of death and corruption we are still all together!

Drum streitet, Thoren, ferner nicht,
Ob Ihr im Geist unsterblich seid!
Denn keines Todes Macht zerbricht
Der Dinge Unvergänglichkeit,
Die Alles was da ist und lebt,
In einem ew'gen Kreise führt
Und, wo sie zur Vernichtung strebt,
Die Flammen neuen Lebens schürt!
Unsterblich ist der kleinste Wurm,
Unsterblich auch des Menschen Geist,
Den jeder neue Todessturm
In immer neue Bahnen reisst!
So lebet Ihr, gestorben auch,
In künftigen Geschlechtern fort,
Und dieser ewige Gebrauch
Verwechselt nichts als Zeit und Ort!

Just as no single atom or smallest conceivable particle of matter can disappear or be destroyed in the life of nature in general, so not the smallest deed or most insignificant thought of a man can perish or be lost in the general life of mankind. For both propagate themselves in unending sequence, by virtue of the impulse given by them, just as the oscillations of the surface of a piece of water produced by a falling stone vibrate

onwards in constantly larger and weaker circles.   And although
this movement itself must by degrees be lost or come to rest
just like these oscillations, it has in the meanwhile set free a
certain number of other (physical or intellectual) movements,
which on their part renew and continue the same action.   Thus
the life of the individual is at the same time the life of humanity,
and the life of humanity that of the individual !   Whoever cannot or will not allow this great truth to suffice for him, whoever
is unable to find in it a sufficient impulse to virtue and honesty,
will also be incapable of being kept permanently in the right
path by any external force or agency.   Neither philosophical
nor religious creeds are capable of furnishing even distantly an
equivalent for it, or of replacing by means of their mixed egotistical and imaginary motives that firm moral position which
the individual must attain by the recognition of the imperish-
ableness of his being in connection with humanity at large.

MATERIALISM AND IDEALISM.

MATERIALISM and idealism are usually regarded as absolute opposites.   Materialism is represented as a miserable, comfortless, hopeless, sad and empty theory, only fit for
hypochondriacs, misanthropes or pure rationalists ; whilst in
opposition to this the so-called idealism professes to satisfy the
higher intellectual and spiritual necessities of man and to raise
him, by a higher conception of the world and of life, above the
deficiencies and nothingnesses of this earthly life.   In truth,
however, this is so incorrect that the Materialism of Science
may rather with perfect justice be described as the highest
idealism of life.   For (and the author has already elsewhere
discu sed this more in detail) the more we free ourselves from
all delusive imaginations of a world above us and outside of us,
or of a so-called *Future*, the more do we find ourselves naturally
directed with all our forces and endeavors to the *present*, or to
the world in which we are living, and feel the necessity of arranging this world and our life as beautifully and advanta-
geously as possible both for the individual and for the whole.   It
is clear that thus a perfectly immeasurable field of exertion and
action is opened up for the idealism or the idealistic striving of
human nature,—a field, it is true, which no longer lies beyond
the stars, but under our feet, and sets reality in place of imagination.   There are consequently no more zealous pioneers of
progress, no greater friends of freedom and no more spirited
defenders of the general equality of mankind in rights and happiness than the materialists and free-thinkers.   Their faith (for

even the materialists have a faith) is that man is better than he
seems, that he can do more than he thinks, and that he deserves to be happier than he is.   Heaven and hell, those primeval bugbears of spiritual despotism, exist also for the materialist ; but he seeks and finds them, not, as of old, outside
of man, but within him, and shows that it depends solely upon
man himself and his conduct, whether he shall have a heaven
or a hell upon earth !

This striving for human perfection, or for earthly improvement and felicity, has given rise to the further objection to materialism, that its sole object is sensual satisfaction and enjoyment, and that therefore, in the satisfaction of the mere animal
impulses, it neglects the higher spiritual needs of man, the interests of his soul.   This objection rests upon so absurd and
evident a confusion of scientific or theoretical materialism, with
practical materialism or the materialism of life, that it scarcely
deserves serious refutation.   The materialism of science and
the materialism of life are things which differ *toto coelo*, and
which can be confounded with each other only by malevolence
or incompetency.   Whoever sacrifices his life to investigation,
his personal interest to the truth, and the force of his activity
to the improvement of the lot of humanity, has no leisure to
run after sensual enjoyments, and is in reality a far greater
idealist than those who find in their idealism a means of obtaining great offices, fat livings, rich salaries or brilliant distinctions.   But even should materialism, when more widely
diffused among mankind, contribute (except among its scientific
supporters) to strengthen the striving after the enjoyments of
this world, which indeed is already sufficiently strong, this could
only be greeted with satisfaction in the interests of progress,—
always supposing that the kind of enjoyment was such, in the
sense of the scientifico-materialistic conception of the universe,
as did not merely satisfy the gross and animal impulses, but at
the same time acted ennoblingly upon the body and mind.

By this means we should again approach that cheerful and joyous conception of the Universe which was held by classical antiquity, from which we have been unfortunately carried far away by monkery and ecclesiastical greed of power ; and those innumerable and immense aids to civilization, which we have and the ancients did not possess, would incalculably facilitate, increase and ennoble our enjoyments.

All this shows that materialism and idealism are not, as so many suppose, born enemies, but that at the bottom they are only different expressions for one and the same thing. In *theory*, materialism far exceeds the old idealistic philosophy in ideal value, inasmuch as it does not, like the latter, assume a multitude of observational facts as inexplicable, and therefore deduce them from supernatural or innate causes (*e. g.*, the mind), but it goes to the bottom of things and seeks to embrace their most intimate and final connection. In *practice* it exceeds all other systems and conceptions of the universe by setting the ideal world *within* us in place of the ideal world *without* us, and endeavors to guide it towards realization. No other philosophy has ever stood like this in the closest connection with life itself; and the best touchstone of its value and correctness will be found in the influence which it has already exerted and will yet exert upon life and its forms. Just as its theory is simple, unitary, clear and definite, so also is its practical tendency ; and its whole programme with regard to the future of man and of the human race may be expressed in six words, which contain all that can be theoretically or practically required for this future, namely :

FREEDOM, CULTURE AND PROSPERITY FOR ALL.

APPENDIX.

NOTES, EXPLANATIONS AND ADDITIONS.

(1.) Formerly it was supposed that the *past* of our earth was clearly separated from its *present*, and it was imagined that the earth and its course of formation had now entered upon a period of rest or of exhaustion, or complete equilibrium of forces, whilst previously great revolutions and catastrophes, terrible changes with periodical destructions of all organized being had taken place. These two periods of the past and present were then thought to be separated by a great waterflood or "Deluge," which occurred not long before the commencement of historical chronology and destroyed all the then existing organic creation, and this at once. The expression "primitive world," (*Vorwelt*) or "antediluvian," (*Vorweltlich*) is therefore synonymous with the expression "Anterior to the sin-flood," (*vorsündfluthlich*), which is still so frequently employed. But it may be remarked in passing that the word "sin-flood" (*Sündfluth*) is of quite incorrect formation' and leads to the false belief that this flood was intended to destroy "sinful" men. But the word really lying at the root of the word "*Sündfluth*," is the old German "*sin*" or "*sint*," which signifies great, mighty or of long duration, and therefore it expresses only the idea of a great or enormous deluge. The only correct orthography is therefore "*Sintfluth*."

This entire conception is geologically incorrect. It is indeed probable that, especially at the cessation of the so-called "glacial period" (a subdivision of the quaternary epoch), certain great floods may have taken place, but no one such as could have produced a simultaneous submergence of the entire surface of the earth. These floods, moreover, were not produced by a single rapid catastrophe, but by many processes following one upon another, and in long periods of time. The powerful animals of the period in question became extinct quite gradually and not all at once, and there is consequently no decided division between the *past* and *present*, between the so-called *antediluvian* and *postdiluvian* times. In fact we only know of gradual transitions in an uninterrupted chain of geological phenomena. Even at the present day the same essential processes and forces are at work in the formation of the earth's surface, as in former times. Nevertheless there does exist a great difference between *then* and *now*, inasmuch as at the diluvial period we meet with essentially changed conditions, such as a different form of the surface of the earth, a different and higher course for the rivers, a different proportion of land and water, a difference in the deposits formed and above all a totally different fauna and flora, among which are especially to be noted the characteristic diluvial animals already mentioned.

(277)

The Diluvium is followed immediately by the so-called *Alluvium*, which consists of the deposits of the existing rivers on their banks or at their openings into the sea. This period presupposes essentially the same conditions of the surface of the earth that now exist, and especially a fauna and flora perfectly similar to those now living. There is no clear boundary line between the two periods, but they pass gradually into one another. We may therefore still further employ the often used expression "antediluvian" (*vorweltlich* or *vorsündfluthlich*), taking it as synonymous with the still more frequently employed denomination "fossil" or "petrified," but we must at the same time carefully avoid connecting with it an erroneous idea belonging to former geological theories. Taken in this sense therefore, as stated in the text, the discovery of Aurignac gives evidence of the antediluvian, (*vorweltliche* or *vorsündfluthliche*), existence of man, who evidently lived at that spot *contemporaneously* with the extinct animals of that period. This result completely annihilates the notion, formerly universally regarded as correct, *that man only made his appearance upon the earth during the period of the alluvium.*

However, nearly all the tribes of the earth have the tradition of a great deluge (*Sündfluth*), which destroyed the greater number of living creatures, only leaving a few from which all subsequent races are descended ; and from this circumstance it has been supposed that the actual *universality* of this great deluge might be deduced. The Catholic Church which was at first inclined to set up the universality of the deluge as an article of faith, finally in 1686 decided in favor of the opposite view and left opinion upon this point free, in consequence of a report from the French Benedictine Mabillon.

(2.) The best known case of this kind is the celebrated or notorious *Homo diluvii testis* or Antediluvian Man of Professor Scheuchzer of Zurich. Professor Scheuchzer in 1726 discovered in a celebrated fossiliferous deposit near Oeningen in Baden, a completely fossilized skeleton which he regarded as the remains of a child of four years old (Andrias Scheuchzeri), and which inspired a theologian of the period with the celebrated verses :

> "Betrübtes Beingerüst von einem armen Sünder,
> Erweiche Herz und Sinn der neuen Bosheitskinder, &c."

Subsequently it proved to be the skeleton of a gigantic Salamander.

Another very amusing affair of the same kind took place in 1616. Near Chaumont in the south of France, the bones of a Mammoth or antediluvian Elephant were dug out, and these were declared by a speculative doctor, named Mazurier, to be the petrified remains of the celebrated Cimbrian King, Teutobochus Rex, who was taken prisoner by Marius in the great battle of *Aquae Sextiae*, (Aix), in the year 102 B. C., and of whom tradition says that he was so large that he overlooked the standards of the army, and that he had jumped over six horses at once. Mazurier exhibited the bones for money and obtained considerable sums, until at last after the publication of several learned treatises and after many learned discussions the fraud was brought to light. This and similar discoveries may have aided in producing the belief in the former existence of a race of human giants which was once so widely spread. In the same way the remains of a Hippopotamus dug up in Sicily were long regarded as the bones of one of those heaven-storming giants which play so prominent a part in the Greek Mythology.

(3.) A more recent discovery exactly similar to this is described in the memoir entitled, *Note sur la découverte d' Ossements fossiles humains dans le Lehm de la vallée du Rhin, etc.*, (Colmar, 1867.) In the year 1865 human bones were found in the Loess of the Rhine at Eguisheim, near Colmar (Alsace), with all the indications of fossilization and in the same bed with bones of extinct animals, (Mammoth, Horse, Stag, Aurochs, etc.) The results at which the author, (Dr. Faudel), arrives, after a thorough examination of the case, are as follows:

1. The bed in question is undoubtedly Alpine Loam of the Rhine valley, (*i. e.* Loess.)

2. In this undisturbed soil contemporaneous fossil bones of animals and human remains were found.

3. Both have undergone the same changes of tissue and composition, and both occurred under absolutely the same circumstances.

4. Hence we may conclude that man lived in Alsace at the time when the Alpine loam was deposited, and contemporaneously with animals of the Quaternary epoch, such as the Gigantic Deer, the Bison, the Mammoth, etc. As regards the human bones in particular, they consisted of two fragments of the skull, and showed a depressed forehead, strongly projecting superciliary arches, and a type on the whole approaching the so-called *dolichocephalic* or long-headed form,—consequently a great resemblance to the celebrated Neanderthal skull.

A very accurate chemical investigation and comparison of the bones of man and animals here found, undertaken by M. Scheurer-Kestner, led to the general result that "from a chemical point of view the contemporaneity of man with the extinct species of animals must be regarded as proved."

(4.) This locality is particularly remarkable because it has enabled us to recognize a regular superposition of three distinct phases of civilization. It is a cone consisting of sand, gravel and rolled pebbles which the little river Tinière has gradually deposited at its opening into the Lake of Geneva, and has been cut through for a length of 133 meters and to a depth of about 7 metres or 23 feet by the railway. This cutting has laid open three layers of civilization (*Cultur-schichten.*) The uppermost, a layer of 4-6 inches in thickness at a depth of four feet, contained ancient Roman tiles and coins, and must therefore be referred to the time of the Roman occupation. In the next layer, 6 inches in thickness and at a depth of 10 feet, there were distinct traces of the so-called Bronze-period; and third and last layer, 6-7 inches thick and at a depth of 19 feet, contained rude pottery, fractured bones of animals, wood charcoal, &c.,—and may therefore be assigned to the last divisions of the so-called Stone-period. The three layers were separated by deposits of rubbish, and the whole appeared so regular, that it could not be regarded as having been brought together by a stream, but by a slow and regular process of deposition. From the relative thickness of the deposits, and the historical datum of the Roman time, Morlot calculates for the bronze-layer an approximate age of 3-4000 years, and for the stone-layer an age of 4-7000 years, whilst the deposition of the entire cone must have required a period of 10,000 years.

These estimates, however, have lately had some doubts thrown upon them by an American savant, Professor Andrews of Chicago, who has reduced them, by his own calculations, more than one half; whether with justice the future must decide.

I must, remark however, that, as stated by Carl Vogt, (*Vorlesungen über den Menschen*), a human skeleton was found in the stone-layer of the cone under consideration, and that its "very round, very small, and very thick skull had the type of a Mongolian brachycephalan." Unfortunately Vogt could ascertain nothing further about this skull.

(5.) In the winter of 1853–54, by taking advantage of a very low level of the water in the lake of Zurich, Dr. Keller discovered the first traces of the *lake-dwellings* or *pile-buildings*, which have since been found in so many places and become so famous. They have been detected in great abundance in nearly all the lakes of Switzerland, and also in the Bavarian and North-Italian lakes, in the peat-bogs of Mecklenburg and Pomerania, the remains of former lakes, &c. Within historical times Herodotus and Hippocrates mention certain tribes in Thrace and on the river Phasis who dwelt in pile-villages. This was 23 centuries ago; but even at the present day many savage tribes still live in similar settlements, such as were met with and represented by Dumont d'Urville in his voyage of discovery to New Guinea. Moritz Wagner also makes a similar report in his journey to Colchis and the country of the Caucasus. Incredible quantities of bones, remains of food, and articles of human industry of all kin. s, which have been found in the bottoms of the lakes beneath the former dwellings and amongst the piles, generally in a very good state of preservation, have enabled students to sketch a tolerably distinct picture of the life and doings of the ancient inhabitants of the pile-buildings, of which details may be found in the numerous reports and memoirs of Keller, Rütimeyer, Troyon, Messikomer, Heer, Desor, Lisch, Lyell, Vogt, Virchow and others. Many pile-buildings, especially those of the bronze-period, are so large that no fewer than 100,000 piles have been found driven close together at a certain distance from the shore; and their number is so great that in the Swiss lakes we already know far more than 200, and in the Neuenburg lake alone 46 such lake-stations. The object of the pile-buildings was evidently the protection of the inhabitants from wild animals, the attacks of enemies, &c., besides the ready obtaining of food by fishing. The inhabitants of the pile-dwellings appear, however, to have been cannibals; at least the human bones which have been found scorched, broken and, apparently, gnawed by human teeth, are in favor of this opinion.

As regards the antiquity of the pile-dwellings they seem certainly to have existed for a very long time, as we find in them remains of the stone, bronze, and iron-periods, sometimes separate, sometimes intermixed. But however ancient even the oldest of them may be, they all belong to the alluvial period, and probably their last offshoots extend far down into the historical period. Many pile-buildings may have been inhabited down to the time of the Romans, and the most recent dredging operations in the bed of the Rhine near Mayence have even furnished evidence that Roman colonists on the Rhine dwelt in pile-villages. At any rate the pile-buildings furnish a proof of what is most important for our present purpose, namely, that thousands of years before the historical period, the human race had already acquired so high a degree of civilization as to be able to erect such dwelling places as these, with all things belonging to them.

(6.) The Danish peat-bogs, which have been chiefly investigated by Steenstrup, are very rich in bones and remains of human activity; we might almost say, with

Steenstrup, that there is scarcely a square yard of them that does not furnish proofs of the existence of prehistoric man. Their depth amounts to from 10 to 40 feet or even more, although the peat grows so slowly that old peat-diggers deny its increase because they have been unable to observe it during their lives. To form a layer of peat of 10 to 20 feet in thickness takes, according to Steenstrup, *at least* 4000 years, and perhaps even from three to four times this period. Now according to the species of trees the remains of which are found in the peat-bogs, three periods of peat-deposition in Denmark have been distinguished, and these are designated the periods of the fir, oak and beech. The lowermost, the *Scotch Fir*, (*Pinus sylvestris*), indicates the most ancient period; this is very old, as this tree never was indigenous in the Danish islands in historical times, and must have become extinct there time out of mind. This was followed by the *Oak*, which has also been for a very long time extinct in Denmark, and has given place to the *Beech*, the true, historical tree of that country. Now even in the lowest deposit, among the trunks of the Firs, traces of man have been met with in the form of worked flints and bones; whilst in the superjacent layers of the Oak-period implements of bronze have occurred and in the uppermost or Beech-layers implements, weapons and coins of iron, and even indications of the Roman invasion. The historical period consequently belongs only to the last of the three periods, or the *Beech-period*.

That there must be a certain parallelism in time between the Danish Fir-period and the formation of the Kjökkenmöddings is shown by the fact that in the latter the bones of the Capercailzie, which feeds in spring upon the young shoots of the Fir, have been met with. Human bones of that time have also been found in the peat-bogs and in tumuli; the skulls are narrow and round and have a projecting ridge above the eyebrows, so that the ancient race was small and roundheaded, with overhanging eyebrows, and thus possessed a great resemblance to the existing Laplanders, who are probably a remnant of this primitive population of the north. Their place is taken during the iron age by a perfectly different type with an elongated, oval head and of far more powerful structure. This is the case also with the dog, which was smallest and weakest in the stone-age and strongest in the iron-age.

(7.) In the thirteenth century the expression "giants' graves" or "giants' mounds," first makes its appearance, and certainly many of these immense burying places which were scattered in the solitude of vast forests and moors, and are now for the most part destroyed by agricultural and roadmaking operations, fully deserved that name. Constructed of immense blocks and masses of stone, they were either placed upon natural hills, or artificially elevated into hills, which were afterwards planted with great trees. In the interior of the sepulchres, composed of huge, rough slabs of stone, objects of the stone, bronze and iron-ages have been found, but bronze objects greatly predominate. On the Island of Schonen near Kivik a gigantic grave of this kind was met with, in which the drawings made upon the sandstone slabs enclosing the grave left no doubt that at this place human sacrifices were offered to the Sungod!

The northern antiquaries are of opinion that these giants' graves are the productions of that Lappo-Finnish race which inhabited the whole of Northern Europe, before the immigration of the Scandinavio-Germanic races, and were driven back by this immigration to the extreme north where it still leads an indigent nomadic life.

Still older than the so-called "giants' graves," are the *Dolmens* or stone tables (also called *Cromlecks* or *Menhirs*), very ancient stone edifices, which have been found especially well-represented in Brittany. They consist of upright stones covered with slabs laid transversely upon them and are reproduced, more or less numerously in almost all the countries bordering the Mediterranean. Under some of these remarkable monuments, corpse-chambers containing abundant treasures of objects of art and human remains have been found. The earthen vessels found stand on a much higher technical ground than the vessels from the Swiss pile-buildings. With regard to the purpose of these edifices and the nature of their builders we have as yet nothing but suppositions. One of the grandest and most enigmatical of these monuments is the celebrated Stonehenge.

Moreover, according to a communication made by Dr. Hooker, to the Meeting of the British Association in the year 1868, the Khasias of eastern Bengal even at the present day erect similar dolmens or stone-tables, merely with the aid of levers and ropes. (See *Globus*, vol. XIV, part 4.) See also with regard to this subject *The Transactions of the International Congress for Archaio-Anthropology for the year 1867,—on Megalithic Monuments.* According to a report there published by M. Bertrand, the stone-monuments are graves and belong for the most part to the *third* Stone-age, or the age of *polished* stones.

(8.) About the middle of the great tertiary epoch a tropical climate and tropical fauna and flora spread over the whole of Europe even into high northern latitudes,—Palms, Cedars, Laurels and Cinnamon trees and other tropical plants had flourished for example in the valleys of Switzerland; and more than thirty. different oaks with evergreen leaves adorned the forests of that time,—Crocodiles had lived in our rivers, and Tapirs, Mastodons, Mammoths, Rhinoceroses, &c., in the forests;—but towards the end of the tertiary period the temperature fell over the northern hemisphere, Europe began to assume a different form, and in consequence of the gradually changing physical influences the southern character of the fauna and flora disappeared, to give place finally, during the so-called glacial epoch, to a perfectly arctic or northern assemblage of animals and plants. Both in the north and in the south of Europe enormous glaciers were formed, their starting points being the high mountains; and these, either directly or by means of drift-ice, scattered gigantic fragments of rock torn from the Alpine heights over the low lands. Once, however, during the quaternary epoch, a retrogression of these great glaciers took place, for which reason geologists distinguish a first and a second glacial epoch, separated by an interglacial period. But while plants and animals suffered the greatest changes by this great change of climate and of the formation of the land, man, furnished with intellectual powers, knew how to resist these influences, especially by the aid of fire; and in fact he lived through the two glacial epochs in which many centuries passed in the gradual increase and diminution of the great glaciers, man giving way before the increasing glaciers and following them up as they diminished in size. In the construction of a canal in the neighborhood of Stockholm they cut through one of those hills called *Osars*, which were deposited by drift-ice during the glacial epoch upon the Swedish plain, then sunk in the sea and subsequently elevated.

In this, under an immense accumulation of erratic blocks, with shells and sand, there was discovered at a depth of 18 metres, or about 60 feet, a circular mass of stones, forming a *hearth*, in the middle of which there were wood-coals. No other hand than that of man, could have performed this piece of work!

In order to obtain a notion of the enormous period of time which must have elapsed since the manufacture of the flint axes of the Diluvium, we must have before us a data which M. Delanoue has given with regard to the geological constitution of the valley of the Somme. In the environs of Amiens, beneath the Alluvium and beneath the Loess, a product of glaciers, which sometimes attains a thickness of ten metres, there are two diluvial strata :— a *red* superficial one which is characterized by having its flints angular and not very numerous,— and a deeper one of *grey* color, the rounded flints in which furnish evidence of strong rolling. These two diluvial ledges, each of which is several metres in thickness, are separated by a layer of freshwater deposits, which contains river shells and is sometimes as much as five metres thick. Now it is the grey or lower Diluvium, lying immediately upon the tertiary formations, that contains the remains of human skill together with the bones of the Mammoth and fossil Rhinoceros. Consequently after the lapse of the first or earliest diluvial epoch a long period of repose must have occurred, during which the fresh-water deposits above the grey Diluvium were formed; then a fresh geological change caused the formation of the upper Diluvium ; and still later under new conditions again a thick layer of Loess covered the flint axes of the second diluvial epoch. Finally the Alluvium was deposited upon the Loess. Hence, since the hand of man made the first flint axes of the valley of the Somme, its geological conditions have changed no less than four times, and the duration of these periods of change is truly incalculable, (See Broca; *Histoire des Travaux de la Société d' Anthropologie de Paris, 1863*). Further details upon the Glacial epoch and its relations to the question of the antiquity of the Human race will be found in the works of Lyell, Vogt and others already mentioned. Lyell, especially, (in his *Antiquity of Man,*) has given a very accurate summary of the facts relating to the Glacial epoch and the traces of human existence contained in its deposits.

To the above demonstration of the high antiquity of the objects found in the valley of the Somme, it might also be added, that in that valley a peat of great thickness (often as much as 30 feet), belonging to the alluvial period, occurs. In the upper layers of this, Roman and Celtic monuments are contained, and its growth was so slow, that it must have taken thousands of years. Nevertheless it is much later than the old gravel-deposits with Mammoth-bones and flint axes which lies beneath it. Moreover, some of these gravel-deposits were accumulated in river-courses which formerly flowed a hundred feet higher than the present stream, and before the valley had acquired its present form and depth. What a length of time must consequently have elapsed since the deposition of those axe-bearing beds!

(9) "The Chronology of the ancient Egyptians handed down by Manetho* and others," says F. Rolle, (*Der Mensch*, &c , 1866), "like the race-traditions of other

* Manetho, high priest of Heliopolis, who lived 350 years B. C., calculates for 375 Pharaohs a reigning period of 6117 years, which, together with the present era, makes about 8330 years. His statements have been frequently declared unworthy of belief, but they have finally proved to be thoroughly trustworthy.

ancient peoples, was regarded by Cuvier as unworthy of credit in comparison with the Mosaic records, and he assumed that in accordance with the latter the creation of Man took place about 6000 years ago. Nevertheless the historical part of Manetho's report has since proved to be more authentic than Cuvier's geological views.

"Even in 1845 Wagner asserted that the Mosaic record of Creation could establish its claim to be the most ancient composition above all other traditions, and that nothing but a deficiency of the necessary linguistic knowledge has led to other opinions; with the exception of the Hebrew the extant histories of the most ancient peoples, including the Egyptians, reaches back at the utmost to about 2000 years B. C.

"Nevertheless the investigation of the ancient Egyptian monuments and the deciphering of the Egyptian hieroglyphs, which has attained a high degree of certainty, have since proved the historical truth of a great part of Manetho's reports, and shown that he was no mere fabulous writer, but that he drew his materials from ancient Egyptian historical springs, was very well-informed, and one of the most trustworthy of the writers of antiquity, &c.

"The kingdom of the ancient Egyptians, according to Lepsius, was already a well-ordered state under the so-called *fourth Dynasty* about the year 3400 B. C. Arts and Sciences flourished. Hieroglyphic writing was already invented, and the characters drawn in this early period are now the most ancient, perfectly authentic, written records which the Archaologist has any where at his command.

"Beyond the fourth ancient Egyptian Dynasty the elucidation of history by the deciphering of contemporary inscriptions has certainly made but little way. It is, however, certain that the development of the Egyptian civilization is much older than even the dominion of the fourth Pharaonic dynasty. The attainment of so high a degree of civilization as that, which already prevailed in Egypt about the year 3500 B. C., *presupposes a period of several thousands of years* during which man elevated himself by gradual progress from a condition of rude savagery."

The celebrated French orientalist and Christologist, Ernest Renan, has also done good service in connection with the elucidation of ancient Egyptian chronology. According to him, *before* the year 970 B. C., when Sesac appears as the first ruler of the twenty-second Dynasty, twenty-one Dynasties must be brought into the Egyptian history, during which this stood in its highest lustre. The greatest epoch of Egypt commences 1700 years B. C., and therefore at a time when Greece and Rome were still nothing, and when Nineveh and Babylon were far from having attained the pinnacle of their greatness. Before the eighteenth Dynasty comes the epoch of the conquering Hyksos or Shepherd kings. It lasted 511 years and commenced 2000 years B. C. Before the Shepherds, Manetho reckons fourteen dynasties with 2800 years; his testimony is good. The dynasties also were not merely local but extended their sway over the whole of Egypt. Manetho's first ten dynasties cannot be reckoned otherwise than from 5000 to 2000 years B. C., and in them falls the brilliant period of the Pyramids and their architects. Great light has been thrown upon this epoch by Mariette's excavations; he discovered sculptures, inscriptions and statues which reached up to 4000 or 4500 years B. C. It is remarkable that in the graves and sepulchres of this period, which already showed a high grade of civilization, no trace was to be found of warlike life which afterwards became so important; nor did anything appear connected with religion or ritual. Not a single picture of any deity occurred; everything related solely to *Death*.

According to J. Braun, (*Geschichte der Kunst in ihrem Entwickelungsgang durch alle Völker der alten Welt, &c.*), Egypt is the most ancient of the great powers and the most ancient of civilized peoples. 450 years B. C., the Egyptian priests showed Herodotus (to whom the wonders of ancient Egypt must have been greater mysteries than to our living Egyptologists) on the outer walls of the great temple in Thebes, 345 mummy-chests i 1 which lay the bodies of high-priests who had ruled from father to son in Thebes for an equal number of ages; it was a pontificial monarchy of several thousand years. According to Braun the Greek civilization originated chiefly from Egypt; and in his opinion and that of Roeth the most important dogmas of Christianity are borrowed from the Egyptian theology.

We cannot but be astonished, when we consider, that at a time, when in Europe the aborigines chased the wild animals with miserable weapons of stone, or dwelt in wooden huts over the water, and obtained their food by hunting and fishing, on the other side of the great Mediterranean sea, in that fortunate country through which the Nile flows, mighty cities flourished in beauty and grandeur, and arts and sciences were cultivated, whilst a powerful priesthood held the reins of a regular government with a firm hand, and probably maintained a flourishing commerce along the shores of the Mediterranean! And what a length of time must have elapsed between that period, when the Egyptian aborigines themselves fought with weapons of stone and the time when they had attained the degree of civilization just described!

In an interesting little book on *The Origin and Destiny of Man*, (published in London in 1868), after a very exact demonstration of the ancient Egyptian chronology founded upon Mariette's discoveries and Manetho's statements, the author, Mr. J. P. Lesley, an American, sums up the results of Egyptian investigation as follows: "Such has been the history of Egypt! Seven thousand years have passed since the fourth king of the first dynasty built the first pyramid of Cochomé, the first which greets the traveller going forth into the desert from the gates of Cairo. Yet even then Egypt was an old country; its people civilized; its architecture grand in idea and perfect in execution; its statuary natural; its language not only formed, but reduced to writing; its agricultural life rich with oxen, asses, dogs and monkeys, antelopes and gazelles, geese, ducks, and swans, and slaves of Numidia. . . . That they enjoyed a happy, peaceful, and sometimes a jolly life, is easy to see, for the walls of the Memphite tombs are covered with pictures of feasts, and games, and dances, and boat tournaments, such as amuse the populace of Paris in July; there you see poets chanting verses and dancing girls with hair dressed up with plates of gold. But you may look around in vain for the symbols of any kind of warfare. Not a trace of military life is visible on any monument previous to the twelfth dynasty, and very little trace of religion. . . . The deity had neither name nor image. Osiris was unknown. The dog Anubis is the only guardian of these primeval mansions of the dead;—the first deity, as the first friend of man. We can make out only the signs of a purely patriarchal civilization, in a land of peace and plenty. Each tomb is built by each farmer for his eternal residence. His effigy is seen in it, surrounded by the pictures of his wife, his children, his servants, his scribes, his dogs and green monkeys and his household goods.   And all this 3000 years before Solomon built his temple on Mount Moriah, or the Assyrian his palace on the platform of Koujunjik.

"For the present let me leave, impressed upon your imaginations, one clear image, the contrast, the marvelous contrast, between the two pictures I have drawn.   On the one hand we have this picture of peace and plenty among the ancient landholders of the valley of the Nile.   On the other hand, we have that picture of want and warfare dominating the life of the wretched savages in the pine-woods of Scandinavia, and standing for the condition of the human race, or rather of all the other human races existing at that ancient epoch, outside of the valley of the Sphinx.

"Yet such a contrast still exists in all its grim integrity upon the earth.   Compare the palaces and parks of England and New England with the wigwams of the west or the slave-cabins of the south; with the utter homelessness of the Hottentot and Australian in the one hemisphere, or the wretched reflection of primæval barbarism among '*les miserables*' in Paris or in London.   And so the world hoards up its old letters, although they can be only re-read with shudderings and tears."

(10) It is a common but erroneous opinion that culture and civilization weaken and corporeally degrade Man.   In general, most certainly the reverse is the case. Better habitations, better nourishment, better clothing and greater protection from diseases and from the manifold injurious actions of external nature cannot act disadvantageously upon man and his corporeal growth, but must be to his advantage. This applies especially to those countries and climates which do not spontaneously pour what he requires into the lap of man, and which do not relieve him of all care about his habitation and clothing.   On the other hand it certainly cannot be denied that civilization brings with it much that is injurious, weakening and enervating or excessively exciting, and therefore must be accompanied by disadvantages of which man in a state of nature is ignorant.   But this cannot upset the general rule, which is indeed abundantly confirmed by experience.   For wherever civilized peoples come in contact with savages or with tribes in a natural state, the latter yield before the greater power and strength of the former; nay, they even die out when in contact with civilization, as if touched by a pestilential breath, as has been the case in America and Australia.   It is true that here the enormous preponderance of greater intellectual development comes into play, and associated with it the increased power of material agencies and of greater moral force.

As regards the primeval man of Europe and his bodily structure, it would appear, judging from the discoveries hitherto made, that he not only belonged to a peculiar race, but that the prehistoric races of Europe differed greatly among themselves.   According to Vogt and Pruner-Bey there certainly existed *two* different, prehistoric races, of which one was large and dolichocephalic, the other small and brachycephalic.   But Vogt regards the former as the most ancient. Professor Wilson, who has investigated the prehistoric times of Scotland, is also of opinion that a dolichocephalic race was conquered and subjected by a later, intrusive, brachycephalic one, whilst the latter in its turn, after making considerable advances in the bronze age, was destroyed by the Celts who introduced iron. According to Professor Schaaffhausen also, the oldest skull was probably dolichocephalic, thick-walled and small.

Stone-weapons are generally found associated with long, negro-like skulls; bronze-weapons with short, mongoliform skulls. Even in the present day these two forms of skull represent those two of the three principal races of man, Negroes, Mongols and Europeans, which have remained most stationary in the general development of civilization ; whilst the type of the *oval* or average head is that of European and other civilized peoples. This type has probably been produced by an intermixture of the prehistoric races with the conquering people who introduced the Aryan languages and the use of metals into Europe. For these conquerors did not destroy the conquered peoples, but mixed with and changed them. Since then, fresh immigrations and intermixtures have been constantly taking place. At the present day, according to Broca, (*Report 1865-67*), the two extremes of these mixtures are represented by the Basques and Fins, of which the former are dolichocephalic and the latter brachycephalic. Broca is moreover of opinion that dolichocephalism and brachycephalism have no definite relation to intellectual development, and that among the European autochthones or aborigines living before the Indo-Germanic immigration, many were dolichocephalic and many brachycephalic, some large and others small in stature. The mixture of these with the Indo-Germanic immigrants, according to him, produced the many differences of the existing European peoples.

According to Professor Schaaffhausen, (*Ueber die Urform des menschlichen Schädels, 1868*), the dolichocephalic type of the most ancient skulls is lower than the brachycephalic, and must therefore be regarded as older ; but it might nevertheless possibly be that it migrated into Europe at a later period and, being a ruder but physically more powerful race, overcame and displaced the brachycephalic type. This would explain why so many ancient skulls of a brachycephalic race have been discovered in Scandinavia, England and western Europe generally. Perhaps also, immigrations of both races into Europe may have taken place from time to time, (from Asia, where the brachycephalic, and from Africa, where the dolichocephalic type predominates.)

All the prehistoric men of Europe, like most savages even of the historical period, were cannibals, as appears from the numerous discoveries of broken and scorched human bones.

" If we uplift the deposits of the earth's surface," says R. Schweichel in an essay on the present state of linguistic and natural science with relation to the primitive history of man, (Leipzig, 1868), " there appears as the first inhabitant of Central Europe a man, whose protruding jaws and nearly deficient forehead betray a savage animal character. The elongated skull with its strongly projecting eyebrows reminds one of the Negro, the Mongol, the Hottentot and the Australian. This autochthon, the associate of the Elephant, Rhinoceros and Hyena, was followed by a nobler, broad-headed, slender race with small hands and feet, which points towards Asia. It approaches the existing Lapps, Fins and Esthonians. Its associate in time was the reindeer. This race never entirely disappeared. Its traces are still to be found everywhere among the present population of Europe. Professor Fraas has called attention to them in Swabia, where they had previously been regarded as a residue of the invasions of the Huns.

"The agricultural man belongs to another race which made its appearance in the later Stone-age, especially in the pile-buildings, and was the principal occupant of Central Europe throughout the whole Bronze-age. The rounded skull, rather broad than long, indicates an energetic muscular people. That they had small hands is proved by the remarkably short handles of their bronze swords, which are much too small for a hand of the present day. In the north of Switzerland this type has maintained itself to the present day."

(11) Dr. Spring, a distinguished savant of the University of Liége, a long time ago made an extremely remarkable discovery on the bank of the Maas in the neighborhood of Chauvaux. About a hundred feet above the present level of the river there was a small bone-cave, in the deposits of loam and stalagmite of which there were numerous bones of animals and men lying intermixed. The condition of these bones, which were generally split and broken, led Spring to conclude with perfect justice that they were the remains of a feast of cannibals or man-eaters. The human skulls and fragments of skulls found here all showed a form approaching that of the Negro rather than that of the European. The skull appeared to be absolutely, and especially in proportion to the jaws, very small, the forehead depressed, the temples flattened, the nostrils broad, the dental arches very prominent and the teeth obliquely placed. The facial angle scarcely amounted to 70o. Judging from the length of the other bones, especially the thigh-bones, the race must have been of small stature. Roughly worked stone-axes and fragments of burnt clay accompanied the remains.

According to Vogt, (*Köhlerglaube und Wissenschaft, 1855,*) all these characters "indicate a primitive kind of man more nearly resembling the oblique-toothed Alfuru, the Negro, and generally the whole lower type of human structure, than the higher one."

Among the numerous discoveries made by Dr. Schmerling in the Belgian caves and described by him, the so-called *Engis-skull*, (from the cave of Engis on the bank of the Maas), has attained the greatest celebrity. In its length and narrowness, the slight elevation of its forehead, the form of the widely separated orbits and the well-developed supraorbital arches, it resembles, especially when viewed from above, the celebrated Neanderthal skull, with which it has often been compared, but nevertheless in general is far superior to this in its structure. Vogt nevertheless thinks it should occupy a middle place between the skulls of the Eskimo and the Australian, and regards it with reference to the proportion of length to breadth, as one of the most ill-favored, animal-like and simian of skulls. However, in judging of the Engi--kull we must not forget that although it was found with extinct species of animals it was nevertheless also accompanied by remains of many still living species, and that consequently its former possessor must in all probability have belonged to a comparatively more recent epoch.

Exactly opposite the Engis cave, on the other bank of the Maas, is the cave of Engihoul in which Schmerling also discovered numerous human bones mixed with bones of extin t animals; but these were chiefly bones of the extremities, and only two small fragments of skulls could be found. They were accompanied by a few rude stone implements; indeed these objects, often associated with worked bones, occurred in nearly all the caves investigated by Schmerling.

The Engihoul cave was visited in 1860 in company with Professor Malaise of Liége by the famous geologist Lyell, who had had his first meeting with Schmerling

26 years before. Additional fragments of bones of man and animals were found, and are figured by M. Malaise in the Bulletin of the Royal Academy of Belgium for 1860, (Vol. x. page 546.)

(12) It has been shown, especially by recent investigations, that even the *first* or *earliest* stone period is represented in the caves, which was previously doubted or left as an open question. In some caves, (such as the Trou Marguerite in Belgium), stone implements exactly of the character of those found in the valley of the Somme, (Moustier and St. Acheul), occurred with enormous quantites of bones of the extinct Diluvial animals, (Rhinoceros, Hyena, Lion and Mammoth), but certainly together with many stone knives and worked Reindeer horns, like those from the caves of Perigord in the south of France. Dupont also, the indefatigable Belgian cave-explorer, quite recently, (1867), found in one of his caves a great number of flint knives, (about 300), associated with split bones of the Quaternary period, (Cave-Lion, Cave-Bear, Rhinoceros, &c.), evidently the remains of a feast, and these stone knives were very diferent from those of the Reindeer period.

According to Lartet, the distinguished explorer of the French caves, many of the stone wedges of the caves are perfectly analogous to those of the open diluvial deposits, so that, as he expresses himself, many anthronologists believe that the diluvial man contemporaneously inhabited the river-valleys and the caves. According to him also we must distinguish two periods, in the first of which the caves were only habitations and in the second only places of sepulture, (like the cave of Aurignac). The habitation of the European caves, however, persisted partially into historical times, and many were even occasionally made use of in the middle ages, as, for example, the Cave of the Fort de Tayac which often served as a place of refuge in time of war.

In accordance with this, Lartet, in a discourse delivered at the Congress of 1867, distinguished *three* kinds of caves : 1. *Caves of the diluvial period*, with remains of the Elephant, of the large Cat, of the Cave-Bear, &c.; 2. *Caves of the Reindeer period*, which contain implements made by the hand of man, showing considerable artistic progress; and 3. *Caves of the latest stone-age*, with remains of still-living and domestic animals, with numerous articles of pottery and polished or ground stone-axes.

The caves themselves, according to Desnoyers, originated by fissures in the limestone rocks, which were subsequently washed and made wider and wider by rivers and the action of flowing water.

The use of caves as habitations is still very common among the savage inhabitants of extra-European countries. The number of the *London Anthropological Review* for April, 1869, contains a very interesting account of the cave-inhabiting cannibals of South Africa, by Bowker, Bleek and Beddoe, which furnishes sufficient evidence of the infinite savagery of these African cannibals, whose habits remind us closely of our most ancient predecessors in Europe. The largest cave of this kind, which was visited and examined by the above-mentioned gentlemen, and which was situated in the mountains beyond Thaba Bosigo, contained immense quantities of human bones, especially those of children and young people. Their condition left no doubt for what purpose the individuals to whom these bones had belonged, had been brought to this spot. In the back of the cave there was a space enclosed with stones which had served as a prison and keeping place for the victims, not destined for immediate consumption.

The savages, who until recently had held their human sacrifices here, were not driven to this course by hunger, as they inhabited a fertile country abounding in game, They ate even their own wives, children and invalids; and the bones of one young person were still in so fresh a state that it could only be supposed, that this victim might have undergone his terrible fate within a few months.

Similar caves of smaller size were scattered through the whole district and were still inhabited only thirty years ago by cannibals, who were the dread of the surrounding tribes. They sent out hunting parties who lay in ambush among bushes and rocks or at watering places and carried off women, children and travellers for the purposes of cannibalism. There still remain a good many of these former cannibals, and one of them who lives not far from the cave, an old fellow of some sixty years old, was visited by the travellers.

Dr. Bowker, with some friends, also visited the caves at the sources of the river Caledon, which are still inhabited, although not now, as formerly, by cannibals. Here also they found an old savage of the cannibal times and learned that formerly the people adopted the charming practice of setting traps for the numerous lions which infest the district, by tying firmly in them little children whose crying was to attract the lions. At present nearly all the tribes, by the exertions of their old chief, Moshesch, have given up the horrible practice of cannibalism.

The corpses of the Europeans, who fell in former battles with these savages, were eaten by them, with the notion that by this means the courage of the deceased would pass into their devourers. Usually they ate only the heart, liver and brain; but in times of scarcity they consumed the rest of the flesh.

(13) Up to July, 1866, E. Dupont had examined at the cost of the Belgian government no fewer than twenty-one caves on the banks of the Lesse in the province of Namur. Among these there were *four* in which numerous traces of the Belgian Reindeer-man occurred, namely, the Trou des Noutons, Trou du Frontal, Trou Rosette and Trou de Chaleux. The animals, whose bones were found, belong either to living species or to such as have quitted the country, like the Reindeer. The industrial objects of stone are all stone knives, and, (with the exception of a later discovery mentioned on page 289), neither polished nor diluvial stone axes were found. But in the Trou de Chaleux alone, Dupont found more than thirty thousand such knives together with numerous split bones of animals and an immense mass of objects manufactured chiefly from Reindeer horns, such as needles, arrow heads, daggers, hooks, &c. There were also ornaments made of precious stones, bored shells, &c., pieces of slate with engraved figures, mathematical lines and the like, remains of very coarse pottery, and finally hearths, ashes and charcoal, intermixed with broken bones. To judge from the latter the horse seems to have served as the principal diet of the Reindeer-man, and next to the horse the Fox and the Water-Rat, whilst remains of Fishes occur but sparingly. In the Trou des Noutons no fewer than one hundred and fifty worked Reindeer horns were found; their acute tips may have served chiefly for the manufacture of javelins. The Trou du Frontal, which is analogous to that of Aurignac, has already been described, and contained, besides fourteen human skeletons, numerous flint knives, bones of animals, shells, hearths, coals and traces of fire. The Trou Rosette also concealed the remains of four buried men, whose skulls were completely destroyed.

Dupont distinguishes three epochs for the Belgian cave-fauna, just as Lartet had done with regard to the French caves. Of these the most ancient is repre-sented by extinct animals, such as the Mammoth, Wooly Rhinoceros, Cave-Bear, &c.; the second by species still living but which have emigrated, such as the Reindeer and Chamois; and the third or most recent by living animals, some of which have been extirpated here by man, such as the Stag, Beaver, Bear, &c. According to him all caves must be subordinated to one of these three divisions.

As regards the antiquity of the Belgian caves, all those with contents must, according to Dupont, be more ancient than the so-called " Blocklehm," and their period comes between that of the Boulder drift and stratified Lehm and that of the " Blocklehm."

The men of the Belgian Reindeer period were, according to Dupont, small, muscular, active and subject to diseases. Their skulls had the so-called brachyce-phalic type in a slight degree and ran into a point ; the face was flattened, like that of the Turanian race. The whole aspect of these cave-dwellers must have been very rude.

Similar results were obtained by the examination of the rubbish heap which was accidentally discovered in 1867 at the source of the Schusse in the neighbor-hood of the Black Forest (in Swabia). The Schusse is a little river which flows into the lake of Constance, and the source of which issues upon the high plateau of Upper Swabia between the lake of Constance and the upper course of the Danube, nearly in the middle of the railway between Ulm and Friedrichshafen. Operations undertaken for the improvement of a mill-pool there brought to light the characteristic remains of a complete station of the Reindeer period. More than 600 split flints were found with such a quantity of partly worked and partly untouched antlers and bones of the Reindeer, that Mr. Oscar Fraas was enabled to put together from these remains a complete skeleton of the Reindeer which is now in the Museum at Stuttgart. Most of the bones were split for the purpose of getting the marrow out of them. The bones of a number of other animals, now living only in high northern latitudes, such as the Glutton, the Arctic Fox, &c., were also found. The Reindeer bones and horns showed numerous and un-mistakable traces of their having been operated on by means of stone instruments. There were also numerous remains of Fishes, and a fish-hook manufactured from Reindeer horns.

Not only the careful investigation of the geognostic conditions of the place, but also the flora of the time (for remains of mosses were found which now live only in the extreme north), leave no doubt that the Reindeer station on the Schusse belongs to the Glacial epoch, or that it probably belongs exactly to the interval between the two Glacial epochs which in all probability Switzerland has experienced. Mr. E. Desor, at the Anthropological Congress of 1867, declared the deposit in question to be *the terminal moraine of the Rhine-Glacier*, which was formerly very large. Moreover, according to him, this discovery at Schussen-ried is particularly remarkable, because it is the first example of a station of the Reindeer-men in a free and open deposit, their remains having hitherto been found only in caves.

(14) P. Gleisberg (*Kritische Darstellung der Urgeschichte des Menschen*, Dres-den, 1868) is absolutely of opinion that in prehistoric times African and Asiatic races of men immigrated repeatedly and alternately into Europe, and thus gave

the main impulse to the development of civilization. Even if this should be correct it would at any rate furnish no objection to the theory of development in
general, inasmuch as these immigrant races must have become developed in their
own homes from rude primitive conditions, and unmistakable traces of the stone
age and its various phases have been detected in different parts both of Asia and
Africa (Palestine, Syria, India, the Cape of Good Hope, Madras, &c.)

J. P. Lesley also (*Man's Origin and Destiny*) calls civilization "the blossom
of the migration of tribes," and is of opinion that every great section of history
has started from some barbaric invasion, as also that the most nobly organized
races of men had the greatest tendency to migrate. According to his representation, the north of Europe has seen *three* different races of men, corresponding to
the three sections of the stone, bronze and iron ages, of which the bronze-men,
who came from a great distance, first introduced the knowledge of metals and
their working, together with the sense of art and the custom of burning the dead ;
whilst the tall, strong, long-headed men of the iron age represent the taste for
war and conquest, and brought the tribes which preceded them into subjection.

(15) Proof of this is furnished by the very interesting speech on *Primeval Man
and his Progress*, made by Sir John Lubbock in the year 1867 at the Meeting of
the British Association at Dundee, in opposition to Archbishop Whateley, who
had defended the old theory of perfection. Lubbock proves by convincing arguments that Whateley's theory is scientifically quite untenable, and that not only
do savages always show traces of gradual although very slow progress, but traces
of former barbarism are by no means wanting even among the most civilized nations. Many a fishing village on the English coast is still exactly in the same
state in which it was 120 years ago It is true that there are here and there peoples who have gone back instead of advancing ; but these cases can only be regarded as exceptions, whilst in general there is no foundation in fact for the assumption of a former condition of perfection. Metal implements and traces of
pottery, which is so persistent, have never been met with among peoples who
were unacquainted with metals, as in Australia, New Zealand, Polynesia, &c.
The art of spinning also and the use of the bow are unknown to many savages ;
and yet these are arts which, once known, would never have been lost. It is the
same with house-building or with religion, of which no trace could be found
among many savages, and which nevertheless, if once existent, could not easily
have been lost ;—or with the art of numeration which arose very gradually by
counting on the fingers and toes,* and even at the present day among many
tribes of Brazil, Australia, &c., does not go beyond the numbers 2—4 ;— or with
the use of fire which is still unknown to many tribes, such as the Dokos in Abyssinia (who know nothing of marriage or family, but go quite naked and live together like animals), and which, if once known, would certainly not have been
lost ;—or with language, which is so scanty among the Australians, for example,
as to possess only a few hundred words and among these none to express general
ideas ;—or with the notions of marriage, family, paternity and the like, which
are perfectly unknown to many savages, and which can be demonstrated to have
made their way only with the gradual advance of civilization.

* Even among civilized nations, counting by the fingers and toes, (5, 10, 20,) is
still quite common.

Many savages (Australians, Fiji or South Sea Islanders, &c.) only recognize maternal descent, and the Egyptians, Chinese, Greeks and Jews actually have traditions as to the introduction of marriage.

Everywhere, even among the most civilized peoples, we find in superabundance the unmistakable traces of a former state of barbarism and of the extension of a stone age over nearly the whole earth.

That people like Archbishop Whateley are not wanting even in Germany is proved by an essay (of which a second edition has just appeared), on *The Commencement of Organisms*, by Professor J. P. Baltzer of Breslau, who takes the field against Carl Vogt and his Lectures on *The Primitive History of Man*, with what he calls scientific arguments, but in reality with the whole theological armor of the middle ages, and likewise endeavors to save the " Man of Paradise " from his expulsion by modern science. Any one who is interested to learn how this science looks in the eyes of a theologian and Professor of Divinity in the present day, may amuse himself for a few hours by reading this essay.

The biblical Adam and the whole Judæo-Christian idea of Creation connected with him, can in the present day and in the present state of science only be held by those who, like the theologians, will not and therefore cannot be convinced by scientific arguments. Thousands of preachers, without troubling themselves about the clear demonstrations of science, continue every Sunday, to narrate to the public again and again their childish tales about Paradise, the Fall of Man, the Creation of the World in six days, &c., &c., and millions of hearers say "amen" to them every Sunday. And what are the scientific men doing while this is going on ? They smile over these old Jewish legends and fables and mix indifferently in the midst of a multitude which appears as if bewitched, without making what must appear to them the desperate attempt to waken the sleepers out of their dreams. And yet, as J. P. Lesley says in his excellent work which has been so often cited, we might as well believe in Aladdin's Wonderful Lamp, or that the Cathedral of Cologne was begun and finished before breakfast yesterday, as that man was created only 6,000 years ago and in a single day ! " There is no alliance possible," he continues, " between Jewish theology and modern science ; they are irreconcilable enemies. Geology in its present advancement cannot be brought more easily into harmony with the Mosaic cosmogony, than with the Gnostic, the Vedic or the Scandinavian. It has escaped fully and finally from its subjection to the Creed. . . . Nor is the difficulty diminished by calling a day a thousand *years*. We have in palæontology the records of a thousand *ages*. Many of the old limestone strata are entirely made up of corals, and their triturated *débris*. Some of the old Devonian mud-rocks are mere masses of the casts of Brachiopods, of every size from the youngest to the oldest. Some of the coal-measure shales are leaved like a book, and every leaf glistens with delicate fresh-water shells. In the Deep-river basin of North Carolina millions of fish-teeth lie packed away between two layers of coal which lie but two feet apart. There are more than a hundred beds of coal in a single coal system, each of which is the result of the growth of a peat-bog, swamp and forest of a separate age ; to say nothing of the many fathoms of rocks which intervene between each one coal-bed and the next in order over it ; during which long interval of time the land must have been too deep below the water-level to permit of vegetation.—The fossil dung of the fish which swam the seas during the deposition of the chalk of England, was so abundant, that the farmers about Cambridge collect it, as it is set free from the mother-rock by denudation, and use it to manure their lands.".

(16) "Linné, in his system, united man with the apes proper, the Prosimiæ and the bats in an order which he named *Primates*,—that is, sovereigns, or as it were the highest dignitaries of the animal kingdom. Blumenbach, on the contrary, separated man as a special order, under the name of *Bimana* or two-handed, to which he opposed the united apes and Prosimiæ under the name of *Quadrumana*, or four-handed. This division was adopted by Cuvier and most of the zoologists who succeeded him. It was only in 1863 that it was shown by Huxley, in his excellent *Evidence as to Man's Place in Nature*, that this rested on false views, and that the pretended 'four-handed' animals (apes and Prosimiæ) are just as truly 'two-handed' as man himself. In all these relations the apes and Prosimiæ are circumstanced exactly as man ; and hence it was altogether wrong to separate him from the former as a special order on the ground of the differentiation (distinctive formation, perfection) of his hand and foot. But the case is just the same with all other physical characters by which one might endeavor to separate man from the apes—the relative length of the limbs, the structure of the skull, the brain, &c. In all these respects without exception, the differences between man and the higher apes are less than the corresponding differences between the higher and the lower apes."—Prof. E. Hæckel's *Natürliche Schöpfungsgeschichte*, (Berlin, 1868), pp. 490–91. Compare, in reference to further details, the Author's *Vorlesungen über Darwin* (Leipzig, 1868), p. 147 *et seq.*

That, moreover, the above alteration of the original Linnean system, proposed and introduced by Blumenbach in 1799, was early recognized as false and decidedly condemned from the anatomico-zoological point of view, may be shown by the following words of the celebrated Geoffroy St.-Hilaire :—"When man is regarded as a group of the value of an order, and a position is assigned him as remote from the ape, as the latter is from the Carnivora, he stands at the same time too near to and too remote from the higher mammalia,—too near if the exalted faculties which place man above all organized beings be taken into account, too far if only the organic affinities which unite him with the Quadrumana and especially with the true apes, be considered ; *for in a physical point of view the latter are much nearer to man than to their proper relatives*, the so-called Prosimiæ. What, then, is the significance of the order Bimana of Blumenbach and Cuvier? An impracticable compromise between two opposed and incompatible systems, it is one of those bastard-like assumptions, one of those equivocal resources, which, more nearly considered, satisfy no one, just because they are meant to please every body. It is probably a half truth, but also a half falsehood ; for in science what is a half truth but an error ?" At all events this passage proves that Huxley's startling announcement relative to the anatomico-zoological position of man can lay no claim to novelty.

(17) The whole arrangement is as follows :

1. ANTHROPINI. This family comprises man only.

2. CATARRHINI, or *narrow-nosed*, comprising the true apes of the Old World.

3. PLATYRRHINI, or *flat-nosed*, comprising the true apes of the New World or America.

4. ARCTOPITHECINI, comprising the sahuis, marmosets, or American clawed apes.

5. LEMURINI, comprising the so-called *Lemures* or Prosimiæ.

6. CHEIROMYINI, including only the *Cheiromys*.

7. GALEOPITHECINI, comprising only the flying lemur,—a remarkable form, which almost touches the bats in a similar manner to that in which *Cheiromys* approaches the Rodentia, and *Lemur* the Insectivora.

The singularity and ambiguous nature of *Galeopithecus* have procured for it the most various names, as the flying dog or fox, flying cat, winged ape, &c. ; and its arrangement in the system has occasioned to zoologists much perplexity. Combining in itself some characters of the ape and of the bat respectively, it at the same time presents a further series of peculiarities which have no closer systematic connection. Its arms, legs and tail are enclosed in a thick and densely hairy fold of skin, which commences at the neck, extends down the flanks and joins together both the fingers and the toes like the web of a water fowl ; yet this cannot serve for flight, but only as a parachute, by means of which the animal swings itself from branch to branch.

(18) It appears from these communications that (independently of ancient myths) the first authentic account of such an animal proceeded from an Englishman (Andrew Battel) in the celebrated old book *Purchas, his Pilgrimage*, (1613). From A. Battel, who had lived for years in the kingdom of Congo, and nine or ten months in the forests there, Purchas heard "of a kind of Great Apes, if they might so be termed, of the height of a man, but twice as bigge in feature of their limmes, with strength proportionable, hairie all over, otherwise altogether like men and women in their whole bodily shape. They lived on such wilde frui's as the trees and woods yielded, and in the night time lodged on the trees."

In a later account by the same narrator (1625), where two anthropoid apes are spoken of, he says of the *Pongo*, represented as the larger :—"This Pongo is in all proportion like a man ; but that he is more like a giant in stature than a man ; for he is very tall, and hath a man's face, hollow-eyed, with long hair upon his browes. His face and eares are without haire, and his hands also. His bodie is full of haire, but not very thicke ; and it is of a dunnish color. He differeth not from a man but in his legs ; for they have no calfe. He goeth alwaies upon his legs ; and carrieth his hands clasped in the nape of his necke when he goeth upon the ground. They sleepe in the trees, and build shelters for the raine. . . . . . They cannot speake, and have no understanding more than a beaste. . . . . Those Pongoes are never taken alive because they are so strong that ten men cannot hold one of them. . . . When they die among themselves, they cover the dead with great heaps of boughs and wood, which is commonly found in the forest. . . . One of those Pongoes tooke a negro boy of his which lived a moneth with them."

A generation later, Tulpius was the first to give a picture, taken from life, of " *Satyrus indicus*," "called by the Indians orang-outang or man of the woods," which was evidently a young chimpanzee. Then the existence of other Asiatic anthropoid apes became known, though at first the accounts were largely mixed with fable; and as early as 1699 the Royal Society published a very good and serviceable anatomical comparison of a so-called "Pygmie" (a young Chimpan-

zee from Angola in Africa), with a tailed and a tailless Monkey, and with Man—
a work which has served as a model for many later writers. The author, Tyson,
starting even then from views similar to those of Huxley in our own day, enumerates forty-seven points in which the *Pygmie* has a greater resemblance to man
than to the tailed and tailless Monkies; and thirty-four in which the reverse is
the case, and names it the most human-like animal that has yet occurred to him.
In 1744, William Smith (*A New Voyage to Guinea*) describes very accurately an
upright-going anthropoid ape from the neighborhood of Sierra Leone, under the
name of *Mandrill* (man-ape), which likewise must have been a chimpanzee.
Linné knew no anthropoid ape from his own observation ; yet he enumerates
four as "Anthropomorphæ" (in the treatise of his disciple Hoppius), and even
speaks of one of them as "*Homo caudatus*" (tailed man). Buffon, who saw a
young chimpanzee alive, and became possessed of an adult anthropoid ape from
Asia, which he called a *Gibbon*, gives very excellent descriptions of these animals ; while a Dutch naturalist, Vosmaer, in 1778 published a very good figure
and description of a young orang which had been brought alive to Holland ; and
at the same time his celebrated countryman, Peter Camper (1779) composed a
treatise on the *Orang-utan*, in which he showed that it formed by itself a perfectly distinct species. He dissected several of these animals of young age. A
full-grown orang of 49 inches height was shot by a Dutch resident in Rembang,
Borneo, at the end of the last century, and very accurately described by von
Wurmb, a German officer. The papers he has left contain further descriptions
of this kind, as that of a specimen 4 feet 5 inches in height. At present we are
more intimately acquainted with the orang-outan than with any other of the
anthropoid apes. Besides it, we know in Asia only the gibbon, which is indeed
more widely distributed and hence more accessible to observation, but, on account of its smaller size, has attracted less attention.

In Africa, on the other hand, the accounts of the old English adventurer Battel
have been splendidly confirmed by modern discoveries. Since 1835, not only has
the skeleton of the adult chimpanzee (*Troglodytes niger*), which is evidently the
smaller of the two mentioned by Battel, and named by him (as it is now in that
country) the *engeko*, become intimately known through Prof. Owen's excellent
work, but in 1819 Bowdich found strong proofs of the existence of the larger
anthropoid ape, named by Battel the *pongo*, by the natives the *ingena*, or *engena*,
"five feet high, and four across the shoulder," builder of a house, outside of
which it sleeps. In 1847, Dr. Savage saw in the house of the missionary, Wilson,
on the Gaboon river, the skeleton of this animal ; and further inquiries led to so
accurate a knowledge of it that Prof. Wyman was able to give a description of
its osseous structure. Battel's pongo was thus discovered afresh ; but the frequent misuse of that name induced Dr. Savage to apply to the animal the name
of *Gorilla* (borrowed from the *Periplus* of Hanno, the Carthaginian). The skeleton of the Gorilla has since been investigated by Owen and Duvernoy ; while
other African missionaries and travellers have increased our knowledge in other
respects of an animal which has had the rare fortune to be, of the anthropoid
apes, the first made known to the world (by Battel), and the last investigated
scientifically.

According to Huxley, all the anthropoid apes have certain morphological characters in common. Thus, they all have the same number of teeth as man ; the

nasal cavities are divided by a narrow septum and are directed downward ; the arms are longer than the legs and end in hands which are provided with thumbs, while the great toe is always smaller and more mobile than in Man, and opposable, like a thumb, to the rest of the foot. None of them has a tail or the cheek-pouches common in Monkeys ; and all of them are inhabitants of the Old World. The accurate investigation of their mode of life has ever been extremely difficult, as they inhabit only the deepest forests of Asia and Africa. The gibbons are the best known, after them the orangs, while of the mode of life of the chimpanzee and gorilla we have the least knowledge from the direct testimony of the Europeans. Of the Gibbon there are about half a dozen species distributed over the Asiatic islands of Java, Sumatra and Borneo, and in Malacca, Siam, Arakan and Hindostan. They are only about three feet in height (thus the smallest of the anthropoid apes) and very slender ; they live on trees, and in the evening descend in troops to the open country. They have a very loud and piercing voice, and *readily and willingly assume the upright gait ;* they can also in this position, with a little assistance from their very long arms and hands, run swiftly ; in fact, testimonies are unanimous that, *on level ground, this is their usual and habitual practice.* Their dexterity in climbing and leaping is astonishing. They drink by dipping their fingers in the liquid and then licking them, and sleep in a sitting posture. *Duvaucel asserts, that he has seen the mothers carry their young ones to the water and wash their faces!* In captivity they exhibit intelligence, cunning, mischievousness, and a sort of *conscience*, as is shown by an anecdote told by Mr. Bennett. The *Orangs* seldom reach a height of more than four feet ; but some are said to have been found between five and six feet high.* They dwell in the densest forests of Sumatra and Borneo, and, as a rule, the old males live alone, except at pairing-time. They live perhaps forty or fifty years, are indolent, and prepare themselves a bed of boughs and leaves, between or under the trees, with dexterity and quickness. They generally lie on their back or side, resting their head on their hands. In cold, windy and rainy nights, they cover themselves with branches, and hide their heads therein. They climb very slowly and cautiously, more like a man than an ape, never make a spring, and first test the branches as to whether they will bear, by shaking them. In the wild state very shy and even dangerous, they are easily tamed and attachable. When pursued they throw branches and heavy fruits from the trees. An orang examined by Dr. Müller in captivity, was found by him to possess great intelligence (*Verhandlungen über die Naturgeschichte der überseeischen Besitzungen von Holland*, 1839–45). The Dyaks of Borneo distinguish several species of Orang ; but these perhaps may correspond to individual variations, which among the orangs are very great. The skulls available show as great variation as the most pronounced forms of the Caucasian and the African races in Man. Similar facts are met with in considering the two African apes, the *Chimpanzee* and the *Gorilla*. Of the adult *Chimpanzees* measured by Dr. Savage *none* exceeded five feet in height. They stand upright, leaning somewhat forwards, but readily fall again upon all fours, in which position the hands touch the ground, not with the inner

---

* According to Spencer St. John, (*Life in the forests of the Far East ;* London, 1862,) the orang-outan attains in Borneo the height of five feet two inches ; while among the natives even five feet five inches is considered a tall stature, and the average is five feet three inches.

surface, but with the thickened ossicles of the outer side. They are good climbers, live in company, yet seldom more than five together; they defend themselves chiefly with their teeth, make nests, or beds on the lower branches of the trees, show in their habits a high degree of intelligence, especially much affection for their young, and are said by the hunters to display, when pursued and wounded, a very human-like deportment. The natives say that the chimpanzees were once members of the human race, but were excluded from the society of man on account of bad conduct, and little by little degenerated to their present condition.* The chimpanzee is found from Sierra Leone to Congo, and it appears that there are several species of them.

The *Gorilla* or pongo (the latter name probably a corruption of *Mpongwe*, the name of the race of men in whose country the gorilla is met with), dwells on both sides of the river Gaboon, in Lower Guinea, West Africa; it is named *Engena* by the natives, attains a height of about 5 feet, is very broad between the shoulders, and quite covered with coarse black hair, which with age becomes grey—except the face and ears, which are naked and of a dark brown color; the skull bears a strong longitudinal and a slighter transverse hairy crest, which the animal can move up and down. The neck is short and thick; the arms are very long, reaching below the knee, and the hands very large. The gait is waddling, and the motion of the forward-leaning body rolling, or from side to side. Like the chimpanzee, the animal reaches its long arms to the ground and then throws the body forward between them with a half springing, half swinging motion. When it assumes the erect position (to which it is said to be much inclined), it balances its huge body by bending its arms upward. The gorillas also live in companies, which, however, are less numerous than those of the chimpanzees, and, as a rule, contain only one full-grown male; for as soon as the young males become adult they fight for the supremacy, and the strongest kills or drives away the rest. Their dwellings are like those of the chimpanzee. The gorillas are very savage and dangerous, and never flee from man, as the chimpanzees do; they are hence objects of terror to the natives, and are never attacked by them. In time of danger the females and young hide themselves, while the male furiously rushes on the foe. These communications from Dr. Savage were confirmed by a letter from Mr. Ford to the Academy of Sciences, Philadelphia, in 1852. He says that the gorilla inhabits the mountain-ranges of the interior of Guinea, from the Cameroon in the north to Angola in the south, and about 100 miles inland, and only in the south approaches within 10 miles of the coast. Formerly, he said, it was found only in the neighborhood of the sources

* The apes are more acknowledged as brothers by savage or primitive tribes than by our modern civilization. According to a communication from Prof. Bischoff, the negroes in Guinea and the natives of Java and Sumatra look upon the orang-outan, (a word signifying "wild man," "man of the woods,") and the chimpanzee as men who could speak, if they would, but who, from mere laziness, behave as if they could not. The Siamese say: "The ape is a man, certainly not very handsome, but nevertheless a brother." (Bowring, *Mission to Siam*, 1855.) And in the ancient Indian heroic poem *Ramajana*, the wild tribes constituting the aboriginal population of the Dekhan, against whom Rama fights, are called "apes" or "men of the woods," the island of Ceylon appears as "Laaka," and its inhabitants as apes or the offspring of apes.—*Note by the Author*.

of the Gaboon, while recently it boldly approaches the plantations of the Mpongwe. This may be the reason that formerly we had scarcely any information about it. A specimen examined by Ford weighed 170 lb. without the viscera, and measured 4 ft. 4 inch. round the chest. According to the same author, it attacks in an erect position, with a furious bellowing, that may be heard to a great distance, and, having thrown down its adversary, lacerates him with its teeth. A young one, taken alive, proved perfectly untamable, and died at the end of four months. Similar testimonies are given by French authors ; and after what we already know of the gibbon, orang and chimpanzee, they cannot very much astonish us. Particularly, as it has been proved that the gibbon readily assumes the erect position, the gorilla is in its entire structure much better adapted for doing the same. Hence the distrust with which the statements of a recent traveller (Du Chaillu) have been regarded is scarcely justified, since every thing essential was known before. There is absolutely nothing improbable even in his accounts respecting the *Nschiego-Mbouvé* and the *Koolou-Kamba*. Nevertheless, just on account of this distrust, not yet removed, Huxley has avoided quoting Du Chaillu's book in any way. The author has briefly given the essence of Du Chaillu's account of the gorilla, the particularly anthropoid koolou-kamba, and the nest-building ape, the nschiegombouvé, in his work, *Aus Natur und Wissenschaft, Studien, Kritiken und Abhandlungen* (Leipzig, 1869), II. Ed. p. 297.

(19) Thus, although in proportion to its size it has the largest brain of all the anthropoids, yet the chimpanzee, and especially the variety of it the koolou-kamba, which has a very broad forehead, has a better formed skull, the orang a better formed brain, and the gibbon is superior in the formation of his trunk-skeleton, which is very similar to that of man. On the other hand, the gorilla has the shortest arms of all and the greatest resemblance to man with respect to the shoulder-blades and the proportion between the humerus and forearm. The same holds good with respect to the more elevated nasal bones, the less-projecting intermaxillaries and the human-like shape of the ear. The broad, human-like pelvis, the stronger development of the sciatic muscles, and the so-called *mastoid* processes of the skull, developed in the gorilla alone, lead to the conclusion that he is more adapted than other apes for standing erect. The hand is peculiarly human-like, having a proper thumb and short fingers, and is attached to the arm by *eight* carpal bones, as in man, not *nine* as in other apes. It is just the same with the lower limbs, which are distinguished by a proportionally strong development of the heel, making the gorilla more *plantigrade* than the chimpanzee. The number of the vertebræ in each of the anthropoids is the same as in man ; on the other hand, the gorilla and chimpanzee come nearer to man in the number of their ribs, which amounts to 13, while man, as a rule, has 12 (sometimes 11 or 13), and the other apes possess 14. The full-grown male gorilla has also a longitudinal crest-elevation on the forehead, which is not generally possessed by the other apes. The large occipital foramen, the more forward position of which in man makes it possible for him to maintain the erect posture, occupies nearly the same place in the skull of some of the apes ; and the number, arrangement and nature of the teeth are alike in man and ape.

In the autumn of 1864, at the meeting of the Natural History Society of

Rhenish Prussia and Westphalia, Prof. Schaaffhausen exhibited three excellently
finished plaster busts of the gorilla, as well as casts of the brain, hand and foot,
executed by Zeiller, the sculptor, in Munich, from the animals which W. Schmidt,
of Offenbach, has prepared and stuffed for the city of Lubeck. At the same
time he exhibited photographs of the specimens in London, Paris, Vienna and
Lubeck. On the basis of the Lubeck animals, and availing himself of Prof.
Owen's celebrated memoir, P. Meyer, M. D., Offenbach, composed his exhaustive
treatise : *The Gorilla, with a Consideration of the Differences between Man and
Ape, and the new Theory of the Transformation of Species.* Subsequently,
two more examples arriving at Offenbach from Lubeck, one of them a large, very
strong, full-grown male, he added an appendix of further details. Both of these,
especially the latter, are illustrated with very good figures, true to nature, in
which the animal stands as he is described by Winwood Reade in his most recent
account of his travels (1864)— erect on his feet, and holding by the hands to the
branches of the trees. The measurement of the facial angle of a skull sent with
them, which must have belonged to a very old animal, gave, according to Meyer,
55°, the capacity of the cranium being 26 cubic inches. The occipital foramen
was situated well forward towards the centre of the basis cranii ; and the two
sole remaining lateral cutting-teeth were strikingly like human incisors.

(20) The following may be regarded as the most essential marks of distinction
of man from the animals most nearly related to him :— the shortness of the upper
and the length of the lower limbs in proportion to the trunk ; the broader pelvis
and scapula or shoulder-blade ; the accurate curve of the vertebral column, and
the whole formation of the skeleton, favoring the upright gait, and the corresponding parts of the muscular system ; the shortness of the spinous processes
of the cervical vertebræ ; the more perfectly formed hand, with its very mobile
and opposable thumb, its use favored by the facility of movement of the arm ;
the greater contrast in form and function between hand and foot, and the increased division of labor effected thereby ; the globose form and the size of the
skull, and its height and largeness in relation to the more retreating face and the
less-projecting jaws ; the quicker coalescence of the so-called intermaxillary bones
and the greater perfection of the so-called mastoid processes of the skull ; the
prominent nasal bones, the projecting chin, the mouth with lips ; the smaller
teeth, constituting an uninterrupted series of nearly equal height ; the larger and
better formed brain, &c., &c. All these, however, are more or less relative and
are balanced by manifold intermediate and transitional stages in savage and extinct races of man and other animals. Here, too, as everywhere, Nature knows
no abrupt transitions, but only variations in a gradual development which everywhere pursues the same fundamental plan. The oft-quoted J. P. Lesley, here
again, well says : '' The differences which subsist between man and ape and between the different races of man, as well as those between the different races of
apes, are only variations of the great fundamental plan common to all. Take
for example the ideal brain-case. It may be more simioid or more anthropoid ;
it may be dolicho or brachycephalic, have a low, retreating, or a high, erect forehead ; it may exhibit a perfectly even rotundity, or be lumpy and knotty like the
root of a bay tree ; it may be high and pointed, or enormously depressed between
the ears ; it may bulge out over the ears, or before and behind, and be ridged and

channelled from side to side; yet all these are differences we are accustomed to see daily, and which we should see if we extended our steps to the forest of the tropics. The whole thing is of one of *degree*, or, st'll better, of execution in details. In like manner an architect, having explained to his pupils the plan common to all Gothic churches, would show them the different modes in which the fundamental idea of this plan is carried out in the different churches of Europe."

(21) "The human body," says George Pouchet in an excellent treatise on anthropological studies (*Revue de la Philosophie positive*, 1866, No. 2), "furnishes to general anatomy not a single new fact. It neither possesses any special tissue nor any special anatomical element; nay, it even lacks certain anatomical elementary parts which are found in other Vertebrates—for example, the so-called electric tissue. This positively established point in general anatomy, as well as everything we know of the properties of organized matter, enables us already to recognize the worthlessness of certain anthropological theories. It is now fully proved that all functions and all faculties of the living being can be reduced to the properties of the elements and tissues of which it is composed. We prefer the term *function* for the phenomena of what is called vegetative life, and faculty for certain phenomena of 'animal life;' but the faculties just as much as the functions, are only the external manifestation or interpretation (*traduction*) of certain properties which reside in organized matter, and especially in certain anatomical elements. In order, therefore, to justify the admission of the existence of a new and essentially peculiar faculty in man, such, for instance, as has been made out of "*religiousness*," at least a peculiar anatomical tissue for it would have to be specified; for a faculty unconnected with the other animal faculties, and independent of an organic basis, is now-a-days inconceivable, except in contradiction to all our anatomical knowledge.

"If we pass from general to comparative anatomy, we here also find no phenomenon of importance which is absolutely proper to man, except the volume of his cerebral hemispheres. All the other characters are subordinate and of equal value with the differences observed between the Mammalia themselves. If we were determined to find the sign of man's predominance in his upright gait or in the arrangement of the tendons of his hands, our judgment would be like that of the Athenian philosopher who defined man as 'an animal with two legs and without feathers.' Diogenes threw a plucked fowl to him over the walls of the academy, thus ridiculing the wretched logic of the master."

(22) On this affair of Professor Owen, and on the general question of man's place in nature, Prof. Broca, in his Report for 1863, (*Report on the Transactions of the Anthropological Society of Paris*), expresses himself as follows:

"From the zoological or anatomical point of view, man differs less from the four higher Apes than they do from the rest of the apes. With them he constitutes a natural group, the *Anthropomorpha*, of which he forms only the first subdivision; and our learned colleague, Prof. Charles Martins, of Montpellier, has made us acquainted with two new osteological characters which are met with in this group alone. . . . Man is man through his intellect; and if he be distinct from the lower animals, he must be so by virtue of his brain, which is the organ of intelligence. Nevertheless anatomy finds between the brain of the chimpanzee and that of the lord of the earth only slight differences of form and constitution, which have been pointed out by M. Auburtin. The distinctive marks asserted by Prof. Owen have been repeatedly recognized as inaccurate. The higher apes, like ourselves, possess a posterior lobe of the cerebrum, a posterior cornu of the large lateral ventricle of the brain, and a hippocampus minor ; and nothing in the order of things, except the very considerable difference of volume and the unequal abundance of the secondary convolutions, entitles us to assume a decided, absolute difference between the brain of the lowest man and that of the highest ape."

(23) As early as 1861, Huxley pointed out, as the only differences between the brain of the ape and that of man, the following :— 1, in the ape the brain, in comparison with the nerves which issue from it, is smaller than in man ; 2, in the ape the cerebrum, in comparison with the cerebellum, is not so large as in man ; 3, the convolutions are less complex and more symmetrical in the simian than in the human brain ; 4, the hemispheres are rounder and deeper, and the proportions of the individual lobes to one another more varied. Finally, in the simian brain certain windings and furrows are altogether wanting or only present in a rudimentary condition. At the meeting of the British Association in 1862, the anatomist Flower and Prof. Rolleston took part with Huxley in opposition to Owen ; and Rolleston would only admit as valid four differences between the human and the simian brain—two qualitative and two *quantitative*. These differences relate, 1, to weight and height ; 2, to the facial angle and the division of the windings and foldings of the brain. Thus Owen was quite isolated.

In an altogether similar manner the French *savant* Gratiolet, perhaps the highest authority in the department of cerebral anatomy, expresses himself on the difference between the human and the simian brain. He says that the former has throughout, the same type (character of formation) as the brain of the ape. The cerebellum of the ape is quite covered behind by the cerebrum. This latter has very much reduced olfactory lobes, and large cornua to the lateral ventricles. The optic nerve vanishes, as in man, almost entirely in the large hemispheres of the brain ; while in the other Mammalia it has its own centre, the *corpora quad-rigemina*. The convolutions, too, are essentially the same, even to some variations. Hence all the differences relate only to subordinate characters ; and the most essential of them relate to the development of the convolutions during fœtal life.

Mayer (*Verhandl. der Niederrhein. Gesellschaft für Naturkunde*, Nov. 7, 1862) indicates as a principal characteristic of the brain of the ape in comparison with that of man, together with the smoother upper surface of the posterior lobe, "the tapering of the anterior lobe, and the great concavity of its under surface." Indeed, besides the difference of size, the development of the anterior or frontal lobes being so much inferior to that of the rest of the brain, may establish the most essential distinction of the simian from the human brain ; as is well known, the frontal lobes stand in an altogether special relation to intelligence and have recently been recognized as the proper seat of the organs of the exceedingly important *faculty of speech*. Hence, then, by his protruding, broad and strongly developed forehead, which corresponds to the fore part of the cerebrum, man is very essentially distinguished, even at the first glance, from all animals, and especially from his cousins, the anthropoid apes. In this respect a transition between man and animal is formed by the *negro*, whose narrow and retreating form of forehead is likewise connected with a proportionately smaller development of the anterior lobes of the cerebrum, and who not in this respect alone, but also in the formation of the rest of his brain, as well as the structure of his whole body, is well known to have many perceptible resemblances to the ape. According to Huschke, the brain of the negro, by the preponderance of its long diameter, the incompleteness of its convolutions, the shallowness and narrowness of its anterior hemispheres, the roundish form of its cerebellum, the largeness of its so-called vermiform process and the proportionally larger pineal gland, stands decidedly at a lower and less perfect stage of development, corresponding on the one hand to the form of a new-born European infant, and on the other to that of the animals next to man. Generally, the differences in brain between higher and lower races of men are quite the same as those between the brains of man and ape. Prof. J. Marshall (*Proceedings of the Royal Society*) found in the brain of an old Bushwoman, which was very small (weighing only $21\frac{1}{4}$ ounces), the convolutions much less developed, simpler and less marked by secondary furrows (*sulci*) than the brain of European women,—as generally a stronger or more numerous formation of sulci, according to R. Wagner (*Vor-studien*, &c.), occurs in the brains of persons of extraordinary intelligence, and is characteristic of them. The observations of the same gentleman have established the important fact that in the brains of human fœtuses of five or six months there is met with a formation perfectly like that in the lowest ape. This fact confirms afresh the old principle of organic morphology, that the human embryo repeats in its successive transformations the forms of the lower animals, which have remained at those lower stages of development.

In relation to the distinction of the human from the animal brain, the greatest weight has always, and rightly, been attached to *relative size*, although size by itself is only a rough or imperfect standard for the determination of the mental value of a brain ; for, on the one hand, it is essential to consider the ratio of the size of the body to that of the brain, and, on the other, the *grey* substance only, which covers the surface of the brain, can be regarded as the seat of consciousness and of the higher mental activities, while the *white* substance is rather the conductor and medium of the nerve-forces which flow to and from the brain. Hence, then, the great value and significance of the furrows and convolutions of the brain ; for the more numerous and deeper these are, the greater the development of the grey substance.

It is not surprising then, if, for example, the brain of the elephant, weighing from 8 to 10 lbs., exceeds the human brain in absolute size by more than as much again ; yet the ratio of its weight to that of the whole animal amounts to only $\frac{1}{3800}$, while the human brain makes up $\frac{1}{35}$ or $\frac{1}{37}$ of the whole body. The whale's brain also exceeds the human brain in absolute size. The brain of man and that of an anthropoid ape are more comparable in respect of absolute size, since here the proportions of the size of the body nearly agree, while the human brain far exceeds that of these apes in volume and weight ; for while Welcker estimates the average cranial capacity of an adult man to be 1375 cubic centimètres, he says that of the largest of the anthropoids, the gorilla, never exceeds 500. Expressed in cubic inches, the cranial capacity of the Gorilla varies from 26 to 34 cubic inches, while that of Caucasian man amounts to from 92–114, and in individual cases still more. Of course this very considerable difference is again very much reduced in the case of the colored or lower races of men, as Malays, Chinese, negroes, American Indians, &c., the capacities of whose crania, according to the accurate measurements of Morton, Prof. Wyman and others, are as low as from 85 to 75 cubic inches, and those of the Hottentots and Alfurus have minima of 65 and 63 cubic inches. Individual Hindoo skulls are said to have been met with having an internal capacity of no more than 46 cubic inches. The *average* cranial capacity of the gorilla amounts to 26–29 cubic inches, that of various apes or the much smaller chimpanzee to 21–26. The cranial space of human microcephali or "small heads" may even fall considerably *below* the mean of the simian.

As to *weight*, human brains have been known of 2, 3, 4, and even nearly 5 pounds, while the brain of a large ox or horse does not weigh 2 pounds. *Negro-*brains weigh, on the average, about 3 lb.* ; while the weight of brain of the large anthropoid apes varies from 10 to 20 oz. According to Huxley, it is doubtful whether a healthy brain of an adult man ever weighs less than 31 or 32 ounces (or about 2 lb.), and whether the heaviest gorilla-brain ever exceeded 20 ounces ; while he gives the weight of the largest known human brain as 65 or 66 ounces (4 lb. 2 oz.). Moreover, R. Owen, in the 3rd vol. of his *Anatomy of the Verte-brata* (1868), states that the brain of an Australian woman weighed 32 ounces, that of a Bushwoman only 30¾ ounces, while the brain of Cuvier, the celebrated anatomist, weighed 64 ounces (or 4 lb.).

The so-called Camper's facial angle, which is a good index of the development of the anterior portion of the brain, amounts in the Caucasian race to 80–85°, in the negro to 65–70°, in the Neanderthal skull to 56–66°, and in the orang and chimpanzee to not quite 50°. Besides, *all* the proportions of the skull and brain are disproportionately more favorable as to form in *young* apes than in full-grown or old ones, the chief reason being that after birth the simian skull no longer continues to advance *pari passu* with the other parts, but is retarded in its development and finally remains stationary, similarly to the skulls of microcephalic or little-headed men.

(24) These lowest kinds of organic propagation were for a long time, during the earliest periods of the earth's history and its peopling with organic life, the only ones generally subsisting, and are even now widespread in the lowest regions of animal and vegetable life, under the name of *asexual propagation* or *amphigony* (Hæckel). The simplest organic corpuscles we are acquainted with, and which consist of merely an amorphous minute clot of mucus, the so-called *Monera*, propagate themselves only by a circular constriction of the substance of their body and a consequent *self-division*. The so-called *cells*, and those organisms which consist only of simple cells (as for example, the *Amœba*), do the same only with this difference, that in them a constriction and division of the nucleus precedes. Higher organisms, those consisting of groups of cells, also propagate themselves by division—as, for instance, the *coral-animals.— Gemmation* is not less widespread than propagation by division ; it takes place by a prominence

* In the American war 141 negro brains were weighed, the average weight of which amounted to 46. 96 oz., while the weighings of another observer brought out a mean of 45 oz. The largest of these 141 brains weighed 56 oz., or 3½ lb., the smallest, only 35 ¾ oz.

rising from the original (one- or more-celled) organism, becoming larger and larger, and finally either separating from the parent organism as an independent being, or else, while remaining connected with the latter, yet carrying on an independent life and growth of its own. Bud-formation is more general in the vegetable than in the animal kingdom.— With bud-formation is closely connected a third and a fourth mode of asexual propagation, or that by the formation of *spores* and *germ-buds*, in which the parent organism forms in its interior single cells or groups of cells, which afterwards quit it and are further developed by themselves. This formation, in which only a very minute portion of the producing organism effects the propagation, conducts us at once to *sexual generation*, which is the usual one among all the higher animals and plants ; its characteristic is that the female ovum or germ-cell must be fertilized by. male semen in order to attain the capability of further development. Moreover, two separate individuals of different sexes are not always required, since in the case of *hermaphrodites* a single individual combines in itself both generative elements. It is evident that the separation of the sexes was developed from the formation of hermaphrodites and first took place at a much later period in the earth's history. It is now the general mode of propagation of the higher animals, while, on the contrary, it is found in a smaller number of cases among plants. In it the female individuals form only *ova*, the male only *semen*, or (among plants) pollen-grains. An interesting transition-form between asexual and sexual generation is what is called *partheno-genesis* or (*virgin generation*), which is frequent among the Articulata ; here the germ-cells, perfectly resembling in appearance ovum-cells, develop into new individuals without any need of the fertilizing semen. In many cases, from the same germ-cells different individuals spring, according to whether they have been fertilized or not : thus, of the honey-bees, males (the *drones*) spring from not fertilized, females or workers from fertilized ova. (According to Hæckel : *Natürliche Schöpfungsgeschichte*, 1868.)

(25) The discovery of this pair of bones, which, present in all Mammalia, are situated between the upper jaw-bones proper, and bear the four upper incisors, was rendered difficult in man because they very early coalesce with the upper jaw-bones (maxillaries), and are only recognizable in the skulls of very young subjects. In human embryos the intermaxillary may be exhibited at any time ; and in some few individuals it is preserved distinct during their whole life. This discovery, of course, rendered quite untenable the opinion of the older naturalists, that the intermaxillary constituted a prime mark of distinction between man and ape.

Moreover, Dr. Carus has recently discovered an independent intermaxillary in the skulls of two Greenlanders and expressed his opinion that this character is perhaps common to *all* Greenlanders' skulls. The separation is described by Carus as like that found in the skulls of the foetus, as well as in those of quadrupeds ; hence it points to an approximation towards the formation belonging to the lower animals.

(26) In support of his views M. Schaaffhausen called attention to a series of facts and investigations which have now become the common talk of the day, as : —the existence of the large anthropoid apes (which even in Cuvier's time were held to be fabulous animals), and their approach to the human form ; the forms,

discovered by geology and palæontology, showing the transition from tertiary to recent times; the probability of the discovery of fossil or petrified human bones; the investigations concerning primitive man and his rude, animal-like condition; the resemblance of the lower human races, and especially the negro, to apes and other animals; the occasional approximations of the human structure to that of beasts; the importance of inheritance in relation to body and mind; the necessary connection between bodily (especially cerebral) organization and intelligence, &c., &c. As regards the human *reason*, which is generally considered an insurmountable barrier between man and animal, it is, according to Schaaffhausen, only "the result of a finer and more complete organization," as the human body can only be regarded as the finest and most perfect expression of animal organization,—it is not a gift of Heaven bestowed equally on all men, nations and times, but a result of universal human education; while even in beasts an incipient tendency to all the activities of the human mind is to be pointed out, and in a higher degree the nearer they approach to man; for in the animal mind, banished to a narrow sphere, the fundamental forces of the human mind are latent. Thus reason is "that higher qualification which proceeds from the proportionate development and completion of all our soul's faculties, to which the human family has been gradually matured, and which will conduct it to ever greater intelligence," &c. "The speech, too, of wild tribes, compared with the languages of cultivated peoples, is poor in words and inflections; many sounds are absent. What is there against the supposition that it has been developed from rude beginnings, from simple tones?"

In a treatise written in 1853 (therefore six years previous to Darwin's) on the constancy and the transformation of species, which already with forcible reasons combated the dogma of their unalterability and vindicated the transformation theory even against men like Baer, Vogt and Burmeister, we read: "Should it be thought derogatory to man to regard him as the last and highest development of animal life, and derive all the superiority of his nature from the perfection of his organism . . . especially as a series of most telling facts evidence the approximation of the most highly developed ape to the lowest type of man most clearly? But if all the facts speak convincingly for a gradual transition from the most recent geological period to the present state of things, a like conclusion must be valid also for the earlier periods less known to us, and the whole creation must appear as a series of organisms connected by propagation and development."

A few years later the author, in his lecture *Ueber den Zusammenhang der Natur- und Lebens-Erscheinungen* (1858), felt himself justified in expressing positively his conviction of the grand unity of all nature, animate and inanimate, and all her phenomena — a unity which previously scarcely any one had ventured to anticipate. "Superstition and miracle," says the author, "it is true, vanish before the new natural philosophy, but not the greatest miracle, the self-consistent universe! Knowledge is never a clog to the freest thought; it can only give new wings to the imagination." The discourse concluded with the prophetic words:

"It has always been conceded that the idea of a gradual development of organic life by a continually operating creation is bold and magnificent; but it was supposed to be void of truth. *It will be no little satisfaction to the often erring human mind when it shall be shown that the most exalted thought we can conceive of nature is also the truest!*"

(27) Nevertheless, and in spite of the materialistic sentiment here and elsewhere so openly expressed, Mr. Huxley (probably alarmed at his own boldness and vexed at the shock given to his bigoted and stiff-minded countrymen) has recently thought it necessary to give a categorical negative to the worn-out, but still always dreaded, accusation of materialism, thus abjuring, at least to a certain degree, the bold spirit with which he six years previously opposed the prejudices of his time and the outcry of ignorance. At any rate, the defence contained in an article in the February number of the *Fortnightly Review* for 1869 (which created so great a sensation in England that several editions of the number containing it quickly followed one another) is so ambiguous in expression that at its conclusion the reader is not at all sure whether Mr. Huxley has been pleading for or against materialism. Only one thing is clear, namely, the declaration, "personally I am not a materialist; on the contrary, I believe that materialism contains grave philosophic error." Nevertheless all the arguments in the article are as materialistic as possible and are sustained by a materialistic sentiment and fundamental view, and the conclusions arrived at are altogether materialistic. That anti-materialistic avowal, therefore, can only have been possible to Mr. Huxley by his accepting a current error which has been a hundred times refuted, but still is ever repeated, and taking materialism in the sense of a philosophic system resting on *à priori* speculation. This designation may, *perhaps*, have been deserved by the materialism of former ages, although *that* always, far more than all the opposite tendencies, relied on experience and actual fact; while the materialism of modern times does *not* deserve that designation and ought much rather to be named a *method* than a *system*. The distinction made by Mr. Huxley between materialistic method and materialistic system, adopting the former and rejecting the latter, is quite inadmissible. No one, Mr. Huxley included, can now say whither the materialistic method, which now a-days is universally predominant in natural science, will in time lead us in the explanation of natural occurrences, and whether it may not even bring us nearer and nearer to the much-abused materialistic *system*. It is therefore very precipitate and at least imprudent, to turn round upon general consequences or convictions, to the bringing on of which the works of those who now oppose them have most of all contributed. Science cannot advance merely by experiment and observation; supposition and hypothesis are also necessary and have always been the most decided pioneers of scientific progress. What we do not know, we try to guess; what we are unable to guess, we try to investigate; and what we cannot yet investigate, we must at least try to define as sharply as possible as a problem for future investigation. No means must appear to us too insignificant by which we may hope to come nearer the truth. Nothing, then, is more ridiculous than that pride of not knowing, with which so many respectable men of science are at present fond of acting in opposition to materialistic endeavors. Apart from the fact that actual ignorance often hides behind this pompous profession of not knowing, it betrays very little ardor for investigation when men are always trying to push into the foreground the *unknown*, and very little penetration not to see that the entirely relative conceptions of *knowing* and *not knowing* cannot in this wise be pushed asunder and contrasted; for, however much we may know, learn, and experience, behind it all there will always remain the territory of the unknown, immeasurable and to our power of conception, impossible to estimate. Then always forward

into this unknown land ! never backward ! must be the watchword of every investigator and man of science animated by a genuine love of truth.

Yet we find Mr. Huxley himself, in the above-mentioned article, induced to
declare that the order of nature is determinable by our faculties to an unbounded
degree, and in another place he puts without hesitation "matter" and "natural
law" as the two conceptions which in future are destined to set aside all other
methods of explanation. "And as certainly," he says, "as every future is composed of a present and a past, so surely will the natural science of the future more
and more extend the empire of *matter and natural law*, till it becomes synonymous with knowledge, sense and action ! The consciousness of this great truth
weighs, it seems to me, like a nightmare upon many of the best spirits of the
present time. They watch what they call the spread of materialism with the
same feelings of terror and impotent anguish which the savage experiences, during
a solar eclipse, when he sees the great shadow creeping over the face of the sun."

How little share, moreover, Mr. Huxley's inmost conviction can have in his opposition to materialism, is as evident as such a thing can be from the following
sentences, which he has ventured to write in an article entitled *Positivism and the
Science of the Present* (*Revue des Cours Scientifiques*, Oct., 1869), when endeavoring to repel Mr. Congreve's animadversions on his attacks upon the French
philosopher Comte in his treatise *The Physical Basis of Life* : "If there is any
thing which is clear in the present progress of science, it is the tendency to reduce
all scientific questions, with the exception of purely mathematical ones, to what
is called *molecular physics*, that is, to the attraction, repulsion, motion and combination of the smallest particles of matter." And further : "The phenomena
of biology (the science of life) are as immediately related to molecular physics as
are those of chemistry ; and this is a fact acknowledged by all chemists and biolo-
gists who see beyond their own immediate occupation." If this is not a materialistic confession of faith in its best form, coming very near to "materialism as a
system," the difference between Mr. Huxley's views and those of the Author can
only lie in the difference between their apprehensions of the idea of "materialism."

(28) "The lower jaw from La Naulette," says Prof. Schaaffhausen (*Ueber die
Urform des menschlichen Schädels*, 1868), "shows a clearly animal prognathism
(oblique-toothedness) in the absence of a chin, a feature so important in the expression of the human countenance. Here the upper jaw takes part in the prognathism by forming behind the cutting-teeth an obliquely directed surface. This
striking formation had not hitherto been observed ; it is presented in a less degree in the fossil jaws from Arcy ; I find it also in the very ancient piece of a
lower jaw-bone from Fritzlar, in a young jaw from Uelde, in which the canine
tooth projects nearly 4 millimetres beyond the molar, and in the lower jaw from
Grevenbrück, which also in the elliptic form of the dental arch betrays the low
grade of its possessor." (This ellipticity, which is also possessed by the lower
jaw from La Naulette, is due to the narrow base of the rude human skull and
the projection of its upper jaws ; the dental arch of skulls of noble form being
parabolic. Among savage races, the inferior Negroes, the Australians and
especially the Malays, like the apes, exhibit this lengthened form of the dental
arch.)

"The shape of the forehead of the Neanderthal skull," says Schaaffhausen in another place in the same treatise, "the dentition and the form of the lower jaw from La Naulette and the prognathism of some children's jaws of the Stone Age of Western Europe excel in animal-resemblance any thing of this kind which can be observed among living savages," and, in a *Report on the Transactions of Scientific Congresses*, he connects therewith the amply justified expectation, that "tertiary Man" would "bring us still more distinct tokens of animal form."

A report to the London Anthropological Society by Dr. Carter Blake, the Secretary, on the jaw from La Naulette and the condition of the place where it was found, is contained in the July and October Parts of the *Anthropological Review*, 1867, p. 294 *et seq*. It appears therefrom that with the jaw were found a human ulna, two human teeth and a fragment of a worked Reindeer-horn. After a close comparison with more than 3000 jaws of various races of men, he comes to the conclusion that the Naulette jaw was contemporary with the mammoth and rhinoceros and presents characters which approximate it to those of the colored races of man, especially the Australian, or even go beyond what is found in them. He will not "venture to deny its indubitable similarity to the jaw of a young ape."

(29) If the idea of *species* is indefinite, that of *race* is so, if possible, in a still higher degree, and consequently furnishes the clearest proof of the want of determinate marks of distinction between the different species of man and of the existence of innumerable intermediate forms and transitional stages. The number of human races distinguished by different men of science at different times has varied from two or three to fifteen ! and yet each writer has his special characters, according to which he undertakes the distinction of the races, as color, hair, form of skull or face, geographical distribution, &c. The most popular classification of human races, and at the same time the simplest, is that of Link and Cuvier, who distinguish only Caucasians (white men), Mongols (yellow men), and Ethiopians (black men) ; while the celebrated Blumenbach added the Red or American and the Brown or Malayan Race ; and according to Schaaffhausen there are properly only *two* distinct races — an Asiatic, and an African — between which all the other forms may be arranged. Baer distinguishes *six*, Prichard *seven*, Bromme *ten*, Desmoulins and Pickering *eleven*, Bory de St.-Vincent *fifteen* races, and so on.

Alteration of climate, change of dwelling-place or of external circumstances generally alter races, although never to such a degree as to make them quite unrecognizable ; for a new race is never a simple product, but always a result of *two* causes — one represented by the *primitive race*, and the other by the *nature of the medium*. Hence two different races (for example, the Aryan and the Semitic) may both be very much altered in a foreign climate and yet never become one and the same race. Overlooking this important point gave rise to many misconceptions and false opinions in the old controversy on the unity or plurality of the human species. Moreover, some races can thrive very well, even in foreign climates, and propagate their peculiarities: for instance, the Jews, the Canadians, the New-Hollanders, the European inhabitants of the Cape of Good Hope, &c.

(30) Mr. Wallace (see *The Malayan Archipelago*, London, 1868) was so fortunate as to come into possession of a very young, uninjured female Orang and to keep it alive for nearly three months. During this time he was able to observe

its behavior closely and was astonished to see how much it resembled that of a human child. "Thus," says he, "the poor little thing began to lick its lips, draw in its cheeks and turn up its eyes with an expression of the greatest satisfaction when it got a morsel that suited its taste. On the other hand, when its food was not sufficiently sweet or savory, it turned over the piece a moment with its tongue, as if it would try the flavor, and then spat it out. If the same aliment was continued, it began to scream and to stamp with its feet, just like a child in a passion. It was its usual tactic to scream, if it thought itself neglected and wished to attract attention, although it exhibited its mental superiority to the human child by gradually ceasing to scream when no notice was taken, but immediately began again if it heard any one's footstep. During its illness, which ran its course like an intermittent fever and killed it, it exhibited phenomena altogether human-like."

Mr. Wallace also communicates many interesting details respecting the adult Orang. The most remarkable is its custom of preparing itself a sleeping-place for the night. He saw an animal that had been wounded by a shot, immediately seek for safety at the summit of an immense tree. "It was in the highest degree interesting to me to observe," says our authority, "how excellently he selected his place, and with what agility he stretched out his unwounded arm on all sides, broke off strong boughs with the greatest quickness and ease and placed them one over another, so that in a few moments he had formed a leafy hut that quite concealed him from our view." Mr. Wallace also remarks that on three occasions he saw the Orang, when irritated, hurl branches of trees to the ground. The Orang, moreover, is feared more on account of his strength than his size; and the natives told Mr. Wallace that, of all animals of the forest, only the Crocodile and the gigantic serpent (*Python*) ventured to attack the Orang, and he generally conquered them.

According to Grant (*Account of the Structure of an Orang-outang*, 1828), the Orang, when agreeably excited, is even capable of a sort of laugh; this is especially worthy of notice, because laughter has mostly been designated as an exclusive prerogative of humanity. On the other hand, he gives distinct signs of his desperation or grief. Grant says of the Orang observed by him: "He emptied his porringer upon the ground, whined in a peculiar manner and threw himself vehemently backwards to the earth, while he beat his chest and body with his hands and from time to time uttered a sort of groan." Dr. Yvan, who was attached to the French Expedition to China in the year 1843, tells us (*Voyage et Récits*, Bruxelles, 1853) that Tuan (an Orang from the island of Borneo) clothed himself as soon as ever he could lay hold of any piece of stuff for the purpose.* One day, his master having taken away from him a mango-fruit, he set up a peevish howling, like a vexed child. As this was not successful, he threw himself flat on his belly, beat the ground with his fist, screamed, wept and howled for more than half an hour. When at last the fruit was given back to him, he threw it at his master's head. His favorite companion was a Manilla negrito; he was also fond of playing with children. "One day, when rolling on a mat with a girl between four and five years old, he suddenly ceased playing and devoted himself to the

---

*The wearing of clothes, too, has been indicated as if it were an exclusive prerogative of man, although so many savage peoples go naked, and, as the above example shows, even animals exhibit a disposition to clothe themselves.

closest anatomical investigation of the child. The result much astonished him ; he retired to a corner and repeated on himself the same investigations that he had made on his little comrade."

In the year 1836, the celebrated Geoffroy-St.-Hilaire, the learned naturalist, mingled with the crowd which the arrival of an orang drew to the Paris Zoological Garden, in order to hear an opinion on this animal from the mouths of people entirely without prejudice and unacquainted with the rules of systematic classification. The result surprised the philosopher himself ; all unanimously declared that the animal from Sumatra was neither an ape nor a man. "Neither the one nor the other," this was the universal impression experienced.

Dr. Abel, at Java, had a young Orang-utan who used to prepare himself a proper bed every evening, with boughs and leaves, on a large tamarind tree that stood near the dwelling-house. Afterwards, on the voyage home with Dr. Abel, he used to make himself a bed with sail-cloths and rolled himself up therein. If canvas was not to be had, he would take the sailor's shirts and clothes which were hung up to dry.

Vosmaër had an Orang-utan that exhibited the same cleverness in arranging his bed.

W—r gives a similar account of the life of an Orang (*Gartenlaube*, 1860, No. 2). When the ship, on board of which the ape was, came into colder parts, he never came on deck without bringing his woollen blanket and wrapping himself in it. His bed he accepted gladly, although he had never known such a thing previously ; and before sleeping in it twice or thrice, he made it each time. Every night he slept exactly twelve hours. In the kitchen, in order to play the cook a trick, he used to turn the water-cocks. Glass vessels, &c., in which he received wine or other drink, he never broke, but put them carefully aside after using. His features remained always alike, just as those of savages do. He died through drinking up a bottle of rum, which he had stolen, uncorked and emptied. During his illness, his pulse was often felt ; every time his master came to his bedside he stretched out his paw to him.

A similar account is given of a Chimpanzee, who had been bled during an illness, and every time he felt unwell stretched out his arm.

Generally the large apes become in captivity and in intercourse with man, quite other beings than in the wild state. They become accustomed to wear clothes, drink out of glasses, use a spoon and a fork, uncork bottles, clean boots and brush clothes, and are even said to be employed at the Cape in a number of useful labors of the house and field. It is said that on ship-board they help to reef and furl the sails. They make themselves a bed with a raised pillow, show an inclination for ladies, light a fire and cook food thereon, dust furniture, clean the floor, try to open locks, &c. Buffon's celebrated Chimpanzee extended his hand to visitors, went arm in arm with them, ate at table sitting and with a napkin, used fork and spoon, wiped his mouth, poured out a glass, fetched coffee, put sugar in it, &c. A. Bastian saw on an English man of war, an ape sitting among the sailors and sewing as zealously as they. Josse tells of an Orang that was on good terms with all on board, except the butcher, whom he only approached timidly, cautiously examining his hands. Degrandpré tells of a Chimpanzee that heated the oven, let no coals fall and summoned the baker when the oven was heated. Le Vaillant had an ape, whom he employed for seeking roots and who sought to devour some secretly, but quickly concealed them whenever he was surprised.

Werner Munzinger, the celebrated traveller, informs us that the apes who live in the vicinity of villages (for example, belonging to the famous *Ape-State* near Karen) are familiar with man and never do any thing to injure him ; while those of the lonely parts, who seldom get a sight of him, regard him as an enemy, and attack a solitary individual or only two together, but do not venture to approach several.

The resemblance of the large apes to man makes the hunting of them very exciting and unpleasant ; and Du Chaillu, in his great work, has communicated some very interesting information thereon. Brehm (*Gartenlaube*, 1862, No. 40) says : "There is one thing very characteristic of the ape-hunters : even the most inured hunter cannot get rid of the idea that by killing an ape he has committed a murder. The demeanor of a dying ape is so human, that a cold shiver runs through one's frame when he has to recognize himself as his murderer." (It may here be remarked that the naturalist Schimper, who resided 28 years in Abyssinia, assured Brehm that the accounts of assaults by male apes on human females were no fables.)

One day Dr. Boerlage, in Java, shot at some apes, and hit a mother. She fell, mortally wounded, from the tree, tightly clasping a young one in her arms, and died weeping. The scene was so affecting to him and his hunting companions, that they firmly resolved never again to shoot an ape. The sight of a dying African ape made a like impression on one of the officers of the British exploring expedition under Captain Owen. On the river Zaire he mortally wounded an ape, and was so affected that he determined never to seek such an amusement again.

With regard to the large apes and their intelligence, compare further the statements of the author of the present work, following Du Chaillu, on the gorilla, the kulu-kamba, and the nschiegombouvé or nest-building ape in Africa, at pp. 297–307 of his collected essays *Aus Natur und Wissenschaft*.

(31) There are men and races of men, who have scarcely more understanding than certain animals, and have as little idea of religion or a moral world. The lowest among the Oceanians and Africans (as the aboriginal Australians, the South-Sea negroes, Bushmen, Central-Africans, &c , &c.), are entirely destitute of general ideas or abstract notions   Past and future concern them not; they live only in the present. The *Australian* has no words to express the ideas of God, religion, righteousness, sin, &c. ; he knows almost no other sensation than that of the need of food, which he endeavors in every way to satisfy, and makes known to the traveller by grimaces. "In them the capability of considering and inferring," says Hale (*Natives of Australia*, &c., 1846), "appears to be very imperfectly developed. The reasons which the colonists use in order to convince or persuade them are mostly such as are employed with children and half-imbeciles."

An interesting letter (an abstract of which is given in No. 15 of the *Ausland* for 1861) from a Frankfort lady, wife of Dr. Bingmann, who, with her husband, emigrated to Australia, depicts the natives as a race below all others in the capability of improvement. They live quite naked, in huts of bark, in which they

sleep with their dogs. They indolently endure hunger, thirst, cold and wet, eat
any thing, insects, serpents, worms, roots, berries, &c., have no fixed dwelling-
place, no tribal property and are quite incapable of civilization. The missionaries have long given up every attempt to civilize them ; for if one baptizes them,
it has no more effect than the baptism of a dog or a horse ; they understand nothing of the signification of the act. Each district has a different dialect ; so that
at every 50 or 60 miles distance they cannot understand each other. Marriages
are very loose ; infanticide is universal ; the aged are put to death. At ten or
twelve years of age they are already full-grown ; and they live, on the average,
not more than 36 years. Advanced age is very rare. Mentally, Madame Bing-
man says, they are mere children ; they find amusement only in childish tricks
and trifles. They live only in the present and think neither of the past nor the
future. They cannot be taught any principles ; they are dead to all morality.
They know no sentiment, no spiritual life, no love, no gratitude, but only un-
bridled passion and the sense of their nothingness against the white races. Their
complete extinction is now only a question of time. The men of Australia appear, like the animals and plants of that country, to have remained at an earlier,
imperfect stage, through being cut off from the rest of the world.

In 1864, Prof. Schaaffhausen laid before the *Niederrheinische Gesellschaft für
Natur- und Heilkunde* some photographs of the natives (soon to become extinct) of Van Diemen's Land, which he had received from the Rev. R. R. Nixon,
the English Bishop in Tasmania, and remarked that they showed such a surprising resemblance to the apes as is presented by scarcely any other race of men.
Nixon had been obliged to desist from all attempts at conversion, because the
poverty of their language and conceptions rendered every higher religious idea
impossible to them.

The aborigines of *New Caledonia*, akin to the Fiji-Islanders and belonging to
the Papuan group, have, according to the account of Von Rochas, no shame, go
quite naked, and indulge in a number of sexual excesses of the basest kind. They
have intelligence, as the beasts, *but no moral emotious*, are faithless in the highest
degree, perjured, crafty, will strike any one down from behind, are cannibals,
eating not merely their enemies, but even their own relatives, can only with great
difficulty count the lowest numbers, use strong abortives, and bury the aged
alive. If a chief is hungry, he straightway knocks down one of his subjects.—

Turning from Australia to *Africa*, we encounter among the lowest human
races there the same brutal degradation and irrationality. " It is sufficient,"
says Eichthal (*Briefe über die Negerrasse*, 1839), " to have seen black men and to
have lived some time among them, in order to be convinced that here is presented
a different human nature from that of white men." The experienced English
·traveller Burton depicts the negro of East Africa as a being without any moral
idea, or any thought reaching beyond the narrowest circle of things perceptible
by the senses. He has or knows no conscience, no logic, no history, no poesy,
no belief except the grossest superstition, no domestic life, no attachment to kin-
dred, no inclination to labor, no gratitude, no compassion, no care for the future,
&c. Mentally he is totally barren, and, though he can probably observe, he can
deduce nothing from what he has observed. Hence he has remained at the first
beginnings of civilization, and for thousands of years has made no progress, although he has had sufficient contact with cultivated peoples. He lies, even with-

out aim or profit, and is in the highest degree obstinate and self-willed, just as some animals are accustomed to be. His *fetichism* is only a rude, sensual superstition, the expression of abject terror. If he has killed any one, his only concern is lest the ghost of the murdered man should molest him. He combines all the incapacity and credulity of childhood with the obstinacy and stupidity of age.

Similar was the experience of the celebrated traveller Sir S. W. Baker in the region of the sources of the Nile (*Exploration of the Nile-Sources*, 1866). The Kytsch negroes, on the White Nile, he calls mere apes, and says that for their nourishment they trust solely to what nature supplies. They lie for hours on the ground, waiting till they can seize a field-mouse. They go perfectly naked and smear their body with ashes. " Savages so dreadfully degraded," says Baker, " I never saw before." The mission to the negroes of Sudan is perfectly useless. Moorlang, the missionary, says of them that they are inferior to cattle and inaccessible to all moral feeling. Baker made the same observation among the Latuka negroes, a tribe in the interior of Africa. They know neither gratitude, nor sympathy, nor self-denial ; they have no idea of duty or religion, know nothing that is good, honorable, or honest, but only lust, selfishness, cruelty, and above all, violence. They are thievish, lazy, envious, and ever ready to plunder their weaker fellows and to sell them into slavery.

The same holds good of innumerable other African tribes, as of the Mpongwes in Central Africa (of whom the American missionary John Leighton, who lived four years among them, reports that they possess neither religion, nor priests, nor sacrifice, nor religious assemblies), of the Bechuanas (of whom Livingstone, Andersson and others have given accounts), of the Kaffirs, the Hottentots, the Bushmen (which latter are accustomed to be reckoned among the most degraded of the races of men and live on the steppes of Southern Africa, in holes in the earth dug out with their hands, feeding on insects, worms and small birds, which they swallow unplucked), &c. All that these tribes know, or think they know of God, has first been brought to them by the missionaries.

Moreover, all these tribes are exceeded in brutal ferocity by the Dokos, who inhabit the south of Shoa, an unexplored region of Abyssinia, and of whom the missionary Dr. L. Krapf, in an English work on his eighteen years' stay and his travels in East Africa, gives very copious information from the statements of a slave of Ennrea. The Dokos are human pigmies, growing not higher than 4 feet, their complexion dark olive. They wander in the woods and live in an utterly brutish manner, without habitations, or temples, or holy trees, and so forth. They go quite naked, feed on roots, fruits, mice, serpents, ants and honey, and clamber about the trees like monkeys. They have no chief, no law, no weapons, no wedlock, no family, and indulge in promiscuous intercourse like the beasts, whereby they increase very fast. Mothers suckle their children only a short time and then abandon them. They hunt not, dig not, sow not, and *are not even acquainted with the use of fire*. Yet they decorate themselves with necklaces of snake's bones. They have thick lips, a flat nose, little eyes, long hair and long nails on the fingers and toes, with which they root in the earth. They are taken by stronger races and used as slaves. Du Chaillu, in his travels in Equatorial Africa in 1863–64, found a race of men called the Obongo or dwarfs. Their stature amounts to from 4 to 5 feet ; their skin is dirty yellow, they have a narrow forehead, but prominent cheek-bones, and an untamably fierce look.

Their legs are short, their chest and thighs covered with woolly hair. They live by hunting, on roots and wild fruits, bury their dead in hollow trees, speak a peculiar language, and live in huts made of leaves. (See *Ausland*, 1867, No. 14.)

In Karl von Hügel's work, *Der stille Ocean und die spanischen Besitzungen im ost-indischen Archipel* (Vienna, 1860, printed as a manuscript), there is a very similar communication on the aborigines of the *Philippine Islands*. This distinguished naturalist says (p. 358) :—"The aborigines of the Philippine Islands, as previously mentioned, are *more than probably* that black race of men whom the Spaniards named, on account of their small negro form, *negorillos de montes*, or dwarf negroes of the mountains. I saw several of them in Manilla, who had been captured in childhood and now appeared contented in their condition, perhaps *like a parrot, which becomes tame* if brought up from the nest, and then is contented with its daily food. To the captured adult, on the contrary, as to all these black aborigines, unrestrained freedom is dearer than a life quiet and free from care ; and if compelled to remain, although abundantly supplied with every necessary, it is said they die of home-sickness. This negro lives *like a wild animal* in the mountains and woods ; he is of an ungainly figure, *dwarfish size, with emaciated arms and legs, a lean body covered with black and red hairs;* the hair of his head black and woolly. The wild negrillo *is not a sociable being;* he always lives by himself alone or with his wife if he can procure one. This peculiarity has added to the difficulty of civilizing them or making of them domestic animals. Without any fixed dwelling, they traverse mountains and woods and sleep under trees, which is rendered possible by the absence of voracious beasts. They live by fishing and hunting, and can use their arrows very dexterously. These *negrillos* dwell only on the mountains of St. Matteo and Maribeles and in the province of Ilocos Norte. In the Island of Negros, which is so named from them, they are numerous. That they have a peculiar and probably *very poor language* is a matter of course ; the nature of this, and whether, as is probable, the negrillos in different provinces speak different dialects, I could not ascertain ; no one in Manilla was in a position to inform me ; the negrillos are there generally regarded and treated as nothing better than *a sort of apes.*" The toes of these savages, who dwell either in holes of the earth or in trees, are very movable and more widely separated than ours ; the great toe especially is distant from the rest. With them, as with fingers, they hold themselves fast to boughs of trees and to ropes.

The other islands of the great East-Indian archipelago also harbor numerous similar tribes of men, some of which if possible still nearer approach mere animal nature. In the interior of the large island Borneo, savages 4 feet high, of dark complexion, with wrinkled skin covered with hair, have been found, who know neither dwelling-place nor family, who sleep in caves, or on trees, live on vermin and eat one another. They can neither be tamed nor be employed for any work. They have a human countenance ; but their speech resembles rather a brutal gabble than a human mode of expression. On the island of Sumatra, Mr. Gibson, an American, had an opportunity of seeing a so-called *Orang-Kabu,* or aborigine. He went quite naked ; and his body was covered all over with soft dark hair. It is said that the Orang-Kabu has no language of his own, but only learns with great labor to pronounce a few Malay words. The same traveller mentions another tribe, the Orang-Gugur, whose body likewise exhibits a very great resemblance to an ape's.

De la Gironnière tells of the Ajetas, who inhabit the interior of Luzon (one of the Philippine Islands) :—"The people appeared to me more like a great family of apes than human beings. The sound they made was like the short shriek of those animals ; and their movements were the same. The difference consisted solely in knowing the use of the bow and the spear and how to make a fire." (W. Earl, *Native Races of the Indian Archipelago*, London, 1853.)—

If we turn from the Indian islands to the *continent of Asia*, we meet here also, in the inaccessible wilds of India, with human beings (probably the remains of the ancient primitive population), who at first sight leave the observer in doubt whether he has before him men or anthropoid apes. One day, in the solitudes of the vast jungles, the Old Shikari (*The Hunting-grounds of the Old World*, by the Old Shekarry, quoted in the *Ausland*, 1860, No. 39), met with wild men who lived on trees. There were a man, a woman and a child, dark olive-colored, the largest of them not higher than 4 feet. They had no clothing ; their eyes were small and piercing and their face wrinkled ; the nose was flat, the mouth wide, the teeth large and yellow, the arms long and shrivelled, the nails like claws. The discoverer took them at first to be in fact apes, and had to look at them some time in order to become convinced that they were human. With this agrees the information given by Piddington, an English colonist, in the *Journal of the Asiatic Society of Bengal*, vol. XXIV., p. 207 (quoted in the *Ausland*, 1855, No. 50), on the Indian "ape men," as well as the account given by von Hügel (*Amtlicher Bericht der Versammlung deutscher Naturforscher und Aerzte in Prag*, 1837, p. 44), of the inhabitants of some of the hill-parts of India, whom he classes with the New-Hollanders, because they had not yet arrived at forming a horde, and scarcely a family was found united. Man and woman live isolated ; and when by chance any one meets with them they take refuge like monkeys on the trees. Piddington describes the one seen by him as "small, flat-nosed, with gaping arched wrinkles round the mouth and on the cheeks, with very long arms, and with reddish hair on the coarse black skin. "Had he been seen," he adds, "crouching in a dark corner or on a tree, he would have been taken for a large orang-utan."

One of the newest reports on wild tribes of men in India was read before the London Anthropological Society, in 1865, by Dr. Shortt Zillah, a physician in Chingleput. One of the most remarkable of them are the so-called Leaf-wearers, who inhabit some districts of Orissa. They do not grow higher than 4 or 5 feet ; and the women clothe themselves only with boughs, which they fasten round the waist with strings. They are regarded as the dregs of the province, of which they inhabit the remotest and wildest parts. They live partly on boiled rice, partly on wild fruits, roots, &c., have no priests, no education, no worship, &c., but, on the other hand, they have some superstitious customs. Their only implements are the bow and arrow and an axe for felling timber.

The *American continent* furnishes an equal abundance of information relative to the wild or primitive condition of our race. The Indians of Ucayale, writes Castelnau, (*Travels in Peru*), appear scarcely to belong to our human kind. Their brown color, their big, almost spherical belly, their meagre arms and legs and the strange shape of their (artificially deformed) head make them appear like beings of quite another sort. The Cahibes, in South America, just like the already described Australian blacks (who, according to the experienced traveller Moritz Wagner, without huts, traffic, or clothes, live on roots, fruits, snails, and, in case of need, *on their own children*, and, on account of their unbounded stupidity, cannot even be used as slaves), are obstinate *cannibals*, who even devour their own children and the aged. The Digger or Pau-Eutaw-Indians are depicted, by the author of "*A Ride across the great American Desert and the Rocky Mountains*, as "the most degraded and wretched beings that inhabit the North-American continent; their food is horrible; the Chinese roasted dogs and rats are epicurean dishes in comparison. Some of them brought with them lizards to the camp and ate them raw with no other preparation than pulling out the tails. Their hair is long and almost as coarse as a mule's mane. Their face is void of all mental expression; and, excepting the eye, which is remarkably fierce, the features are nowise noteworthy. The traveller can only discover a striking resemblance between them and wild beasts, both as regards their manners and their exterior. I have often observed how in walking they turn the head quickly from left to right, exactly as the prairie-wolf does. In their voracity they have more resemblance to an anaconda than a human being. I have been told, by those intimately acquainted with their manners, that five or six of these Indians will seat themselves round a dead horse and eat till nothing is left but the bones.

"We gave them the remnant of our dried beef, which was putrid and mouldy. This they ate greedily; and when they saw that nothing more was to be had, they expressed their satisfaction by rubbing their bellies and grunting in a way that would have well suited a herd of swine."

"The Indians," says the author of the account of a journey from New-York to California, in Diezmann's *Aus der Fremde*, "are *children*. Their arts, wars, transactions, &c., belong to the lowest condition of human society. A company of boys from ten to fifteen years old is quite as well able to govern itself as an Indian tribe; and the primitive inhabitants of America will within fifty years have vanished from the soil of their fathers. . . . The Indian depicted by Cooper and Longfellow is only visible to the eye of the poet; to the prosaic observer the Indian appears a creature which has altogether failed to reach the dignity of human nature, a slave of appetite and sloth," &c.

The Brazilian man of the woods, or Botokudo, is according to Dr. Robert Avé-Lallemant (*Journey through North Brazil*, 1859), quite naked and without the slightest sentiment of modesty. He has thin thighs and calves, long, slender hands, a large trunk, big belly and a depressed, narrow and bony forehead. He is not interested by any thing uncommon; his eyes are without lustre and soul; his look is staring, dull and without intelligence. In the presence of an European he is shy, embarrassed, and slips aside. He wears wooden plugs in his lips and ear-lobes, is considerably smaller than the European, and appears, on close intercourse, like a good-natured ape. When Lallemant endeavored to make him understand anything by signs, he imitated every action, just as apes do. "I was convinced," he says, "with deep sadness, that they were two-handed apes." They are also cannibals and quite incapable of seeing the abominableness of the practice. Nothing excites their curiosity or attention. They speak little to one another, but rather mutually grunt and snuffle. They are quite destitute of moral notions. To them a man is either a friend and then *good*, or an enemy and then *b.id.* In eating they make a smacking noise, like swine.— In the *Revue des deux Mondes*, 1863, Adolphe d'Assier says of the Brazilian Botokudo that he is entirely destitute of moral ideas. Immorality is normal, morality sporadic or exceptional; an honest man is called " not a thief,"— truth, " not a lie."

On the 19th September, 1868, at the fourth session of the International Congress for Archæology and History in Bonn (Section for Primeval History), Otto Schmitz gave a very full report on the wild Apaches Indians, whose country lies between the Rio Grande del Norte and the Rio Colorado, among whom he had been compelled to live several months, and who exhibit the utmost degree of brutal barbarism. They go quite naked, their leather-like skin seeming to compensate for the want of clothing; sleep in hollows in the ground, feed on fruits, berries, vermin and stolen horses or asses, have no other implements than bow and spear, and go singly or in small troops without a chief; only for marauding expeditions on a larger scale than usual do they unite under chieftains. They know no marriage, but only a longer or shorter cohabitation of the sexes, the children being quickly lost in the horde, have no notion of their age or of counting years, they are unacquainted with *physicians*, do not wash their children, but powder them with sand, leave their sick and dead on the road, and have scarcely any idea of wailing for the dead. " They have no idea that the dead live on, that there may be something better elsewhere than here, or a conception of the great Spirit, such as is found among many Indians. The only festival they observe is that of the full moon." Beasts are not slaughtered, but torn asunder. In a marauding expedition the weak or the crippled are left behind to starve, or are slain. The Apache speaks little, and rather in gestures than in sounds, has no notion of greeting, either at meeting or parting, speaks more in broken sentences than in coherent words; guttural sounds so predominate that loud discourse is almost impossible. The important auxiliary verb "to be" does not exist. Their numeral system is decimal, like that of most savage peoples.

The inhabitants of Tierra del Fuego, at the southern extremity of America, are, according to the Duke of Argyll (*Primeval Man*, 1869, p. 167), perhaps inferior to all other races of men. They are habitual cannibals; they will sooner kill and eat their old women than their dogs; go perfectly naked, have an ugly countenance bedaubed with paint, a dirty, greasy skin, tangled hair, unharmonious voices and violent manners. " When we see such men," says Darwin (*Voyage of the Beagle*), " we can hardly persuade ourselves that they are creatures like ourselves and inhabitants of the same world."—

If we repair from the extreme south to the extreme north of our globe, we find also here a similar spectacle among the inhabitants of the Arctic Ocean, the Eskimos. " The Eskimo," says John Ross (*Narrative of a Second Voyage*, &c., 1835, p. 448), " is a beast of prey, without any other pleasure than that of eating; without any principle or rational emotion, he devours as long as he can, and as much as he can get, like the vulture or the tiger. . . . He eats only to sleep, and sleeps only as soon as possible to eat again." As to their mental capabilities, they have, according to Whitebourne, no knowledge of God, and live without any form of civil government. On this point John Ross says : " I could not be clear whether they understood any thing of what I endeavored to make intelligible to them by explaining the simplest things in the simplest manner. Should I have accomplished more, if I had understood their language better ? I have very much reason to doubt it. That they must have had a certain sort of moral law written on the heart I could not doubt, for their behavior proved it ; but beyond this all my searches were vain, and no effort led to anything worth mention. Relative to their opinions on the essentials of that from which the presence of a sort of religion might have been concluded, I was at last compelled to give up the attempt in despair." (*Loc. cit.*, p. 548).

This hasty sketch of the natural and moral history of savage peoples may suffice in this place, although by similar or analogous delineations by transatlantic travellers from the most diverse regions of the inhabited earth it might have been much further extended. The rude savage or primitive man is, even as to his whole essence, so very different from the civilized and cultivated man, who is accustomed to fixed civil and social arrangements and educated by the culture of thousands of years, that it is impossible to place the two on one level and from them, after the manner of the idealistic philosophers, construct an ideal universal "essence of man." It is only education, improvement, experience, the inheritance of acquired capabilities and the innumerable aids and incitements of culture that make the civilized man what he is now and what he must be, and probably will in process of time continually still more transform him and remove him still further from his original brutish condition. It is true that some have endeavored to diminish the force of all those observations of savage peoples, which we have urged, by laboring to represent them as *degenerate*, fallen from a previous better condition of culture, and hence abnormally departing from the idea of humanity. But, apart from isolated cases with which that opinion agrees, there are no facts to confirm such a view, or even to make it appear probable. It is a universal law of nature that degeneration leads to premature extinction ; but some of these tribes have already existed from time immemorial, and many of them enjoy a *fecundity* too great to be reconcilable with the fact of degeneration.

"The immediate impression," says Prof. Schaaffhausen (*Ueber den Zustand der wilden Völker*, p. 164), "made by all the phenomena of savage peoples, their intimate connection with the nature of the country they inhabit, the absence of any reminiscence of any better condition, the bodily health and physical strength in which, when out of contact with the influences of civilization, they are preserved, the peculiarities of their organization (which betray a lower stage of development), finally the absence of such signs of decay as we perceive in certain cases — all this leads us to think that most of the savage tribes have never been in possession of a higher culture. This view is also favored by the circumstance that many of the most polished nations of the present day were in ancient times at a like stage of barbarism."

(32) Besides those contained in Appendix 31, numerous examples of savage nations who are destitute of this belief and even have no words in their languages to express the ideas *God, religion, justice, sin*, &c., may be gleaned from the Author's *Kraft und Stoff*, ii edition, p. 201 *et seqq.* "Three large sections of the earth's surface," says G. Pouchet, "which are still inhabited by savages, appear to have remained till now exempt from religious notions : they are the interior of Africa, Australia, and the polar regions — consequently the three most difficult to explore, and hence the least known portions of the world. Latham says that the Australians have not yet gone so far as to form by themselves even

the rudest elements of a religion, and that their minds seem to be actually too inert for superstition. A missionary says of them : " What can be undertaken with a people whose language knows no expressions for ' righteousness,' ' sin,' and the like, and to whose minds the ideas which those words are intended to express are utterly unexplainable ?" Of the Latukas (region of the Nile sources) Sir S. W. Baker states (*The Albert Nyanza*, 1867), that the idea of a Deity does not exist among them, and they have no sort of religion, not even the rudest fetish-worship.

The belief in a God is not any thing original or innate, but something made or grown, and first results from a certain amount of reflection by the uneducated human mind on the surrounding natural phenomena, which, from defective knowledge of the laws of nature and of their intimate connection, he cannot explain in a natural way, and hence refers them to an invisible, mysterious cause ; while the *wholly* uncultivated savage does not feel the need of even such a superficial method of explanation. Science is a continued struggle with this notion ; and with every step she makes forwards she drives back the belief in supernatural forces, or the need of such a belief, into more remote and untenable positions. Hence every science, and especially every philosophy, that seeks reality instead of appearance, truth instead of pretence, *must necessarily be atheistic ;* otherwise it blocks up against itself the path to its end—the truth. As soon, then, as in a *philosophic* book the word " God " occurs, except in criticism or reference, one may confidently lay it aside ; in it will be found nothing capable of promoting the real progress of knowledge. In properly scientific works the word will be seldom met with ; for in scientific matters the word " God " is only another expression for our ignorance ; in like manner as on more special occasions the words " vital force," " instinct," " soul," &c.

That, moreover, for religion itself the idea of a Deity is not indispensable, is proved by the well-known and oft-cited example of the most wide-spread religious system in the world, *Buddhism*. Barthélemy St.-Hilaire, the author of the excellent work *Buddha and his Religion*, (1862), says :—" There is not found even the least trace of the belief in a Deity in the whole of Buddhism ; and the assertion that it assumes the absorption of the human soul in the divine or the soul of the universe is an altogether arbitrary supposition, which in Buddha's notion is not even possible. In order to believe that man can lose himself by union with God, one must first believe in God himself. But one can scarcely even assert that Buddha did *not* believe in him. He ignores God so completely that he does not once endeavor to deny him. He neither mentions him to explain the origin and the earlier life of man, nor to advance a conjecture concerning his future destiny. Buddhism knows God in no wise," &c.

The same writer adds to this statement the following words (certainly very worthy of being laid to heart) :—" The human mind has hitherto been observed scarcely anywhere else than among the races to which we ourselves· belong. These races doubtless deserve a very large place in our studies ; but although they are the most important, they are not the only ones. Must not the others also be taken into consideration, however inferior we may deem them ? If they do not fit into the hastily constructed frame, must we distort them in order to be able to adapt them to our too contracted theories ? or is it not better to acknowledge that the old systems are defective, and that they cannot comprehend the whole of that which they pretend to explain ?"

(33) That the art of numeration, and the science of mathematics erected thereon, is not any thing innate in the human mind, but is only gradually developed by education and cultivation, is proved by the example of the savage tribes of Australia and Brazil who have not carried their numeral system beyond three or four, and can only indicate higher numbers by *gestures.* Oldfield even describes a tribe who count no further than the number *two* and designate all beyond by the word *bool-tha*, which signifies "many." A native of this tribe, wishing to give the narrator an idea of the number of men killed in a battle, tried at first by mentioning the names of those who had fallen, and at the mention of each name he stretched out a finger; but after several vain attempts of this sort, he ended by raising one hand three times in succession, by which he wished it to be understood that the number amounted to fifteen.

Generally, *all* numeration began with the fingers or toes; and among most savage tribes it has remained at that stage to the present time. Hence, *five, ten* and *twenty* everywhere form the fundamental numbers; and indeed the verbal signs for these numbers agree with the names of those parts of the body. Among many savage tribes of Africa, America, &c., for example, the number *five* is called "a whole hand," the number *ten* "two hands," *twenty* "a whole man." The number *six* is denoted by the expression " one of the other hand," &c. ; the number *eleven* is called "one of the foot," and so on. *Twenty-one* is called " one of the hand of another Indian," &c. In some instances words expressing number are taken from the properties of the individual fingers; in others the names of other natural objects which are present once or oftener, serve as numeral designations. Thus the ancient Indians said earth or moon for *one*, eye or arm or wing for *two;* for *three* Rama, or fire, or property, because they accepted three Ramas, three kinds of fire, and three properties; for *four* they said age or Veda, because they accepted four ages and four Vedas, and so on. For *four* the *Abipoins* in America say "ostrich-foot," because it has four toes. The custom of tying up pine-cones in parcels of four has in some of the South-Sea Islands led to the number four being denoted by the word "pono," which signifies a packet, while for ten and a hundred the words for bundle and great packet are used.

Moreover, counting by 5, 10 or 20, or the number of the fingers and toes, is so general that departures from it must be regarded only as exceptions : and it lies at bottom of the numeral systems of the most advanced nations.

Some observations seem to prove that the *beasts* also are able to count. A mouse, from whom nine young ones had been taken, came nine times, to fetch them back one by one, and then no more, although she had not been able to look into the cap in which they were imprisoned. The *magpie* can count to four, but no further. If four hunters hide themselves before her eyes, and three of them go away, she knows that one is still there, and is on her guard ; but if, on the contrary, there are five of them, and four go away, she thinks that all are gone, and becomes careless.

(34) Animals also use tools. Apes push stones between the open valves of the mussel-shell to prevent their closing, and open the shells of oysters by striking them with stones. Still better known is the fact that apes defend themselves with sticks or cudgels, and hurl down branches or heavy fruits from the trees upon their pursuers. And Forbes observes (*Eleven Years in Ceylon*) that wild

elephants break off boughs from the trees to use them for keeping off the flies. It is well known that, when tamed or under training, beasts learn to use all manner of tools with great dexterity. On the other hand, it is related of many wild tribes that they have scarcely any idea of using tools. Thus the *Mincopies* (the black inhabitants of the Andaman Islands, in the Bay of Bengal), according to a report made by travellers to the Paris Anthropological Society, possess neither dwellings nor hatchets or the like. They know not the use of fire, leave their dead unburied, have no regulation or custom concerning marriage, and appear in respect to their *social* instincts to be lower than the beasts. Of them, of whom Colebroke said that their form and features expressed the extreme of wretchedness and savagery, and more recent accounts mention incredible traits of animal barbarism, R. Owen has lately (as Schaaffhausen says in a communication to the *Niederrheinische Gesellschaft für Natur- und Heilkunde*, June 8, 1864) been able to prove that in some characteristics of their bodily structure, especially of their bony system, they exhibit a lower grade of organization — which, in connection with their mental rudeness, must appear specially worthy of notice.

(35) That many wild tribes of Africa, America, Australia and Asia, as well as the islands of Oceania, have no idea of the use of clothing and go *perfectly naked*, is well known and is sufficiently proved by the testimonies already adduced. Indeed, when clothing is offered to them, they scorn it. In 1858 the American frigate "Niagara" rescued 455 Africans from the slave-ship "Elcho," in order to carry them back to their native country. Dr. Rainey, who accompanied them, writes of these savages :—" They are altogether very dirty and refuse to wear any clothes. They cannot be prevailed upon to comply with even those measures of cleanliness which are absolutely indispensable for the preservation of health. The clothes which were given them in Charleston they immediately rent to pieces. It is seldom that one cares for another ; the utmost they will do is to assist each other if their back itches. Even for their sick and dying they have not the least concern. If one of them has died, they let the corpse lie amongst them for hours, as if nothing had happened. But scarcely has the last sign of life disappeared ere they take possession without ceremony, of his coverlet, his spoon, and whatever else he may have used. They are the most imbecile, brutish, pitiable creatures I ever came across." (See *Allgem. Zeitung*, 1858, No. 313.) Similarly Wilhelm Bischoff (*Ausland*, 1860, No. 3) states, concerning his impressions in the American slave-States :—" The *genuine woolly-head*, especially as he is not seldom found among the plantation-negroes, makes upon the European, who is not accustomed to such a sight, an extremely disagreeable impression, which is aggravated by their character being, as a rule, in perfect correspondence with their ugly exterior. It would be difficult in Europe, especially in Germany, to find a stock that could, even remotely, be compared with this race. Except speech and form, these negroes have in them scarcely one mark of humanity ; all their movements, their entire deportment, remind one rather of the brute; and they seem totally incapable of any higher culture," &c. "Almost all are thieves and liars ; hence the evidence of a black has no validity in a court of justice. It is useless trouble to make them understand the wrong of this, because they are altogether ignorant of the word *shame*," &c.

Of the Nuehr negroes in Africa, Sir S. W. Baker (*l. c.*) says : " They carry the nature of savages pretty well to the highest pitch. The men go as naked as they were born; their bodies are rubbed in with ashes, and their hair dyed red with a wash of ashes and cow's urine. These fellows are the veriest devils I ever saw; there is no other expression for them. Even the unmarried women are quite naked; the married wear a fringe of grass round their loins." The same author gives a similar account of the negroes of Kytschland, of the Latukas in the region of the Nile-sources, &c.

(36) The speech of the Fans of West Africa is, Du Chaillu says, a collection of guttural tones which no one can understand; and still worse and harsher is the speech of the Oschebas. De la Gironnière, who staid some days among the Ajetas on the Philippine island of Luzon, says that the people appeared to him like a large family of apes, and that *the sounds they uttered resembled the short shriek of those animals*, and their movements also were the same. The Brazilian Botokudo has, according to Adolphe d'Assier (*l. c.*) an extremely imperfect language, indicating by the same word a number of tolerably diverse objects. Thus the word *tschohn* signifies at the same time tree, beam, twig, chip; the word *po:* foot, hand, finger, toe, nail, heel, &c. The Australian language is very poor, possessing only a few hundred words, and among them not one to express a general idea. Thus they have denominations for individual trees, but no word for the notion "tree." The same is true of the languages of many savage peoples, which, as a rule, are quite destitute of expressions for general notions of properties which at the same time belong to different bodies, as "color," "tone," "tree," &c. They have a special word for each kind of color, for each kind of tree, but no general designation. The language of the savages of Borneo and Sumatra is said to be rather a sort of brutish cackle or croak than a real human mode of expression. The speech of the Hottentots and Bushmen, too, is distinguished by its poverty in words. Generally, savages are accustomed to talk more by gestures and looks than by actual tones. The lower in the scale a people or a man is, the poorer are they in words, while wealth of words is a special characteristic of superior minds; for word is nothing else but the incarnation of thought. The Veddahs in Ceylon, Sir Emerson Tennent tells us, mutually make themselves understood almost entirely by signs, grimaces and guttural sounds, which have little resemblance to definite words or language in general.

That language, however, is not exclusively the property of man is shown by the circumstance that brutes also possess the faculty of mutual converse and communication in a very high degree. The brutes understand each other, they understand us and make themselves understood by us, all which cannot be done without a sort of language. It is very well known that dogs know how to inform their masters, in relation to very definite matters, by gestures, looks, play of the eyes, barking, whining, &c.; and it is as well known that dogs understand exactly what is said of them, or when orders are given to them. Every animal has its peculiar language and a number of determined sounds to express its wishes, wants, sensations, &c. Thus Dupont has, by close observation, found that pigeons and fowls have twelve different tones, dogs have fifteen, cats fourteen, horned cattle twenty-two, &c.—an estimate which is probably much too low. At first all the tones were "guttural" or throat-tones, as is still the case with brutes and savages; later the "labial sounds" were added. Besides, as Pouchet justly remarks, *language*, which is only a simple means of communication between two living beings, and as sign- and tone-language, though not as verbal language, belongs at the same time to man and beast, must be distinguished from *speech*,— which is exclusively the property of man, but is only possible with a certain development of articulate verbal language and the existence of designations for general ideas. There is, according to Clémence Royer, a greater difference between the most highly developed analytical languages, or between the language of a Shakespeare or Corneille, and that of a Papuan negro, than between the latter and the stammering cry of an angry ape when scolding his female or young. Also the tones which apes are accustomed to utter exhibit a close approximation to the lowest primitive forms of human speech. "Language," says H. Tuttle, "is the expression of thought; and even if the thoughts which the brutes unmistakably communicate to one another are not identical with the human, at any rate they are analogous. The dog calls his companions or his master by means of an altogether peculiar baying; in the roaring of the lion, the snarl of the tiger, the song of the bird and the thousand-fold modes of sound of the insect world are found all the modulations of the expression of feeling and mutual intelligence, from the alluring call to the warning signal, from love to fury, &c., &c. Lastly, in the comparison of brute with human language, it must not be forgotten that parrots, starlings, ravens, &c., are able to utter articulate sounds, and many words very distinctly, and, in fact, with consciousness of their purport, even without having been expressly taught, and merely from voluntary imitation and independent observation.

(37) According to the distinguished linguist A. Schleicher (*Ueber die Bedeutung der Sprache für die Naturgeschichte des Menschen*, 1865), language is something which has gradually grown, and which once was not existing. All the more highly organized languages have little by little arisen or been developed from simple language-organisms in the course of enormous periods. The languages of simplest construction have been gradually formed out of so-called *vocal gestures* and *imitative sounds*, such as the brutes also possess; and language itself is the product of a gradual growth according to vital laws which, in their essential features, we are able to indicate. This growth took place in connection and simultaneously with the greater improvement of the brain and the vocal organs.

Schleicher, however, in contradiction to M. Pouchet, defines language as the expression of thought by means of words; and he holds it to be exclusively characteristic of man, while *vocal gesture* belongs to the brute also. Since, according to him, language first made the man, our ancestors were not from the beginning that which we now call man; and hence the results of linguistic science also just, like those of natural science, lead "decidedly to the adoption of a gradual development of man out of lower forms."

J. Grimm, also, the renowned German etymologist, in his well-known pamphlet on the origin of language (*Ueber den Ursprung der Sprache*, VI. Aufl., Berlin, 1866), calls the latter "a progressive work," "a difficult acquisition" of man, and says expressly that it is not innate, but, in its origin as well as its progress, is "acquired" by us. Language, according to him, was imperfect at first and has gradually increased in value; hence it cannot have emanated from God. All verbal roots contain *sensuous* representations; and all ideas originate from the intuitions of the *senses*. From the notion of *breathing* comes that of living; from the idea of *expiring* (breathing out) that of dying; from that of *crowing*, the idea of a cock, &c., &c.

According to J. P. Lesley (*l. c.*), every language has a certain number of roots (200–600) from which it has been developed. Now, for the origin of these roots or germs there are only three possibilities:— they were either communicated by divine revelation or the gift of a *ready-made* language, or resulted from the gift of a *capacity* of language to the first men, or finally, were produced by a higher, a human development of a faculty of expression diffused throughout the animal world. Now-a-days, says Lesley, the first of these possibilities can only be entertained by those who believe in Adam and Eve, and is inadmissible on account of the *multiplicity* of languages. *Scientifically* only the last two can now be spoken of, while the circumstance that all animals have a sort of language, and that the human faculty of speech is greater only because the human brain is larger and more finely organized, speaks decidedly in favor of the last of these possibilities. At any rate, according to Lesley, the original development of language was just as gradual as that which we now observe in every child; and the language of a nation grows and changes with its changing mental condition. We shall never fathom the languages of the so-called Stone-age; they have long ago been lost and replaced by others. Language is a portion of natural science; words and language live and become extinct, exactly as living beings do, and like them become *fossil* also.

The following are dead, having completed their cycle of life :— Sanskrit, Pehlvi, Egyptian, Chaldee, Hebrew, Greek, and Latin.

(38) The limited nature of our physical knowledge and the change or addition which the things to be known undergo or receive within our physical means of knowledge or senses, form the last citadel within which philosophical spiritualism has retreated, after it has been victoriously driven from the field at all other points by philosophical materialism or realism. Sulking solitary upon deserted rocks, it hopes at some more favorable time to be able from this point again to reconquer the lost territory. But there is this in opposition to it, that it is equally or perhaps even less able than its opponent to give any account of what the so-called *thing* is in itself, or of what the thing is without its phenomena. Things, or more properly speaking, the material movements of the external world within our organs of sense may indeed only then receive the properties which we ascribe to them,— tones, colors, odors, nay, even sensations of heat, light, taste, &c., may only be additions of our subjective I to the objective external world,— and the latter, when we deprive it of these additions, may appear to be only an accumulation or sum of innumerable atoms or particles of matter vibrating against and among each other in the most multifarious forms and relations, but nevertheless these movements or in general things are not on this account less real or actual, and in the form of contemplative ideas constitute the foundation of all human knowledge. Locke, the celebrated founder of sensualism, knew this very well, for he ascribed a great part of the properties of bodies to our sensitivity and distinguished between what he called *primary* and *secondary* properties of things, referring to the former, extension, impermeability, form, motion or rest and number, and to the latter color, tone, taste, odor, hardness, softness, roughness, &c.

The materialistic philosophers of antiquity also, such as Epicurus, distinguished between the sensorial qualities of things or the sensation of the organized animal body, and the things themselves, but added that *beyond* the things of the phenomenal world nothing existed and there was nothing to seek. It is therefore a grievous error when, as we so often hear in the present day, this distinction is described as a bran-new discovery of science (*especially* the physiology of the organs of the senses), whilst even the simplest consideration without any scientific cultivation leads us to separate our sensation from the action causing the sensation. And it is incomprehensible, how so acute a thinker as F. A. Lange, could allow himself in his well-known *History of Materialism* (Iserlohn, 1866) to be led by this circumstance and the well-known distinction by Kant of the *thing itself* from the *phenomenon* to go directly against materialism and even in accord with Kant to support the maxim, *that our ideas do not accommodate themselves to the objects, but the objects to our ideas.* The simple consequence of this conception would be the absurd assumption that all that we recognize is only an illusion of the senses,—an assumption which must make an end not only of all philosophy but of all knowledge. Even the imperfection and the sufficiently demonstrated limitation of our sensorial perception, which does not even possess a direct organ of perfection for so many motions which occur in nature, and in this respect is perhaps exceeded by many animals, will not suffice to furnish a scientific foundation for the doctrine of Kant, which is derived from pure speculation. Kant's "thing itself" is a purely ideal entity, or a logical and empirical nonentity, of the connection of which with our *conception* proceeding from sensorial recognition no conception can possibly be formed. A "thing itself" is inconceivable for the very reason that all things exist only for each other, and without reciprocal relations have no significance. But even if there were a "thing itself," it would be absolutely inconceivable or unrecognizable and could claim no value either for our action or for our thought. We know things every where all the better, the better we investigate their manifold relations to each other and to other things. Even the qualities or properties which things acquire within our organs and our capacity of conception and which are usually designated by the philosophers as "appearance" in contradistinction to the "thing itself," are therefore no less actual and always represent perfectly definite and equally actual conditions or movements of the external world. Hence, when Lange calls the world of sense "a product of our organization," this opinion rests upon a perfectly one-sided conception of the actually existing relations and upon an artificial confusion of the state of the case which is in itself very simple. If the senses sometimes deceive us by a false appearance, as, for example, in the movements of the celestial bodies, we correct the error thus produced by contemplation, that is, by the application of natural laws, which, again, we have ascertained only by means and as a consequence of sensorial impressions. The *deceptivity* of sensorial appearances *in particular cases* is therefore established by their *truthfulness* in general.

The author proposes hereafter and in a more suitable place to express himself in more detail upon the whole of the very important matter here touched upon, and in the mean while recommends those philosophers by profession who still believe in the "Ding an sich," and without any appearance of a reason regard it as the sole determinant, to set the following song to music and to have it sung at their assemblies in place of the grace usual among theologians:

> O Ding an sich,
> Wie lieb' ich Dich,
> Du aller Dinge Ding!
> Nur blinder Wahn
> Sieht schief Dich an
> Und achtet Dich gering.
>
> Zwar weiss ich nicht,
> Ob Dein Gesicht
> Ist hässlich oder schön?
> Und ob Du wohl,
> Fest oder hohl,
> Magst liegen oder stehn?
>
> Ob jung, ob alt,
> Ob warm, ob kalt,
> Ob grade oder krumm,
> Ob Du voll Zwist,
> Ob sanft Du bist,
> Ob pfiffig oder dumm?
>
> Doch einerlei!
> Dir bleib' ich treu
> Und unveränderlich,
> Und thue dar,
> Dass nichts ist wahr,
> Als nur "das Ding an sich!"

(39) The greater development and increased perfection of the brain in the higher races of men and in proportion to the advance of civilization is a fact as well demonstrated, as the gradual improvement of the brain and its individual parts in the Vertebrate series. This applies especially to the anterior or frontal portions of the brain, whilst the posterior parts appear to have become more flattened with advancing civilization, so that a kind of greater erection of the whole brain accompanied by a widening appears to have been a chief characteristic of its civilizatory development. This, however, relates only to the very rough character of size and external form, whilst the internal improvement of structure, composition, formation of the different parts, &c., generally remains concealed from the eye of the anatomist. But it is in this, and in the more fully developed function of the activity of the organ that we have the main lever of its relative superiority and also of its continued development in the future. It is therefore a sign of great want of knowledge or judgment when we find in many works written in opposition to the theory of evolution, and especially against the consequences deduced from it by Carl Vogt with regard to the future development of the human race, that the following absurd objection is brought forward, namely, that an enormous and injurious development of the brain and skull or a morbid macrocephalism (big-headedness) must be the necessary consequence of that development in accordance with the Darwinian doctrine of evolution. Even within the space now furnished by the human skull, the growth of which is subjected to definite laws, prescribed by the type and mutual relations with the other organs and parts of the body, there is still so much superfluous room for the further development of the organ of thought in its indivividual and more delicate parts, as

may suffice for thousands of years and for a civilizatory development of the widest kind.   Moreover, we must not forget that by means of its present form and constitution the organ is already capable of an evolution of its function or activity by use and practice, such as we know it attains only in very few men.   It is a fact sufficiently well-known to physiologists that the structure and function of an organ do not always stand in an equal ratio to each other, but often in a very unequal ratio, so that the hand, for example, which in the animals most nearly allied to man serves almost entirely as a grasping or motory organ, although approaching very near to that of man, and which probably served only for the simplest purposes in primeval man, is capable in the more highly developed men of an almost marvellous perfection and adroitness.   In the same way the brain of man also by practice and cultivation becomes capable of performances which appear simply incomprehensible to the simple and uninstructed understanding.   If we add to this that a brain thus developed and trained under otherwise favorable circumstances transfers its acquired improvements in accordance with the law of inheritance to its descendants, we shall easily see, how, by this means, a sufficient material foundation is furnished for an unlimited intellectual progress, without its being necessary for the organ of thought itself to become inflated to a bulk inconsistent with the laws of structure in general.   Finally, it must not be forgotten that the brain of the cultivated man nowadays acquires with comparatively less effort and in a very short time a whole series of ideas conceptions and knowledge, on the creation or establishment of which the intellectual powers of many generations of men before us have exhausted themselves. The present treasure of civilization possessed by man, like his material possessions, is the result of the life and activity of the whole human race during the hundreds and thousands of years that have passed away!   The individual succeeding at once to the whole of this valuable inheritance and taking his stand upon it works on further, and this it is above all that, together with his more perfect organization, confers upon man his immense superiority over the animal. *Corporeally* man is in fact nothing but an ennobled and more perfectly organized ape ; but *intellectually* he is, in comparison to animals, a demi-god, that is, he has become so by the gradual evolution of his powers !

(40) The principle of the division of labor, as Professor E. Haeckel has shown in an admirable discourse on that subject, (Berlin, 1869), is diffused throughout the whole organic world, and exerts itself not only in the arrangement of the individual organism but also in the social and confederate combinations of the individual species of animals.   Life, according to Haeckel, is nothing but the mechanical total result of the performances of the different organs, separated by the division of labor ; and these organs on their part have been developed into their various forms from simpler and very simple forms,—the so-called primitive and fundamental organs,—in consequence of a progressive division of labor.   The simplest or primitive form of organic life is, as is well-known, the *cell*, which, as the smallest organic individual or as the elementary organism, constitutes all organs whether simple or complicated.   " The apparent vital unity of every multicellular organism, like the political unity of every human state, is the combined result of the union and division of labor of these little citizens."   Every cell in the body of the animal or plant has thus up to a certain degree an independent life.   Those cells which are the most favored or the most highly endowed undertake the high-

est function of the animal body, that of self-consciousness or of sensation, thought and will.

The division of labor of the organism itself is a result of the struggle for existence in the course of many, many millions of years under the pressure of the external conditions of life, and guided by the principles of variability and inheritance.

(41) Although it must be regarded as a very just principle that "Whoever does not work, shall not eat," nevertheless daily experience teaches that a great many do eat, who do not work, and never have worked ; and from this it follows as an inevitable consequence, that those who do work must do so not only for themselves but also for the nourishment of a whole army of idlers. And this makes it appear the more unjust that those portions of the happiness of life which fall to the lot of the individual, are usually smaller in proportion as the exertion of his forces for the maintenance of his own existence and that of others is great, whilst the best and largest shares are in general carried off by those who have made very slight, if any, efforts to deserve them. It must not be objected to this that these people live upon the exertions or services of their ancestors, because the most essential necessaries of life are exactly those which cannot be created beforehand, and when they are consumed, must necessarily have been produced by the exertions of contemporaries.

What applies to *bodily* work, applies also, and almost in a higher degree, to *intellectual* labor, which usually becomes less remunerative and more proletarian, the more it is directed towards the highest and most truly ideal problems of humanity. Philosophers and poets are born proletaires, except when the luck of property has smiled upon them in their cradle, and even in business the heaviest and most wearing intellectual labor is generally performed by those who are worst paid for it. It is a very poor consolation, and moreover untrue, to say, that want drives great intellects to the production of extraordinary works, and that wealth and comfort keep them from it. Whoever is kept back from intellectual creation by wealth or comfort, is really destitute of the characters of prominent and creative spirits, for whom the outpouring of their inward thoughts into the bosom of mankind is as much a necessity as eating, drinking and sleeping. On the other hand, want and privation make people discontented, inattentive and slow of thought, and rob those who are subjected to them of those external and internal incitements which are so absolutely necessary for the development even of the greatest intellect. The leisure which is indispensable to the poet, the philosopher, &c., is wanting to the man who is pressed by want and the cares of life, and the scattering of his powers which is caused thereby makes him attain that which forms and must form a mainspring to the progress of the creative spirit,—namely, *success*,—too late, if at all. Of course so long as the principles which now govern society with regard to the struggle for existence prevail, it is useless to think of improving these conditions, as only such intellectual work as furnishes or promises to furnish a direct material benefit, is remunerated. What an infinitely injurious influence upon the quality of our modern literature this circumstance has exerted is too well-known to render any further reference to it necessary. Professorial detail-work or hasty workshop-work speculating upon the pocket of the reader, with abject subjection to the temporarily prevailing spirit or taste of the reader, is the predominant character of our literature, whilst manly *rectitude* and philosophical conviction are seen to encounter everywhere a mountain of vulgarity, ignorance and calumny.

(42) The present foundations of society according to Radenhausen (*Isis*, Band IV.) are *mistrust*, mutual *plunder* and *egotism ;* it is a war of every one against every one, in which it is not philanthropy, but only an insatiable striving after gain that forms the mainspring. F. A. Lange (*J. S. Mill's Ansichten über die sociale Frage*, &c., Duisburg, 1866), who like us regards the struggle for existence as the essential spring of social movement, also calls *egotism* the mainspring of our society. In opposition to this, according to Lange, the principles of *justice* and *fraternity* which have hitherto played only a secondary part in the state and in society, must be made the principal thing. In theory we possess a far higher ideal of true humanity than that which actually exists. Morals must be introduced into national economy, and by this means that hateful contradiction between theory and practice which moves our existing society to its misfortune must be got rid of. Morality itself must, however, as even Adam Smith recommended, be founded upon *sympathy ;* it is the regard of the individual for the whole that settles morality.

In the first edition of his work *Force and Matter* (pp. 256–57), the author wrote the following passage (afterwards omitted) on the present state of our society :— "And finally let us once more look a little more closely into human society and enquire whether, or not it acts upon moral impulses. Is it not in fact a *bellum omnium contra omnes ?* A universal race in which every one strives to outrun or even to destroy every body else ? Could we not almost represent it as Burmeister does the Brazilians : ' Every one does what he thinks he may do without punishment ; cheats, takes advantage of, deceives and makes use of the others as well as he can, with the conviction that no one would treat him any better. In general they regard any one who does not take this course as too stupid and silly to be able to follow it,' &c." Every one does what agrees with his nature and follows the impulses communicated to him either by this or by the external conditions of life ; he does what appears to him to be advantageous and suitable for himself and for the attainment of his objects, without troubling himself about moral principles which have not become positive. "All men are practical atheists" (Feuerbach). A man who cares more for others than for himself is usually, as Cotta says, called a " good silly fellow."

(43) M. Busch (*Wanderungen zwischen Hudson und Mississippi*, pp. 129 et seq., Stuttg., 1854,) describes the Shaker town of Watervliet in America, which had adopted the principles of community of all property and non-compulsory labor (work at pleasure). The colony was in a state of the highest prosperity. Pohl, a Scotchman, founded, also in America, a colony in which all constraint was to be done away with, and every one was to work only according to his inclination and powers. The idea of this was given to Pohl by his own factory in Scotland, in which he brought up poor children. The colony, which had also adopted the principle of community of women, proved a failure. The most celebrated of the many societies arranged in accordance with socialistic principles is the great Phalanstère of New Jersey in America, which only broke up after thirteen years of a flourishing existence. Active philauthropy served this society as a

guiding principle. The land belonged to all in common ; all also dwelt and ate together. Every one worked at what he pleased and as much as he liked; his work was estimated and put to his credit as a certain sum. Every week a balancing of accounts took place, when the liabilities and assets of each individual were settled according to his work and the amount due by him to the society for his maintenance. There was no religion or church, but good schools. The women had exactly the same rights as the men, even to the right of voting; and a select committee governed and decided upon the reception of new members, who had to submit to a year of trial. The circumstance that many availed themselves of the Phalanstère and its cheap mode of life only in order to save up a capital for themselves, together with the other circumstance that the *capitalists not belonging to the Society* who had lent the money for the purchase of the land called it in for the purpose of getting possession of the well-situated and beautifully cultivated ground in order to sell it at a high price, caused the overthrow of the undertaking.

Even in the prosaic land of China communism has taken root. For there has existed in that country since the beginning of the present century a secret society called Thiantihoei (or the union of Heaven and earth), which has extended itself from Canton to Malacca, Java and the Indian Archipelago, was discovered in the year 1824, and made itself remarkable by a rising in Malacca in the year 1836. The adherents of this sect desire to overcome the terrible contrast between poverty and riches, and start from the principle that all men have an equal right to the possession of the earth and of their properties. They have nothing but precepts of brotherly love and practical benovolence, and strive after the liberation of mankind from misery and oppression. (See Milne, *Transact. of the Asiatic Soc.*, 1827, Vol. I. and: *Thian-thi-hoih: Geschichte der Brüderschaft des Himmels und der Erde, der communistischen Propaganda China's.* Berlin, 1852.)

That community of goods was a recognized principle, carried out in a greater or less degree by many religious sects of ancient and modern times, is a matter of history. I shall refer only to the Jewish sect of the Essenes, to the first Christian communities, the Albigenses, Waldenses, Bohemian brothers, Herrnhuter, &c.

(44) Radenhausen in his *Isis* (Vol. IV. pp. 445 *et secq.*) admirably expounds the economical and other advantages of a *community of goods*. Distrust, the thirst for unfair gain, plunder, selfishness, &c., which at present form the foundations of intercourse, would be got rid of; and in the same proportion culture, conscientiousness, trust, moral worth, &c , would increase. "Whilst at present very many, and precisely those who are in an influential position, seek out of selfishness, to obstruct culture—the community, on the contrary, would seek to foster it for its own benefit, in order that each individual might be the more profitable to the whole." The striving after enjoyment would be ennobled ; the maintenance of existence would be much facilitated, as communities can always exist much more cheaply than individuals ; work, when carried on in common, would become easier, more agreeable, more healthy and more profitable; the money-slavery of small manufactories would cease ; age and sickness would affect the individual with respect to his material existence no more than temporary want of work ; the knowledge and skill of individuals would not be lost at their death, but would benefit the community and their successors ; the love of work

itself, which would no longer be mere hired work but would be for the service of all in common, would increase extraordinarily, &c., &c.

Even the transition from individual life to community would not be so rugged as it would appear, since our present life is already interwoven much more than is usually supposed with communism.   The direct and indirect savings in governmental arrangements which are now so costly, and in the many devices for the security and maintenance of private property, would be incalculably great; whilst the numerous losses produced by the whole army of evil inclinations, such as avarice, hatred, envy, revenge, calumny, hard-heartedness, &c., by which mankind is more severely punished than by a plague, would cease.   The *worth of man*, hitherto almost disregarded or despised, would come into its right estimation, and a free son of man would no longer, as heretofore, be less estimated, as regards his worth, than a sucking pig or a lamb or the child of a slave, &c., &c.

(45) That the proprietary classes should fear and detest the social revolution from personal and class interests is intelligible and excusable, although the notions which are usually formed of such revolutions and their consequences are generally much more dreadful than the things themselves.   On the other hand, it is incomprehensible and inexcusable that these same classes should be just as shy and recusant as towards the social revolution itself, towards all proposals intended to check social evils in a *peaceable* manner and to lead, by gradual reform, to a better state of things.   The more we refuse to see and acknowledge the social evils, the more strongly will these spring up in silence, and the less possible will it be in the end to escape from a solution of them *by force*.   Therefore instead of pursuing with hatred and calumny those who drag the mischief to light and propose means for its cure, they should be greeted with thanks and listened to quietly and intelligently.   Most certainly our wealthy burgher-class or the so-called *Bourgeoisie*, in which, at present, the most political influence is concentrated, are destitute of the most necessary qualification for this purpose, namely, *cultivation*.   Having sprung from the lower state of society and gradually attained to riches and influence by the unexampled progress of industry, trade and commerce, generally to their own astonishment, they know nothing higher than the assertion of this position and material comfort, and despise everything else as unpractical enthusiasm and ideology.   The words "Money," "Credit," "Parliament," "Ministerial Responsibility," &c., exhaust the whole treasury of their social and political ideas,—the highest flight they can take is to the requirement of a "free course for every one," which they regard as the *Non plus ultra* of liberalism, or to the removal of all those medieval obstacles which still stand in the way of free labor.   But they forget that the free course alone, on which the best places are already occupied, and on which those who go on foot can often scarcely find room among the crushing wheels of those who travel in carriages, will by no means do, and that we must not talk about freedom of labor, so long as this is subservient to private capital or private possessions.   In point of fact it is still exactly as it was formerly, when the noble made his serfs work for him; only the parts have been changed, and the moral pressure which Capital and possessions nowadays exert upon the laborer, is often harder than the old physical compulsion.   That this cannot remain so permanently is clear, and it will depend entirely upon the intelligence or want of intelligence of our present Bour-

geoisie, or independent middle class, with regard to social questions, whether we are now advancing towards a social *revolution*, with all its terrible and incalculable consequences, or towards a peaceful and gradual *reform.*

(46) As a matter of course there can be no question here of a formal expropriation or expulsion of the owners of the soil for the benefit of the state, but only of a redemption of the land, that is to say, a repurchase of it for moderate sums to be settled by estimate. In the case of small properties or pieces of ground, especially where these form the sole possession of a man or a family, this estimate must come very near their real value ; whilst larger properties, whole manors and the like must be subject to a certain reduction in the estimate. It is well known that very many and perhaps the most important of the titles to the private possession of the soil which was originally in general a common possession, by no means originated in honest acquisition, but from the times of conquest, feudalism and forcible dominion, and for this reason alone we might have the less hesitation about their retransfer into the possession of the community. Nevertheless as, after the lapse of so long a time investigations of the justice of the titles of acquisition can no longer be instituted, and as we cannot make the descendants answerable for the sins of their forefathers, no one should be injured in his existing rights, but only compelled to give back his possessions to the state for a sufficient compensation.

Such a restoration of the property in the land to the community, moreover, even if we leave entirely out of consideration all social reasons or scruples of justice, is an *economical* or political necessity, and therefore cannot be avoided at last in spite of all resistance. For the more the population increases, the more necessary does it become to obtain from the existing soil the utmost that it is capable of furnishing both in quantity and kind. It can, therefore, no longer be left to the individual possessor of a piece of ground to decide whether and how far he will make it capable of bearing, but, as we have said, in the interest of the community as much must be got out of it as it is capable of producing. This, however, can of course only be done by cultivation on the large scale carried on, on the principles of scientific agriculture, and by rendering every spot of earth capable of cultivation in accordance with its position and nature, whilst private possession acts in this respect quite arbitrarily and often very irrationally. Thus in England great stretches of cultivable land are either left entirely unemployed by their possessors or converted into meadows, parks, race-courses, grand gardens, &c., which serve only for the gratification of individuals, but by no means for the general benefit* ; and the same thing occurs everywhere, although not to so great an extent as in England.

Whether the state or community itself will undertake the cultivation of the soil or leave it, under certain guarantees and regulations, to agricultural societies, to the country communities, or, by agreement, to private individuals, is a question of secondary importance, which will probably be settled in different ways in different places in accordance with the conditions of the country.

The *land-question* has, as is well-known, become most pressing in the country

* The county of Sutherland contains more than a million acres of land which belong to *two* owners, and of which only 23,000 acres are under cultivation. The English Lords prefer making sheep-runs, hunting grounds or enormous parks out of cultivable soil.

of political freedom, England, in consequence of the peculiar conditions of the possession of land, and here the agitation in favor of community in possession of land or at least for a thorough-going reform of the existing state of things has already made itself felt and obtained many adherents. According to Radenhausen (*Isis*, Vol. III., p. 354), *land-slavery* in England has been one of the principal means of making the high nobility enormously rich, whilst, on the other hand, it has placed the greatest difficulties in the way of the agricultural improvement of the soil, which is so necessary.

Ground rents appear to be most unjust when they are produced by simple increase of the population and the augmented value of landed property caused thereby. This is most striking in and near large, growing cities, where pieces of land, which were previously almost of no value, often become real gold-fields within a short time. This kind of rent or augmentation of property is evidently produced without any assistance from the individual, merely by the industry and activity of the community, which nevertheless leaves this result of its industry to the individual owner of the property without any deduction. Here, even *without* the introduction of communistic possession of the soil, the community even now, by suitable taxation, might be made at least a joint proprietor of the benefit created by itself.

(47) This proposition is very different from that which has also been made of a total abolition of the right of inheritance ; an abolition which must cause such a profound alteration of all social conditions, that its sudden introduction cannot be imagined except by means of the most reckless power. Social reforms cannot, like political ones, be *suddenly* organized, since for their introduction a certain agreement of public opinion or of the classes of society is absolutely necessary. But it is exactly in this respect that the proposed method of a limitation of the right of inheritance particularly recommends itself to notice, as it is one that conducts quite gradually from the present social state to a better one, without disturbing any one in his possessions during his life, and may be increased or made more energetic according to circumstances. As a principle the limitation of the right of inheritance has long been recognized in the form of the *succession* and *legacy duties* which have probably been introduced in all countries ; and in point of fact no juster and less pressing duty can be imagined than the duty on inheritances, especially when these are indirect. The individual has acquired what he possesses in and with the aid of the community, and it must therefore be regarded only as just and equitable, that after his death he should be compelled to give up to the community a portion of what he has acquired and can no longer make use of ! Arbitrary or absurd legacies, such, for instance, as that of the rich Englishman who left his whole property to a lady with whom he had not the slightest acquaintance, simply from his admiration for her beautiful nose, or legacies to very distant lateral lines who are not in want of them, would of course meet with as little toleration on the part of the state, as the enormous private properties, maintained by constant inheritance, which constitute a state within the state, a power of money within the power of the state, and exert both on their possessors and on their families an unnatural influence injurious to the welfare of the community. The place of the former aristocracy of birth has been gradually taken by an *aristocracy of wealth*, which at least is as strongly opposed to demo-

cratic principles and good taste, as the former, and hereafter, if a barrier is not raised against it, will acquire a constantly increasing preponderance.

It may, indeed, be objected that great properties generally split up or become divided among several distinct branches by inheritance. Nevertheless experience teaches that great wealth is generally maintained in individual families (to which the circumstance that the rich always marry among the rich may essentially contribute) ; and on the other hand, great properties often collect by inheritance in individual hands, by the flowing together of many sources from various sides. The presumptive heirs of great wealth are generally regarded by most people with quite different eyes from ordinary men, and indeed nearly as beings of a higher kind ; they have the privilege of being stupid, lazy, rude, presumptuous, and even uncultivated, without losing much respect ; for one is certain that they will one day easily compensate for all these deficiencies by their wealth, and in spite of them take a prominent and influential position in Society. They also generally do not regard it as their duty to learn or do much, or to be very just in their other duties to Society, as they are usually quite sure of their advantageous lot without any exertion of their own.

In concluding this note it may be remarked, moreover, that the prohibition of the right of possession and inheritance is by no means a discovery of modern times, but is already thousands of years old. At the most different times intelligent and right-thinking men have proposed or introduced regulations leading towards it. See upon this subject Radenhausen's *Isis* (Band III., pp. 376 *et seqq.*), where it is demonstrated that at various periods attacks have been made on behalf of the common weal upon the right of possession and inheritance. Moreover, it must not be forgotten that even under present conditions in the State, the community, the family, unions, &c., we already possess an infinity of communistic arrangements, all of which, if the Manchester-theory were correct, ought to be got rid of and left solely to private activity, which is almost always insufficient.

(48) The desolate condition of descendants incapable of inheritance and left solely to public beneficence by the death, age or illness of their supporter forms one of the most crying and obstinate of social evils. It is true, indeed, that privately by means of committees and benefit societies, as well as by the numerous life assurance offices, and publicly by means of parochial and other arrangements, the misery thus produced is as far as possible counteracted. But every one who has attained even a little insight or experience in these matters is well aware how insufficient and defective all these arrangements are, what danger of loss there is in them, and how they leave one in the lurch precisely in the worst cases. The object would be attained quite differently and better if the state or the community were to take charge over these natural cares and to a certain extent form a great and universal mutual assurance institution, under which innocent destitution would be an impossibility. The contribution which every individual gives towards the burdens of the state, or the taxes, would of course have to be increased in such a measure as would cover the expenses thus arising ; but the obligatory contribution of all (each individual according to his powers or the amount of his income) would probably make the increase very small. It is impossible that a community ordered upon humane principles should tolerate that

the *invalids of labor*, as they may be called, after having devoted their whole life and their powers to the service and purposes of this community, should when old or sick be compelled to want or even to die of hunger, or that their unendowed descendants, children, women, &c., should be pitilessly flung into the arms of wan distress. The poor's rates and other arrangements for the relief of the poor at present existing do not generally fulfill the purpose for which they were intended, and are often better fitted to develop ragamuffins and idle paupers or to help beggary, than to relieve real and innocent poverty. Nor can they prevent the most terrible and heart-breaking scenes of social misery, slow starvation, desperate suicides, &c., from taking place almost daily in the midst of a society which is rolling in superfluity.

(49) It is mere nonsense to reject the assistance of the state upon principles and arguments derived from the nature of the state itself, as Wackernagel, for example, has done, in his essay against Lassalle. The state is not, as the present Bourgeois-party think in their stupidity, merely a mutual law and protection office, but only the external form within which the great advances in civilization of mankind have to be performed. Everything therefore is an object of the state which promises to advance the intellectual or corporeal happiness and comfort of the citizens, its individual members, and which the majority of these citizens regards at any given moment as serviceable to the common welfare. Men without state are inconceivable; hence we cannot separate the individuals from the idea of the state and consider them without reference to it. They are men in our sense of the word only by their living together with other men in a political union, and the latter itself changes in its nature every moment with the changing necessities or degrees of cultivation of those of whom it is composed. In this sense State-aid is nothing more than the assistance which the community offers to the individual, and the more extensively this is done the more will the great objects of humanity and Manhood be attained. Hence state-aid itself is not in question, but only the *mode* in which it shall be exerted. All disputes about the nature and purpose of the State become unnecessary as soon as the principle of the *sovereignty of the people* is fully recognized, and it is admitted that everything must be law that the majority of the people will. The individual freedom of which the adherents of the Bourgeois-State speak so much, really exists only on paper, because so long as social equality does not exist it becomes force and club-law in opposition to those who are least favored. Of what use to the poor workman is the power of moving about freely, when he finds the same misery wherever he goes? Of what use is freedom of trade to him when he must everywhere work only for those who alone have the instruments of production in their hands? Where is the individual freedom of all those poor people or workmen whom we can at any moment throw upon the streets and consign to the extreme of want, by depriving them of their scanty employment? Freedom of labor, which the opponents of State-aid and the defenders of the Bourgeois-state praise so highly, is in fact attained by State-aid or the assistance of the less-favored by the community, so that every honest, healthy man who is willing to work will find it possible to earn his independent existence by work, and not always to serve as the slave of others. If it depended only upon freedom of labor in the liberalistic sense or the removal of political hindrances which narrow this freedom, England and America would

necessarily be the most blessed countries in the world, whilst in reality the work-men there have exactly the same and in part still greater grievances than in other countries, and in the former country the social contradictions and injustices are greater and more monstrous than anywhere else. Here and everywhere, if things continue as they are and industry on a large scale continues to overgrow small businesses in the same proportion as hitherto, it will finally come to pass that there will be only one God with unlimited power in the world, namely, Mammon, or property, money ; and human society will consist only of a small number of millionaires or great capitalists and an enormous army of proletaires,— the latter apparently existing solely for the purpose of consuming their lives in the service of the former.

(50) The evident decline of our Universities or High Schools as seminaries of free and independent science, which has been increasing from year to year and is pretty generally admitted, is due to a series of causes, of which the following are among the principal :—

1. The pressure exerted by the existing government upon the teachers or es-tablished representatives of science in the Universities, which renders it more or less impossible for the individual to teach anything which is in opposition to the views or necessities of the Government and its generally reactionary endeavors. By this means a checking bridle is put upon every new and suggestive investiga-tion, and an almost insuperable obstacle is opposed to everything that rises above the ordinary level. Men who form the ornaments of science and who will shine upon future generations as stars of the first magnitude, are hunted or juggled away from the universities in consequence of this system ; whilst men of small intellects and narrow minded pedlars of scientific details usurp the lofty thrones from which the light of enlightenment and intelligence should shine down upon the nation. If we add to this the incredible diffusion of *cliquism* in our High Schools, the bad payment, the mean and dishonoring hunting after hearers or stu-dents, the depressed position of the private tutors, the submissive feeling of all those who hope for advancement or increase of pay, and many other things, we shall easily understand what must become of science under such circumstances and in such hands, and what would long since have become of it, if it did not bear in itself a force of attraction and elevation which nothing can destroy.

2. The extraordinary universalization of culture, which draws the means of culture and in part the interest in culture away from the universities, which are usually situated in small and imperfectly developed towns, and towards the great central points of intercourse, the populous cities containing a numerous and in-telligent population. In many of these cities (for example, in Frankfort on the Main) more is often done, merely by private activity, for science and scientific de-velopment, than in the actual seminaries destined for that purpose and supported by the state as well as by old donations and privileges.

3. The antiquated form or constitution of our Universities, derived from the middle ages and contrasting with the whole spirit of modern times, which exerts the most unfavorable influence not only upon the *teachers*, but also, and almost more, upon the *taught*, producing the absurd, renommistic, ragamuffin student-life, with its innumerable barbarisms, injury to character and health, squandered powers, &c.

4. The extraordinarily advanced importance and increase of printed books which conveys to the public all scientific and literary productions and all intellectual creations, much better, more easily and more quickly than could be done by the Universities which were formerly to a certain extent regarded as individual central suns of cultivation. Nowadays we can learn nearly every thing from books, and often better than by oral intercourse with teachers; and only the practical branches of knowledge depending upon inspection, observation and experiment, constitute, to a certain degree, an exception. But often enough the oral discourse of the University teacher is nothing more than a tedious repetition from some Compendium or Textbook compiled by himself or by others.

5. The general materialistic Tendency of the times, which has extended even to the higher affairs of education and causes only those branches of knowledge to appear of importance and use which, as Schiller says, look like milking cows capable of supplying butter. All the higher and highest, truly humanistic studies are thus pushed into a corner and so neglected that we can hardly blame any one if he turns his powers and efforts towards other objects. And nevertheless the necessity for a purely human or universal University-culture, without any consideration of the purposes of any calling, is at present stronger and more pressing than ever, because there are a great number of young people belonging to the higher mercantile or industrial station, who do not intend to adopt a learned career and yet imperatively need such culture. At our present Universities which almost entirely devote themselves to the purposes of the learned callings, and whose lists of lectures put forth in the public journals as regards humanistic studies, in general only effect a pleasant delusion of themselves and others, they cannot attain this object, and they either do not visit them at all, or pass the time destined for that purpose in trifling pursuits. What we require at present above all, therefore, especially in Germany, is the establishment of a few High Schools or Universities which would leave entirely out of consideration all learned professions and only cultivate a general course of study, developing the mind in the various principal branches of knowledge. As a matter of course these institutions must be free from all governmental or other influence, and must furnish free space for every philosophical or other line of thought so far as it moves within scientific bounds. These free Universities, moreover, would not only benefit the unlearned callings, but also the learned professions, for which they would form an admirable and really indispensably necessary preparation.

(51) The diminution of the daily period of labor and the establishment of a normal working-day of from 8 to 10 hours by the state is one of the most justifiable requirements of the working class, and one which will certainly in time be fulfilled. If the German workingmen who for the last nine years have spent their force in the Lassallean agitation for universal suffrage and state-help, which are perfectly useless under present circumstances and have not advanced one hair's breadth nearer to their object, had selected *this* requirement as the subject of their agitation, they would by this time probably have been further advanced than they are at present. It is true that the opponents of an abridged term of labor assert that the workmen would not occupy those hours which would thus be set free for them in useful or improving occupations, but pass them in the public house. With some exceptions this may be correct so long as the present

rudeness and want of cultivation, which stand in necessary connection with the position in life of the workman, continues. But it will be otherwise as soon as the workman is differently educated and cultivated, and as soon as he can see that there is a possibility in his future life of giving a further development to the foundations thus laid, whilst under present circumstances we can scarcely blame him, if he seeks to forget in sensual enjoyments his unfortunate and unimprovable position during the few minutes of his daily freedom. The objections raised from the economical point of view also do not seem to be tenable, seeing that by the better preservation of the power and good will to work, more may generally be done in a shorter time of labor than in a longer one, which produces dejection and laxity, and permanently exhausts the powers by excessive effort and the want of recreation.

(52) One of the principal sources of good actions, especially as regards our behavior towards our fellow men, is *pity*. But at the bottom even this highest of all noble sentiments is nothing but the efflux of a refined egotism. For when we see a fellow man suffering we immediately put ourselves in imagination in the place of the sufferer and ask ourselves what would be our own feelings if we should be assisted or neglected by others. The disagreeable sentiment, of the imagined helplessness in ourselves becomes immediately converted into the agreeable one of aid conferred and liberation from a depressed position as soon as we have actually given our assistance to the sufferer. Of course this presupposes a certain development of the powers of sentiment and imagination in which rude nations or individuals are more or less deficient; this want of the sentiment of pity renders them cruel and spiteful towards their fellow man, whilst the opposite character is produced by higher cultivation of the mind and heart. Moreover, we act well, as regards our behavior towards mankind in general, out of consideration for our own weal or advantage, for our good fame, our social position, &c., as well as out of respect for the laws and fear of punishment, whilst all these motives would fall away as soon as, being merely limited to ourselves, we could follow our own egotistical impulses, just as the animals do. It is only his social relations, considerations of the common weal and the conviction that it is his duty to act for humanity to which the individual is indebted for everything that makes man a *man*, and renders him that moral being which the moralists and theolologians imagine him to have been created at the beginning. Even the *wickedness* which is the source of all *bad* actions towards our fellow men, just as pity is the source of all our *good* ones, depends ultimately upon a want of recognition of this relation and is therefore finally, like everything evil, a product of want of cultivation and ignorance. Even moral indifference, or the mere abstaining from bad actions towards our fellow men, depends ultimately upon an egotism refined by culture, inasmuch as we partially feel the evil that we inflict, or think to inflict upon others, in consequence of the process of thought above described, as if it were inflicted, or to be inflicted upon ourselves and abstain from the action in order to escape from this disagreeable feeling.

CHIMPANZEE.

BORNEAN ORANG.

INDEX.

The SOCIAL CONTRACT,

Or PRINCIPLES OF POLITICAL LAW.

Also, A PROJECT FOR A PERPETUAL PEACE,

BY

JEAN JACQUES ROUSSEAU, *Citizen of Geneva.*

One volume, post 8vo, 238 pages, with portrait, extra vellum cloth, 75c., paper 50c.

The writings of Rousseau, says Thomas Paine, in his *Rights of Man*, contain "a loveliness of sentiment in favor of Liberty that excites respect and elevates the human faculties."

"He was the most directly revolutionary of all the speculative precursors. His writings produced that glow of enthusiastic feeling in France, which led to the all-important assistance rendered by that country to the American colonists in a struggle so momentous for mankind. It was from his writings that the Americans took *the ideas and the phrases of their great Charter*. It was his work more than that of any other one man, that France arose from the deadly decay which laid hold of her whole social and political system, and found that irresistible energy which warded off dissolution within, and partition from without."—JOHN MORLEY.

"He could be cooped up in garrets, laughed at as a maniac, left to starve like a wild beast in a cage,—but he could not be hindered from setting the world on fire.—THOMAS CARLYLE.

PROFESSION OF FAITH of the Vicar of Savoy,

BY JEAN JACQUES ROUSSEAU.

Also, A SEARCH FOR TRUTH, by Olive Schreiner.

Post 8vo, 128 pages, with portrait, Vellum Cloth 50c., paper 25c.

ROCHEFOUCAULD'S MORAL MAXIMS.

Containing 541 Maxims and Moral Sentences, by Francis, Duke of Rochefoucauld ; together with 144 Maxims and Reflections by Stanislaus, King of Poland. Also Maxims to Live by, and Traits of Moral Courage in every-day life. 12mo, 186 pages, cloth, 75 cts.

> " As Rochefoucauld his maxims drew
> From Nature,—I believe them true.
> They argue no corrupted mind
> In him—the fault is in mankind !"—*Swift.*

FAWCETT'S AGNOSTICISM

AND OTHER ESSAYS, with a Prologue by ROBERT G. INGERSOLL.
One volume, 12mo, 277 pages. Cloth, 75 cts.

SALTUS' ANATOMY OF NEGATION.

Intended to convey a tableau of anti-Theism from Kapila to Leconte de Lisle. 12mo, 218 pages, cloth, 75 cts.

Saltus' Philosophy of Disenchantment.

A critical examination of the Pessimistic Philosophy of Shopenhauer. 233 pages, cloth, 75 cts.

Goodloe's Birth of the Republic.

Compiled from the National and Colonial Histories and Historical Collections, from the American Archives, from Memoirs and from the Journals and Proceedings of the British Parliament. Containing the Resolutions, Declarations, and Addresses adopted by the Continental Congress, the Provincial Congresses, Conventions and Assemblies, of the County and Town Meetings, and the Committees of Safety, in all the Colonies, from the year 1765 to 1776, to which is added the articles of Confederation, a history of the formation and adoption of the Constitution, the election of President Washington, his Inauguration, April 30, 1789, a copy of the Constitution, and Washington's Inaugural Speech. 12mo, 400 pages, cloth, $1.00.

SUNDAY
UNDER THREE HEADS.

AS IT IS.

AS SABBATH BILLS WOULD MAKE IT.

AS IT MIGHT BE MADE.

BY

CHARLES DICKENS,

(TIMOTHY SPARKS.)

One volume, with portrait. Illustrated by "*Phiz.*" Paper 25c., clo. 50c.

———

The idea of "making a man truly moral through the ministry of constables, and sincerely religious under the influence of penalties," seemed so incongruous and absurd to CHARLES DICKENS — the true and sympathetic friend of the toiling masses — that he was induced to write in their behalf, in his remarkably unique and inimitable style, this eloquent protest against religious intolerance — this trenchent argument in favor of personal liberty — liberty to enjoy respite from the carking cares of every-day life, — even if this liberty should be enjoyed on the *Sun*-day. — the day known to the ancient Pagan idolaters as the "Venerable day of the Sun." — *Preface.*